BWB 2019

Keep.

V

"David is a brilliant social architect who is able to see key patterns and princi-ples between levels of change—from the individual, to the household, to the neighborhood, to the community, to cities, to states and nations, and to the entire planet. His knowledge about the process of social innovation and dif-fusion and his discoveries over decades of experimentation and research in large system change efforts merit serious consideration by all of us who seek a more hopeful future for our human community. His work illuminates our common yearning for connection with others, and provides the practical tools needed to achieve it at every level necessary to invent our world anew. I loved the way this book stimulated my thinking and spirit."

—Juanita Brown, Co-Founder, The World Café

"David Gershon, an unusually talented and effective organizer, has spent most of his adult life teaching people how to take control of their destinies. The world has changed dramatically during those years, and David has been astute and nimble enough to change with it. His attitudes and tech-niques are different today from when I first met him a quarter-century ago, though his values remain intact. *Social Change 2.0* is an insightful summary of what David has learned during a career of helping to build a better world. Anyone who wants to effect change—whether to promote a global clean-tech revolution, or to organize a preschool program in their neighborhood—will find valuable truths here."

—Denis Hayes, CEO, Bullitt Foundation, and Co-Founder, Earth Day

"I met David twenty years ago when he was the inspiration behind the Global Action Plan sustainable lifestyle movement. With *Social Change 2.0* he demonstrates that he has lost none of his brilliance in the intervening years. I predict that this book will become the defining resource for those wishing to create sustainable, low carbon communities, and social change in general. It is a must-read for helping us traverse the challenging times ahead."

—Lawrence C. Bloom, Chairman, World Economic Forum,
Global Agenda Council on Urban Management

"Governments have limitations in leading complex social change, and increasingly progressive leaders are recognizing that such challenges can only be effectively addressed through the innovation and passion of grassroots people power. In *Social Change 2.0*, David Gershon offers us a way to draw on this power to make a difference in the saving of our planet. In doing so he argues for nothing less than a reinvention of the way we think, value, and do things. It's a big ask and it's not going to happen overnight—but Gershon offers us a compelling blueprint and a doer's toolbox of social marketing strategies and empowerment tools, which, if used by enough communities, might just get us there. Simply, he helps make our global future something we can act on."

> —John Cole PH.D, Professor and Director, Centre for Sustainable Business and Development, the University of Southern Queensland, Australia, and formerly Chief Officer, Office of Clean Energy, Queensland Government

"*Social Change 2.0* is a visionary and pragmatic book that strikes at the essence of what is needed right now to help our social systems, which are at long last opening to transformative change, achieve it. It offers those of us on the front lines of that change—in my case of America's health care system—the invaluable resource of a tested roadmap and toolkit for social transformation. David's book should be read by all those ready to seize this extraordinary time for change in society."

> —Kenneth J. Abrams, M.D., Senior Vice President, Clinical Operations, North Shore-LIJ Health System

"For those of us in the community-capacity-building sector, David Gershon is not only a dear and trusted resource, but also a living reminder that the work to which we have dedicated our lives can have important tangible outcomes. Building capacity among community members is a complex and intense process that often progresses at a glacial pace. *Social Change 2.0* enables community organizers to take this work to the level of craft. Reading this book re-energizes our conviction not only that this work is important, but that it really is possible to help communities transition to a new paradigm. Thank you, David, for your life's work!"

> —Daniel Homsey, Director of Strategic Initiatives and the Neighborhood Empowerment Network, City of San Francisco

"In *Social Change 2.0* David Gershon presents an inspiring vision and a realistic roadmap for how we can reinvent our world through empowering grassroots leaders. The proven strategies, practices, and tools Gershon provides are powerful and will deliver results. I wish I'd had access to them when I was mayor."

—Graham Richard, mayor (2000-2007), Fort Wayne, Indiana, and author of *Performance is the Best Politics: How to Create High Performance Government*

"This book offers an inspiring evolutionary blueprint for transforming our social systems, and provides some of the most effective organizing principles, empowerment processes, and movement strategies that are emerging in our time. For our rising generation of Millennial activists, student organizers, and young social entrepreneurs, *Social Change 2.0* will unquestionably play a significant role in bringing forth the next great wave of social change."

—Joshua Gorman, founder of Generation Waking Up

"*Social Change 2.0* is the call to a new generation of leadership, a generation that feels instinctively what David teaches explicitly: that the progress of our society requires us to rebuild our communities house by house and neighborhood by neighborhood. And this book shows us how! If enough change agents apply the highly effective strategies and tools in this book, it will be a game changer for our world."

—Rob Garrity, Executive Director, Massachusetts Climate Action Network

"This book is a voyage of discovery and learning. Not only does it describe the journey of one man's life and his commitment to broad-scale systems change, it captures his and others' learnings about what it takes to create the generative changes so needed in our communities, institutions, and world at this unique moment in time. David's writing provides a wonderful invitation to reflect on our values and aspirations for the differences we want to make. He then proceeds to provide insights, ideas, and a tested framework for action, for those who aspire to truly reinvent the world."

—Charles Homes, Learning Strategies Group, Simon Fraser University

"We all know we need to change our social systems, but few of us realize that the means for this change lies untapped in us all. David's genius lies in knowing how to access the innate resources each one of us holds, and his book is a guide to awakening these possibilities and helping us shift our society to be truly sustainable for the next seven plus generations."

—Gregor Barnum, Director of Corporate Consciousness, Seventh Generation

"*Social Change 2.0* shows us how to release the human intangibles of hope, aspiration, and vision, and combine them with the processes needed to achieve sustainable behavior change at the personal, organizational, community, and social system levels. This book is a major contribution to all who wish to bring about change in our world."

—Kathy Castro, Director, University of Rhode Island Sea Grant Program

"Gershon writes from the front lines of social change with practical information flowing off the pages. Like a social change superhero, he demonstrates on every page the power of living with a no-limitations philosophy, showing us how we, too, can be the architects of a better world. This book will influence every project I take up in my life. I now know there is a pattern language for making social change happen."

—Craig Hamilton, New Dimensions radio host, former editor of *EnlightenNext* magazine, and founder of IntegralEnlightenment.com

"David Gershon is one of the most accomplished social innovators alive today. This timely book offers the rare gift of proven and transferable solutions that can be applied to a wide range of problems confronting humanity. I have seen and experienced firsthand the effectiveness of this social change model. If you wish to change the world, I cannot recommend this book too highly!"

—Michael Dowd, author of *Thank God for Evolution: How the Marriage of Science and Religion Will Transform Your Life and Our World*

SOCIAL CHANGE 2.0

A BLUEPRINT FOR REINVENTING OUR WORLD

DAVID GERSHON

High Point / Chelsea Green
1649 Route 28A
West Hurley, New York 12491

10–9–8–7–6–5–4–3–2–1

First Edition: September 2009
Printed in the United States of America

⊗ This edition is printed on acid-free paper that meets the
American National Standards Institute z39.48 Standard.

Design and composition: Stephen Busch, dogwood studio
Cover photo: Kevin Kelley and NASA
First Earth Run photos: Haroldo DeFaria Castro and Robert Goodearl

Cataloging Data
Gershon, David.
Social change 2.0: a blueprint for reinventing our world /
David Gershon.
p.–cm.
bibliographical references and index.
isbn 978-0-9630327-7-5 (alk. paper)
1. Social change. 2. Social entrepreneurship.
3. Transformative change strategies. 4. Empowerment
Library of Congress Control Number: 2009927049

This book is printed on 30% postconsumer waste, Forest Stewardship,
and Rainforest Alliance Certified recycled paper, using plant-based inks,
and processed chlorine-free. As a result, for this printing we have saved:

73 Trees (40' tall and 6-8" diameter)
13,984 Gallons of Wastewater
10 million BTUs of Total Energy
849 Pounds of Solid Waste
2,904 Pounds of Greenhouse Gases

Environmental impact estimates were made using the Environmental Defense
Fund Paper Calculator. For more information visit: www.edf.org/papercalculator.

To those called to the great adventure of reinventing our world

Contents

REINVENTING SOCIAL CHANGE

Every few hundred years in Western history there occurs a sharp transformation. Within a few short decades, society—its world view, its basic values, its social and political structures, its key institutions—rearranges itself. We are currently living through such a time.

—Peter Drucker

In my dream the angel shrugged and said, if we fail this time, it will be a failure of imagination. And then she placed the world gently in the palm of my hand.

—Bryan Andreas

I came of age in the 1960s, when, with the music of the Beatles serving as the soundscape, America was stirred by antiwar protests, civil rights marches, and dreams of a better world. This heady time impressed on my young psyche both the firm belief that we can change the world, and the equally firm desire to do so. My favorite Beatles song, although he was not still a Beatle at the time, was John Lennon's "Imagine." I loved the song then, and I still love it today, because it is unapologetically visionary and optimistic about what is possible for our world. Its power comes from Lennon's willingness to dream and his courage to share his dream with others. "You may say I'm a dreamer," he told us, "but I'm not the only one." (In a 2007 global jukebox poll "Imagine" was voted the world's favorite song ever. In fact, former U.S. President Jimmy Carter once remarked that when visiting countries around the world "you hear 'Imagine' used almost equally with national anthems.")

Like John Lennon and so many others, I dream of a world that is possible but does not yet exist. In large and small ways I have spent most of my adult life attempting to create such a world. Along the way I discovered the secret of being a dreamer. If your dream is compelling enough it draws forth your passion and this keeps you motivated to stay with it even when the odds are against you. And if you stay with something long enough, eventually you wring out the truths needed to bring it to fruition.

I also draw inspiration from how Thomas Jefferson handled the assignment given to him by John Adams and Benjamin Franklin to write a statement declaring America's independence from Great Britain. Jefferson transformed what could have been a mundane document into a transcendent vision of possibility for how human beings might live. His dream for America stunned Adams and Franklin and became the rallying motto of the American Revolution. Thomas Jefferson was inspired. He tapped deeply into his imagination and crafted a document that would come to epitomize the American dream and inspire many to seek this country's shores in search of it.

He courageously envisioned the world anew and then helped create it. Some have called the creation of America one of the great social innovations of human civilization. The boldness of this dream inspired him and stirred the blood of his fellow patriots. With this inspiration they were willing to release their attachment to a known but deeply compromised reality and embark on a transformative journey to create a world of fresh possibilities.

It is time to dream again. So many of the assumptions we have been operating with as a human community have proved faulty that this generation must literally re-envision them. And with the accelerating unraveling of our planet's life support system and the deterioration of so many of our social systems, we are being called to create *rapid* transformative change. But the current social change tools at our disposal—passing laws, adjusting tax policy, and public protest—were designed for slow-moving incremental change.

We are being called to reinvent not only our world, but also the process by which we achieve this reinvention. If the current social change tools of carrots, sticks, and protests are not sufficient, what else do we have? Are there assumptions we might rethink about what motivates people to change? Taking a page from Jefferson's playbook, might we be able to motivate people to change because of a dream that inspires their imagination, enlivens their sense of possibility, and lifts their spirit as human beings? Or to ask this question in a more tangible way, how might we empower people to voluntarily adopt new behaviors that help them, their community, and their organizations operate at a higher level of social value so we can realize more of our potential as a human species?

I have been attempting to answer this question over the past three decades, at the individual, local, national, and international levels; working with government agencies, nonprofit organizations, corporations, and ad-hoc community groups; in developed and developing countries alike, and around a multiplicity of issues.

My research has taught me that **people are willing to change if they have a compelling vision and are provided tools to help them bring it into being.** The vision must touch their core to engender the necessary passion and commitment needed to overcome the inevitable obstacles on the path of realization. They need others of like mind going on the journey with them to stay motivated. And with a well-designed transformative change platform that is replicable, these behavior changes can be widely disseminated throughout a community, organization, country, and across the planet.

I have also seen that when individuals become personally part of the solution it creates a new dynamic in the way we tackle large societal challenges. We are able to see beyond the traditional social change formula of business as the problem and government as the solution, with nonprofits lobbying government for better regulations against business and citizens sitting on the sidelines complaining about the coziness between politicians and business.

When citizens are empowered to adopt socially beneficial behaviors, such as a green lifestyle, for example, an opening can occur for traditionally adversarial relationships to establish new arrangements of cooperation and collaboration in service of this new voting constituency and purchasing community. When all the parts of a system begin working together and there is no "other" to combat or protect against, more innovative and generative solutions start to emerge. I call the process of bringing the whole system into collaboration building a *unitive field*.

The model of social change that I have been describing represents what systems theory calls *second order change*—change that transforms and reorganizes a system to a higher level of performance. When the easier-to-implement change solutions are exhausted and prove inadequate for the magnitude of change required, the system goes into stress and must either evolve or breakdown. This book represents an attempt to expand the parameters for social change solutions so that we can evolve our social systems. I call it "Social Change 2.0." It stands on the shoulders of "Social Change 1.0"—command and control, financial incentives, and protest—because it could not function optimally without the rule of law and a democratic form of government that allow for free expression. But it is designed to go beyond the constraints purposefully built into this more incremental approach to change.

The Social Change 2.0 framework aspires to tread in the territory where some have thrown up their hands and wondered if change was really possible. It addresses issues that are complex and require many people to change fundamentally; issues for which there are no easy solutions and those that exist are exceedingly difficult to implement and require the cooperation of the whole system; issues which if not adequately addressed will cause an ecological or social system to break down. These issues include global warming, depletion of our nonrenewable natural resources, chronic poverty, disease epidemics, terrorism, ethnic and racial animosity, the disenfranchisement of women and minorities, and overpopulation.

Global warming is a prime example of the need for a second order change solution. Al Gore calls this a "planetary emergency" because our future well-being as a human species is at stake. Jim Hansen, NASA's chief climate scientist, says we have at most ten years to start turning global warming around or "suffer a planet that is not conducive to human life." The New York Times says the "climate crisis is at its very bottom a crisis of lifestyle. The Big Problem is nothing more or less than the sum total of countless little choices. Most of them made by us (consumer spending makes up 70 percent of our economy) and most of the rest of them made in the name of our needs and desires and preferences."

In a democratic society we can't legislate the kind of lifestyle change that would be necessary to have a major impact on global warming. Passing a law that commands people to change their behavior and then penalizing them if they don't is not acceptable or practical. Offering people financial incentives to change is sending the right signal, but people are still free not to avail themselves of these incentives. If people are not already predisposed to changing, financial incentives have a limited effect. And even when people aren't averse to changing, financial incentives take us down a slow, politically cumbersome path not well suited to making the major and rapid transformative changes scientists tell us are needed.

Social protest is a gift of our democracy that has allowed Americans to speak out against injustice and government policies with which we disagree. It contributed to ending an unpopular war in Vietnam and furthering the civil rights of the disenfranchised members of our society. But as important as social protest has been and always will be in a democratic society, it is reactionary and defined by the problem. It is a great tool for objecting to what is wrong in society, but not for creating what is right. Saying no to global warming and lamenting the lack of bold and effective political leadership are very different from providing a viable alternative.

I have no pretensions to believe that the Social Change 2.0 design principles and practices described in this book are the solution for any of these enormous challenges facing us as a human community. The nature of these problems defies any single approach to change. And this framework is still very much a work in progress. But I have seen enough evidence applying these tools over the past thirty years to believe that they can make a contribution, either in whole or in part, to tackling issues requiring fundamental transformative change.

It is also my hope that this book will contribute to a revolution in thinking about the very nature of social change itself and spawn many more second order change solutions. This will require a special type of thinking which I call "social creativity." The objective of social creativity is twofold: to evolve the existing social systems and institutions we have created, which in turn have created the boundaries of our assumptions and expectations of what is possible; and to generate the new social innovations that are now needed by society.

This is the type of thinking that Jefferson and his fellow founders employed to create the social experiment of America. But Jefferson went one step further. He provided us with a core design principle for his social change philosophy considered so important by future generations that they etched it in stone on the fourth panel of the Jefferson Memorial in Washington, D.C. He said:

> Laws and institutions must go hand in hand with the progress of the human mind. As that becomes more developed, more enlightened, as new discoveries are made, new truths disclosed, and manners and opinions change with the change of circumstances,

institutions must advance also, and keep pace with the times. We might as well require a man to wear still the same coat which fitted him when a boy, as civilized society to remain ever under the regimen of their barbarous ancestors.

In short, we must continually evolve our social systems to reflect the changes occurring in our world and humankind's development. To be able to do this successfully with the civilization-threatening challenges we now face will require us to dig deep into our reservoir of social creativity. But humanity's survival instinct and inventiveness have always been at their best when backed against the wall. That is why we are still here as a species. It is also during these times of greatest need that the most visionary, talented, and passionate among us are aroused to action. That was the case in Jefferson's time and it is happening once again.

This book is written for these people. It has a simple and some might say radical premise: that the natural starting point for changing our world for the better is *us*. That taking personal responsibility to make the needed changes within ourselves and our communities is the foundation for changing our institutions, not the other way around. That people are willing to make these changes if empowered by a personal vision and the means to bring it to fruition. That these changes can be accelerated and reinforced with the right laws and financial incentives, but it begins with us.

In *Guns, Germs, and Steel*, his Pulitzer Prize-winning book on the history of human civilization, Jared Diamond describes two principal methods by which ideas have been disseminated over the millennia. One he calls "idea diffusion" and the other "blueprint copying." He said the least effective method is when you just get the idea and you have to figure out the rest on your own. The most efficient is when you get the entire blueprint. Those civilizations that received language blueprints versus just the idea for instance, were able to accelerate the development of a written language by thousands of years. The intention of this book is to describe a transformative social change blueprint in enough detail so it can be both understood *and* put into practice. It is organized into three parts: stories, principles and practices, and game-changing strategies.

In the first part I share four in-depth stories that I call experiments in societal transformation. Each reflects a different scale of change, from the individual, to the block, to the community, to the planet. Each looks at transformative social change through the prism of a foundational societal issue for the twenty-first century: environmentally sustainable lifestyles, livable neighborhoods, disaster-resilient communities, and peaceful coexistence on our planet. Each is described in enough detail that it can be a useful blueprint for similar or complementary social change initiatives. And each describes my personal journey of learning and growth, illuminating the social entrepreneurial challenges, pitfalls, rewards, and strategic thinking process.

The second part describes the five design principles that undergird these experiments and collectively represent the Social Change 2.0 framework. It amplifies these principles with practices and lessons learned from these four social change stories and others. The five design principles and practices described are:

- empowering people to voluntarily adopt new behaviors beneficial to themselves and society

- transforming dysfunctional or marginally effective social systems so they can achieve a higher level of performance and social value

- inventing and implementing transformative social innovations

- building a more collaborative playing field to maximize the potential of a social system or social innovation

- leveraging and disseminating social innovations at larger levels of scale

The third part addresses three major rites of passage human civilization must pass through to avoid collapse and evolve to the next level of our potential: the ability to address global warming effectively, to transform the paradigm of war, and to build the leadership capacity to bring about the needed societal transformations. In this section the new social change framework described in Parts One and Two is put through its paces to address these issues.

And for readers wishing guidance in applying the principles and practices described in this book to a specific social change initiative of their own, I have included questions at the end of each chapter to stimulate your thinking. I call it a "Social Change 2.0 Practitioner's Guide."

I have great faith in humanity's imagination, ingenuity, and will to create our world anew. My work is grounded in the belief that many people will be inspired to serve in this noble endeavor if their odds for success are increased. *Social Change 2.0* seeks to increase these odds by providing a blueprint for transformative social change. Changing the world is not for the fainthearted, so it also attempts to provide fire for the soul of those embarked on this great transformative adventure.

The human species—willingly, or fighting and kicking—will need to engage in momentous change over the next decades. How we fare on this journey will determine the fate for generations into the foreseeable future. Whether you are a social activist, social entrepreneur, or community organizer; elected official or civil servant; foundation program officer or social venture capitalist; business leader responsible for developing a corporate social engagement strategy or running a social benefit division; teacher or researcher of social change; Boomer looking for a way to give back; or a Millennial just starting your first career and raring to go, it is my hope that this book will help raise the quality of your contribution. It is time to reinvent the world. Let's get started.

IT ALWAYS SEEMS IMPOSSIBLE UNTIL IT'S DONE:

FOUR EXPERIMENTS IN SOCIETAL TRANSFORMATION

IT ALWAYS SEEMS IMPOSSIBLE

UNTIL IT'S DONE:

FOUR EXPERIMENTS IN SOCIETAL TRANSFORMATION

It is the social entrepreneur's need to achieve major impact that leads to the years of experimentation and adjustment that culminates in a blueprint.

—David Bornstein, *How to Change the World:*
Social Entrepreneurs and the Power of New Ideas

The four stories in this section describe the thirty-year learning journey that gave birth to the Social Change 2.0 blueprint. This learning journey can be viewed from three perspectives—its process, context, and content. The process is the aspiration and specific experiences that enabled the development of this social change framework. The context is the common path all social entrepreneurs must walk. And the content is the specific societal issues this second order change solution addressed.

To understand the versatility of this social change *process* one needs to be aware of the problems it was designed to solve, the milieus in which it operated, and the resistances it pushed up against, each of which contributed to shaping this unique set of solutions. And to recognize its usefulness one must see it demonstrating social value. This section will take you under the hood to examine this social learning process in action. It is a learning process, I might add, that can be applied to any manner of social change endeavor.

These stories also describe the path on which all social innovations must travel—their *context*. A change agent identifies a societal problem or unmet societal need and invents a possible solution. He or she then builds and tests a social innovation until it produces a consistently workable solution that can be replicated and brought to scale. All along the way the change agent must generate the resources to keep this creative endeavor going so it has the possibility to achieve its social impact, almost always against major obstacles. Being able to get all these elements to work in tandem is the path of a social entrepreneur. It is a path anyone attempting to further social change must walk to a greater or lesser degree.

Finally, this section offers insight into four distinct societal issues, or the *content* to which this social change framework was applied. In each case we explore a societal issue from the vantage point of the individual, who, if empowered, can play a major role in its transformation and evolution.

- Chapter 1 explores the question of how to engage the planet's citizens in shifting the energy of a world poised on the brink of nuclear self-destruction.

- Chapter 2 asks the question of how to get Americans whose lifestyles are a major cause of the planet's rapid ecological unraveling to live within the means of the Earth and even become change agents.

- Chapter 3 looks at the question of how to help those living in crime-ridden and blighted inner-city communities develop a sense of efficacy so they can regain control of their lives and neighborhoods.

- Chapter 4 takes up the question of how to build the resiliency of citizens and neighborhoods so that they can respond skillfully to the ever-increasing incidence of global warming-induced natural disasters like Hurricane Katrina, and the ever-present threat of terrorist incidents like 9/11.

These four stories will be layered into the *Social Change 2.0* principles described in Part Two and built on in the strategies described in Part Three. Enjoy the ride.

THE WORLD AT THE BRINK:

CREATING A BETTER GAME THAN WAR

In 1983, I decided to swallow the world whole on my first bite. They say if it doesn't kill you, it will make you stronger, and I can attest to that. In a literal crucible of fire, the social change framework that I would come to flesh out over the next decades was born, and it was basically a combination of beginner's luck, timing, a modicum of knowledge about transformation, intuition, and a lot of perseverance that kept me holding on to fan the flames.

In that year a nuclear war seemed very, very possible. And in November, half of America and the largest audience ever for a TV movie tuned to ABC to watch *The Day After*, a simulated nuclear holocaust. In this apocalyptic film nightmare, America is destroyed by a nuclear attack launched by the Soviet Union. The movie created an almost palpable shock among Americans as we sat in our living rooms and watched the annihilation of tens of millions of fictional fellow citizens. It was as if Americans had had a collective near-death experience.

It was a time when the two most powerful nations on Earth kept their deadliest weapons trained at each other in a doomsday scenario of mutually assured destruction. Children were in despair of ever having a future and the smartest political strategists on the planet could not imagine a way out. The world was enveloped in a profound psychological darkness.

13

Out of this paralysis a small opening occurred in the American psyche for something innovative to enter. It was into this opening that I entered with a dream: to carry a torch, person to person, country to country, leader to leader, extending a band of light around the world. In my dream, the torch would ignite and unite the people and political leaders of the planet in a shared vision and experience of living together in harmony. And, I hoped it would help to create an opening in the global psyche for something new to be born—what I would come to call a planetary unitive field.

The odds against this coming to pass were immense. Who would help organize an almost impossible dream? Who would be willing to finance such a risky and unprecedented undertaking? What organizations could meet the logistical challenges? What political leaders would put their reputations on the line for such a wildly improbable idea? And if I could somehow defy all these odds and bring this dream into reality, would it really make any difference, given the monolithic forces at play? How much, after all, could a symbolic gesture accomplish?

While I clearly had a lot to learn about the world's geopolitical complexity, I did have an interesting history. I had organized the Olympic Torch Relay for the 1980 Lake Placid Games and was a seasoned management consultant. I may have been naïve, but I couldn't be completely discounted.

My first recruit, I hoped, would be a sure thing.

I had met Gail Straub three years earlier right after organizing the Olympic Torch Relay. She had short blonde hair, a radiant smile, and a contagious *joie de vivre*. There was no doubt that she was my soul mate and we instantly fell in love. Within a few months we decided to get married and develop a training program that empowered people to envision and manifest their dreams. By the spring of 1983, when this global vision was coming into being, we had been leading this workshop for two years.

I hoped my wife would not only support my dream for the world, but be willing to add her considerable energy, enthusiasm, and expertise to help make it happen. I told her it would certainly be a great adventure. I had had this idea since 1976 when I first tried my hand at large-scale organizing by creating the U.S. Bicentennial Torch Relay. During this relay, a torch was passed nonstop by thirty-two runners for 9,000 miles through America's forty-eight continental states and then flown to Alaska and Hawaii. The event was created to rekindle the values on which America was founded and which were receding into a post-Vietnam War malaise.

I explained to Gail that this self-funded grassroots initiative had captured the imagination of the country, the media, and the White House. Most important, I discovered that the fire had a mythic power that touched people in a profound way. As the event was winding down at Federal Hall in New York City, the site of George Washington's inauguration as America's first president, a thought came to me: Pass the fire, not just around the country, but around the *world*, uniting people everywhere in the spirit of cooperation. Let the passing of the torch serve as a symbolic way to recognize our common aspiration to live in harmony with one another. I felt this idea was so important that I was willing to dedicate several years of my life to making it happen.

I told Gail that after the Bicentennial Torch Relay I had tried for three years to convince people and institutions to participate in this endeavor. While I was able to create a core organizing team and had the goodwill of many, I had received multiple rejections from funding institutions. Having spent my meager savings, I was running out of options. Suddenly, out of the blue, I was offered an opportunity to organize the 1980 Lake Placid Olympic Torch Relay. I had developed an expertise in a most esoteric craft and essentially had cornered the market. I quickly redirected my team.

It was a remarkable experience. President Jimmy Carter offered us his plane, Air Force One, to transport the flame the 5,000 miles from Olympia, Greece, to Langley Air Force Base in Virginia, from which we would relay it to Lake Placid, New York. The awe of the flight attendants when they viewed the Olympic Flame was perhaps my first real experience of the full extent of the power of this symbol. I kept the fire in a draft-proof miner's lamp next to my seat on this surprisingly ordinary-looking plane, and each of the attendants made a point of coming over to look at it. One commented to me: "I have had the pleasure of being host to many important guests on this plane, but the Olympic Flame is *the* most important." Their awe was echoed and repeated all along the relay route and once again, I saw the fire's power to transform and uplift all who gazed on it.

I told Gail that given the credibility I'd gained from organizing the Olympic Torch Relay and the pervasive fear of our planet's imminent peril, I thought people might now be more willing to embrace this vision. I cautioned her that if we went for this dream, we would need to devote the majority of our time to organizing, which might put our young empowerment training business at risk. We would also have to invest the small inheritance I had recently received from my mother's death as the start-up capital. Since no one had ever done anything of this global and logistical magnitude before, it would also be very, very hard to do. But *if* we were able to pull this off, I felt it might just provide enough inspiration to nudge the world in the right direction. Was she up for it? If she wasn't, I assured her that I certainly would understand.

Her answer was immediate. "If it could make the kind of difference you describe," she said, "I'm willing to go for it." After a hug, my next question was, "Do you know anyone who lives in a foreign country?"

"Well," she said, then paused to think, "I know someone who used to live in England; perhaps she could help us find people."

So began our odyssey to convince the world to participate in this mythic transformative act. What transpired over the next three years demanded more of us than we could ever have imagined.

CALL OF THE DREAM

One by one we began assembling the team. I honed my recruitment pitch to: "Long hours, no pay, and no guarantee of success, but a vision that just might change the world!" It was right out of the classic Japanese movie *Seven Samurai*, in which a small group of warriors is recruited to save a city under siege by an invading army. Each samurai was accomplished and masterful in his specialty. Each was willing to step out of his life and courageously dedicate himself to a very difficult and highly challenging assignment. It was moving to watch this heroic impulse come alive within a small band of people in the here-and-now.

Soon we had graduated from convincing individuals to convincing organizations to help us arrange for the passage of the torch through their country. One such organization was the Jaycees, an international association of young leaders dedicated to community service. I was invited to their annual international meeting in Cartegena, Colombia, to present my idea. I made a speech to the entire group hoping for a great reception, but there was no immediate response. How in the world, I wondered, was I was going to find the organizers that I needed?

My opportunity came a day later during the Jaycees' traditional parade through the city. Each contingent of young leaders was lined up behind their national flag and an accompanying placard with their country's name on it. I realized this could be a bonanza! I darted from placard to placard giving my pitch and setting up meetings for the next few days. In three hours I had identified individuals from eight countries, most of whom signed on to help.

On one trip Gail went to meet with a number of possible organizers in India, Bangladesh, Singapore, Malaysia, and Indonesia. She gave herself ten days to get five organizers. She came back a week and a half later with dysentery, many stories—and the five organizers she sought.

The vision was becoming a reality: One country at a time, the world was demonstrating a desire to receive the flame.

Serving as our international director, Gail created a seventy-five-page "how-to" manual that was distributed to each country's organizing committee. This was to be their primary organizing tool. The only long-distance communications available at that time were cables and phone, both of which were cost prohibitive. The manual explained how to organize the torch relay in their country including financing, publicizing, and creating public ceremonies around it. It also explained a component of the larger initiative that we called "What's Working in the World"

With "What's Working in the World," we wanted to honor and replicate at the community level what was being created with the torch at a global level: people using their imaginations in the spirit of cooperation to find solutions to important problems. Each community the torch passed through was asked to select the three most successful self-help projects. These self-help projects were to be a celebration of the best of humanity's ingenuity, and a collection of the most successful community change strategies and practices from around the world.

At each community ceremony, the torch would "shed light" on what was working in the world. Our goal was to disseminate these local solutions to other communities so they could become global solutions.

The relay team was a group of runners who served as keepers of the fire and escorts for the torch runners in each country. Our strategy was to divide the world into sixteen geographic regions. The dream, like a beautiful song bird, attracted runners from each of these regions who were willing to add their unique spirit to this epic adventure in the making. They came from Argentina, Australia, Brazil, Canada, China, Costa Rica, Hungary, India, Japan, Kenya, Malaysia, New Zealand, Nigeria, Russia, United Kingdom, and the United States. They were women and men, Hindus, Muslims, Jews and Christians, recreational runners and Olympians. The world's rich cultural and religious diversity was being assembled and would be placed together for eighty-six days.

The core responsibility of the relay team was to serve as emissaries—welcoming and accompanying each of the thousands of runners from around the world who would carry the torch. They were also charged with assuring the original fire stored in draft-proof miner's lamps always remained lit. They would face many challenges, from helping runners safely navigate through the massive uncontrolled crowds, to convincing airlines that it was safe to fly with a live flame, to living with others who were so different from themselves.

RUNNING ON AN EMPTY STOMACH

So how do you transport a multicultural group of people, a live flame, and torches through a different country almost every day? How do you successfully guide people with limited experience in this sort of thing to organize hundreds of community events with millions of people? How do you go about convincing dozens of heads of state to participate? How do you persuade airlines to go against their regulations and allow a live flame on board? How do you get the world's media to follow this adventure as it circumnavigates the planet? The organizing, logistical, and political challenges were unending. It was like mounting-an-expedition-to-scale-Everest-for-the-first-time meets producing-the-Olympic-Opening-Ceremony!

While these challenges were being confronted, a most daunting one still lay ahead: attracting the several million dollars of financing needed to make all this happen. I needed to provide assurances to the sponsors about our team's ability to pull off an immensely complex global event that had never been done before. While I had secured seed capital to pay some staff, with six months left to go there was still no major sponsorship. As the seed funding and Gail's and my financial resources were dwindling, I felt a growing sense of unease. Here we were persuading people all over the world to invest their time and hope, in some cases at the cost of economic hardship, and I might not be able to raise the money to make this happen. Our Japanese organizer, Atsuo Shiga, summed up the situation this way: "How far can one run on an empty stomach?"

For about a year, we had been having discussions with the United Nations Children's Fund (UNICEF) about a partnership. As our international organization grew and momentum built, their interest was piqued. Ultimately I met with Jim Grant, UNICEF's visionary leader, who agreed to have his organization become an in-kind sponsor, using the event to celebrate their fortieth anniversary. They would also be a recipient of any funds raised. In return, they would provide office space in their Manhattan headquarters, active support reaching out to heads of state through their international network, and a state-of-the-art communication infrastructure. In the mid-1980s, this meant an in-house telex machine to receive cable messages; there were no fax machines or e-mail. Our team moved into wonderful new digs overlooking Manhattan's East River. We were motivated to keep running on an empty stomach.

Soon the media caught wind of this initiative. Stories began appearing in the *New York Times* and on the major TV networks for what was now being called the First Earth Run and the "torch of peace." One team member, Hal Uplinger, who had helped produce the mega rock concert fundraiser for famine relief in Africa, "Live Aid," used his contacts to bring ABC Television on as the media sponsor. They committed to providing coverage of the torch's 12-week passage around the world every Wednesday morning on *Good Morning America*. This inspired other media across the planet to do the same thing.

Then the political leadership support began falling into place, including U.S. President Ronald Reagan, the Soviet Union's President Mikhail Gorbachev, and China's President Li Xiannian. As the momentum built, requests started coming from many heads of state asking that the flame go through their country. One of the most meaningful requests came from King Birendra of Nepal. He wished the torch of peace to light an eternal flame he would erect at the pilgrimage birthplace of the Buddha in Lumbini. He said he wanted the millions of Buddhist pilgrims who come to Lumbini to be inspired by this act of peace building. The mythic power of the dream was generating a magic that was captivating all who heard it.

A member of the core team, Brooke Newell, a vice president of the large multinational Chase Manhattan Bank, had begun soliciting her company to sponsor the event from its very inception. As the senior leadership heard of the growing support and momentum that was building, they became more and more interested, concluding that, "this is one of the truly extraordinary activities of our time and is an unparalleled opportunity for our company." Soon we were negotiating in earnest for a multimillion dollar sponsorship. The only issues were how much they would pay and how they would promote it. Needless to say, this news gave everyone on the organizing team a collective sigh of relief.

Then, one day about three months before the event, Brooke requested a meeting with me. We had been meeting frequently about the negotiations with Chase, but this day Brooke had an ominous look about her. She got right to it. After a hard-headed analysis at the highest levels of the organization, Chase had decided to pull back from sponsorship. They had determined this was too risky an undertaking. So many things could go wrong. They ticked off the potential pitfalls one after the other.

- Without consistently professional crowd control the runners, spectators and team were in danger of bodily harm or even death.

- It was such a high-profile event that it could easily be hijacked by a fringe group for its own political purposes.

- The level of organization was uneven and in any number of countries the event could fall on its face with minimal participation.

- If it was used as a propaganda event by communist dictators it would reflect poorly on the company.

In short, it was just way too risky a venture for them and they were unwilling to go forward.

We were definitely at a moment of truth. Should I thank my amazing team for their efforts and faith in me as a leader, but tell them there just wasn't enough time to find another sponsor? That we needed to call this off before more expectations were raised? I had invested so many years of work and we were so, so close. I was at a complete loss as to what to do.

I sought support and counsel from my dear wife, Gail, who had been there 110 percent at every step of the journey. She held me and advised me to pray for guidance and sleep on it. I followed her advice and when I woke up the next day, I was clear.

I called our core team of about twenty-five people together in our United Nations offices. They assembled in the only location where everyone could fit—a corridor between our tightly packed offices. Calmly, but with my heart in my throat, I told them: "Chase Manhattan Bank has decided to pull out as a sponsor. We have no other prospects at the moment, as Chase had wished to be the sole sponsor. It would be extremely hard to find a multimillion dollar sponsorship on this short notice.

"Everyone's faith and dedication has brought us to this point and now we all need to determine where we stand. I have decided to go forward and I ask each of you to think hard about what you want to do. I will understand if you aren't willing or able to hang in any longer. After all, most of you have not been paid, and those who have have received only a survival level salary. Our workload is relentless—ten- to twelve-hour days. For every logistical and political challenge we solve, two new ones appear. In spite of this major setback, I will do whatever it takes to find another source of funding."

The team did not hesitate. They unanimously decided to go forward. They determined they would keep running on an empty stomach.

I decided my best chance was to speak to UNICEF's executive director, Jim Grant, and ask for his financial support. From several communications, I knew Jim had become a real partner. He had told me he was in awe of the response this project was getting from usually reticent political leaders all over the world. He had said that although he was getting some resistance from his country directors, the positive association of people and political leaders around the world toward UNICEF would make their work much easier in the future. He also hoped it would assist their fund-raising efforts both through the event and in the future by the increased visibility. But the bottom line was that he was putting his organization behind this initiative because he believed it was the right thing to do.

I arranged a meeting with Jim the next day to explain what had happened. By the time I arrived, Jim had already heard that Chase had pulled out. When I asked him to consider funding the whole thing, he was ready with an answer. He said, "We will make it happen!" I could not hold back my tears of relief and joy.

This moment marked a phenomenon that became a hallmark: Each time we were faced with a seemingly insurmountable challenge, if we kept the faith, help came. UNICEF became the underwriter, and a better sponsor for a global humanitarian mission of this magnitude could not have been found. We all concluded this dream was blessed with grace.

THE DREAM GOES LIVE

With funding finally secured, the effort and response from around the world leapt to another level of intensity and scrutiny. I was summoned to meet with senior government leadership in both Moscow and Beijing. High-level officials asked me probing questions seeking to understand how this project had come to be, who was behind it, and what their motivations were. They wanted to know why they should encourage the people of their countries to get involved.

I told them my story and they must have believed me because both countries committed themselves to providing runners for the international team and supporting this event in their countries. In the Soviet Union 60 cities would participate throughout the fifteen Soviet Socialist Republics that made up the country, with huge events planned for Leningrad (now St. Petersburg) and Moscow. In China, large events would be held in Beijing and Shanghai with hundreds of thousands of runners joining a run to the Great Wall. In both countries, the heads of state would honor the flame's arrival.

Other amazing things were happening. President Daniel Ortega of Nicaragua and his arch enemy, Adolfo Calero, leader of the guerilla group the Contras, would declare a cease-fire for the day and have their children carry the torch together through the capital city of Managua. Jewish and Arab children were going to carry the torch into the Knesset, the Israeli parliament building, in Jerusalem. In Northern Ireland, Catholic and Protestant runners were going to pass the torch from one to another. The president of Iceland wished the torch to be brought to Reykjavik to light a world peace cauldron outside the building where Gorbachev and Reagan were to have their historic first summit meeting. It was as though the geopolitical chessboard were given a second dimension to play on and previously unimagined new moves were being invented.

The lighting and launch of the torch of peace on its journey around the world were to take place at the United Nations in New York. The torch was to be lit from a fire created at a sunrise ceremony on the grounds of the United Nations by two Native American elders, Chief Shenandoah of the Iroquois Nation and Grandmother Caroline of the Hopi Nation. Among the native cultures, the Iroquois are the "keepers of the sacred fire." It is they who are charged among all the native tribes to provide the fire necessary to realize dreams. The Hopi are the "keepers of the dream." They serve as stewards of the most profound belief and hope on the planet: that human beings can live in harmony with one another and the Earth.

The Hopi people are also keepers of the Hopi Prophecies, reverently handed down from one generation to the next for more than a thousand years. The most important of these prophecies states that when humanity is on the brink of self-destruction, the Hopi must deliver a message at the great hall of mica. If this message is received, the world will begin the "great turning" toward a thousand years of peace. If it is not received, the world will continue its direction and enter into a thousand years of darkness and war. The prophecy states that the Hopi will have four attempts to deliver this message.

The Hopi elders determined that the time described in the prophecy had come, and the great hall of mica was the glass United Nations building on Manhattan's East Side. For the sake of the world, they diligently sought an audience with the leadership of the United Nations. Their previous requests for an audience with the United Nations had been turned down three times, so this was their final chance. The native cultures were closely tracking what they felt was a momentous opportunity for humanity.

It was a beautiful sunrise in Manhattan. It had rained overnight so the air was pure and the sky was clear. Sunlight was gleaming off the tall rectangular glass United Nations building and surrounding skyscrapers. Political dignitaries, rock stars, and the United Nations secretary general were preparing to participate. It was September 16, 1986, the opening day of the U.N. General Assembly—the international day of peace in the international year of peace.

The evening before, a ceremonial site had been prepared on the U.N. grounds by Chief Shenandoah. There was a little chill in the air that September morning as Chief Shenandoah of the Iroquois Nation rubbed two sticks together, in the ancient way, until a spark was ignited into kindling. The kindling was placed on combustible grasses until a small flame grew into a blazing fire. Many political dignitaries and media were on hand to hear Grandmother Caroline offer the prophecy the Hopi had been stewarding for a millennium.

"Humanity" she said in her soft voice, "is at a crossroads. To continue on this planet, we are being called to achieve a higher level of global community, where we can experience that which unites us. The fire symbolizes the light within that connects us all. As this light goes around the world it will awaken in humanity a deep yearning to live in harmony with each other and the Earth. This will leave a lasting imprint in our memory and initiate the great turning that was prophesized. Learn to interpret the signs. They will be there."

Her profound message of hope inspired everyone in attendance. Over the next eighty-six days, it would be communicated in one form or another to the twenty-five million people and forty-five heads of state in sixty-two countries who would directly participate in the passage of the fire, and to the billion more who would follow it through the media. (See Figures 1.1 to 1.8, pages 24–27, for the First Earth Run map and photographs.)

— First Earth Run Map and Photos —

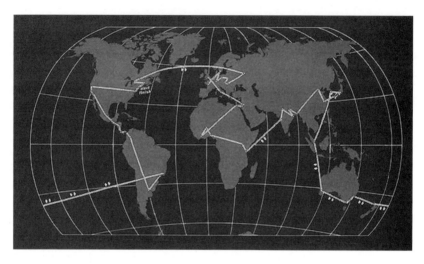

Figure 1.1—Transworld route, September 16–December 11, 1986.

*Figure 1.2—Child reading her message to dignitaries, including
(in the foreground from left to right) UN Secretary General Javier Perez and UNICEF
Execuive Director Jim Grant at opening ceremony. New York City, United States.*

Figure 1.3—Thousands of villagers welcome the torch of peace to Burkina Faso, Africa.

*Figure 1.4—David hands the torch to China's president, Li Xiannian,
at Great Hall of People, Beijing, China.*

*Figure 1.5—President Li Xiannian in a light moment with
First Earth Run International Director, Gail Straub, Beijing, China.*

*Figure 1.6—Arab and Jewish children from the Neva Shalom community
carry the torch of peace together on the way to Jerusalem, Israel.*

Figure 1.7—In Red Square, Moscow, Russia.
Many torches were dispersed throughout the country,
and a strong message of support was delivered by President Mikhail Gorbachev.

Figure 1.8—Young boy holds candle lit from the torch of peace with First Earth Run
banner in the background, Warsaw, Poland.

The eighty-six-day journey of the fire around the world was an extraordinary moment on the planet. Wherever the flame traveled, conflict stopped and adversaries cooperated. The anticipated fear of crowds being out of control did not materialize; even when they were wildly enthusiastic, they were also very respectful because of the awe evoked by the fire. There were no injuries, not even a single burn. On more than one occasion, it was raining when the flame arrived, but when the ceremony began, the rain ceased and the sun came out. Airline pilots welcomed the flame onto their planes as a distinguished guest. Inspired art, music, dance, and poetry were created as part of the many ceremonies that greeted the flame, touching people's spirits and uniting them. Each community proudly shared success stories of how its citizens had cooperated for the common good and achieved something great. And the torch arrived on time for every scheduled ceremony. For eighty-six days, wherever the flame went there was peace and goodwill. These "signs" were noticed by all.

When the flame arrived back at the United Nations in New York, a special session was held in the U.N. General Assembly Hall. Delegates shared story after story of how the people of their countries were uplifted by the fire, united by their common aspirations for a better world, and hopeful now that perhaps it would be possible to create it.

INITIATED BY THE DREAM

On a personal level I had an experience similar to that described by astronaut Rusty Schweikert, who, on seeing the awesome beauty of the Earth from space, described himself as a "sensing mechanism for humanity." In this case I felt like humanity's sensing mechanism on the Earth, experiencing our beauty up close. I experienced the depth of our common humanity and our wondrous diversity. I saw firsthand our ability to rise beyond that which separates us and find ways to cooperate. I witnessed our courage to risk believing, in spite of much evidence to the contrary, that we can create a better world. I also came to believe that yes, anything is possible.

Did the flame's journey change our world in any demonstrable way? A story will illustrate the mysterious effects of the fire on a few of the mortals playing out one of the great dramas of that time.

The prime minister of the United Kingdom, Margaret Thatcher, known as the "Iron Lady" because of her toughness, had been reluctant to participate in the First Earth Run, thinking it was all a colossal waste of time. But when the groundswell of political support had grown to include Presidents Mikhail Gorbachev of the Soviet Union, Ronald Reagan of the United States, and Li Xiannian of China, she finally accepted the invitation to take part. Children from each of the major ethnic groups in London were invited to 10 Downing Street for a short candle-lighting ceremony.

The flame was carried in by a runner and each child was offered a candle to light from the torch. One by one, as they lit their candles, the children became transfixed, hardly able to move. It was as if in receiving fire from the torch, they had received the collective goodwill of all those people who had transported it and witnessed it in its journey so far. The entire room was transformed. What had been planned as a simple ten-minute ceremony evolved into a two-hour tour through the rich history of this historic building that for 250 years had served as the country's seat of power, with the prime minister as guide. She told the children of the many important events and decisions that had transpired in those chambers, and impressed on them the need to use their experience with the flame to inspire others in their communities. The powerful presence of the fire had warmed the "Iron Lady," allowing her momentarily to shed her armor.

A few weeks later she was to be the first Western political leader to meet with President Mikhail Gorbachev of Russia. Her assignment was to determine if he could be trusted and the world could be brought back from the precipice. Knowing that the peace flame had also just passed through Moscow, she shared her candle-lighting experience with one of the meeting organizers. When she arrived in Russia for her historic meeting, she was invited to participate with Gorbachev in a candle-lighting ceremony in the Kremlin similar to the one at Downing Street, with Soviet children representing the country's many ethnic groups. In this instance they used fire lit from the peace torch that had been maintained in seven day candles. The fire again had a transforming effect, allowing these two cold warriors to relate to one another in a context of peace and goodwill. The distrust softened in both of them, allowing for intelligence to transcend political posturing. Her communication to the world after their meeting was, "We can do business with him."

Another example of the alchemical power of the fire and the dream occurred when it penetrated what was then called the Iron Curtain. When the flame arrived in the Soviet Union and Eastern Europe it elicited a palpable emotional response. You could see it in the teary eyes of the tens of thousands of enthusiastic participants who lined the torch relay routes three deep to catch a glimpse of the fire. You could see it in the loving way parents gazed at their children after the flame had passed. And you could most certainly see it in the spontaneous organization of dozens of auxiliary relays that spun off the main route to bring the fire to hundreds more cities throughout these countries.

It was as if an intoxicating fragrance was wafting through the air. What had been an airtight container was now being permeated with the freshness of innovative new ideas. They were breathing in what free will could achieve. They were breathing in hope and possibility for their lives.

So did the fire and the dream cause a demonstrable change in the world? Thousands of people around the world with whom I have shared the video documenting the story have weighed in with their opinions. Some said it helped catalyze a shift toward a more unitive consciousness on the planet. Some said it created the *non sequitur* needed to allow the two superpower adversaries to find new footing in their relationship. Some said it empowered the thought leaders in Eastern Europe with a sense of hope and possibility which contributed to the Velvet Revolution and the tearing down of the Berlin Wall. Some said all this would have happened anyway.

Ultimately no one will ever really know if the fire's influence on the hearts and minds of the many around the world translated into these outcomes. What is certain is that a world poised on the precipice of nuclear war somehow miraculously survived, and that people under communist oppression miraculously rose up and with minimal bloodshed threw off their bondage. Were these signs of the great turning foretold by Grandmother Caroline?

And what is the legacy of the fire and the dream? While there are many aspects that affect people, one universally emerges every time I tell this story: the simple fact that this seemingly impossible dream for our world overcame the immense odds against it and actually happened. If this could happen, why couldn't other acts of seemingly impossible transformation occur as well? The First Earth Run's legacy is that it fuels people's imagination and willingness to believe in and create profound transformative change in our world.

Let me close with a story related to me by a Dutch delegate who participated in the negotiations attempting to transform the European Economic Community from a trade organization into the politically and economically integrated European Union. During one of their crucial meetings, its opponents had enumerated the reasons that substantive cooperation could never be achieved.

They said, "We will lose our individuality and unique cultures. We will have to depend on others who may not be economically and politically reliable. There is just no way we will be able to put aside all our past history and animosity." When the arguments had been laid out, it was obvious there was no rational counterargument to these fears. A fundamental leap of faith was required that could not be made with logic. A continent was being asked to trust that something better could work in spite of its prior experiences of war and cultural animosity.

It was at this moment that a leading advocate for the European Union from the Netherlands reminded everyone about the story of the flame. He stated: "They, too, faced immense resistances that seemed impossible to overcome. Yet they overcame these formidable obstacles and birthed an unprecedented experience of cooperation around the world. Given the opportunity, people were willing to transcend their historic differences and allow themselves to be united by their common desire for a better world. It is now our time to do the same thing."

The delegates realized that a moment had come to trust without proof and hope that when people from their countries came together they would see that that which united them was stronger than that which had historically separated them. It was clear that the people of Europe could not get to their next level of societal development without an act of trust. The story of the fire contributed to building this safety net of trust. And they took their historic leap into the unknown.

As we face the many monumental global challenges that seem impossible to overcome, it is my hope that the story of the First Earth Run will provide a safety net of trust beneath the dreams of those willing to imagine the impossible. Nelson Mandela, a seasoned veteran of such endeavors, says it well, "It always seems impossible until it's done." The next story continues down this path of exploring the boundaries of the possible.

CHAPTER 1: SOCIAL CHANGE 2.0 PRACTITIONER'S GUIDE

1. What is your dream—large or small—for making our world a better place?

2. What about it inspires you?

3. What about it do you think will inspire others to participate in it?

4. What are you doing to bring it into realization?

5. What allows you to keep your faith in its possibility?

CHAPTER 2

ENVIRONMENTALLY SUSTAINABLE LIFESTYLES

IN AMERICA:

PSST—SAVE THE PLANET, PASS IT ON

After the First Earth Run experience Gail and I needed time to decompress. The preparation and the event—three years in the making and three months in the execution—were both extraordinarily exhilarating and physically exhausting. To recuperate and take stock of this experience we went to the two places that had most touched us on our planetary journey. For one restful month we soaked up the sensual beauty and gentleness of the island of Bali. Then we moved on to the rugged and awe-inspiring mountain peaks of Nepal for another month. As I trekked through the dramatic landscape gazing at majestic snow-capped mountains each day, my mind emptied. This was the perfect place to begin integrating my experience and ponder some large questions. What had I learned? How should I use this experience? What was most needed in the world? *What called me?*

As I was considering all this, I received an invitation in early 1988 from Ted Turner, to participate in the startup of a new television program he was developing to focus on the environment. He had heard of my experience with mass mobilization and empowerment and hoped that I might have ideas that would help inspire viewers to take personal action. In the course of my meetings with Ted, a colorful, larger-than-life personality with a passionate commitment to the environment, he gave me a copy of a book called *Our Common Future.*

The book, which had just been published, was authored by the U.N. World Commission on Environment and Development, an independent commission established by the United Nations to examine the critical environment and development problems on the planet and to formulate realistic proposals to solve them. It coined a new term, *sustainable development*, to describe an approach to reconciling the two opposing forces causing an environmental stalemate. The authors proposed the notion that countries need *both* to grow economically *and* to protect the environment. They moved the debate from either/or to both/and thinking, creating an opening for collaboration among business, government, and environmental organizations. While not strong on specifics, the book was an important first step toward finding a more transformative approach to environmental change.

I dove in to learn more. All the books and reports I read described the problems our planet faces in excruciating detail and then saved the last few pages, or a chapter at the most, for a solution. They would offer a few sketchy ideas and then conclude by saying we just need to generate the political will. But how was that to happen?

There were many environmental groups working to protect different parts of the ecosystem—animals, land, air, and water. I could not, however, find any comprehensive global environmental action plan or any organization responsible for implementing it. The planet's ecosystem was unraveling and no one was in charge.

If there was a likely candidate for such a job, it was the United Nations. It was not hard to arrange a visit to a colleague I had met during the First Earth Run, Noel Brown, the North American regional director of the U.N. Environment Programme. Noel, a Jamaican with a strong international and diplomatic background, was an astute and creative planetary thinker. He had proposed that we plant trees around the planet as a legacy wherever the torch went. We were not able to make this happen, but I always thought it was a great idea. He was also an eloquent and inspiring speaker. Every speech I heard from him left me informed and fired up.

I met with him in at the U.N. office complex on the East Side of Manhattan—a familiar haunt to me by now. We held our meeting in a conference room with maps of the world's environmental hot spots plastered all over the walls. "What was going on with the United Nations as far as environmental action was concerned?" I asked. "Who was in charge of it? Was there a plan?"

Noel quickly enlightened me as to the international politics of environmental change. "If countries agreed to measurable international environmental goals," he said, "there would be pressure on them to achieve them. Governments are not ready at this point in time to take on this responsibility. As a consequence, the U.N., as an institution of national governments, has no mandate to go beyond the analysis of the problem, and a philosophy of change."

No goals, no plan, and no leadership. Not good.

Way Out of My League

I thanked him for his time and insight. As I got up to leave the meeting, Noel coyly offered, with a smile, "If you want a global action plan you will need to create it yourself."

"Way out of my league," I told him. I laughed and shook my head.

But the idea started gnawing on me. Our planet is facing this huge problem, I thought. I have some credibility from successfully mounting a large global initiative. I have a great international network, and I know a bunch about empowering people to take action. It would not be the first time that I have traveled where angels feared to tread. Why not give it a try? And so began my next big adventure.

My first step was to understand what it would take to transform our planet's unsustainable environmental trajectory. This translated into three concrete questions.

- What are the measurable goals to get our planet on a sustainable path?

- What are the leverage points in society to achieve them?

- How do we get people to participate?

A friend of mine, Denis Hayes, was organizing Earth Day 1990. This was the twentieth anniversary of the first Earth Day event, which he also helped organize. I had met Denis the prior year and immediately found him to be a kindred spirit. He had a big vision for changing the world and knew how to empower people to step up to the challenge. I rarely met people willing to think and act at this level, and fewer still that had his degree of organizing and strategic know-how. Denis's presence on the planet was very reassuring to me. Perhaps I was not completely out of my mind since there was someone else who was willing to think and take action at this scale.

Earth Day was picking up steam both here in the United States and internationally. Since the Earth Day network was in 140 countries it would be a perfect grassroots platform for launching a set of global environmental goals. I approached Denis and he loved the idea immediately. He thought this would add a strong legacy component to Earth Day and provide credibility for the many grassroots organizers around the planet working on one or more of these specific environmental goals. We agreed that I would pull together the initial research and his team would review it and integrate it into the Earth Day materials and communications.

Now that I had a platform from which to deliver a set of planet-wide environmental goals to the world, all I needed to do was to figure out the goals. Oh, and to make sure they were credible enough to stand up to critical scrutiny by scientists, environmentalists, and politicians. No big deal. My off-handed remark to Noel was prescient. This *was* way out of my league.

I plowed ahead and began looking for funding to hire a person who did know something about this topic. I was able to secure a small grant, and my first choice was Robert Gilman. After the First Earth Run he had interviewed me for *In Context*, a quarterly magazine he founded on sustainable humane culture. I was impressed by the thoughtful and out-of-the-box quality of his questions. I also loved his writing. Robert's prose makes complex planetary issues eminently understandable to the layperson.

With a Ph.D. from Princeton in astrophysics, he could also bring the needed scientific rigor to this research helping protect us against those who might try to discredit this endeavor. A comment he made when I was interviewing him for the position clearly demonstrated that he had the soul of a change agent lurking beneath his scientific mind. "The stars can wait," he said, "but the planet can't." Robert would not be intimidated by the scope of this project. To my delight and relief he agreed to come on board.

We developed five criteria for the project:

- Address the major issues necessary for the planet to move on to an environmentally sustainable path.

- Express them in quantifiable terms that could be measured.

- Base our recommendations on the research of well-recognized authorities and institutes.

- Base our recommendations on science and human capability.

- Key to the year 2000 to provide a realistic time frame for mobilizing action and measuring progress.

We created fifteen environmental action goals divided into five categories: preserving the climate and atmosphere, preserving biological diversity, reducing waste, using water wisely, and stabilizing human population. We created a matrix connecting each global goal with specific actions people could take at the personal, workplace, and community levels. (See Figure 2.1, page 38, for the detailed goals.)

We called it the Earth Day "Agenda for the Green Decade." On April 22, 1990, we launched these goals across the planet. As Denis and I had hoped, they immediately began stimulating powerful conversations among thousands of grassroots change leaders. Many of these leaders thanked us for putting together what began to be called "a people's agenda for the planet." Some told us that these credible and measurable metrics strengthened the case they were making to political and funding institutions for support of their efforts. Some translated the global template we developed into complimentary local sustainability goals.

One of the most significant effects of the Earth Day goals was how they served as a call to action by the people of our planet for political leaders to move our governments into alignment. True to the saying—*when the people lead, the leaders will follow*—in 1992 in Rio de Janeiro, Brazil, the United Nations hosted a large intergovernmental environmental conference. Representatives of all of the world's governments gathered to start addressing the planet's environmental problems and to craft a plan of action. Although this "Earth Summit," as it was called, was already in the works before we launched the Earth Day goals, the response to the Agenda for the Green Decade demonstrated across the planet that there was political will and demand for government leaders to create tangible goals and a substantive action plan.

What came out of this historic conference was the first-ever comprehensive governmental consensus document on the environment, "Agenda 21." It both described the need to take planetary action to restore our planet's damaged ecosystem and offered a set of goals to achieve this restoration. Because of the many political compromises needed to achieve consensus, these goals were far more modest than the planet needed. But Agenda 21 was a huge step forward. We now had international governmental buy-in for the importance of humanity getting on an environmentally sustainable path, and consensus on our first map for heading there.

Figure 2.1—Agenda for the Green Decade

GLOBAL ENVIRONMENTAL ACTION GOALS
TO BE ACHIEVED BY THE YEAR 2000

PRESERVE THE CLIMATE AND ATMOSPHERE

- Decrease carbon dioxide emissions by 20% through increased energy efficiency and increased use of renewable energy sources to slow global warming.
- Eliminate emissions of and production of CFCs and other ozone-depleting chemicals.
- Decrease emissions of sulfur dioxide by 90% and nitrogen oxides by 75% to abate acid rain.
- Improve urban air quality in the world's cities by reducing all automobile pollutants at least 50%.

PRESERVE BIOLOGICAL DIVERSITY

- Triple the area of protected ecological preserves for species preservation.
- Reduce deforestation by 50%.
- Increase reforestation enough to offset deforestation by planting 100 billion trees.
- Shift 50% of agricultural production to low-input sustainable agriculture
- Reduce global pesticide use by 75%.

REDUCE WASTE

- Reduce solid waste by 75% through recycling, source reduction and composting.
- Cut the production of hazardous waste by 80%.
- Clean up all existing toxic, hazardous, and nuclear waste sites to acceptable levels of safety.

USE WATER WISELY

- Reduce water use by a third or more through more efficient use in agriculture, industry, and households.
- Provide safe drinking water for all.

STABILIZE HUMANITY

- Reduce the rate of world population growth by 50%.
- Eliminate hunger.

One statement that came out of the *Agenda 21* report became the rallying cry for my work: *The single greatest cause of the deterioration of the planet's ecosystem is the unsustainable patterns of consumption and production of natural resources in the industrialized countries. The industrialized countries of the world need to take responsibility to lead the way.*

This simple, straightforward analysis confirmed and legitimized Robert and my conclusion that we needed to change how we lived in order for the planet to get on a sustainable path. I now had answers to my first two questions about the goals and leverage points, and was ready to answer the third. *How do we change the consumption patterns of people in the industrialized nations of the world?* Although I did not know about second order change at the time, I was learning firsthand how to define it—it always seems impossible.

A Change in Behavior

In the early 1990s America and the other industrialized countries were waking up to the realization that our environmental problems were not exclusively the result of pollution caused by big business, and that therefore the necessary solutions were not going to come exclusively from governments regulating those businesses.

Through the research I was doing I learned that America, as 5 percent of the planet's population, consumes *one-third of the planet's natural resources.* We consume these resources—oil, timber, minerals, among others—directly through our daily lifestyle choices. Incredibly, we also influence the other two-thirds indirectly through the products we buy. And here's the kicker. As Americans we waste up to 75 percent of what we consume through our lack of awareness and efficiency. Said another way, we waste up to 75 percent of our hugely disproportionate share of the Earth's bounty.

The bad news is that as individuals the ways in which we use the planet's natural resources on a daily basis are a major part of the problem. The good news is that if we are a major part of the problem, we can also be a major part of the solution, *if* we can adopt more environmentally sustainable lifestyle practices.

So we needed to change our lifestyles. Simple enough. Earth Day 1990 helped spawn a cottage industry of "how-to" books ranging from 50 to 1,000 things individuals could do to lessen their environmental toll on the planet, and this seemed to be a promising start. But studies were showing that books and media campaigns imploring people were not translating into changing behavior. Yes, we were beginning to leave our newspapers tied in bundles at the curb, but that was just the tip of the iceberg.

To better understand this disconnect between people's growing environmental awareness and their lack of behavior change I began asking everyone I knew and even some I didn't this question: What would help you translate what you know about the environment into new behaviors in your life?

Here's what came back to me:

- Where do I start?

- Which are the important actions?

- How do I implement these actions?

- Does what I do actually make a difference?

I knew that if people were to be a solution, there needed to be good answers to these questions and the frustration underlying them. I was speaking to people of goodwill who wanted to do the right thing. But they were frustrated and questioned whether or not change was really possible. Some had lost ground to cynicism.

What was needed was becoming clearer.

DESIGNING A BEHAVIOR-CHANGE SOLUTION

I knew I had to develop credible answers to these four questions or I would be wasting my time. I began by organizing the plethora of existing how-to environmental information so it could be more easily acted on. I decided to use a design format we had developed for our Empowerment Workshop. In that training, to help people make changes we divided life up into seven areas: relationships, work, body, money, emotions, sexuality, and spirituality. People focused on one area before moving to the next. In each area they developed a vision of what they wished to accomplish and then developed a plan to implement it.

Translating this design framework was straightforward. Together Robert and I developed a workbook based on the five major areas in which a household impacts the environment—solid waste, energy, water, transportation, and purchasing. We added another section on empowering others so that people could encourage friends and neighbors to make changes, too.

In each of these five topic areas we developed a menu of possible actions. Each action was written as a one-page recipe with the time and materials required, the resources saved, a number indicating its degree of difficulty, and a playful cartoon illustration. (See Figures 2.2 and 2.3, pages 42–43 for sample actions.)

This programmatic approach was a major improvement over a simple list of disconnected actions. But to get people actually to take action would require some form of motivation. Again I turned to our Empowerment Workshop for inspiration. What were the essential elements that motivated people to change? The empowerment tools we offered were certainly important, but they were not motivational. *What actually motivated people to change was witnessing and engaging with other people who were changing in front of their eyes.* Many workshop participants commented that they had personal growth breakthroughs in this group setting that they would never have had on their own. It was the group format that inspired people to change. Yes, a support group might just be the yeast needed to raise this dough into bread.

I called the support group an EcoTeam and developed basic guidelines for conducting meetings. Different team members would each lead one of the topic meetings every two weeks. At these EcoTeam meetings everyone would share which actions they would take before the next meeting. At the next gathering, they would then report on what they had actually done. They would also tell the group if they had encountered any problems, and if so how they addressed them so others could learn from their experiences. If they wished help in implementing a particular action they were encouraged to ask their teammates for support. They were also asked to take the program seriously by agreeing to be accountable for taking the actions to which they committed themselves.

An environmental behavior-change program was born. I called it EcoTeam: A Six Step Program to Create an Environmentally Sustainable Lifestyle (later changed to the *Green Living Handbook*). I started introducing the book at conferences and through environmental networks such as the community of Earth Day organizers. People were immediately attracted to it. They liked the program structure, the support system that established accountability for taking action, the easy-to-use recipe format of the actions, and the opportunity to express their environmental values in such a concrete way.

EcoTeams began sprouting up all over the place. Within a few months there were more than fifty teams spread across the country, then a hundred.

A-MEND

REPAIRING ITEMS INSTEAD OF THROWING THEM AWAY

WHY ACT? If you take an inventory of personal or household items not being used because they need repair, the results might surprise you. This Earth Action will help you breathe new life into a lot of unused items. Consider this action especially for large bulky items that have greater impact on landfills.

RESOURCE SAVINGS

For every item you repair, you lessen the demand for resources to produce a similar item. Allow yourself to feel a sense of pride for everything you mend instead of throw away.

EARTH ACTION

- Make an inventory of the personal or household items that are broken or need repair.
- Separate what can realistically be repaired from what is no longer usable, and recycle as much of the latter as possible.
- Make a plan with dates and times to repair what you can easily mend.
- For items you can't personally repair, look through your local Yellow Pages and locate the businesses that will fix the items: electrical and appliance repair services, shoe repair persons, seamstresses and tailors, and mechanics. Call or drop by for an estimate.
- If some items prove too costly to fix, see if you can find service organizations like Goodwill or Salvation Army that would be happy to have them as is.

MATERIALS

- Things that need repair; tools; Yellow Pages; phone.

TIME

- An afternoon to round up the items, contact the repair services, and drop them off; more time if you mend the items yourself.

GARBAGE   12

Figure 2.2

DRIVE EARTH-SMART

DEVELOPING FUEL-EFFICIENT DRIVING HABITS

 Did you know you can save gasoline, the air pollution it causes, and 10–30% of your car's fuel costs just by driving smart? This Earth Action will not only improve the quality of the air we all breathe, and save you money, but also encourage you to drive more safely.

RESOURCE SAVINGS

You improve air quality, reduce global warming, and save gasoline and money. While you are helping to make our environment cleaner, you are also making it safer. You're letting the Earth—and those living on it— know how much you care.

EARTH ACTION

Here's how to drive smart:
- Before you even pull out of the driveway:
  - If your household has more than one vehicle, always drive the more fuel-efficient model if you have a choice.
  - Plan your route, including commutes to work. The best route may not be the shortest, but the one that prevents idling in traffic. In city driving, up to one-third of a fuel's potential energy can be wasted through idling.
  - Rid your car of any unnecessary weight. You lose about 1% of fuel efficiency for every extra 100 pounds.
  - Minimize cold starts and limit warmups to 30 seconds.
- When driving on the highway:
  - Maintain a steady speed, using your cruise control device if you have one. While 55 mph may no longer be the speed limit, it's still the most fuel-efficient highway speed and will save you up to 30% in fuel costs compared with driving at 75 mph. It's also safer.
  - Keep windows closed for better aerodynamics, which, in turn, saves fuel.
- When driving on secondary roads:
  - Anticipate stops and slowdowns. Accelerate, decelerate, and brake steadily to save gas.
  - When appropriate, drive between 35 and 45 mph, the most fuel-efficient range.
  - Save gasoline at bank drive-through windows and fast-food restaurants by not using them if there is a long line of cars ahead of you. Park and go inside instead.
  - Consider turning off your car engine when your car is stopped for a minute or two, as when waiting for a train to pass.
- Limit short trips. Most of the particulate pollution that a car generates occurs in the first few miles. For short trips, a bike may be faster anyway.

MATERIALS
- A light foot on the pedal.

TIME
- No time at all.

TRANSPORTATION 72

Figure 2.3

They continued to proliferate and soon were taking many different forms. They were occurring among friends, in faith communities, workplaces, neighborhoods, and service organizations. The program was adaptable enough to fit into each of these unique cultures.

I also shared the program with international friends and colleagues I had worked with during the First Earth Run. A number of them ended up asking if they could translate and adapt the workbook to their cultures. I eagerly supported this adaptation process and the program rapidly spread in these countries as well. And as word got out, I started receiving more and more requests from different parts of the globe.

GETTING STRATEGIC

Management guru Tom Peters describes the typical creation process for new ideas as "ready, fire, aim." I had fired and now it was time to aim. This is the hard-work phase of maturing a social innovation. It meant I had to become strategic about what I was doing. Until now I had accomplished whatever I had accomplished with my own money and a small research grant. If I hoped to make any kind of meaningful change I needed to establish an international organization to implement it. I went about creating a nonprofit arm to my Empowerment Institute so I could attract philanthropic support, and I called it Global Action Plan for the Earth or GAP for short. Although the means were limited at the moment, the vision was not.

Because I had established a successful track record by mounting the First Earth Run, and because this program struck a chord in society, I was able to secure two six-figure foundation grants. I now had the financing for the "aiming" phase of refining and disseminating this program. It was time to address my next set of "how-to" questions.

- Was this program effective in helping people change their behavior and achieve substantive environmental improvements?

- If so, could these behavior changes be sustained over time?

- What was the best way to disseminate the program?

The questions would take me most of the 1990s to answer.

This was an iterative and slow learning process. Because the program was four months long it took as much as a year, or in some cases two, to find out if a particular strategy was working. We would try out a new behavior change or organizing strategy, make some progress and then it would stall. We would tweak the strategy and have to wait another few months before we could find out if that change was successful. If not, we were back to the drawing board.

With the initial funding I was able to hire staff to help me track results. We developed a pre- and postprogram participation survey called a Sustainable Lifestyle Assessment. We created a computer program to calculate the results we got from this assessment and then provided this feedback to participants.

Although people were not interested in doing their own calculations, they were willing to fill out these pre- and postprogram assessments. On the front end they found the process of assessing the environmental sustainability of their lifestyle fascinating and relevant for deciding which actions they would take. On the back end they wanted to learn what resource savings they had achieved, provided we crunched the numbers for them. This was a win-win because we were eager to learn how effective the program was in achieving measurable behavior change.

The initial test results from the first 200 households were very promising. These households on average reduced their annual solid waste by 40 percent, water use by 32 percent, energy use by 17 percent, vehicle miles traveled by 8 percent, CO_2 emissions by 15 percent, and achieved financial savings of $255.

We were very heartened by these results. Because there is so much room for environmental improvement in the American lifestyle, these high numbers made sense intuitively. Having done the calculations ourselves we could vouch for their accuracy, provided that people were filling out the assessments honestly. Several of our funders, including the U.S. Environmental Protection Agency (EPA), studied these numbers and our process for crunching the data, and concluded that this data was trustworthy. That said, there was nothing to compare this against. We were blazing a new trail and learning as we went along.

As more people participated in the program, we kept getting consistent results. Eventually we would collect data from 20,000 people with comparable resource and financial savings. The program had passed its first test. It had demonstrated it could help people substantially reduce their environmental footprint.

The next big question was now upon us. Were these reductions in natural resource use being sustained over time? The greatest challenge in the behavior-change world is recidivism. Think weight loss. Would people go back to their old environmental habits in six months or a year or two years? Or would they be able to keep the belt cinched once they reduced their use of natural resources?

My hunch was that they would. My reasoning was that once you develop a new household system, like recycling, it is actually hard to go back to the old system. And people were taking these actions because it was the right thing to do. No one was forcing them. They wanted to act on their values. I would ask people who were now recycling what it was like to go to a place where you couldn't recycle, and the consistent response was a cringe. It was painful for them to throw away recyclable materials. But until I had some real data it was just my speculation—and perhaps wishful thinking.

Because everyone who funded this program wanted to find out if it was a worthwhile investment, there was no lack of opportunity to start answering this question. Over a number of years we conducted seven independent longitudinal studies funded by foundations and government agencies both in the United States and Europe. The most in-depth study was a two-year longitudinal study funded by the Netherlands Ministry of Environment. It was conducted by Paul Harland and Henk Staats of Leiden University's Centre for Environmental and Energy Research.

They studied 150 households who had participated on EcoTeams as part of our sustainable lifestyle program. What they found was that on average these households adopted twenty-six new proenvironment behaviors as a result of the program. Two years later they had sustained their changes in nineteen of these behaviors and continued to improve in seven of them. They had also adopted four new proenvironment behaviors. In other words, not only had they sustained the behavior changes, they had advanced them. In addition, 53 percent of the people in the study transferred what they learned to their workplaces, further leveraging the positive impact of the changes. Based on a thorough literature search, Harland and Staats concluded that our sustainable lifestyle program "was unprecedented in achieving significant and sustainable behavior change." The other studies validated this conclusion.

Having an environmental program that can produce and sustain behavior change was exciting. I was now asked to speak at many conferences and my colleagues around the world were also getting much recognition. The funding for our sustainable lifestyle program was growing. In the Netherlands, the program received more funding from the Ministry of Environment than any other environmental initiative. The program also began winning environmental awards both in America and Europe.

There was now interest in implementing our program coming from local, state, and federal government agencies in the United States. These agencies were increasingly confronting environmental issues that required citizens to adopt behaviors such as conserving water and energy; reducing or eliminating household and lawn chemicals that were polluting local water bodies; and being more efficient in driving to reduce air pollution, traffic congestion, road construction, and greenhouse gases. The director of the Oregon Department of Environmental Quality, Lang Marsh, with whom we would work in Portland, stated his agency's problem this way: "Citizen behavior change has been one of our most difficult challenges in advancing environmental protection."

From a systems point of view, the environmental outcomes these government agencies were seeking required a shift from first to second order change solutions. First-order change solutions, in this context, addressed the easy-to-reach low-hanging fruit of obvious environmental problems and were focused on regulating easily identifiable polluting companies. Second order change solutions required climbing higher into the tree, so to speak, and were far more complex to implement because they involved getting millions of people to change their lifestyles.

The government's first-order change tool of command and control was exactly right for addressing environmental protection when business was the problem. A company could be regulated and fined based on what came out of its smokestack. But when the daily lifestyle of individual human beings became the problem, the government was at a loss for meaningful action. You can't legislate lifestyle change. Financial incentives are not only just marginally effective, but politically difficult to implement. And information campaigns aimed at encouraging citizens to adopt more environmentally friendly lifestyle practices are also only marginally effective for behavior change. The research data on this last strategy are quite emphatic about its limitations.

Sharon Dunwoody, Professor of Journalism and Mass Communication at the University of Wisconsin, states:

> When social problems erupt, one classic response of governments and organizations is to wage an information campaign. The goals are often noble ones, the dollars spent gargantuan, and the outcomes

all too predictable: Messages seem to change the behavior of some people some of the time, but have almost no discernible impact on most people most of the time. This situation has so discouraged policy-makers in the past that the pattern was given its own dismal label: "minimal effects."

Local and state government agencies needed a better way to create behavior change and our sustainable lifestyle program was the right tool at the right time. As a result I soon had my first contract. The city of Portland, Oregon, having heard about our program from an enthusiastic EcoTeam member and respected civic leader, wanted the program. I remember well the date that the municipal ordinance was passed by the city council providing funding. It was October 16, on my fiftieth birthday. What a great birthday present!

I had now answered my first two questions in the affirmative. Could this program help people change their behaviors and achieve substantive environmental improvements; and were these behaviors sustained over time? My final question, which had been looming large in my mind but never been answered, was now upon me. Could I scale up this program?

LEARNING HOW TO SCALE

From my initial research I had learned that one of the biggest obstacles limiting people from taking action was their belief that they were just a drop in the bucket, so why bother? To address this issue we developed the final topic area in the EcoTeam's agenda which we called "Empowering Others."

The appeal to people was this. You want to make a difference or you wouldn't be doing this program. To make any meaningful positive impact on the environment, many of us need to make changes in our daily lifestyle practices. This program is designed to help *you* adopt sustainable lifestyle practices and then encourage *others* to do the same. We need to be role models and we need to get others involved. If enough of us do this, *rather than being drops in the bucket, our drops will actually fill the bucket.*

And reaching out to friends and neighbors is socially rewarding. We heard from many people who were grateful for the chance to create more of a sense of community where they lived. "I've lived in the neighborhood for twenty-one years, but getting to know my neighbors [only] started three years ago with an EcoTeam," wrote Sarah Conn on West Newton, Massachusetts in a representative letter. "There is a lot more friendliness on the streets now. It's given us the feeling of being embedded in the community and having roots." It was a sentiment we heard echoed again and again.

Through making the intention to multiply one's impact an explicit part of the program and providing people the tools to share their natural enthusiasm for their experience, many of the teams were spawning other teams. In several cases, as many as eight new EcoTeams came from a single team. This was, however, a hit-or-miss process. Was there a way to make this ripple effect more systematic and replicable?

Portland would provide the opportunity to find out how. To start with I needed to recruit two local program managers to be responsible for managing the outreach effort. I was very fortunate to find two outstanding individuals, Llyn Peabody and Michael Dowd, both of whom are imaginative, enthusiastic, and very smart about community organizing. Along with my program director, Eve Baer, another gifted community organizer, we created what we called the Portland Sustainable Lifestyle Campaign. Our goal was to form sixty EcoTeams in year one. To do this we would need to find people willing to start the EcoTeams and then convince each team to start at least one new team.

We were lucky to begin this learning adventure in a city known for its environmental consciousness and accomplishments. There was a lot of buzz around the sustainable lifestyle campaign; it was seen as the next new environmental thing. But could we build this buzz into something that was self-generating?

Hello, I Am Your Neighbor

By now I had discovered that while social networks of friends were naturals for starting teams, you soon exhausted the number of people in those networks. As a consequence this was not a strategic pathway for systematically expanding the program. The neighborhood, however, was attractive because there were no built-in limitations for expansion. On several occasions the number of teams being formed kept growing from block to block, as neighbors told other neighbors about the program. It also provided people the very important motivating benefit of getting to know their neighbors.

It was a daunting thought, however, to imagine building this program around a neighborhood dissemination process. The conventional wisdom is that in America we don't know our neighbors and that's just fine; we are an individualistic society and people like their privacy. But my intuition told me this was not what people really felt. Given a chance, I believed, people really would like to know their neighbors. They just did not know how to go about it.

Prior to starting work in Portland, I had gotten a small grant to test-market the idea of a neighbor-to-neighbor organizing model. We hired a market research firm to test a script for organizing at the most local of levels—the block. We developed the script based on what we learned from debriefing both those people who had successfully started teams on their blocks and those who had been unsuccessful.

> Hi, I am your neighbor from up the street. I would like to invite you to my home to hear about a new program sponsored by (city's name). Its purpose is to help us better conserve our environment's natural resources for the sake of our children, get to know each other better as neighbors, and make our neighborhood a healthier and safer place to live. The meeting is at (location, day, and time). Can you make it?

We had tested the script over the phone in four regions of the country: Northwest, Northeast, Midwest, and Southeast. Forty-three percent of the people we reached said they would be very likely to attend the meeting and 42 percent said they would be somewhat likely to attend. We were encouraged by this response, but of course this was a phone survey. We would soon find out if we could really get these results.

Michael was a natural-born salesman. He used to be an evangelical minister, so he knew how to inspire people with his passion. Llyn was charming and had an engaging way of being with people. They were a perfect pair for recruiting EcoTeam leaders and they found them in a variety of places. Some were from likely places like environmental groups, but Michael and Llyn were also successful with neighborhood associations and civic groups. They recruited the first batch of ten EcoTeam leaders by offering the same three benefits used in the telephone script: learning how to conserve natural resources, getting to know their neighbors better, and making their neighborhood a healthier and safer place to live.

These leaders all believed in the cause and were willing to reach out to others, but knocking on their neighbors' doors filled some of them with dread. Many of them admitted that they were afraid of being rejected or, even worse, thought of as pushy. We tried to bolster their confidence by telling them about the very encouraging results from our market research. We also told them that if they were getting doors slammed in their faces, they certainly did not need to continue.

The big door-knocking event would take place on a Saturday afternoon from 11 AM to 2 PM. The leaders were taught the simple script and Michael or Llyn offered to walk with any of them who needed their confidence bolstered. We were all eager to see what kind of response these brave souls would get to their reaching out in a society acculturated to neighborhoods of isolation.

Michael and Llyn called me that night bubbling over with excitement and enthusiasm. "It worked so well," they exclaimed.

The feedback from the leaders was consistent. Rather than having doors slammed in their faces, they had been greeted quite warmly. In fact, almost everyone said they were interested in attending the information meeting. Some had to check their calendars or speak with a spouse, but as the market research had predicted, there was clear and genuine interest.

Michael and Llyn debriefed the leaders carefully so we could learn as much as possible. The leaders reported that many of their neighbors said that no neighbor had ever knocked on their door before. They described how many of the people they spoke to were touched by this experience, and quite excited to meet other neighbors at the upcoming meeting. Many individuals told them they had wanted to do something for the environment but aside from recycling did not know how to go further. People consistently thanked these intrepid team leaders for taking the time to do this.

After our initial euphoria of thinking we might have a breakthrough for organizing EcoTeams, it occurred to me that this was a far more profound learning. We had touched a nerve in the modern American psyche. *I don't know my neighbors and would like to know them. I don't wish to remain isolated, but I don't know what to do about it.* Unwittingly, we had stumbled on a way to reinvent community in our modern disconnected neighborhoods. I would spend many years unpacking this insight.

The neighborhood gatherings in the ten team leaders' homes were scheduled for one week later. The big question was: Would the people who said they were coming actually attend? The team leaders were instructed to call them the night before to remind them and to confirm their attendance.

The evening arrived. The market research had indicated that 43 percent of the people were "very likely" to come, and that was exactly what happened.

The "very likely" group came and the "somewhat likely" group did not. They were predisposed, but not quite ready to put this on the top of the list. They would, however, be good prospects for the next round of teams once this program was a more known commodity on the block.

Of those who attended, approximately 75 percent decided to join a team. Some who did not choose to participate would have, but scheduling was an issue. For others, the time commitment was more than they were ready to make, or they felt they were doing enough already. *Ultimately, a remarkable 25 percent of everybody approached agreed to participate in a seven-meeting program over four months!*

This was unprecedented in community organizing and we were thrilled. Equally important was the fact that most of these participants were not what one would call "true believer" environmentalists, but rather they were their *neighbors*. This neighborhood-based approach was able to tap into a much wider circle of possible participants than our previous approaches had been able to do. The additional benefits of getting to know your neighbors and improving the neighborhood were very strong motivators. We would come to see over time that they were actually the strongest motivators.

As this initial round of teams completed the program they were encouraged to reach out to others on their block. On some of the blocks most of the households ended up joining EcoTeams. The momentum began spreading to neighboring blocks and it became clear that we had laid the foundation for a repeatable way to grow the program. In a number of Portland neighborhoods, "EcoTeam" became a household word.

SPREADING THE PROGRAM TO OTHER CITIES

A program that could help residents of a city successfully adopt environmentally sustainable behaviors, maintain them over time, and recruit program participants with some consistency was a winning combination. Knowledge of Portland's achievement began spreading to other cities through the local government networks. Mike Lindberg, Portland's visionary commissioner of public utilities and a city council member who had championed this program, began receiving invitations to speak about it at local government conferences, and so did I.

At one meeting of twenty innovative large U.S. cities we generated so much interest that this group of government officials decided to make their next meeting a field trip to Portland to study the sustainable lifestyle campaign firsthand. They wanted to determine if this was just a Portland phenomenon or if the program could work elsewhere. I wondered the same thing myself.

When the time came, Mike arranged for our meeting to take place in one of Portland's landmark Greek restaurants—where, as it turned out, a band was playing very lively Greek music in another room. Not the best of environments to make a presentation to a group of tired, demanding city officials who had flown in from around the country. But in spite of this distraction, the Portland citizens and city officials we had asked to speak rose to the occasion. Program participants passionately shared about meeting their neighbors for the first time, and how much fun they had, and, of course, their environmental improvements. City government officials talked about how exciting it was to partner with committed citizens and how much was possible when you have an engaged citizenry. It went on like this for about an hour. Then challenging questions started coming from these somewhat incredulous visiting city officials. There were good answers, but I could sense that there was still skepticism. This was not how they had always done business and they weren't sure if they wanted to change.

I will always remember the meeting the next morning in Portland City Hall when the city officials gathered and began describing the experience of hearing about the program. "I felt like I was attending a revival meeting," said one with more than a hint of sarcasm in his voice. Others indicated how impressive this outpouring of enthusiasm was in Portland. But the general sense was that although this was all well and good for Portland, it could never work in their cities. Their citizens were just not ready to make these changes. Their city councils would not get behind something like this. They had already tried citizen engagement and it hadn't worked. Their city was just too *fill in the blank*. After hearing them throw cold water on the Portland experience for fifteen minutes I decided to chime in.

"The term 'revival meeting' is actually apt, but not exactly how you mean it," I suggested. "This program offers a revival of something that has been lost or severely reduced in American life—citizenship. What you heard were not angry activists criticizing the government, which is certainly needed sometimes, but ordinary citizens saying, 'we are doing our part and we'd like to partner with our government so we can take it further.'

"You heard city agencies acknowledging citizens for doing their part and saying, 'Yes, let's take it further,'" I continued. "You also heard residents who had become neighbors and built community where they lived, around issues that mattered. What you experienced was a new civic model—city and citizens as partners. It beats getting yelled at by disgruntled citizens and as a result wishing to avoid them."

I smiled, and couldn't resist closing by saying, "Try it, you'll like it."

We were successful in recruiting two cities: Kansas City, Missouri, and Columbus, Ohio. Now I had to face the music. Was this a Portland phenomenon, as they had wondered, only possible in a progressive city with environmentally conscious citizens, or was this model transferable and universal? Many initiatives developed in progressive cities don't transfer well because they are unique to those cities' populations and local government officials. We would soon find out about ours because these two cities were not considered environmentally progressive in the least. In fact, Kansas City, Missouri was still struggling to get a curbside recycling ordinance passed.

We went forward hoping for the best. We created a program manager job description, and coined the term "living-room friendly" to describe how the person needed to be someone who people would want to invite into their homes. We looked for people with a passion for doing environmental work, community-organizing experience, excellent communication skills, enthusiasm, a comfort in selling ideas to people, a pioneering spirit, and a can-do attitude.

If a candidate got this far, there was a final threshold that would determine whether or not he or she was really suited for the experience. In a recruitment pitch, well honed from my First Earth Run days, I told them. "This job will require long hours and a lot of time on evenings and weekends," I continued, "and we can only offer you a modest salary since we are not able to charge much for an unproven product. There is no guarantee of success and in fact the odds are against us. But if we are successful we will have a shot at changing the world." On hearing this, some candidates ran the other way, but there were enough people, I am happy to say for our world, who found this opportunity very appealing.

We worked hard to get various city agencies and elected officials on board. While this is never easy, it was quite challenging in these cities where they were definitely not as enlightened about environmental matters as the government officials in Portland. We ultimately had to work with a smaller base of official support, but we had enough to move forward.

We used the same selling points to recruit team leaders. Again, while not as easy a sell because of the lower level of environmental consciousness, we were still able to find willing people because of the co-benefits of meeting neighbors and improving the neighborhood. From all the EcoTeams we had formed around the country and world, I was confident that the program would deliver behavior change if people were willing to participate. Participation was our crucible. Would our three selling points appeal to people in neighborhoods that did not have Portland's environmental awareness?

We were committed to making sure our new program managers had the benefit of all our learning in Portland. If we were to fall short of our goals, it would not be for lack of our best effort. We created master classes where Michael and Llyn shared the various recruitment and training techniques they had found successful as well as those that had not worked. They, along with Eve and me, were in constant communication with our new program managers. We debriefed them regularly to see what worked and helped them make course corrections where necessary. Because of the length of the program and the steep learning curve of bringing new program managers on line, it would take us awhile to know how we were doing.

As we were going through this learning process in Kansas City and Columbus, word about the program kept spreading and more municipalities signed on: Madison and Dane County in Wisconsin; Bend and Deschuttes County in Oregon; Issaquah and King County in Washington; Rockland County in New York, and the cities of Philadelphia, Pennsylvania, and Chattanooga, Tennessee. We now had cities and counties representing a wide diversity of size, governmental structure, and environmental awareness among citizens.

With more cities and people in the game, the number of ideas and social innovations for how to get people to participate increased multifold. We learned how to form mutually beneficial partnerships with local nonprofits, faith-based groups, businesses, and government agencies in which they would help recruit neighborhood team leaders. We kept improving our techniques for helping team leaders succeed in their outreach efforts to their neighbors. We developed personalized support systems for these team leaders by providing them trained coaches who had successfully been through the program.

And most important, we discovered that no matter what city the program landed in, our three benefits were universally appealing. People everywhere care about the quality of life they will leave to their children, and they want to reduce the toll they take on the environment. If given the opportunity, they wish to know their neighbors and to build a greater sense of community where they live. Improving their neighborhood is a wonderful extra benefit, attractive to everyone. While there needed to be adjustments for the culture and environmental circumstances of each city, the program and recruitment process was successful in each of these very diverse communities. It worked better in some than others, but in no community did we get less than a 15 percent recruitment rate on the block. In Bend, Oregon, we got an astonishing recruitment rate of 32 percent—higher even than Portland.

We had proved this program was transferable and could be successful just about anywhere. It was hard work. It was labor intensive. It required the right people on the ground. It required a willing local government. It was not inexpensive, but relative to media information campaigns aimed at changing behavior, it was quite cost effective. And it actually changed behavior! In short, it was successful. We had set out to create a new social innovation to measurably reduce the significant impact our lifestyles take on the environment and successfully disseminate it, and we had done it.

Sustainable lifestyle campaigns would continue to expand in these and other cities, both in the United States and throughout the world, ultimately encompassing some 200 communities with the participation of several million people in twenty-two countries. They would also provide a new policy option for local and state governments and undergird a budding sustainable community movement. But little did I envision the foundation all this would lay for a future none of us could yet imagine.

In 2007 the U.N. Intergovernmental Panel on Climate Change would inform the world in no uncertain terms that either we significantly change our behaviors or face an inhospitable world for human beings. In Chapter 11, I will share how the sustainable lifestyle campaign morphed into a solution to take on the issue of global warming—household by household, community by community. Until that time however, I still had more learning opportunities.

WATER STEWARDSHIP: TEACHING OTHERS HOW TO FISH

It wasn't long before a request came to adapt the sustainable lifestyle campaign approach. In May 2001 I was asked to speak at an EPA conference in Chicago on the tongue-twisting theme of "nonpoint source water pollution education and outreach."

The conference was tackling the question of how to clean up the 70 percent of America's water bodies being polluted by the fertilizers, pesticides, dog poop, and assorted chemicals that run off our lawns, roads, and other surfaces during storms. Only a small percentage of the country's storm drains connect to sewage treatment facilities. For the most part, storm drains mainline their contents straight into our local watersheds, which consist of an intricate network of underground aquifers, streams, rivers, lakes, estuaries, wetlands, bays, and even oceans. Each household's small amount of pollutants when multiplied by the thousands and millions are causing havoc in our water bodies.

Because of the seriousness of this problem, before it would provide a permit to operate water treatment facilities, EPA started mandating that local governments educate their citizens in the prevention of these harmful pollution practices. But with the only tool being information campaigns, local governments and watershed education groups had become painfully aware that raised awareness does not translate into changed behavior. Everyone knew the brochures and television ads were not working, but no one knew what to do.

That was the backdrop. I had been invited to keynote the conference in order to share the behavior-change and recruitment results we had been achieving with our sustainable lifestyle campaign. I did not go into the gathering with the thought that I would challenge the status quo, but effectively my talk started a mini-revolution.

Three hundred and fifty education and outreach practitioners from state and local government and watershed organizations now saw there was another way. They were tantalized by the idea that there was a social technology that had been proven to achieve public participation and change behavior and they were intrigued by the invitation to rethink how they measured their success. Counting how many glossy brochures they had distributed or how many compelling advertisements they had run, or even just measuring the impact of the pollution was no longer acceptable. They had been introduced to a second order change solution and they were ready to respond.

During the conference several leaders from EPA, assorted state environmental agencies, and the National Fish and Wildlife Foundation asked if I would be willing to adapt our sustainable lifestyle program to address these water quality issues. Because of the increasing incidence of droughts they also wished me to include a section on water conservation.

I agreed to take on the project. I liked that local government agencies and watershed organizations clearly saw the need for this program. It's much easier to offer up a social innovation when the demand for it already exists, especially if the demand is an urgent one. I also liked that this project would provide me an opportunity to build the *capacity of other organizations.* I had learned that while I could come into a community and hire staff to do the organizing, it was a lot of extra work to get a program up and running when we did not already have the networks in place. And this certainly would be more cost effective for local government agencies if they could use their own staffs. With a now-proved environmental behavior-change tool, it was time for me to train others in how to manage these campaigns.

I called the program Water Stewardship and applied our core behavior-change process: carefully crafted action recipes combined with structured peer support and focused, in this case, on water quality and water conservation.

The program took about six months to develop. With grant funding available, three Northern Virginia municipalities lined up to test-drive it: Arlington County, Falls Church, and Fairfax. These communities were in the Four Mile Run watershed surrounding the Potomac River just outside of Washington D.C. They formed a partnership consisting of the three municipalities and a local environmental organization, Arlingtonians for a Clean Environment.

Three powerhouse women from these organizations helped us develop the water quality part of the program. Elenor Hodges, Aileen Winquist, and Annette Mills represented the best of grassroots change leaders. It was a pleasure working with them and they gave me the confidence that the knowledge I was handing off would be put to good use.

A watershed organization, Friends of the Rappahannock, also signed on to pilot the program. Its executive director, John Tippett, was exceedingly challenged in protecting the scenic Rappahannock River from the residential runoff of fertilizers generated by the rapid suburban growth of Fredricksburg. "All those Washington D.C. commuters want their pristine green lawns," he told me with a shake of his head. John had been around the block enough times trying various approaches to behavior change that he was genuinely ready for something that had a chance of getting the job done.

Another community to come forward was progressive Boulder, Colorado. Boulder is always ahead of the curve so I was not surprised to see its interest. The Boulder initiative was led by a dynamic local government watershed educator, Curry Rosato, who exudes positive energy and enthusiasm. I was confident she would be successful with this program, and, for that matter, anything else she was promoting. She and her team would also train several other communities in their watershed.

With competent and committed people in the field, my goal was to do everything I could to help them succeed through comprehensive training and follow-up coaching. While this process was relatively straightforward to implement, the program managers needed to be disciplined in following each of the steps. Otherwise they would fall short of getting the results they desired.

The plan was for me to lead a two-day training, followed by monthly coaching calls over twelve months led by our program director, Eve Baer. I had already learned from working with my staff that the training, while providing essential knowledge and tools, was theoretical until people actually had to apply it in the field. It was 20 percent of what they needed to be successful. The other 80 percent came through learning by doing with real-time follow-up coaching.

Based on my past experience, I was confident the behavior-change aspect of the program would be successful. I was hopeful that if the local water issue was understood, the program's community-building would provide the extra edge needed to get people to participate. But most important we needed to build the competency of these local government and watershed organizations to lead this program effectively. This would be our first test in transferring this capability to external change agents.

A Tool That Really Works

These three efforts were successful by both the standards of the communities implementing them and by ours. They achieved the behavior-change and recruitment results they wanted, and we transferred this social technology so that it was theirs to use permanently. Because of the unique local nature and relevance of water issues, they were able to achieve a remarkable 40 percent participation rate through the neighbor-to-neighbor outreach process. Participating households averaged ten water stewardship actions each and achieved impressive water usage savings of 44 percent, or 20,000 gallons per year per participant.

The accomplishment and satisfaction of the program participants and their civic partners were gratifying for everyone involved. "My neighbors responded very enthusiastically to the invitation to join a Water Stewardship EcoTeam," said team leader Katie Watters, "and were ready to move into action immediately." And so they did. Not only did team members take significant protection and conservation measures, but they also held a cleanup of the alley behind their own house one weekend. Like most teams, this one rated getting to know one another better very highly.

Aileen Winquist, an environmental planner for the Department of Environmental Services in Arlington County and an organizing partner in the program, was particularly excited about having a means to track exactly what changes people made in their lifestyles, and to estimate the pollution reduction that resulted from those changes. And after struggling for years to develop an effective way to motivate citizens to change the behaviors that pollute their beautiful river, John Tippet of Friends of the Rappahannock was delighted and relieved to find "a tool that really works."

This decade-long quest had been an extremely gratifying journey. We had learned how to achieve and promote environmentally sustainable lifestyles so vital to our planet's well-being; further a new social compact between a city and its citizens as partners in social change; and shift neighborhoods from residential isolation to genuine community, often for the very first time. I had also learned, on a more personal level, about the process of developing a social innovation and the path of the social entrepreneur, which I will talk about in Chapter 7.

But perhaps the most important learning, certainly from the point of view of social change, was cracking the code of an essential factor for second order change. *We had learned how to achieve measurable behavior change in people's lives on the street where they lived—the epicenter for social change.* I would soon be asked to apply this knowledge to another daunting challenge: improving the livability of inner-city neighborhoods.

CHAPTER 2: SOCIAL CHANGE 2.0 PRACTITIONER'S GUIDE

1. What is the societal problem or unmet societal need your initiative addresses?

2. What are the "how-to" questions you must answer for your social change initiative to be perceived as effective?

3. What is the social learning process you need to develop to answer these questions?

4. What does success look like for your social change initiative and how will you measure it?

5. What are the benefits your social change strategy offers to attract people to participate?

NEIGHBORHOOD LIVABILITY IN INNER-CITY

PHILADELPHIA: AGAINST THE ODDS

I arrived in the picturesque port city of Annapolis, Maryland, on a bright spring day in the year 1999, greeted by its charming early American buildings and an array of sailboats bobbing in the harbor. Both President Clinton's Council on Sustainable Development and Renew America had recently recognized our work in the area of community sustainability, and I had been invited by the U.S. Environmental Protection Agency to keynote a national conference convened to review the effectiveness of community sustainability initiatives. My assignment was to offer an assessment of the current state of community sustainability tools in America and a vision for the direction we needed to head in the future.

The people attending the conference were sustainability thought leaders consisting of roll-up-your-sleeve community organizers, sustainability tool designers, and managers of government environmental programs. To put what I said to them in context, I will share my observation of community sustainability work in the 1990s. (Those readers who wish to skip this context can jump ahead to the section *Sustainable Communities Meet Livable Neighborhoods* on page 69.)

SUSTAINABLE DEVELOPMENT BECOMES LOCAL

In 1992 the U.N. Earth Summit helped introduce the term *sustainable development* into the vocabulary of community change agents. This grew out of the agreement signed by all the governments attending this conference to create national sustainability plans. In the United States, President Clinton and Vice President Gore created the President's Council on Sustainable Development to develop the American plan.

Molly Olson, the newly appointed executive director, was a charismatic leader who combined a rare talent for being able to integrate public policy formulation with grassroots organizing. Her résumé contained leadership stints at both the U.S. Department of the Interior and Greenpeace. One of her responsibilities was to stay informed on the sustainability plans and programs of other countries through attending periodic conferences at the United Nations.

Because of the success and growing international presence of our work, we had just recently partnered with the United Nations Environment Programme (UNEP). They were keen to help countries put sustainable development on the ground in communities and very much liked our program as a practical and replicable international model. Executive Director Elizabeth Dowdswell and I had just developed an initiative we called "The North Puts Its House in Order: Household by Household," and she invited me to lead a workshop about this initiative at one of these U.N. conferences. Ironically, my old friend Noel Brown, who ran the UNEP North American office and who had contributed to my getting involved in environmental work years earlier, was asked to co-lead the workshop with me. That is how I met Molly.

After the presentation, Molly made a beeline for me with what I would come to discover was her trademark enthusiasm and passion. I remember the entreaty quite well. "This is fantastic! You must come to Washington, D.C., and talk with me and my staff more about your work. I wish I could make another trip to New York to learn more, but I have used up my carbon budget." To have been living on a carbon budget in 1995 says a lot about Molly. Our friendship still continues except that now she lives in Australia, has always used up her carbon budget, and her entreaties continue as I grow deeper into carbon debt.

I flew to Washington to meet with Molly and her team in one of the White House's executive offices, an old converted three-story home on

Jackson Place. Over a brown-bag lunch in a conference room filled with plants, Molly shared with me that because they were the official U.S. government organization addressing sustainability policy, communities across the country were flocking to them for guidance and tools. But they did not have the right guidance and tools to disperse, and so were looking for help. Like Elizabeth Dowdswell, Molly wanted to make sustainability more relevant to the day-to-day lives of residents in a community.

She invited me to share my vision and my research with her fifteen staff members. She and her team were very much aligned with this vision and fascinated by the research. They were also interested in the policy implications of this work. They peppered me with questions to learn more about any political or economic changes the sustainable lifestyle campaigns were furthering in these communities.

I told them how EcoTeams, to better live their sustainable lifestyle choices, had become advocates in their communities for bike lanes, better public transportation, curbside recycling, the collection of more types of recyclable items, and incentives for going solar. I shared how EcoTeam members were getting appointed to city council environmental advisory committees or running for elected office on sustainability platforms to get this done. I also shared how they began creating active demand for local businesses to supply them with green products and services—from increased recycled-content paper products to nontoxic cleaners to green energy choices.

As policy wonks they were intrigued by how personal action was leading to a demand for policy change and driving green economic development, and by how seamlessly the sustainable lifestyle campaign connected these two domains and catalyzed the creation of a more sustainable community. I was so obsessed with the behavior-change and community-organizing aspects of our program that I hadn't really spent much time thinking about the larger policy and economic development outcomes that were organically emerging. This was exciting!

There was a natural synergy between the President's Council on Sustainable Development and my work with sustainable lifestyle campaigns and so we decided to form a strategic partnership. Molly invited me to serve on two task forces—Education and Outreach, and Consumption and Population—to help the council create a sustainability blueprint for the country. She also actively promoted our work as a resource in their various communications and newsletters and invited us to present at their regional workshops.

With this influential organization spreading the word about our program, I was now being invited to speak in many communities across the country. Even though several of these cities were ready to start sustainable lifestyle campaigns, these visits turned out to be more about my learning than about anything else. I was provided a front-row seat to observe an unprecedented community transformation process sprouting from the grassroots. A shift was occurring across America in how communities thought about and planned for their future. Citizen groups were becoming empowered to take responsibility for creating more sustainable communities. The landscape looked incredibly promising—but the road through it would be a very bumpy one.

REINVENTING COMMUNITIES

As sustainable development wound its way down to the local level, its value as a change strategy was viewed through the eyes of the beholder. Everyone wanted a piece of it, but as a consequence, the term became so watered down and amorphous that it was hard to easily define and equally hard to measure. Ultimately it was defined as an integration of environmental, economic and social sustainability.

In the 1990s understanding, assessing and envisioning sustainability became the starting point for most of the community efforts. At that time, local government urban planners developing business-as-usual plans were surprised to discover a new player emerging on the scene—citizen sustainability groups. These groups began developing projections for the current land, transportation, energy, and water use patterns of their community. As they crunched the numbers, it became apparent that their communities were on environmentally unsustainable paths, and these groups were determined to change this trajectory.

They concluded that the best way to achieve this transformation was by actively engaging their fellow citizens in envisioning a different possibility for the future of their community. To do this these sustainability groups developed two new tools—*sustainability indicators* and *sustainable community visioning processes.*

A *sustainability indicator* points a community toward a more sustainable future and then measures the community's progress in getting there. One environmental sustainability indicator, for example, might be the reduction of vehicle miles traveled by a certain percentage of the population over a specific period of time. A social sustainability indicator might be the increase of students who graduate from high school, or a decrease in crime by a certain percentage. An economic sustainability indicator might be the percentage of new green businesses in the community over a certain period of time.

Sustainable Seattle, a citizen group in Seattle was one of the first communities to develop sustainability indicators. They spent several years developing a robust set of indicators. These were so well conceived that they ultimately became a template for citizen groups and local governments nationwide.

A *community visioning process* starts when the residents are invited to a large civic gathering to create a preferred future for their community. It is built around many different themes, including environmental quality, social development, and economic prosperity. It is often a several-day event with follow-up task forces assigned to flesh out the vision with specific measurable targets. Chattanooga, Tennessee, winner of the ignominious label as one of the dirtiest cities in America, organized a very successful community visioning event to clean up their city. Their very inclusive citizen participation process and subsequent success implementing their vision spurred on many communities to follow in their footsteps.

All across the country literally hundreds of communities were sprouting sustainability projects. It was citizen engagement and empowerment at its best.

In my travels I had the privilege to speak with many of the community activists who were leading these initiatives. I was deeply inspired by their passion and commitment to improve their communities. They poured their hearts into these initiatives, usually as volunteers. They were empowered as active contributors to their communities' future. But there was also frustration in their voices as they described their struggles to implement these community sustainability visions and to work with the entrenched local infrastructure, government policies, and inertia.

They discovered that many utilities and so much of their community's infrastructure were designed unsustainably. Municipal water utilities had financial incentives to sell more water to pay for the loans they had taken out to meet the increasing demand for water that was being used wastefully. Although a number of these communities had water-conservation programs, the utilities were ambivalent about implementing them because they reduced revenues. More new roads were being built and people were driving more miles, causing more traffic congestion, air pollution, and global warming—but public transportation alternatives were rejected as too expensive or unwieldy. Sprawl was out of control in many of these cities, with no re-course in sight. Similarly, increased solid waste generation required the building of more landfills, or the carting of waste further and further away from the city.

Their communities were wastefully and inefficiently using natural re-sources and spending increasingly larger amounts of limited tax revenues to subsidize the unsustainable practices of citizens and businesses. They were trapped in endemic and unsustainable natural resource use patterns and these change leaders did not know how to get them unstuck.

Furthermore, they told me that by the time they had done all the re-search and organized these community engagement events, they had spent most of their energy and money and had little left for tackling these sub-stantial implementation challenges, even if they knew how. It was frustrat-ing for them to have all these inspiring visions, plans, and recommendations sitting on their office shelves. They were also saddened by hearing from fel-low citizens who were becoming disillusioned about civic engagement be-cause their ideas and passion were not going anywhere.

Most of these sustainability initiatives did not partner with the local governments responsible for the community's infrastructure, and therefore lacked the buy-in of these agencies. Sometimes there was outright resist-ance to change because it "wasn't invented here." But just as often it was sim-ple frustration because the things these groups wished to measure, for example, were inconsistent with the data the agencies collected. This was not an insurmountable obstacle, but it would require two steps backward before one step forward could be taken. Constrained government budgets and a lack of resources on the part of the community groups added to the challenge of implementation.

Not all community sustainability initiatives were driven by citizen groups, though; some local governments were also actively involved. But the mirror opposite was occurring with local governments. They were creating sustainability indicator projects without the participation of citizen groups. When it came time to implement these policies they had not gotten the cit-izen buy-in or generated the political will to support the changes they were advocating. Local government agencies had not fully understood that when embarking on a major community sustainability venture they needed to en-gage their residents as partners.

It was cathartic for the community and local government leaders to have someone to talk to about their innovative efforts. As I listened deeply

I became aware of just how hard it is to create profound change in communities. And these communities actually had leaders who wanted to create change! The traditional social change tools were proving insufficient. Laws, taxes, financial incentives, and protest, while having their own roles to play, were not designed for the type of fundamental communitywide transformation for which people were longing.

There was a need for a better way, but how? I did not have any grand plan, but I did believe there were better ways to think about, implement, and organize people around the process of community change. When I delivered my talk that day to the gathering in Annapolis, I would attempt to lay out some of these design principles.

SUSTAINABLE COMMUNITIES MEET LIVABLE NEIGHBORHOODS

I began my talk by challenging everyone to radically rethink how we design and implement community change processes. We needed to think harder, design smarter, and work together better, I posited, and I offered seven broad ways in which we could all begin.

Use people's time more efficiently. The goodwill and limited discretionary time of citizens is precious, and needs to be used much more effectively. I challenged us to reevaluate our assumptions about what had become the dominant formula for citizen engagement processes. Intensive community visioning and indicator projects that left citizens and community groups so depleted that they had no energy left to implement their initiatives were not furthering the cause of community change. What if we could reverse this formula so that we only needed to invest 10 or 20 percent of the goodwill of citizens in visioning, since most of the desired solutions are already understood, and then spend the remaining 80 or 90 percent of their time implementing these solutions in our neighborhoods and homes?

Make community change relevant to people's lives. To engage more people and increase their investment in implementing solutions, we need to make community sustainability more immediately relevant to people's lives. I shared our successful appeals to people around the idea of an environmentally sustainable lifestyle, getting to know your neighbors, and making your neighborhood more livable. I suggested that it would be much easier to create a sustainable community from the bottom up by helping people create solutions at the block level. This is where most people express their quality-of-life concerns and are open to participating in a community.

Make it easier for people to participate. I challenged community groups and local governments to think about change from a resident-centric point of view. In other words, to imagine their own experience as a community resident being approached by a dozen city agencies and community groups, each with their own message of what they wish them to do: Recycle these items, drop off their household hazardous waste on this day, water their lawn at this time, carpool, start a block watch, prepare for emergencies, avoid contaminating watersheds with pesticides—the list goes on and on. To be bombarded by assorted agencies providing information, making different appeals, and offering an array of services is overwhelming for already oversaturated residents, and causes many people to tune out.

To overcome these challenges, I recommended local governments and community groups consider a coordinated neighborhood-based program that combined all pertinent information and services into a single offering. I explained that this was the framework that allowed our sustainable lifestyle program to be so well received by community residents and participating cities. It is one-stop shopping for both residents around creating a sustainable lifestyle and for a city disseminating these practices communitywide.

Organize citizens to take on more responsibility. I suggested that this model could be adapted for neighborhood livability issues like safety, health, greening, and beautification, among others. Many of the issues traditionally managed by city agencies could actually be handled directly by block residents if neighbors were more connected and better organized. Helping neighbors get to know and support one another to make life better in their neighborhoods is key to tapping the vast citizen potential available to improve our communities.

Empower local government employees as agents for change. The other huge untapped resource is civil servants. Most of these individuals enter public service with the express purpose of making a difference. Serving the community is their explicit job description, but they are often frustrated by the inefficiency and dysfunction of the government bureaucracies in which they work. They are rewarded for not rocking the boat. In combination with being put off by the confrontational approach of some community groups, this has caused many government employees to resist change. They need to be empowered, encouraged, and held accountable for civic change, with their performance evaluated by measurable outcomes. To attract and retain the best and the brightest talent in public service, they need to know that they are expected and rewarded for making a real difference.

Design a whole-system approach to community change. The goodwill and desire in citizens and city employees to improve our communities is right below the surface waiting for a catalyst. To tap into it requires that we build imaginative new partnerships. This partnership approach between city and citizen directly contributed to the success of our sustainable lifestyle campaigns. Activating the whole system is the key to building truly sustainable communities.

Raise the level of play. I concluded by saying that the people attending the conference represented some of the most innovative social architects, community organizers, and progressive government agencies in the country. The desire for change was bubbling up in communities all across America and people were ready to take action. It was time to invent the next generation of sustainability tools and strategies and diligently pursue them until we got them to work. It was time to raise the level of play.

A CONVERSATION BEGINS

After my talk, a slight, brown-haired, middle-aged woman from the U.S. Environmental Protection Agency, Susan McDowell, came up to me and said quite matter-of-factly, "What you described is really needed. I think *you* should implement a block-based sustainable community initiative and I would like to help." She explained that she had developed a "Green Communities" how-to web resource, and suggested that maybe it could be useful to me.

I had too much on my plate to start a new program like this, and so I politely declined and wished her well. But she was unwilling to take no for an answer. She suggested that we experiment to see if we could get EcoTeams to take on sustainable community projects at the neighborhood level, and offered to build her online resource at the neighborhood scale, as well. Then she threw in the fact that she would help find a pilot community in her region, and oh, by the way, pony up funding from EPA. What could I say but, "Yes, let's do it and learn!"

Susan's determination and can-do attitude were attributes that she would continue to demonstrate as we embarked on what would prove to be my next major community change initiation.

Susan was based in EPA Region 3, which encompasses the Mid-Atlantic States from Virginia to New Jersey. She began putting out feelers to find a city interested in implementing a sustainable lifestyle campaign. Some of the likely suspects were not interested, or were in the middle of a sustainability visioning process and did not have the resources to invest in another initiative. However, Susan did get an enthusiastic response from an unlikely person in an unlikely city.

Shirley Kitchen, a state senator from inner-city Philadelphia, wished to talk with us. Shirley is a force of nature. She has a strong community-organizing background and represented a low- to middle-income, mostly African-American district, in North Philadelphia. She was street smart, did not mince words, and was known for being highly effective in the rough and tumble politics of Philadelphia.

Hers was one of the toughest districts in a city with one of the highest murder rates in the country. Crime, drugs, and blight were rampant. Given the issues of her constituents, Shirley was the most unlikely advocate for our sustainable lifestyle campaign that I had come across over the past decade. In fact, Susan and I were sure she did not really understand that this was more a middle-class program for save-the-planet types like Susan and me. I did not expect it was something that would be of much interest to people struggling with more basic life issues. We expected when she learned more about it she would say, thanks, but no thanks.

We scheduled a meeting with Shirley Kitchen and her staff at EPA Headquarters in Philadelphia. In a small conference room with no windows and one long conference table, I made a slide presentation describing how the program worked and the results we had achieved. Shirley didn't ask a lot of questions so it was hard to get a read on what she thought; I was pretty sure she was not interested.

When the presentation was over she simply said. "If it can help the environment, I'm on board. Let's do it. How much money do you need from the state and city to make this happen?"

Susan and I smiled bemusedly at each other. I was most impressed that Senator Kitchen (you quickly learned that was how you addressed her) saw this program as something larger than meeting the immediate needs of her constituents. "If it could help the environment," was all that she demanded. We could deliver on that. I didn't argue with her and we took common cause. So began a relationship of most improbable bedfellows.

We could not have had a better champion. She approached then-Mayor Ed Rendell for support. He liked the idea (or else he just didn't want to mess with Shirley Kitchen), so he came on board with eighteen months of city funding. She then procured state funding from their Community Development Block Grant program. We threw in the EPA funding that Susan had secured, and we launched the Philadelphia Sustainable Lifestyle Campaign. I was most curious to see how our program would do in a highly urban city not known for an environmental orientation.

We hired and trained two staffers and were able to get them up to speed quickly using the knowledge we had acquired over the past few years in combination with peer-to-peer mentoring. What had previously taken six months was now compressed to two.

In spite of the modest level of environmental awareness in Philadelphia, the co-benefits of getting to know one's neighbors and improving the neighborhood, in conjunction with conserving natural resources, proved to be attractive. Working in middle-class neighborhoods, we formed fifty-three block-based EcoTeams with resource savings comparable with those in other cities. Our recruitment rate of 22 percent, while a little lower than our national average of 25 percent, was still quite respectable. But while we were winning the battle, we were losing the war. We were not addressing the issues most critical to the city of Philadelphia.

Senator Kitchen's district was challenged by serious urban blight. This blight was caused by a number of factors including population loss, a declining housing market, and contagion from other abandoned properties. As a result, these neighborhoods were breeding grounds for crime and drug dealers. The population loss also eroded the city's tax base and many of these neighborhoods were not receiving adequate services. When they did receive services like street and vacant lot cleanups, these restored conditions were rarely maintained and so these city agencies were not motivated to come back. This in turn caused the neighborhood to be even less attractive. It was a vicious cycle with people leaving the neighborhood, if they could, which contributed to more blight. Those that could not afford to leave developed a bunker mentality for self-protection.

By the time we approached the city for the next round of financing, the program's initial champion, Mayor Ed Rendell, had been elected governor of the state and was no longer available to support it. The new mayor, John Street, was too busy getting his administration in gear to have any time to meet. So Senator Kitchen and I went to Philadelphia's managing director, Joseph Martz—the person responsible for day-to-day operation of the thirteen city agencies, to see if we could get him on board.

He seemed genuinely impressed with the program's success, respected Senator Kitchen, and wanted to find some way to make this work. But he explained that a program that focused on conserving natural resources, while laudable, was just not in line with Mayor Street's "Neighborhood Transformation Initiative," which addressed the urgent local issue of urban blight. He left the door ajar by saying he liked the behavior-change and community-organizing aspect of the program and would be willing to invest in something like this if it could help the city address these livability issues.

Shirley Kitchen was a fighter, but could see we were swimming upstream. Without the city as a partner we could not continue to get state or federal funding. Creating a program to address neighborhood livability issues was clearly a better fit for her district. It was also much closer to what Susan had originally wanted.

We all decided this was the obvious way forward, and without a lot of deliberation we went for it. Shirley got the buy-in of the managing director who in turn got the mayor's support. She used that leverage to get more state financing. Susan used the city and state commitment to get the next round of financing from EPA and the active support of the head of her agency, the regional director. I accepted the charge of developing a neighborhood livability program. This was a teachable moment for the evolution of this social technology. It was time for me to put my thinking where my mouth had been eighteen months earlier in Annapolis.

THE PHILADELPHIA LIVABLE NEIGHBORHOOD PROGRAM IS BORN

I had discovered that a by-product of our community-organizing strategy was what is called "social capital," which can be loosely defined as the informal web of relationships and trust that exist in a neighborhood when people have opportunities to connect with one another. Many EcoTeams had organically begun investing the social capital they generated into tackling neighborhood-level issues such as cleaning up neighborhood alleys, planting community gardens, and creating block watches. The cities we had worked with were eager to explore how to use these block-based teams to help them improve their communities. It was time to activate all this potential.

I had delivered the basic framework for such a program in Annapolis. The major ideas were all there, and now I needed to pull them together, make them coherent, and design an empowerment process to engage people on their blocks around *livability* issues as I had previously done around *sustainability* issues.

I spoke with many of our Philadelphia block-based EcoTeam leaders. I spoke with the managing director's office to understand how the city was organized to deliver services. I studied the city of Philadelphia's web site to better understand the various services provided to neighborhoods, and their outreach strategies. I met with the heads of many city agencies to get a firsthand sense of the challenges they faced in delivering their services. I interviewed several of the city's nonprofits that delivered neighborhood services. I talked to my network of government agency partners, elected officials, and program managers in the other cities where we worked. I also spoke with several of the community organizers around the country who had led successful visioning projects to learn about the outcomes people most desired for their neighborhoods.

I asked our block-based EcoTeam leaders three questions. What do you most love and value about your block? What are you most concerned about on your block? If you could have it the way you wanted, what would you like your block to be like?

People appreciated the opportunity to think about what they most loved. Their answers ranged from particular people and houses to their favorite trees and birds. People had many concerns about their blocks, from the very serious to the merely annoying. They talked about issues ranging from crime and drug dealing, to dirty streets, to speeding cars, to not knowing people, to someone's irritating choice of music. Their answers about what they would most like their block to be like were often profound and generally spoke to their yearning for more community and connection with their neighbors.

Analyzing the programs various local government agencies delivered to neighborhoods both in Philadelphia and other cities was both enlightening and essential. I learned which ones were successful and why, as well as which ones were struggling and what might enable them to be more successful. I asked what types of people were participating in these programs and what were the strategies used to recruit them. I asked about the greatest challenges facing the agencies and solicited any suggestions their directors might have for those facing similar challenges. Their answers ranged from the political to the practical to the philosophical.

My final question asked them to step out of their comfort zone as an implementer of government programs and policies and dream a bit with me. If they could have it anyway they wanted, what would they like their relationship to look like with the citizens they served? It was quite touching to watch the protective layers start to fall away as they gave themselves permission to touch their deeper aspiration for public service. My experience of those in public service is that this desire to make a difference lies just below the surface. It is one of the major untapped resources for community change.

My conversations with community organizers offered insight into the actual delivery and participation side of neighborhood improvement strategies. They shared their challenges and best practices in recruiting people, helping them successfully implement their projects, and keeping them engaged.

This very rich information-gathering process which took three months of full-time research generated about fifty neighborhood improvement actions and different strategies for delivering them. We boiled these down to thirty-five distinct activities that reflected four fundamental needs people expressed.

- They wanted a safe and healthy street to live on.

- They wanted it to be clean and look nice.

- They wanted to be able to ask a neighbor for help in a pinch.

- And they wanted to know their neighbors better and feel a greater sense of community.

We designed the Philadelphia Livable Neighborhood Program using our sustainable lifestyle program as the template. We translated the four needs people had expressed into four topic areas: neighborhood health and safety, neighborhood beautification and greening, neighborhood resource sharing, and neighborhood building. Each section had eight or nine action plans designed in a recipe format for improving some aspect of life on the block—how to set up a neighborhood watch for instance, or beautify their street, or establish a child care program among parents, or resolve conflicts among neighbors.

We adapted our self-directed meeting guide tools for working at the block level. At each meeting, the team would select the actions they wished to take from the existing menu and then decide who would do what. Within about thirty minutes the team would be able to decide on their priorities and then form different subteams to implement them.

Many of the actions were designed to be taken at two levels: actions that could be done on the block by residents and those that required government or nonprofit services. As we got into the actual creation of the action plans, it was a revelation that so many of the neighborhood improvement activities could be implemented without the need of external resources. For example, people could clean up their own streets. Or better yet, create an ethic of cleanliness and beauty on their block. The missing piece was getting neighbors organized. This had major implications for the city government because it provided the possibility of reducing demand on the city's limited service delivery resources.

A key to designing any program is figuring out how to get the participation of your target audience. It is one thing to want things to be "better" where you live; it is something else to be willing to spend time making it better. What I had learned from the EcoTeam experience was the power of working at the block level. The block represents most people's definition of neighborhood and the level at which they can most benefit from their investment of time. This was also the place where they wanted more connection.

Getting to know their neighbors meant the people who lived next door, across the street, and the ones they saw when they were walking, jogging, cutting their lawn, or gardening. The crime they were most wishing to prevent was on their block. The vacant lot they most wished to clean up was on their street. If they needed to borrow something from a neighbor, it was the one next door.

I also thought hard about what I was hearing from city agencies who delivered services to lower-income neighborhoods. They were frustrated by the fact that they would clean up a vacant lot and it would be trashed one month later. They would clean a street and it would be full of litter in a few days. They would start a neighborhood watch program and it would immediately dissolve. As a result, they would often not provide the same level of service to these neighborhoods. This in turn would cause resentment from these underserved neighborhoods.

What if we could create mutual accountability and mutual benefits between citizens and their city government? What if we were able to redefine the implicit social contract between a community resident who pays taxes and a city that delivers services? What if the city prioritized municipal services to those neighborhoods who organized themselves to maintain these services? If the city cleans up a vacant lot or street, the block agrees to keep it clean. If the city helps a block start a neighborhood watch program, the neighborhood agrees to sustain it for at least a year. To enable this accountability we could integrate into the relevant actions a brief description of the city service and a specific contact person for the action leader to call or e-mail.

I scheduled a meeting with the person the managing director had assigned to oversee this initiative for the city, John Hadalski. My purpose was to explain the new program that had taken shape and attempt to get the city's support for this mutual accountability aspect.

I explained how blocks would become better organized, enabling them to use city programs more effectively and sustain their use over time. When the city set up a neighborhood watch on a block, for example, it would be maintained because there was now a community of people connected who cared about one another; when the city cleaned a vacant lot, the block would help keep it clean because there was now a committed team in place. Residents would be educated to cease behaviors that increased the need for city services, such as stuffing leaves down catch basins. And ultimately it would improve citizen satisfaction as residents learned about services, were able to access them more easily, and accrued the benefits of a safer, cleaner, and overall more livable neighborhood.

He asked many questions about how the program was designed, our recruitment strategy, and how we anticipated getting participation. He was impressed with the thoroughness of this new program and the fact that our sustainable lifestyle program had been so successful, but he voiced concerns about our ability to break through in Philadelphia's toughest inner-city neighborhoods where many attempts to create change over many years had failed. I acknowledged that I had similar concerns and then shared some others of my own.

"Alone we would not get very far," I said, "but if we work in full partnership we will have a better chance. In particular, we need to demonstrate that the city is willing to go the extra mile by prioritizing services to those neighborhoods that participate. This will provide us the extra incentive to get people's attention, at which point the program would either succeed or fail on its own merits."

He was intrigued, albeit cautious, in his expectations. But he agreed to support this approach and convinced the managing director to get all his departments on board. While neither of us knew what the road ahead would bring, I did know that we would be a lot further down that road because of the new social compact that would be forged between the city of Philadelphia and its most disenfranchised citizens.

John would work with the different agencies and identify the contact people we would list in our program. He would also serve as our go-to person if anything did not work. If an action leader did not get a response, the service was not delivered in a timely manner, or the block did not keep its end of the bargain with the city, John was the man to contact. John is the quintessential civil servant—ready to serve with a cheerful attitude, effective, and committed to excellence. We would test these qualities many times and he would never fail to impress me.

John set up a series of meetings so that I could brief the various department heads about the program and learn about their neighborhood priorities. We would then explore how the program might best help them meet these priorities. We always came up with productive ways to work together. They also shared with me the different programs they or their predecessors had implemented in these neighborhoods. This would inevitably lead to recounting their frustrations, challenges, and failures. It seemed they wished to cushion me from what they felt would be my similar fate of frustration and failure.

Each time I heard these concerns, I tried my best to bolster their confidence (and mine) by launching into all the unique features of this program and the rationale behind each that gave it a chance of being successful. I talked about our research and how we had built this program on the successes and failures of much that had gone before it. They listened politely and asked a few questions, but I could tell they were not convinced. At some level, though, I felt them hoping I was right.

I expected to encounter a similar "What is the use?" attitude in the residents. In spite of the past failures that had likely eroded their spirits, I hoped for a better outcome in convincing them than I had achieved with the city agencies. I was betting on the fact that, faced with the continuation of a diminished quality of life in their neighborhood, they would be willing to try a new program if they believed it could work.

My job was to create a program worthy of their trust. I believed we had done this. We would now need to ask community leaders to be willing to suspend any disbelief they might have and give it a try. Fortunately, with our perennial champion Shirley Kitchen, and the active support of Mayor John Street, we had enough credibility for people to be willing to listen with a somewhat open mind.

Philadelphia Livable Neighborhood Program: Making Life Better on the Street Where You Live was ready to make its maiden voyage. We recruited and trained three staff people in these neighborhoods to serve as program managers. Their first job was to recruit individuals to serve as block leaders. They began by approaching the likely suspects. People who were already block captains, neighborhood association leaders, and volunteers associated with other city programs.

We asked qualified candidates to make a commitment to attend a day-long training to learn our community-organizing model and empowerment coaching skills; start a team on their block within a month of the training; participate in regular coaching with a member of our team; complete the program within six months; and accurately report the final results. We told them if they accomplished this, the city of Philadelphia and Empowerment Institute would certify them as a Livable Neighborhood Block Leader.

We anticipated that these requirements would evoke resistance and require some serious selling. To our surprise, and, quite frankly, amazement, we experienced just the opposite. People were brimming with enthusiasm. We heard comments like "this makes complete sense" and "it could really work on my block." Those we approached were excited by the level of training and the seriousness of our intention. A few commented that they had never had any type of training like this and it was a great opportunity to burnish their résumé or use it in their current job or with their church. Not all of them were ready to make a commitment, but if they weren't, they often pointed us to someone they thought might be interested.

Within three months we had met our initial recruitment goal of twenty block leaders and had scheduled our inaugural Livable Neighborhood Block Leadership Academy at the Nicetown Community Development Center. We had also established our office in this two-story walkup because it provided us free meeting spaces for holding our trainings and was convenient to many of the neighborhoods in which we worked. It was a hotbed of community activity, and we wanted to be where people were expressing their community activism. We invited our three sponsors as special guests to launch the academy and inspire our intrepid pioneering block leaders on their adventure.

We gathered in the large multipurpose meeting room that the next day would host a wedding; it was a modestly appointed room with simple tables and chairs, but most adequate for our needs. Lending their weight and credibility to the program, State Senator Shirley Kitchen, newly appointed Managing Director Estelle Richman, and Donald Welsh, the regional administrator for the U.S. Environmental Protection Agency spoke eloquently about the groundbreaking nature of the program and its potential to improve the quality of life in Philadelphia's inner-city neighborhoods, fostering the sense that this was truly a cooperative venture that could work if everyone involved wanted it to.

Having top city, state, and federal government officials attend the launch of their training in an inner-city Philadelphia neighborhood made the block leaders feel proud to be part of something viewed as so special. I felt the same. With that send-off, we jumped into the training. We taught them our proven neighbor-to-neighbor recruitment process, how to lead the team meetings, and our empowerment coaching techniques for keeping team members on track. We role-played many of the possible issues that could come up in their informational and team meetings. People felt inspired by one another's commitment, and at the end of the day everyone was revved up and ready to change the world—or at least their block.

The Journey of a Hundred Blocks Begins With the First Step

Although many block leaders had been living on their street for many years, and in some cases their entire lives, with few exceptions they did not know their neighbors. Some were excited by this prospect of meeting them and, as we had seen with the sustainable lifestyle program, some were petrified that they would be rejected, or worse.

To increase their self-confidence they once again practiced the simple script they had learned in the training before they ventured out.

Hi, I'm your neighbor from up the street. I would like to invite you to a neighborhood gathering in my home to learn about a program sponsored by the city of Philadelphia to help us create a safer, healthier, and more livable neighborhood and get to know each other better as neighbors. It is this Sunday afternoon at 3 PM at my home. Can you make it?

And then, ready or not, in July of 2001 they began their journey of introducing the Livable Neighborhood Program to some of the toughest neighborhoods in the city of Philadelphia. Given our past experience, I was prepared when the word started coming in. "It worked!" "My neighbors actually thanked me!" "*Everyone* said they will come!" We shared with them that it was the personal connection that made the difference and we encouraged them to speak with all of their neighbors, if possible. Once the block leaders discovered this was an enjoyable experience, they didn't mind going back a second or third time to speak to those neighbors they had missed.

Robert Johnson, an elderly and distinguished-looking man with gray hair, had been living his entire life on the same block but barely knew any of his neighbors. With a friendly and engaging personality he reached out to each of his twenty-two neighbors and invited them to his home on Sunday afternoon at 3 PM. His block in Nicetown consisted of low- to middle-income predominantly African-American families living in older single-family homes. As is typical of many blocks in Philadelphia, there was a vacant lot with trash and several abandoned buildings on the block. His block had also recently experienced some petty drug-related crime.

It was summer and Robert was sitting in an aluminum chair on his front porch wondering if people would actually come to his neighborhood gathering. Almost everyone he spoke with had said they would come, but nothing like this had ever happened on his block before and he didn't know what to expect. He lived on one end of this quiet street and could see, through a few interspersed trees, its entire length.

At approximately 2:55 a few doors started opening, then a few more, and then a few more. As people walked to the end of the road, they began eyeing one another. "It was quite an amazing sight to behold," Robert reported. "Just about everyone on the block was walking to my house."

After about ten minutes of people talking and partaking of cookies, iced tea, and lemonade, Robert invited everyone to sit down. Following the detailed meeting script he had been trained to use, he asked people to introduce themselves, stating why they had come and what they wished from the meeting.

The most common theme was that they had been living on this block, some like Robert their entire life, and they did not know the neighbors they passed daily on the street. They came first of all get to know their neighbors. They also had many things they were concerned about and wondered if this program might help address some of these issues. They were skeptical because they had seen several programs come promising much and delivering little. But they were willing to go to Robert's and at least meet their neighbors.

After people introduced themselves, Robert asked them three questions. "What, if anything, do you most like about living on our block?" "What, if anything, are you most concerned about?" And "If it could be any way you wanted, what would you like our block to be like?"

The answers came pouring out. "I want our block to be safe from the drug dealers who are moving about freely." "I want to see that vacant lot which is an eye sore cleaned up." "I would like people not to throw their litter on streets." "I would like to create a community garden where that vacant lot is." "I would like some help in the winter shoveling snow from the sidewalk, because at 83 I can't do it like I used to."

One of the last to speak, visibly touched, said, "No one in my whole life has ever asked me a question like this. I never knew that we could really make things better. I am so grateful for Robert bringing us together. What I most want for our block, is for it to feel like church, where we are really there for each other."

Robert explained in detail how the program worked, and that there were actions already designed for each of the things mentioned. He reiterated that the neighbors could do most of the actions on their own, but if there was something that required help from the city, the city would prioritize its services to help out because their block was part of the Livable Neighborhood Program. All they needed to do was agree to maintain any of the services delivered.

"I was a bit nervous at the end of saying all this and wondered if people would be willing to try this out." Robert explained. "When I asked who would be interested in joining this livable neighborhood team, I was so happy when *everyone* said yes."

Robert's team met over the next three months and systematically took the actions people talked about at this first meeting. They cleaned up the litter on their block. The called the city to set up a neighborhood watch program to prevent crime and rid themselves of the drug dealers. They asked the city to clean up the vacant lot and they turned it into a community garden. They cleaned up an alley adjoining the next block that had become a junk pile and eyesore. They asked the city to board up the two abandoned buildings that were unsafe. All told, they took eight substantive actions to improve the quality of life on their block. They also reported that the city agencies were prompt in delivering the requested services.

The transformation on their block was contagious. Residents on the block adjoining the alley that had been cleaned saw what had happened and quickly joined the program. Word continued to spread not only in the Nicetown neighborhood, but throughout blocks in North and West Philadelphia. The Livable Neighborhood Program soon began diffusing on its own momentum and required less and less effort on our part to recruit block leaders.

The specific issues people addressed through the program varied from block to block, but the reasons that always rose to the top for participating were getting to know their neighbors and making their block safer and cleaner. Because of the concrete and immediate benefits people were seeing, we achieved a remarkable 63 percent involvement rate of the people on participating blocks.

I remember a conversation with one of our program managers, Angela, after she told me that over 60 percent of the block had attended a recent meeting and 100 percent of the people attending committed themselves to joining the program. I had been in awe of the 25 percent participation rate we had experienced with EcoTeams, and found this new number hard to fathom.

I kept probing and asking Angela questions about what might have been special about that meeting or block to achieve such an extraordinary outcome. She seemed puzzled by my questions. "Every meeting I attend has pretty much the same result. Between 50 and 70 percent of the block shows up for the initial information meeting and almost everyone joins the team. Often people who can't make this initial meeting come to future meetings."

She paused and then smiled. "Why wouldn't someone participate? It's such a great program!" It seems I was the last to understand what others now took for granted. The program was working exactly the way we had hoped it would.

From Residents to Neighbors

It moved me to sit in on some of the meetings and listen to the many stories people told about how life had changed on their blocks. Although numerous large changes, such as reducing crime and cleaning up vacant lots, occurred, it was often the many little changes that really transformed blocks into livable neighborhoods.

On one of the original Livable Neighborhood blocks in North Philadelphia, Samuel Dow helped elderly neighbor Bob Davenport install the door alarm they had received from a city program on family safety. Jeanette Davenport reported that she used to worry that her back door was not secure, but now she felt much safer in her home. Samuel also trimmed a few limbs from the Davenports' tree, which was causing Bob and Jeannette's next-door neighbor some concern. This thrilled the neighbor who then helped repair Bob's fence.

This team has started a newsletter for their block, feeling very strongly that they wanted to share the information about city services they had learned with their other neighbors. They also are continuing to meet as a group, and they use the newsletter as a tool for inviting new neighbors to their meetings and potlucks.

Several team members reported that some of their immediate neighbors who were not participating in the program had cleaned up their property anyway. These nonparticipating neighbors had observed piles of rubbish disappear and houses be painted, so they decided to do the same. There was now a noticeable sense of pride spreading on the block.

In another North Philadelphia neighborhood, Dorothy Roberts and her husband used to be very active in their neighborhood. He had passed away a few years ago and Dorothy hadn't been out of the house much since her stroke. When Viola Brown, the Block Leader, invited her to the first Livable Neighborhood meeting, Dorothy was determined to attend. It took her fifteen minutes to walk next door to the meeting, but she made it, with a grandson on each arm to steady her. The neighbors were moved to tears, and started the meeting with a thankful prayer.

The story doesn't end here. Near the end of the meeting, Dorothy mentioned that she was concerned about her leaking roof; she didn't know how she'd get it fixed. Team members Corliss and Roberta started networking. They raised $50 to cover the cost of materials. In the course of raising the money, one of their neighbors volunteered to fix Dorothy's roof, and he did.

Another team in a high-crime area in Nicetown wanted to bring all the neighbors on their block together to participate in the neighborhood watch program they were implementing. The team organized a gathering literally in the middle of their block one Sunday afternoon. During this gathering, not only did the neighbors learn about the program, but they were given the opportunity to meet both their area police officer and the city's crime pre-vention educator. Everyone at the meeting committed to participate in the neighborhood watch program.

Mrs. Denton had lived in her home in West Philadelphia for 50 years. Mr. Williams had lived three doors down for thirty years. Until this pro-gram was started on the block, they had waved at each other and exchanged social pleasantries, but didn't know each other's name. They've enjoyed get-ting to know each other better through their team. At a meeting Mrs. Den-ton, a widow, remarked that there was a hole in one wall of her home, and that bees were coming into her home—a very uncomfortable situation. She had already been stung three times. Mr. Williams stopped by a few days later and sealed the hole. No more bees!

At the final meeting, one neighbor shared that she goes out on her porch at least once each evening and looks around her block, just making sure everything's okay. She enjoys this feeling of being more connected to her neighbors. She now genuinely cares about them and wants to keep a watch-ful eye out.

"The best thing that happened," says Karen Robertson, "was that through this process we've formed a core group of seven or eight people on our block who are genuinely interested in improving it. They are the foun-dation we'll build on during the coming year as we expand our activities on the block. Now we have a vision of how it can be in the future."

And Dorothy Allen, whose team took a remarkable twelve block-im-provement actions over a year, described her experience of community. "Neighbors are coming together like never before. They're decorating more for Christmas. I used to see lots of strange cars driving by constantly looking to buy drugs. I don't see them anymore. There's increased communication we didn't have before. I've lived in this neighborhood for six years, and for the first time, I feel like I'm part of the neighborhood."

LIVABLE NEIGHBORHOODS TAKE ROOT

Between July 2001 and June 2004 the Livable Neighborhood Program, in partnership with the city of Philadelphia, was successfully implemented in 101 inner-city neighborhoods. Participating blocks successfully took a minimum of three neighborhood improvement actions during the formal program, with most of the teams continuing to meet and take further actions afterward. The program also added an energy efficiency module called "affordable comfort," and participating households reduced their energy bills by 12 percent.

John Hadalski described these results in his report to the managing director and all the participating city agencies.

> The Philadelphia Livable Neighborhood Program has achieved high marks in communities in which it exists, which I might add are some of the lower income neighborhoods of our city. Uniquely, the program has helped us respond to community needs and deliver services more efficiently, while simultaneously creating community involvement to help us sustain this government investment. The program has exceeded our expectations and become one of the true success stories in city government.

This was accomplished because the city of Philadelphia was willing to step out of its comfort zone and take a risk on a new idea and on its citizens. In turn, the citizens of the City of Brotherly Love were willing to reach out and help one another, and to be mutually accountable with their local government for improvements to their neighborhoods. And the premise that people *will* take action to improve themselves and their community, if provided effective tools, had proved true.

Word of this success started spreading, as did the program. The University of Pennsylvania's Fels School of Government, located in West Philadelphia, having gotten a large U.S. Department of Justice grant, asked us to implement the Livable Neighborhood Program in the inner-city neighborhoods bordering the university. Our state partner, the Department of Environmental Protection, wished us to disseminate the program more widely and provided funding to build the capacity of local community-based organizations both in Philadelphia and Pittsburgh. And I was invited to keynote Neighborhood USA's national conference in Pittsburgh, attended by representatives of nearly a thousand neighborhood associations and city agencies. My talk spawned a desire for this program in communities across the country, so I published the Livable Neighborhood book with guidelines on how to implement it. We had lit a fire.

We were now reliably able to change individual *and* neighborhood behavior. We had demonstrated the effectiveness of this social change methodology in a very challenging urban environment. But a new peak beckoned that would put these tools to yet another unique and demanding test.

The aftermath of two national disasters—the events of September 11, 2001, and Hurricane Katrina in August 2005—revealed a deep vulnerability in urban communities. Many elderly and infirm people were stranded in buildings surrounding New York City's Twin Towers after the terrorist attacks. They were not able to evacuate and no one knew they were there. In New Orleans, many of the lives lost in the wake of Katrina could have been spared if their neighborhoods had been more disaster resilient.

In 2003 a fragile energy grid broke down causing half of the country to be without power for a day or more in the blistering heat of August. In many cities, food and water were sold out within three hours. Had the power outage lasted for several days, many people's lives would have been at great risk.

Global-warming-induced natural disasters of flooding, tornadoes, hurricanes, and fires were now becoming commonplace along with the concomitant loss of life and property. Terrorist attacks are now, it must be acknowledged, an ongoing threat. The next frontier beyond sustainability and livability was *resiliency*. For urban communities, disaster resiliency was a new quality-of-life indicator. Could the tools I had been developing over the past two decades be helpful? New York City invited me to find out.

CHAPTER 3: SOCIAL CHANGE 2.0 PRACTITIONER'S GUIDE

1. Within what larger social system does your change strategy fit?

2. How can you improve the social change performance of your initiative by developing synergy among the major stakeholders in this larger system?

3. What percentage of your social change initiative's time is spent on visioning/awareness-raising activities versus measurable behavior change and tangible societal improvements?

4. What can you do to build a more robust back end of measurable behavior change and tangible societal improvements into your initiative?

5. What specific ways can you use community to further the outcomes of your social change initiative?

DISASTER-RESILIENT COMMUNITIES

IN NEW YORK CITY:

ALL TOGETHER NOW

It was right out of the movie *Groundhog Day*. I was co-facilitating a workshop on our sustainable lifestyle campaign to a group of local government leaders I had addressed twice already. The most recent time had been in Portland at the "revival meeting" event that they had written off as a Portland thing. Except this time, their colleagues from Kansas City, Missouri, and Columbus, Ohio, were leading the workshop. The two midwesterners had drunk the Kool-Aid and were still alive to tell the tale. It was a redemption story of sorts for me, proof to this skeptical group that our work in Portland was not just a one-off experience in a green city. Now there were heartland representatives confirming similar results from the "Show Me State" of Missouri, and the ultimate Middle America city of Columbus, Ohio, where corporations go to test out their new products.

Their experience proved to be a tipping point for the government representative from the "show me" city of New York. Alan Leidner was New York City's assistant commissioner for information technology, a cover he used for involving himself in projects he thought were cool and could make a difference. He and I had discussed the sustainable lifestyle campaign several years earlier but according to Alan, it was "not yet ready for Broadway."

Alan is the quintessential New Yorker: effective, direct, and soft-hearted under a brazen exterior, convinced that New York City is the center of the universe. He had established himself as a government change agent and smart operator who got things done and was always on the cutting edge. He was also a community activist and passionate environmentalist. After the workshop he approached me and said, "David, we need to talk."

We pulled up a couple of oversized chairs outside the meeting rooms in the beautifully appointed and environmentally conscious Sofitel Hotel in Atlanta, Georgia. He got right to it. "I would like to champion your work in New York City, but it will need to go through some changes. It needs to have another entry point for people who won't join a team with their neighbors. And we need to address the issue of public safety." He continued, "As much as I personally like the environmental program, your new neighborhood program will be a better fit because New York has many neighborhood associations looking for ways to engage people, and we can build on your action on emergency preparedness."

He continued, "The Office of Emergency Management needs something like this. Right now all they do is make media announcements telling people what to do after an emergency has occurred. By then it is too late."

His idea was that we would rework the program to make preparedness more prominent, but keep the livability components attractive to residents in neighborhoods. "Would you be interested in exploring this path for the program in New York City?" he asked intently.

Having lived in Manhattan in my twenties and thirties I was thrilled at the prospect of taking this work there. I took a breath and said yes. Then Alan and I shook hands and he agreed to call me when he had arranged a meeting with Mike Berkowitz, the Assistant Commissioner for Communications in the NYC Office of Emergency Management (OEM). A few weeks later he called.

The OEM had their offices on the twenty-third floor of 7 World Trade Center, and I was looking forward to this mini sightseeing tour of one of New York City's most famous buildings. It was a warm June day and we met in OEM's modern, and (by government standards) well-appointed conference room. It had a stunning view of New York's harbor surrounding the tip of lower Manhattan.

Michael had a laid-back persona, for a New Yorker, and a boyish face that made him look younger than his thirty-something years. Alan had briefed me not to be deceived by his looks. Behind his youthful exterior was a very sharp communications person who orchestrated Mayor Rudolph Giuliani's frequent high-profile media events in response to the many emergencies New York City faced on a regular basis. Michael worked directly for Mayor Giuliani, who was a demanding task master.

He knew Michael well, so we agreed that Alan should take the lead. He started the conversation by describing the sustainable lifestyle campaign's success in other cites. He explained the new livable neighborhood program, and how we would appeal to people by describing the immediate benefits of improving their neighborhood, then highlight the emergency preparedness action as a smart insurance policy. I provided the color commentary and research findings on behavior change and community organizing. Michael listened patiently and then began asking a battery of questions, each one more pointed than the last.

"New Yorkers are not known for warming up to their neighbors. Why do you think you will get them to work together on teams? We have more diversity in the borough of Queens than any place else on the planet. Each neighborhood is a walking United Nations. How will you address the language and cultural differences? There are eight million people living here. This block-by-block approach will be an organizing nightmare. How do you expect to have any impact with so many people? Given how hard it has been traditionally for cities to get citizens to prioritize emergency preparedness, what makes you think your approach will work?"

It went on like this for about ten minutes. If I had been deceived by Michael's boyish looks, I wasn't anymore. We did not have good answers to any of these questions. After watching Alan and me scramble for awhile, he smiled and said, "Nothing ventured, nothing gained." I didn't understand until he continued. "For me to sell this to my boss, I will need you to speak to the city's Community Assistance Unit responsible for working in neighborhoods. If they like this, it will help our cause."

After our meeting he took us to OEM's famous "Emergency Command Center" and the room where Mayor Giuliani held his media events. Michael had helped design this space and was proud of it; the tour was his way of letting us know we had passed the test. Pointing to a window overlooking the harbor of New York City and the Statue of Liberty, he said, "This is where we do the 'money shots.'"

As we were going down in the elevator Alan smiled at me and said, "David, by New York City standards this was easy, they usually want a pound of your flesh." I didn't realize at the time that he wasn't entirely joking.

Alan arranged a meeting with the Community Assistance Unit of the mayor's office in late July of 2001. We met with August Simmons, the woman who directed the neighborhood outreach department, in a small cramped room in need of a paint job in one of downtown Manhattan's very old city offices. August served as the liaison with the city's many neighborhood associations. She had been doing this work through three different mayoral administrations and knew the neighborhoods like the back of her hand. She was also a community organizer, having created her own neighborhood association in the Bedford Stuyvesant section of Brooklyn. When we explained the Livable Neighborhood Program and our block-by-block organizing approach, her eyes lit up.

August then explained why she thought a program like this could work in New York. "Over 60 percent of the city already has strong block and neighborhood associations, and the rest have a desire or need to create them. These block and neighborhood associations work in cooperation with New York City's fifty-nine government-funded community boards divided over five boroughs. Each borough has an elected president responsible for working directly with these community boards, and through them the block and neighborhood associations. New York City is manageable because so many of its neighborhoods are organized.

"Neighborhoods that are not organized are at a distinct disadvantage in receiving city services and should be open to your approach as a way to organize themselves. You know your way around community organizing well enough to be able to identify neighborhood leaders to play such a role." She nodded her encouragement. "Existing block and neighborhood associations are always struggling to get people involved and should be open to such a practical program, which can help them attract new members and engage existing members."

She then went on to say that she was about to retire. This was very disappointing news to us, as we had quickly come to see what a valuable partner she would be. But she promised her office would be available to help when we were ready.

We thanked August effusively for her tutorial. When we left her office, Alan and I "high fived" and agreed to get a meeting going with Michael in early September, when we both returned from vacation, to report on this very positive endorsement for our neighborhood program.

A TRAGEDY AND A NEW PRIORITY FOR NEW YORK CITY

That meeting was not to be. A little over a month later New York City changed, and with it, the world. I tried to reach Alan to make sure he was okay. Having left messages at his office with no response, I finally tracked him down at his home on the Upper West Side. When he answered the phone I breathed a huge sigh of relief.

He, like all of New York City, was grief stricken and in deep mourning, having lost several friends in the Towers. And if the planes had struck one hour later, he would have been at the World Trade Center in a meeting.

Alan reported that Michael was also okay and was leading the communications effort for New York City's recovery in a makeshift facility on Pier 92 near Fifty-Third Street in midtown Manhattan; the OEM's office had been in the World Trade Center. Alan was with Michael and that was why I had been unable to reach him at his office.

Alan invited me to visit him at Pier 92 to regroup on our plan, saying that what we had been discussing was now needed more than ever. I thought to myself how prescient Alan had been about the need for emergency preparedness.

When I arrived at the building, I needed special clearance to get inside. So many people wanted to volunteer to assist in the recovery effort that the police had to create a barricade to keep them out so that the highly specialized work could get done.

The efforts inside the building were a sight to behold. There were hundreds of people organized around dozens of different disaster recovery functions. One section had maps showing the different parts of the recovery site and the underground basements of the structures that had collapsed; another section was for the search-and-rescue operation; another for grief counseling of survivors; another for the construction crews; another for communications. There were several dozen distinct and specialized operations spanning this block-long structure. It was deeply touching to see people from the many different city agencies and nonprofits that normally work in silos, or compete for visibility and funding, working together seamlessly. There was immense goodwill and determination permeating the building. It was New York City at its best. In fact, it was humanity at its best.

When I arrived Alan and I had a warm hug and he asked if I was hungry and explained that the Red Cross was providing free food to all those working on the recovery effort. Having not yet eaten, I went ahead and availed myself of a free lunch. I did not know at the time that there really are no free lunches in New York, and I would be paying for it for quite a few years.

When I returned, I saw Alan pouring over a large map surrounded by people at dozens of computers. He turned toward me and was more focused than I had ever seen him before. Until now this had simply been a project he thought would be helpful to his city. It was on the cutting edge, where he liked to play, and so it was interesting to him. But now there was a sense of urgency and passion in his voice.

He laid out his plan. "We will need to do this in stages. First we need the support of one of the community boards. I'll arrange a meeting with Penny Ryan who runs the community board where I live. I've been working on an information technology project with her community board and think she'll be interested, particularly if I tie this into that project. If we get a demonstration of interest, I will put up the seed capital from my budget to help us develop the major financing." We had a brief meeting with Michael Berkowitz, who, though completely overwhelmed with the recovery communications effort, indicated that if there was community interest, he was willing to help us get financing from his agency.

Penny Ryan is the district manager for Community Board 7 in Manhattan's Upper West Side. The boundaries of her district start in the south at Central Park and Fifty-Ninth Street and go north to the beginning of Harlem at 110th Street and west from the park to the Hudson River. Its most famous landmark is the cultural Mecca, Lincoln Center. The district represents about 225,000 New Yorkers. Some call it the "Independent Republic of New York" because so many of New York's progressive thinkers, creative types, and artistic community live there. This is where John Lennon lived and died at the Dakota Hotel on Central Park West, and where he is immortalized in the "Strawberry Fields" sanctuary in the park. This had to be one of the most fascinating parts of the world in which to land and attempt to put down roots.

Penny was a dedicated community organizer who because of her passion for new ideas had many things on her plate. Given this penchant, she was interested in meeting with us and learn more about this neighborhood program. She liked the idea, but wondered if busy New Yorkers would take time for something like this and want to form teams with their neighbors.

Most of the community organizing of the neighborhood associations she worked with was based on opposition to something. She thought this program was a bit soft by New York City standards, but she agreed to think about it.

Penny had many bosses: her board of directors, the city council representative from her district, and the borough president. Making a decision to pilot a new program associated with the city in her district was not something she could decide alone. A month later Penny asked for a meeting. She reported, "I spoke with my board of directors, our city council representative, and several of our neighborhood associations. The consensus of opinion was to go forward, but we would like the program to be exclusively about emergency preparedness. In this post-9/11 environment people are afraid and need a way to do something practical to prepare for future emergencies. It will also be a constructive way to channel the strong need people have to build community. If you are interested in developing a program like this, I would be willing to help pilot it in my district."

It was a "yes, but" answer. She wanted us to deliver a very different program. I believed our Livable Neighborhood Program with an action on emergency preparedness would be easier to sell in New York City with its strong focus on neighborhoods. I was not sure about selling emergency preparedness, straight up. But this issue certainly was in people's minds and hearts and it did appear to be a teachable moment for emergency preparedness. I told her that I would like to think about it and discuss it further with Alan.

Penny had not made this request in a vacuum. In the course of our prior conversation, to bolster our credentials on emergency preparedness, I told her about an emergency preparedness program we had developed two years earlier for the Federal Emergency Management Agency (FEMA). They had contracted with us to develop and deliver a program to help communities prepare for the possibility of power outages caused by Year 2000 (Y2K) computer malfunctions. Kay Goss, director of Personal and Community Preparedness, and a real visionary, wished America's citizens to be prepared for the possible disruption of essential services.

Because of the need for such a rapid mobilization and the uncertainty of the threat, we created this as an online emergency preparedness program with teletraining classes. We partnered with the National League of Cities and National Association of Counties to distribute the program to thousands of municipalities. In short, we had a generic program already built that we could adapt for New York City.

Over the next two months I huddled with my team and had a number
of conversations with Alan and Penny, attempting to figure out what might
work. Eventually, I developed a proposal for three phases. Phase one would
be to pilot a New York City adaptation of this program in Penny's district.
We would work with three different types of buildings and demographics
to learn if we could get people to participate in such a program *and* actually
adopt emergency preparedness practices. If that proved successful we would
then do a demonstration project in all five boroughs. If that achieved comparable results we would attempt to take it to scale citywide.

Alan then arranged a meeting with Michael Berkowitz to see if he could
help us get financing from OEM, but as we walked him through the proposal it became clear that he did not have the bandwidth for taking on anything new; the 9/11 recovery effort was all consuming. He also told us not
to expect much success in getting this financed out of the OEM coffers; all
of their discretionary money had gone into the many costs associated with
the recovery effort. But he was willing to set up a meeting with his Commissioner, John Olderman, to explore this further.

The meeting took place in OEM's temporary headquarters, an old
metal-roofed converted warehouse right next to the Brooklyn Bridge. John
Olderman and his senior leadership team, many seconded from the fire and
police departments and representing the city's ethnic and racial diversity,
gathered in a small conference room with large metal heating and air conditioning ducts in the ceiling. It looked like the underbelly of a submarine.

I had sent them the proposal in advance to review so they were familiar
with the project. They asked me very straightforward questions that people
who are daily in the line of fire dealing with emergencies might ask. I liked
the direct and honest manner of these guys. After listening for awhile, John
spoke: "We could definitely benefit from such a program. I am willing to
sponsor it, but I don't have any money in my budget. Please work with my
development person and see if you can get some of the federal money that is
in the pipeline for New York City's recovery." I thanked him for his interest
and support and said I would be happy to pursue this with his development
person.

Getting this person's help was easier said than done. She was too
swamped writing multimillion dollar proposals to provide anything but lip
service to this project. It soon became apparent that if anything was going
to come of this, I would have to pursue the funding on my own. It was beginning to feel like the twelve labors of Hercules. Of course this appealed to

me. I had learned by now that I thrive on large challenges. On a more pro-found level, though, I felt privileged to have an opportunity to make a con-tribution to New York City's healing process. Especially since this was the city I still called home.

To have a chance of securing a federal appropriation, I would need to find a champion for this proposal. My first choice was my newly elected senator, Hillary Clinton, who I knew was very committed to securing fund-ing for New York City's recovery and was known for her "it takes a village" approach to change. I turned to Kay Goss with whom I had worked at FEMA. She had known Hillary since working on emergency preparedness for then-Governor Bill Clinton of Arkansas. She had subsequently worked on his two presidential campaigns and served as one of the highest ranking women in his administration.

Kay was enthusiastic and forthcoming, seeing this as a continuation of the work we had started together. One of the most knowledgeable and re-spected people in the field of emergency preparedness, Kay would prove to be an invaluable ally as I attempted to build out this initiative in New York City. I reinforced Kay's support with a letter from my congressional repre-sentative, Maurice Hinchey, who knew of my work through several EPA funded grants we had secured. He had been a prominent supporter of Hil-lary's run for the Senate and was respected as a man of uncommon integrity.

Through these two supporters, I was able to get Hillary's attention. She was interested and I was contacted by Jason, one of her staff responsible for securing congressional appropriations. He asked me to come to her office in Washington to discuss the proposal with him and the senator. When I got there I learned that Hillary had been called into an urgent meeting and would not be able to meet with me. But she had blessed the proposal and told him to convey to me her sentiments. "This is just what New Yorkers need to heal. It can help them transform their fears into something benefi-cial to their future security and provide a way to reach out to one another for support."

Jason invited me to lunch in the Senate cafeteria, not anything to write home about, where we met for several hours discussing the finer points of the proposal. At the end of our meeting he said this process is a "political crapshoot" so I should not get my hopes up about getting this funding. But he and the Senator would do their best.

Month after month passed with no news and I assumed we had lost in the "political crapshoot." I called Jason to see if he knew what was happening and learned he was no longer working for Senator Clinton. No one in the office knew what was happening or was able to provide much insight into the mysterious process of congressional allocations or "earmarks." I told Alan that we would have to try again next year and we should think about some other source of funding in the short term if we wish to get this going.

Then out of the blue, I got an e-mail from the U.S. Department of Justice. *You have been awarded $500,000 dollars to develop and pilot this program in New York City*, it said. *Please contact us to discuss next steps.* Completely shocked, I picked up the phone immediately "You won't believe this," I said to Alan, "but we just got the funding." Alan's reply touched me, "David, thank you for your perseverance; you are going to make a difference in this city."

My first major decision, a seemingly straightforward one, was wrought with complexity and opened up the many issues we would wrestle with throughout the project. Should I direct the grant to my institute and work with OEM as a partner organization, or to OEM and contract with them to do the work? The first path would be a lot easier and would, I suspected, save me a lot of frustration with red tape, and I would end up with the full grant. At best, the $500,000 would only get us through the first two phases of a three-phase project and we certainly needed it all. I asked Alan for his advice.

First he enumerated the plusses of my keeping all of the money: (1) It was less financing then I had requested to get the job done, so I would have to reduce the scope of work in order to give OEM a percentage of the money. (2) As grant managers, they would be responsible to manage and pay me, and being under the control of a New York City bureaucracy would be quite stifling for a social entrepreneur, especially since OEM was one of the most conservative agencies in the city. (3) The OEM was focused exclusively on emergency recovery. A neighborhood-based behavior-change program was not something with which they had a lot of experience or predisposition. As a result, I may not get much support.

But the minuses didn't sound any better. Alan pointed out that if my institute kept control of the grant, OEM would not own the project and I would be left completely on my own. We needed OEM's support in order to get the buy-in from the borough presidents and community boards, which would play a critical role in helping us get traction in the neighborhoods.

I had learned a lot from watching how sustainable community initiatives had not gotten off the ground because the groups organizing them were not connected with the city agencies responsible for the issues being addressed.

I also watched how well the city of Philadelphia took to integrating their community services into the Livable Neighborhood Program when invited to participate. It was ultimately New York City's responsibility to help New Yorkers prepare for emergencies and care for their safety. I decided the grant should go through the New York City Office of Emergency Management.

I called a meeting with Michael Berkowitz and OEM's development person. I explained to them that I saw us working as partners, but that they should take ownership of this project since preparing New Yorkers for emergencies was their responsibility. I was there as a resource to design and implement the program. I proposed a percentage that they would receive for helping with the program adaptation, outreach to the political leadership and community boards, and managing the grant.

Up until that point in the early part of 2002, New York City had received very little of the post-9/11 money promised to them by Congress. As a relatively small agency with only 80 staff at the time, a federal grant for $500,000 would give them bragging rights across the city. They thanked me for the offer and accepted. They did not ask many questions and express much enthusiasm, which gave me pause. But I decided to enter this relationship with an open mind.

A social entrepreneur, community organizer, change-the-world type partnered with one of the most conservative of New York City agencies that had never ventured into neighborhoods or worked with citizens before, and perhaps had no desire to change now. This should be interesting. I was not sure if this qualified as another labor of Hercules for me or for them.

The person OEM assigned to the project was a former Red Cross volunteer coordinator named Annie Grunwald. She had been hired to head up a new position as OEM liaison with the many volunteer agencies now involved in New York City's recovery. One of only three women who worked there, Annie was their designated "people" person. She had a natural affinity for what we were attempting and in our initial phone conversation was the first person actually to express enthusiasm for the project.

As we sat down for our first meeting, Annie could sense that I was a bit forlorn and wondering what I had gotten myself into. "Don't worry," she reassured me. "My agency is full of good people; they're just not used to working on such a tame project. Their juices flow when they're called into emergencies where they can help save people's lives. Right now this doesn't excite them. But as they come to understand what we're doing, they'll realize that we'll make their work easier because they won't have to save as many lives. You have me as your partner," she concluded. "We will carve out a new capability in this agency and we will make this work."

Annie's pep talk worked. For the first time I felt that there might be a possibility for this partnership to go somewhere. Someone got what we were doing and actually wanted to see it succeed.

Our first job was to adapt the program for New York City. I assumed this would be relatively straightforward and something we could do in a couple of months. After all, the book was written and we just needed to adapt it for the particulars of New York City. We made sure each action worked for both apartment dwellers and single-family homes. We attempted to make it attractive for the diverse socioeconomic and ethnic populations of Manhattan and Queens, Brooklyn, and the Bronx. We also added new actions to address various types of terrorism attacks, an avian flu pandemic, as well as your garden variety three-alarm fires, summer heat waves, and hurricane flooding.

Once we did all this, we needed to get the approval for each customized action from seven different city agencies: the police, fire, health, aging, disabilities, housing, and OEM. This seemed to take forever since no one wanted to be responsible for a mistake and consequently kept passing the buck. They were also not sure what would be the correct action in many cases and it took time to research the different options and then get them approved. When we finally got their feedback, it would be in the form of a mini treatise on the topic. Another round of conversations would ensue as we translated the verbiage into simple actions.

To say this was an arduous process would be an understatement. I certainly came to appreciate what Alan meant when he warned that "being under the control of a New York City bureaucracy will be quite stifling."

Every time I got anxious about yet another bureaucratic delay putting this program behind schedule, Annie would calm me down, "David, please be patient with this process and let it take the time necessary to get everyone on board. It will be worth it when we can say to skeptical New Yorkers who question the program's content that it has been vetted and has the contributions of every relevant government agency in New York City."

What I thought would take two months ended up taking six, but we had the buy-in of all the key agencies. Another Herculean labor had been performed, this one by my partner OEM.

Alan was now singing my praises for getting OEM to own this project and as a result use their influence to get the participation of these other agencies. He reiterated that it would raise the program's credibility level and trustworthiness with hard-headed New Yorkers, reinforcing Annie's comment that we would need all the help we could get in this regard. I can't say I had recognized this need, but I was very grateful that OEM had, and had risen to the occasion.

A SEED GROWS IN MANHATTAN

Given that both Hillary Clinton and Penny Ryan had stressed the need for community building, and that the team process is such an essential element in creating resiliency, I decided to take inspiration from the ever-instructive Beatles for the program name. We christened the initiative All Together Now: Neighbors Helping Neighbors Create a Resilient New York City, and I was happy to see that my newfound fire fighter and police department friends went along with this name with not one raised eyebrow. At least not while I was around.

I got well known *New Yorker* cartoonist Ed Koren to illustrate the book. His cover image perfectly captured the spirit of the program. People of different ethnic and racial backgrounds huddled together under the shelter of a large open umbrella all holding the handle together. A contented dog and cat by their feet. (See Figure 4.1, page 104.)

The simple message we would promote to New Yorkers is that taking prudent precautions against blackouts, natural disasters, and terrorism was nothing more than a form of insurance. The program's title reflected the belief that by far the best insurance is the group insurance we get from teamwork, because our neighbors' security is tied to our own. Taking reasonable steps to protect ourselves and families against disasters was common sense. And while the future is uncertain, what was certain was that being prepared and connected allowed people to face that future with greater security and confidence.

All Together Now used the same structure as the sustainability and livability programs. It consisted of thirty actions divided into three sections: preparing for energy disruptions; preparing for emergencies, natural disasters, and terrorism; and creating a resilient building or block. The actions included purchasing extra food, water, and flashlight supplies to last three to seven days; creating evacuation kits called "go-bags" which people could use if they had to evacuate their homes on very short notice; developing a plan for how to relocate one's family and loved ones if they were separated;

Figure 4.1

learning how to "shelter in place" in case of a biological or chemical attack; identifying and supporting elderly and disabled block or building residents to prepare and create evacuation plans; and creating building or block level actions to help those who did not choose to prepare.

We created another program for those not willing to join a team or invest much time in preparing. Using the same behavior-change format, it concentrated on the eight most essential actions to achieve basic resiliency. Participants had access to the building or block leader for coaching, and would have one large group meeting at the end with the others participating in this program. There, they would have a chance to exchange experiences, report on their results, and form a loose-knit support system. We called it Becoming Resilient. We also created a volunteer program to provide elderly, infirm, or disabled neighbors with evacuation assistance.

My next labor would be to convince skeptical, busy New Yorkers of the value of this investment of their time. The logic of preparedness was unassailable. Given a choice, most people will buy insurance. But preparedness would take time and effort. It was much more demanding than just paying a yearly premium. It was also a relatively new concept. The first challenge was getting busy New Yorkers—known to be the healthiest city residents in the country because they walk so fast (really)—to slow down long enough to give something like this the time of day. There was no immediate safety risk or distress, as in the low-income Philadelphia neighborhoods, or motivation to do good by saving the planet, as in our sustainable lifestyle program. This was taking out insurance against an unknown risk that they did not want to think about and hoped would never materialize.

Over the next six months we would attempt to answer three huge questions.

- Could we find volunteers willing to lead an emergency preparedness program on their block or in their building?

- Could they get people to participate?

- If people did participate, could we get them to adopt emergency preparedness behaviors?

New Yorkers are a feisty bunch, able to endure much. They are always facing mini emergencies like flooded-out subways from underground water pipes bursting, traffic noise in a city that never sleeps, and the intensity of living in tight quarters with many other people. Furthermore, they see their city destroyed in a constant string of Hollywood apocalypses, and shrug it off. But underneath this bravado, many realize just how vulnerable they are living in a city that is the number one target of terrorism from around the world. They know that a severe hurricane could flood their city, which is surrounded by water, and that an avian flu pandemic could hobble it in an instant, and that evacuating several million people via a few bridges is a nonstarter. Would these real threats be enough to motivate busy New Yorkers to participate?

It is one thing to appeal to people with a program that meets their basic security needs; it is another to attract volunteers to run such a program. These volunteers would need to make a serious commitment of time to recruit residents of their building or block to come to an initial information meeting. They would need to manage the three programs, including recruiting and training the volunteers to help the at-risk populations. This would be an iterative process and not something that would be completed and checked off a list.

Penny had been watching and cheering Alan and me on from the stands. Now it was her turn to step up to the plate and help us find three buildings within her district to pilot the program. We wanted enough diversity so we could build a case to different types of buildings and socioeconomic groups in the next phase. Penny delivered.

She chose a 300-unit co-op on Sixty-Sixth Street and got the co-op president, Claresa Fisher, to sign on as the building leader. Claresa recruited Deborah Queller as her deputy. Penny then asked Patricia Ryan, tenant leader of a NYC Housing Authority rent-subsidized building for lower-income New Yorkers on Sixty-Third Street to take on the assignment. Patricia agreed and immediately asked Rebecca Gordon to help as her deputy. The final recruit was Alan, a soft touch, who in turn asked David Reiss to be his deputy. Alan was eager to test-drive the program and see what could happen in his sixty-unit apartment building on 102nd Street and Riverside Drive. We invited a few other buildings to participate so we had backups in case any of the lead buildings did not make it.

I designed a one-day training, modeled after the Livable Neighborhood Block Leadership Academy. It consisted of modules on how to recruit residents of a building, host an information meeting, provide empowerment coaching, and manage the three programs. The Red Cross, which partnered with OEM, provided us, at no charge, one of the training rooms at its headquarters on West End Avenue on Manhattan's Upper West Side, right around the corner from Lincoln Center.

In attendance were our three building leaders and their deputies, along with representatives from two other Upper West Side buildings. We had Annie and her colleagues from OEM. Penny participated with several board members of Community Board 7. The Red Cross sent two staffers to find out what this was all about. And Eve Baer, my trusted colleague, who would be responsible for managing the day-to-day operations of the program, was there assisting with the logistics of the training. In all we had about twenty people.

City Councilperson Gail Brewer, who represented this community board and had given Penny the green light to pilot the program, welcomed the participants. She told everyone how pleased she was to see this coming together, and that the city council was fully behind the program and eager to see it succeed as a model for New York City. She then left and I began explaining the purpose of the training and the philosophy behind the program.

Before I could finish, one of the participants we had invited to represent a backup building shouted out, "There is no way this program would work in my building. No one talks to one another or *wants* to talk to one another. It would be a complete waste of time to do it my building. In fact, I don't think it will work anywhere. This is New York City, and we like our autonomy."

This was followed by Patricia Ryan. "People in my building are so caught up in basic survival that even though this program makes so much sense, they would not take the time to do it." Even Alan threw some warm water on the program, saying that while the program was great and needed, people in his building would probably not want to do it as a team. They were all too private.

The twelve labors of Hercules were beginning not to feel like a joke anymore. I took a breath and told them, "It might not work, but if it did you would make a real difference in the lives of your neighbors and could take personal pride in making a major contribution to your city. I ask that you be willing to engage in this training with an open mind and experience the rest of the day. At that point you will be better able to gauge if this might work in your building." They agreed to give the program, and me, the benefit of the doubt and complete the day.

From the sidelines Annie gave me a thumbs-up when I passed my first test by keeping these skeptics in the room. The participants practiced the neighbor-to-neighbor invitation script with one another. They learned the empowerment coaching techniques to help participants who were committed to the program but needed help following through. They got familiar with the three components of the initiative: the comprehensive team program, the low-investment individual household program, and volunteer program for people with special needs. Almost everyone left in good spirits with a willingness to give it a try. The gentleman who had said, "No way in my building, we don't talk to our neighbors and we like it that way," decided this was not for him. A good choice, I thought.

Claresa Fisher was the first to organize her introduction meeting. In fact, she moved so fast I could barely get it on my calendar. She was a typical New Yorker, which means she was completely overextended—so much so that she did not take the time to return my increasingly more urgent sounding e-mails asking how she was doing in recruiting people for her introduction meeting. As president of her co-op, she knew most of the people in her building, knew how to get things done, and she did not have time for discussions about the process. I never got more than an e-mail with directions to her building and a comment, "Don't worry, we'll get a good turnout."

We got to the community room used for hosting building meetings at 6:45 for the 7:30 meeting. I counted 150 chairs and wondered if we would have been wiser to set up the room for twenty-five people so it would not look so vacant if we didn't get much of a turn out. I really had no idea what to expect, but I knew we would never get enough people to fill a room this large.

People started arriving at about 7:15. First in ones and twos, and then in fives and sixes. They kept coming and coming. Person after person walked straight through the laundry room into this very large community meeting room. There were people in wheel chairs, seniors with walkers, a blind person with her guide dog, thirty-something singles, and young parents with toddlers in tow. Many mingled to talk in the back of the room, availing themselves of apple cider and cookies. We waited ten minutes for late arrivers to settle in. When we began, almost every seat in the room was taken, and by the end of the meeting there was standing room only.

Claresa thanked everyone for coming. She acknowledged that 25 percent of the building was in attendance and how remarkable that was. She shared how exciting it was for their building to be one of only three selected by the city of New York to pilot this important program. She then briefly explained how the program worked, with me amplifying a few points. Knowing the people in her building she kept it short so we would have enough time for questions. Sure enough, when she was done, about thirty hands shot up in the air.

"What should I pack in my 'go bag'?"

"Is New York City the first city to do anything like this?"

"I'm in a wheelchair. What should I do if the elevator power goes out and I need to evacuate?"

"How many days of food and water should we have in our apartments?"

"There is this guy across the street that looks suspicious; what should I do?"

"How will the building deal with those people who choose not to prepare themselves?"

Once they were warmed up, in the inimitable way of New Yorkers, the questions started cutting deeper to the bone.

"I know Claresa, but sir, what are your credentials to lead this program? Why should I trust you?"

"How do I know I can trust the things in this book?"

"The city did not give us honest information about the air quality after 9/11, why should I trust that this is also not government propaganda?"

"How is the city going to evacuate millions of people? It will be mass chaos."

"If we get nuked it is all over anyway. Why should I bother to take time to do this?"

"I lost my son in the World Trade Center, I am not sure I want to participate in a program like this. I am afraid it will stir up all of my pain and sorrow again."

All Together Now touched a deep wound in the psyche of New Yorkers, which in many people had not been tended to in any way. Asking Claresa and me questions provided a conduit for people to surface their unprocessed feelings. We did not pretend to be there as healers or therapists and we did not need to be. The program was creating a safe space for people to talk about multilayered issues in a community of neighbors who had all experienced a similar trauma. Many of the questions asked were more in service of that person's catharsis than in search of a particular answer.

I had known that this program could serve as a vehicle for healing, but my head had been down so long while creating it and wondering if we could get people to participate that I hadn't been thinking about this aspect as we went into the evening. Listening to the emotion-filled questions, it was clear to me that New Yorkers were still shaken by the attack on their city and the death of so many fellow residents. They intuitively seemed to grasp that this program could provide them some level of control for their lives, which, when they paused long enough to think about them, seemed quite vulnerable.

At the end of the meeting, Claresa asked how many people were interested in participating in either the team or single-household program. About three-quarters of the hands went up. Those who did not raise their hands were given a copy of the single-household program as they left and told they could participate in the future if they wished. We arranged people into five teams based on their floor and section of the building. Those who were formally participating in the single-household program were told when to reconvene so that we could debrief them and plug them into the larger building resiliency plan.

As I worked with Claresa getting people on to teams and answering logistical questions, I asked them why they had chosen to participate in this program. Their answers basically boiled down to "it just makes sense" and "all I needed to do was come downstairs in my slippers to participate." I was very encouraged by this start.

Alan Leidner was next up. His building had sixty units, making it 10 percent of the size of Claresa's building. Alan took our recruiting advice very seriously. He personally knocked on every door in his building in order to invite his neighbors to the information meeting. He did a second round of door knocking to invite people who had been out the first time around. If he still had not made personal contact by that point, he left a notice underneath their door. There was a cozy, four-person elevator, which afforded another opportunity for Alan to remind people as they rode up or down with him. People would see Alan coming and preempt his friendly reminder with "I will be there."

He got a great response with about half of the building responding that they would attend. He joked to me, "This response is either out of interest in the program or to avoid having to confront me in the elevator." It did create a problem however—a good problem. Alan's deputy, David Reiss, a successful information technology entrepreneur, would be hosting the information meeting in his beautifully appointed apartment with a view overlooking the Hudson River, but could not accommodate that many people. Their solution was to create two events: one from 6:30 to 8:00 and the other from 8:00 to 9:30.

I attended both events. David prepared a wonderful spread and the first fifteen minutes of each meeting were used for people to socialize with one another. Many commented to Alan that there had never been anything like this before in the building, and that they were enjoying having time to visit with people that they saw in the elevator every day.

Alan began warming up to the possibility that the community-building aspect of the program, rather than being an obstacle, was its secret. The mantra we had been hearing for so many years, "The best thing about this program (whatever program it might be) is getting to know my neighbors" was now working its magic on the issue of emergency preparedness.

People asked some of the same questions I had heard in Claresa's meeting, but because the setting was so intimate they were asked with less of a bite. Alan was a natural. He knew the program and the philosophy behind it so well and was such an advocate that he assuaged any concerns. When he asked how many people were interested in participating on a team, almost all said yes. The ones who did not volunteer said their travel schedules did not permit it, but they would like to participate in the next round. He got the same response at the second meeting.

After the meeting Alan and I got in the elevator, which I had come to call Alan's "secret weapon," to go get my stuff from his apartment. A woman who had attended the first meeting was already in the elevator. "I told my neighbor on the tenth floor about the program, she said, bubbling over with enthusiasm. "She also wants to join the program, is it too late?" "Of course she can join," Alan replied. "Just have her contact me." She exited the elevator one floor later and Alan and I continued riding up to the eleventh floor. As we got out we saw a woman running up the fire exit stairs in her bathrobe and slippers. "Alan, I want to join a team! Please sign me up." Alan was softening more by the minute to this "team" thing.

Eve attended the third of the information meetings in Patricia Ryan's New York City Housing Authority building. Patricia had been a tenant leader for over ten years and was well respected in her building of 200 apartments. Because of her stature, she assumed that if she just posted a meeting flier with her name on it around the building, it would be enough to get people to the information meeting. To create a little more insurance, she held the meeting in the lobby, which everyone needed to pass through to go to their apartments. Without the personal contact with people, the strategy did not work very well and only eight households attended. But she did get all eight of these households to sign up and participate on her team.

We had overcome our first hurdle. Our volunteer leaders had all gotten the program launched in their buildings. Our next challenge: Would people actually take the actions to become more disaster resilient?

The team program performed as I had hoped and expected. Because of the community that was built, almost everyone stayed with the process and completed the program. Predictably the most notable feedback we got when we spoke with our three building leaders was how much people enjoyed the opportunity to meet their neighbors. They also commented on how the formal support structure helped them follow through in taking actions that they would not have done without it.

Leaders and participants alike also spoke about the confidence they now had in their ability to survive a disaster, and about the subtle healing that had taken place. And in the response to the anticipated "No time!" refrain of so many New Yorkers, Claresa Fisher noted that "This is not time consuming! I am so overcommitted in my life, if I can do this anybody can!"

Along with this anecdotal feedback, team leaders asked participants to report on which actions they took. Team participants on average took eleven preparedness actions. In Claresa's building, more than 50 percent of the people who signed up for the single-household program completed it, averaging six preparedness actions per household.

Overall, the most popular actions included: stocking a special supply of food and water to last at least three days; getting flashlights for each member of the family and a good supply of batteries; purchasing (or getting an extra from a neighbor) a nonelectric phone that could be used if the phone line went dead and cell phones didn't work, which had happened after 9/11; getting a portable radio and batteries in order to be able to listen to emergency reports from the city; creating a "go bag" of supplies for three days if it became necessary to evacuate their apartments; planning an evacuation route to a shelter on foot; and determining a meeting place for family members in case they were scattered and could not return to their homes. The last three actions were motivated by watching the reports of the dispossessed in New Orleans.

I was very pleased with these behavioral change results, especially for the experimental single-household program. But I was particularly excited that our recruitment strategy was able to break through the perennial busyness of New Yorkers to get them actually to prepare. Recent surveys had indicated that while New Yorkers believed emergency preparedness was important, few had in fact done anything about it. Getting them to participate actively was an encouraging signal about our neighbor-to-neighbor approach. It was a small sample size, but we now had a proof of concept on which we could build.

Annie and I got a pat on the back from OEM's leadership, but they still had a wait-and-see attitude about all this neighborhood team stuff. They wanted to see how this initiative would play in the "outer boroughs," as they are called, before they took the program seriously. It was one thing to achieve success in the "Independent Republic of the Upper West Side," considered one of the most enlightened communities in New York City. Taking the program to the outer boroughs would be the real test.

They were right. These outer boroughs included a hodgepodge of multi-ethnic communities; small enclaves of immigrants still following customs from the old country; gang violence based on racial and ethnic antipathy; budding gentrification in formerly lower-income neighborhoods; and provincial attitudes. The only thing they had in common was a fierce pride in their borough and an attitude toward people who lived in Manhattan. No doubt about it, this would be a challenging proving ground.

I confessed to Annie, "I had lived in New York City for twenty years and with the exception of my visits to OEM's office in Brooklyn, trips to the airports and immediate surroundings in Queens, and running in the marathon, which touches briefly in all five boroughs, I had not ventured outside the island of Manhattan. I knew nothing of these boroughs or the people who lived there. She smiled and said, "You'll like them."

I knew that I'd have to do more than like them, though. I'd have to understand them, so I rented Ken Burns's brilliant eight-part documentary on New York City. I learned about the unique history and culture of each borough and how it is precisely this diversity that has made New York City the nation's melting pot and a one-of-a-kind city in the world. Henry Ford went so far as describing New York City as its own country. "New York is a different country. Maybe it ought to have a separate government. Everybody thinks differently and acts differently." I have to admit that sometimes I agreed with him.

BUILDING STRATEGIC PARTNERSHIPS

The next Herculean labor, in increasing order of difficulty, was figuring out how to enter into these multiple unknown worlds, "where everyone thinks differently and acts differently," to recruit community organizations and government leaders to be our partners. Penny had told me that although OEM could help us get in front of community boards, getting her counterparts involved would not be easy. She said they were so understaffed and overextended that they had little capacity, even if they were interested, to play much of a role recruiting community groups. She also didn't know if this idea would resonate for them. "To get this to work," she told me, "you will need to get your hands dirty this time and directly recruit the neighborhood organizations yourself." But I didn't even know my way around these boroughs by subway, much less any of the community groups spread out over the 280 square miles that make up Brooklyn, Queens, the Bronx, and Staten Island.

I got lucky. Paula Olsiewski, a savvy program director for the Alfred P. Sloan Foundation, a major funder of emergency preparedness projects, had gotten wind of our work and was keen to meet me. By that point her foundation had spent twelve million dollars on various emergency preparedness projects attempting to change individual behavior. The projects ranged from a web site she helped fund for the Department of Homeland Security, as odd as that might seem; to a media campaign by Steve Brill, a well-known New York businessman-turned-social-entrepreneur; to a basic preparedness brochure Michael Berkowitz had developed and which OEM was now giving out. According to her accounting, none of these projects had demonstrated any proof of changing behavior. She was looking for a better way.

She invited me to meet in the Sloan Foundation office at Rockefeller Center, one of the most prominent buildings in New York City, located in the heart of Midtown Manhattan, and known for its famed ice-skating rink, annual Christmas tree lighting ceremony, and a bronze statue of Atlas holding up the world. Having always been fascinated by the symbols that appear in my life, I was curious what these might portend.

Paula combines a charming, gregarious personality with a razor-sharp intellect, honed as a Ph.D. scientist steeped in the field of bioterrorism. It is a combination not usually found in one person. She is also a primo emergency preparedness networker, who has the "who's who" in this field on her speed dial. I could see I was being interviewed for a place in this club.

We spent an hour and a half discussing her projects and the field at large. As one of the few funders in this field, every project of merit crossed her desk sooner or later seeking funding, and I received quite an education. She asked many probing questions, and I carefully explained the empowerment architecture underlying the larger scale behavior-change methodology, and the approach to community organizing that we had come to through years of trial and error.

She then admitted her frustration in having invested in ad campaigns, brochures, and web sites that had made no demonstrable impact in changing behavior. I reviewed with her the substantive amount of research that had been done on the inability of information and awareness campaigns to make much of a dent in changing behavior, and suggested that she check out some of these studies.

Since I already had funding, I had not planned to ask for money at this meeting, but rather just create our relationship. Of course, in the back of my mind, I had hoped she would be financially helpful down the road. As the conversation was coming to a close, however, Paula volunteered to invest. In all my experiences with funders, an on-the-spot offer like this had never before occurred.

She explained that she would like to make a grant to All Together Now to help in the next phase of our work when our federal funding ran out, and then asked if I would be willing to meet with the president of the foundation, Ralph Gomory, to share both All Together Now and my behavior-change research. "If he likes your program," she said with a smile, "it will help me make the case to our board of directors for the grant. And your practical research could be most helpful to us in making better grants in general."

I would gladly have shared our research for no other reason than that I knew she would put it to good use. Adding money into the mix took this way over the top. I was flattered and thrilled to have the potential for such an intellectually engaged, well-connected, and well-heeled new partner.

Ralph Gomory was the former director of research for IBM, an inventor, and considered by Paula and others to be a "genius type." I looked forward to this conversation and was not disappointed. Ralph asked probing questions about the behavior-change tools, our business model, what it would take to bring All Together Now to scale in this city, and my sense of the psychology of New Yorkers around emergency preparedness at this point in time. He wanted to know if I thought this model would be effective with workers in the city's large office buildings; if it could be transferred to other cities; and useful to other activities his foundation funded. At the end of this robust discussion, he asked if I would be willing to make a presentation on All Together Now and my behavior-change research to his program officers.

After the meeting as Paula walked me to the door she told me that I had done well. "Ralph only invites people to these special 'teas' (served afterward with cookies) if he is interested in funding 'big-ticket' grants. This is the way we learn and it provides us an opportunity to take the measure of a person." I asked her for any tips on what would be helpful for the presentation. She said, "My colleagues, like Ralph, are thinkers, and will want to understand the social change theory and design principles underlying your work as much as the results that prove that it works. But be ready, they take pride in tearing down ideas. You'll do fine."

Of course, it was New York City, and there was that pound of flesh again, but I wasn't worried. I was actually excited to have a rigorous intellectual dialogue about this work. Until I had spoken with Paula and Ralph, conversations about my work were about implementation with practitioners and funders. Preparing for this event, as it turned out, planted the first seed for this book. I had to think through the behavior-change and community empowerment model as it applied to the many different applications I had used it for, and how it might serve as a new tool for social change.

I met with Ralph and eight program officers in Sloan's wood-paneled board room. After my slide presentation, they did what Paula told me they would do, asked hard questions and attempted to find any weak spots in my thinking. Although this model of social change was still a work in progress, it seemed to hold up to the critical scrutiny of their questions and I very much enjoyed this substantive discourse. There was one big question that I did not have an answer to, however, and that was scalability. We had no evidence that this program could work in the outer boroughs, not to mention being taken to scale citywide.

After the meeting Paula, Ralph, and I continued our discussion on how Sloan might be most helpful going forward. Funding at this point wasn't necessary, but I still had a lot of work to prove that we had something worthy of their investment in the next phase. "Perhaps my network of grantees will be helpful, particularly for your community organizing," Paula volunteered. "I had been planning on creating a networking event anyway." Bingo!

Paula organized a beautiful luncheon in one of the Upper East Side's finest restaurants. For the event she rented a room with a hand-laid stone floor and wood-paneled walls with fine wines on the shelves. Elegant floral arrangements elevated the beauty of the setting another notch. I got there a little early, to discover Paula meticulously putting out the seating cards for the fifteen quests that would attend. It was a pleasure watching a master at her craft.

She placed me to her right to demonstrate support for the new kid on the block. On her left was the Deputy Administrator for Communications of the U.S. Department of Homeland Security, who had flown in from Washington just for this event. Sloan was an influential patron of this new federal agency. Across from me was Mayor Bloomberg's newly appointed commissioner for OEM, Joseph Bruno, whom I had not yet met. Next to him was the president of the New York City chapter of the Red Cross, and on his other side the department chair for Columbia University's newly formed Department on Disaster Preparedness. Others of equal stature were dispersed among the fifteen place settings. To my right sat Michael Clark, president of Citizens for New York City (CNYC), a grassroots organization implementing an auxiliary first responders program for community activists called Community Emergency Response Teams (CERTs).

There were many bigwigs that I should have been networking with, but I spent all my time talking to Michael Clark. Paula knew exactly what she was doing placing Michael next to me. We were like two peas in a pod. In fact we hit it off so well that we ended up continuing our conversation for the rest of the afternoon at his office on Seventh Avenue and Twenty-Fourth Street.

Michael was a seasoned veteran of New York City organizing, respected for the quality of his work and his intelligence, wisdom, and wit (he used to do stand-up comedy). He had built up his organization over seventeen years as the go-to place for foundations, government agencies, and community groups wishing to accomplish change at the grassroots level. Given that this was a city of neighborhoods, that meant most institutions interested in change. His organization took on issues important to the city's neighbor-hoods and underserved populations. They ranged from job creation pro-grams for inner-city youth, to health programs like lead paint abatement, to safety programs such as CERT.

He would secure a large grant for these programs and then provide many community groups small grants of $500 to $1,000, along with the technical assistance and capacity-building expertise of his organization. CNYC was accountable to the funders for the desired change, and so was invested in supporting these local groups. The local groups were too small to get funded by these larger foundation and government agencies, and therefore were committed to doing a good job so they could receive future funding from CNYC. I was totally impressed with what a cool niche this was for effecting change in such a large and complex city.

Michael knew his way around New York, having literally put together a map of all the established neighborhood groups and what they did in all five boroughs, and knowing who was who in most of the city's government agencies and foundations. He was also a sophisticated student of social change. He felt our methodology and strategy was exactly what was needed if New York City was to take emergency preparedness seriously. It was a statement of Michael's confidence in himself and his organization that rather than feeling threatened by the new kid on the block, he warmly em-braced us.

Before the afternoon ended I realized Michael and CNYC were the an-swer to my prayers. Here was a potential partner who could teach me the ropes about New York and open the doors to the exact groups we needed to work with. He was familiar with OEM, having worked with Annie on his CERT project, so he could fit right in. He was also excited to have a new audience for his jokes, having long ago worn out the appreciation of those on his team who had been hearing them for years.

I asked him for his help, and, after proffering a rope trick joke which I cannot remember well enough to do it justice, he agreed to give it.

We then entered into an active negotiation, attempting to clarify our ex-pectations of each other. The heart of the negotiation was around how many community groups he thought he could deliver and what it would cost to accomplish this. Neither of us had any idea what to expect, so com-ing up with a number for which he would be accountable and a cost to ac-complish this was a real shot in the dark. OEM could help provide credibility and make contacts with the borough presidents and community boards (from whom Penny had cautioned us not to expect much), but OEM did not have any knowledge of the neighborhood groups. Michael and CNYC would be pretty much on their own to make this happen without any small grants to entice people.

After much wrestling with the number question, we decided on a goal of recruiting 100 building or block organizers in a two-step process. CNYC would recruit qualified community leaders to attend information meetings in each of the five boroughs. I would then be responsible to enroll attendees at these sessions in the one-day leadership training and support them in program implementation. Recruiting 100 community leaders was an ambitious goal, for sure, given how little we actually knew. But Michael said he would make this happen "whatever it takes."

It would be an act of trust on both our parts. For me, it was believing that Michael could accomplish this and that his organization would be willing to work in partnership. For Michael, it was believing that this program would be attractive enough and my pitch effective enough to enroll 100 organizers for the training. And equally important, as a fiercely independent social entrepreneur, I would not attempt to dominate the partnership and browbeat him because I controlled the purse strings.

It was highly unusual for two organizations so freely to share resources, networks, and methodologies. The norm, unfortunately, was groups competing with one another for money, territory, or prestige and keeping their proprietary assets closely under wraps. This project had already pushed the envelope of business-as-usual by attempting to get a conservative local government agency to work collaboratively with an outside organization. The partnership with CNYC would now take that a step further by attempting to get two organizations that would traditionally be viewed as competitors to work together collaboratively. And as hard as this might be to do, the difficulty would be compounded by requiring us both to work collaboratively with OEM.

I had already seen OEM playing way out of their comfort zone on many levels in this project. Having to work with a social entrepreneur constantly innovating new ways to do things, being accountable as the grantee to the Department of Justice for measurable behavior change, and actively engaging in community organizing had them teetering on the edge. They put on a good game face, but it was not hard to tell they would rather just do what they always had done, with a few small enhancements. Bringing in another player in such an intimate way would just add to the already complex nature of this initiative. It certainly would have been easier simply to pay CNYC for their mailing list and Michael's consulting advice, and then hire staff to implement, as I had done in many other cities. Likewise, it would have been easier to get OEM's blessings and manage this project ourselves.

But OEM had confirmed that my intuition was right to invite them in as a full partner. In spite of our occasional culture clashes and conflicts over spending priorities, they had proved themselves to be an excellent and committed partner. They used their clout to get the critical inputs and signoffs we needed from their fellow government agencies, which in turn allowed us to stand confidently before the public with a program vetted and backed by their city. And they were willing to use their credibility to get us in front of borough presidents and community boards. I would need this same quality of partnership and collaboration with CNYC to navigate New York City's grassroots universe. CNYC's credibility, personal relationships, and know-how would be essential to pulling off this complex community-organizing feat in the biggest and most diverse city in America.

OEM had shown me how willing they were to give of themselves if they were generously given to, that is, well remunerated for their time and given visibility for their organization in all of the materials and media communications associated with the project. For CNYC to be fully invested, I would need to do the same with them. I offered them a generous fee for their services (much more than I had planned and a little less than Michael wanted) and equal recognition for their organization on all our materials.

We now had three partners holding up Ed Koren's All Together Now umbrella over New York City. We were beginning to live up to our name.

GETTING OUR HANDS DIRTY

Michael's team began by sending out a blanket mailing, using OEM's imprimatur for credibility, to several thousand community groups, inviting them to contact CNYC to participate in this program. They had been successful in getting people to respond to this approach when offering small grants, and hoped because of the underlying anxiety in the city after 9/11 this program might generate a similar response. In the follow-up phone conversations, CNYC would qualify the candidates to make sure they understood what we were asking of them, namely, to come to a meeting to learn more about the program, and if interested, commit themselves to implementing it in their neighborhood, block, or building. We hoped that this mailing might provide us a quick win. We got a meager response.

Michael went to Plan B, hard-core community organizing. This consisted of intensive phone calling day and night by a dedicated team of CNYC staff attempting to recruit community leaders to attend these information sessions. To make it easier for people to attend, Michael decided that instead of having one information session per borough, as was our original plan, he would have multiple sessions spread throughout the boroughs. His logic was if people didn't need to travel so far, it would raise the likelihood of their attending. He would bring the mountain (me) to the people.

Michael was constantly joking about how happy I should feel each time he added on another information session in some farflung part of one of the five boroughs that would require a long subway and bus ride. "Hey David," he'd say. "I'm providing you with such a great education of New York City you should be paying me, which in fact you are already doing. Smart move!" I smiled and thought about Penny's comment about getting my hands dirty. In my head, Frank Sinatra crooned, "If I can make it there, I'll make it anywhere."

Meanwhile, OEM arranged briefings for us with each of the five borough presidents by putting us on the agenda at their monthly community board meetings. This was an expected courtesy when bringing an official city program into any of the boroughs, and it served the dual purpose of soliciting the community boards' support in recruiting neighborhood organizations. Each of these meetings was a mini information sessions equivalent to what I would be offering to the general public.

As Penny had advised us, finding her equivalents at community boards was not easy, but ultimately we were able to find three, all in Manhattan, out of the fifty-nine community boards willing to organize information events in their district—the East Village, Columbia Heights, and the Upper East Side. I would take what we could get, and turned these leads over to Michael's team.

Our first information session organized by CNYC was held in the historic and ornate wood-paneled meeting chambers of Brooklyn's Borough Hall, recognized as one of New York's great landmark buildings. Borough Hall has been the center of Brooklyn's government for almost 150 years, dating from the time it was an independent city, which it was until 1898. Displayed in the back of the room were the winning paintings from a children's art contest celebrating Brooklyn's ethnic diversity.

We arrived ninety minutes early to set up. CNYC's logistics team led by Debbie Gratton, their program director, arranged a table in the hallway for people to sign in as they arrived. This would allow us to determine who, out of those who had RSVP-ed, actually attended, and who were walk-ins. They set up another table for refreshments. Inside the room they organized a table to register people for the training after the session. They placed fliers on all the seats advertising the training and how to register by phone, in case some people left not ready to make a decision. Eve Baer was supporting CNYC and taking photographs.

Meanwhile, Michael and I were anxiously standing in the hallway counting each arrival and wondering how many people would actually show up. He had RSVPs from sixty-five people and with fifteen minutes to go, only about twenty had arrived. Furthermore, the refreshments, a mainstay of any community event, were nowhere to be seen. Five minutes before we were ready to start, a large number of people finally arrived—and so did the missing refreshments. We waited until 7:05 to start and counted thirty-nine people, not including our team. I said to Michael, "Not bad." But he wanted at least fifty so was a little deflated. Over the next twenty minutes twelve more people meandered in and he had his fifty plus one.

We had all the big guns for this event. Brooklyn Borough President Marty Moscovitz welcomed everyone and talked about the long and rich history of Brooklyn. He spoke of the many firefighters from Brooklyn who had heroically died in the World Trade Center and he honored their sacrifice. He told the participants that Brooklyn had a long tradition of civic engagement and that volunteering their time to help protect the lives of their Brooklyn neighbors was a most noble thing to do. He shared his hopes that this program would help create a more resilient Brooklyn and encouraged everyone to participate and help lead the way for New York City. No mistaking, we were in Brooklyn.

Joe Bruno, commissioner of OEM and a former judge in Brooklyn, not to be outdone, said that he was born in Brooklyn, had lived his whole life there, and planned to die there. He then talked about why the city was so committed to helping people prepare. In case of a major disaster first responders would be hard pressed to serve anyplace other than the disaster scene. That is why New Yorkers need to be able to fend for themselves for at least three days, which should provide the city enough time to sort out the disaster. He ended by encouraging everyone to take advantage of the All Together Now program the city was offering.

I went next. Lacking a Brooklyn affiliation, I jumped into the vision for the program and why it could be helpful to the people they served. I pointed out that if Hurricane Katrina had hit New York City, causing an extended blackout or need for evacuation, residents would not have been ready, and that one of the foremost lessons learned from Katrina was that many lives could have been saved and social disorder reduced if residents had been prepared. During the blackout that had occurred in New York a year or so earlier, I reminded them, food and water were sold out in many parts of the city within three hours. Had this blackout continued for as long as the outages caused by Katrina, people's lives would have been at risk. I then described the three programs and how they worked.

Alan, whom I had invited to do a cameo appearance, of course talked about how he used to live in Brooklyn. He then shared why he felt participating in this program should be a no-brainer, and about the results his team and building had achieved. He ended with his story about a neighbor walking up the fire exit stairs to his floor in her slippers and bathrobe and requesting to join his team.

It was time for questions and they came pouring out; the predominant focus was terrorism.

People wanted to know what to do if there was a chemical attack, a biological attack, a dirty bomb, a nuclear device detonated in a cargo container, or if the Indian Point nuclear facility was attacked. Joe and I answered these questions from our different vantage points. He talked about the city's plans to prevent such occurrences and its emergency response plan if they did occur. He repeated that the people were basically on their own, however, and that was why preparedness was so important. I then explained the relevant actions from the program that would be helpful, such as sheltering in place, a go bag, an evacuation route, and a plan for meeting up with family members. I also told them that their best insurance was the group insurance they get by developing a disaster-resilient community, which was a central part of this program. I concluded by telling them that in some of these scenarios there was little they could do except pray.

I was grateful for Joe's ability to talk about how the city was preparing and doing everything possible to protect New Yorkers from these horrific possibilities. He seemed grateful that I was able to offer an actual preparedness implementation plan, and handle the more emotionally charged questions. Based on the response we were getting from the community leaders in attendance, our partnership seemed to be going over well.

After taking questions for about twenty minutes it was getting close to 8:30, the time we told people we would end. It was the next moment of truth. How many people would be willing to sign up for our leadership training to take this program into their neighborhoods, blocks, or buildings? I asked people to raise their hands if they were interested in attending the leadership training, and about half of the hands in the room shot up. Michael breathed a sigh of relief in the back of the room. Mine was less noticeable in the front. The next day when I spoke with Annie she told me that Joe was very pleased with how the meeting had gone and that there was a lot of positive buzz at OEM. We were ready to take this show on the road.

Sixteen information sessions in all five boroughs under CNYC's leadership would be organized by neighborhood and block associations, community boards, borough presidents, city council representatives, the largest building complexes (Co-op City in the Bronx, Rochdale Village in Queens, and Stuyvesant Town in Manhattan, with some 150 buildings in all), and city agencies serving the at-risk populations of seniors, people with disabilities, and low income. We now had many more hands across the entire city holding up the "All Together Now" umbrella.

Working with these information session organizers, CNYC would turn out between twenty-five and fifty people for each event. These included block or building association presidents, chairs of building safety committees, representatives from nonprofits that worked in the neighborhood, staff from city agencies, elected officials, community board representatives, leaders in the faith community, civically engaged citizens, and individuals interested in their own preparedness.

We would replicate the recruitment success we had in Brooklyn's Borough Hall and average a 40 percent registration rate for the leadership training. While we knew that not all these individuals would show up for the training, it was a clear sign that this issue had resonance among New York City's community leaders. In total, we would have 153 building or block representatives attend the two leadership trainings. Michael would exceed his goal by 50 percent! All building or block leaders were asked to bring a deputy if they could, so we ended up training a total of 257 individuals.

Seeds Grow in Brooklyn, Queens, the Bronx, Staten Island, and Manhattan

We had 110 people in the first leadership training at Red Cross head-quarters in Manhattan. At about 9:25 on a cold and bright blue Saturday in January, after partaking of a light breakfast, people began sitting down and having casual conversations with one another.

We had all been working so hard to get our numbers that we had not taken time to think about who was saying yes at all of these information sessions. When I looked around the room I was taken aback by the diversity. I asked Alan, who was co-facilitating a portion of the training, and Michael if this level of diversity was commonplace for events they had attended before in New York. Both exclaimed, "No way!" Michael commented, "I have never seen such a diversity of New Yorkers in one room in all the years I have been working and living in the city."

An elegantly dressed middle-aged Caucasian woman living in a luxury condominium on Manhattan's exclusive Upper East Side was talking to an African-American tenant leader wearing a Yankee sweat shirt and living in subsidized housing from the Bronx. A construction worker from Queens who had worked at Ground Zero was conversing with a Wall Street stock-broker who had evacuated the World Trade Center. A married couple from Staten Island, both hearing impaired, were signing with the two translators we had hired for the event. Two sight-impaired people with their guide dogs were positioning themselves in their seats with help from those sitting next to them. Accents from a multitude of African, Caribbean, Latin American, and South East Asian countries were colliding with the indigenous dialects of Brooklyn, the Bronx, and Queens. The variety and mixture of sounds, ethnicity, and faces was a picture that could only be seen in New York City.

Here everyone was on an equal playing field. Ethnicity, race, economic status, and street address meant little. Everyone had come together to learn what it would take to live in this new world, and everyone would need everyone else. If the Bronx was prepared and Manhattan wasn't, tony New Yorkers would be migrating there for food and water. Not only was it important to care for your family and neighborhood, it was also important to make sure others did the same. You were as resilient as the larger community was resilient.

There was a magic in the room that day and everyone experienced it in one form or another. People who lived more hand to mouth were teaching survival skills to those who had never had to worry about food or shelter. Relationships were formed during the many small group processes among immigrant groups from the same country or region who back home were sworn enemies. Technology geeks, hip hop artists, and mild-mannered office workers were mixing it up. Brooklyn was talking to the Bronx; Queens to Staten Island; and all the outer boroughs to Manhattan.

The training got so much buzz, it helped us turn out 140 more people for the second one three months later. As successful as these trainings had been, however, we knew that the real work of these volunteer leaders would begin when they left. They would go home and face a building, block, or neighborhood that really had no idea of what to make of this new concept of emergency preparedness and disaster resilience. We were also going into many parts of the city where there would be language and cultural barriers. We had provided a lot of personal attention supporting Claresa, Alan, and Patricia in the pilot, but now, given the number of people involved, we would need to depend on master classes for the program leaders as the primary support system.

We had anticipated there would be attrition and there was. About 40 percent of those we trained never got the program off the ground. For some, life took over and this volunteer effort fell off their plate. Others were frustrated by the effort required to get the formal approval of their blocks or building associations. Others did not wish to do the neighbor-to-neighbor outreach and defaulted to just putting up posters, which produced minimal results. They then decided to throw in the towel rather than go through a more rigorous outreach effort. Many of those struggling and most in need did not partake in the master classes because they felt embarrassed and dropped out of the program.

Those with the staying power adapted the All Together Now seed to their unique soil and microclimate. In Castle Village, a multibuilding residential facility overlooking the Hudson River in northern Manhattan, they wrote regular articles in their newsletter summarizing their efforts and listing local stores that supplied emergency items. They created an in-house video that they broadcasted exclusively to Castle Village residents via cable TV. They connected the program to their fire safety plan, which included evacuation instructions for their large number of seniors and people with disabilities. And they educated their doormen, porters, and custodians in the program so that they could prepare their families, as well as assist Castle Village residents.

Co-op City in the Bronx, New York City's largest housing complex with some 60,000 residents and its own power-generating plant and police unit, was one of the most enthusiastic participants in the program. They had eight people attending the leadership training, and ultimately committed to starting at least one core resiliency team (responsible for all the residents) in each of their forty-two buildings. They also integrated the program into their safety and evacuation planning. Joe Boiko, who was in charge of the Co-op City program, told me that they had been searching for something like this for two years. They had thought they would have to create their own program and were delighted that it already existed.

Of the 60 percent of the volunteer leaders who implemented the program, we were able to collect hard data from half of them. Based on this, we learned that those who followed the format of the information meetings got approximately 70 percent of the attendees to participate in either the single-household or team program. We estimated that 5,000 New Yorkers participated in the program and averaged eight preparedness actions per household. Through the many one-on-one conversations, information meeting notices posted and distributed throughout the buildings, the many newsletter and neighborhood newspaper articles, we estimated that some 300,000 New Yorkers were educated about the program for possible participation in the future.

We organized a special ceremony to honor the stalwart leaders who had successfully shepherded their buildings or blocks through this process. On a snowy February evening at Brooklyn Polytechnic Institute, Joe Bruno and I offered All Together Now leadership certification to all who had completed the journey. Fifty-one building or block leaders attended the evening along with several of our partner organizations. We offered special recognition to those who had gotten over 25 percent of their buildings or blocks to participate. Alan, our superstar, had enrolled over 50 percent of his building.

It was a bittersweet affair for me filled with many emotions. I experienced a parent's pride watching community leaders I knew and had come to respect, honored by their city for exemplary service to their fellow citizens. I was acutely aware of my gratitude to OEM, CNYC, and our Empowerment Institute team for all that they had contributed to enable us to accomplish what we had set out to do. And I felt a profound tiredness from the ride I had been on for almost four years, but which now seemed far from over.

THE FINAL LABOR

I had no idea we would get this far, but now that we had, I felt obligated to see if we could develop the mechanisms to make this an indigenous program for New York City. This got complicated, however, because shortly after the ceremony, Joe Bruno informed me that while OEM would continue to support the initiative, they did not wish to continue on as a full partner. Annie had left the agency a few months earlier to take a new job coordinating the many volunteer disaster agencies in New York City. Without her as an advocate, there was no driving force to continue the partnership.

Michael Clark indicated that he also felt complete. He and CNYC had done their job by helping us build relationships with New York's grassroots organizations. Now that those were established he felt his organization was no longer needed. OEM and CNYC had done their own Herculean labors in helping launch this program, but if it was to go any further, it would be up to those who had experienced its value in the field to take it on the next leg of the journey. It was time to circle the wagons and see if there was the leadership and energy to continue.

I turned to the organizations that had hosted information sessions and the building and block leaders who had successfully taken the program to their communities. I explained that if I was able to secure funding from the Sloan Foundation, this final phase would be to build community capacity throughout the five boroughs to manage this program going forward. Many signaled that they were ready and eager.

I asked Alan for his assessment of the political situation. He acknowledged that without OEM as a full partner it would be harder to get the support of the next wave of political and community groups to whom we would need to reach out. But he also believed with the backing of the NYC Housing Authority and Department of the Aging and with OEM's full blessing, which we also had, we had enough city support to continue. "We owe it to ourselves and the residents of this city to take it as far as we can," Alan said decisively, "I vote to go forward." This show of interest encouraged me to approach Paula for funding.

Being the bottom-line and metric-driven foundation person she is, she went right to the heart of the matter. She asked how we had performed in the mission critical success factors of getting community and government support, recruitment of program participants, and measured behavior change.

I reeled off our data: Sixteen information sessions organized by community and government partners; 153 building or block leaders throughout the five boroughs trained; fifty-one certified; 5,000 program participants completed the program averaging eight preparedness actions per household; and the NYC Housing Authority and Department for the Aging's support and desire to bring the program to their populations. She congratulated me and our partners and asked me to prepare a proposal for their next funding cycle in the spring. This would give me a few months to recuperate from the intensity of the past year.

I prepared a proposal and Paula did her part. The Sloan Foundation would provide funding for this next phase of recruiting and training twenty organizations, who in turn would recruit and train at least ten buildings or blocks within their territory to deliver the program. Our goal was to see if we could effectively build community capacity to make this a free-standing program in all five boroughs.

Through the partnerships we established during the demonstration phase, we were able to recruit a geographically, organizationally and racially diverse group of twenty organizations in all five boroughs. They consisted of members of community boards responsible for the Upper West Side, Upper East Side, Washington Heights, and Lower East Side of Manhattan; representatives from the NYC Department for the Aging who took the program to seniors in high-risk hurricane zones in the Coney Island section of Brooklyn, Far Rockaway section of Queens and Staten Island; representatives for the NYC Housing Authority who took the program to the South Bronx and East Harlem; representatives from OEM's Community Emergency Response Teams who worked within their community board districts in Brooklyn, Queens, Staten Island, and Manhattan; and several neighborhood organizations.

In a two-day capacity-building training we taught thirty-two individuals representing these twenty organizations how to lead the one-day leadership training and recruit building and block leaders. We provided them a 100-page program manager handbook outlining all the tools and materials we had developed. We offered them a ten-minute recruitment video that told the real-life stories of people who had been through the program and what it meant to them and their families and communities. Manhattan Borough President Scott Stringer appeared in it and spoke of its importance, and Kay Goss, from her vantage point as one of the nation's leading authorities on personal and community preparedness, offered a glowing testimonial. Taking a page from Michael's book, we also provided them with a $1,000 seed grant to cover out-of-pocket expenses. We followed up the training with monthly master classes and one-on-one coaching calls.

Three of the twenty program managers made major innovations. The NYC Department for the Aging reformatted the program to serve as a four-part class at the several hundred senior centers they managed. Manhattan's Community Board 3, in the Lower East Side, reformatted the program to serve students living in New York University dormitories. And an OEM Community Emergency Response Team got businesses and the local police department to use the program as a business continuity planning tool through which employees formed workplace teams to prepare their homes and families so they would feel secure reporting to work in an emergency.

Seven program managers dropped out because it was too much work or they could not get it off the ground. The remaining ten followed the structure with minor adaptations and were successful in attracting and training building and block leaders as planned. But unfortunately, these leaders were only modestly successful in getting take-up of the program in their buildings and on their blocks. Some of this may have been because we lost some quality through the train-the-trainer process, but our program managers felt there was a more fundamental challenge. Five years after 9/11, New Yorkers had lost their appetite for emergency preparedness and Mayor Bloomberg did not wish to invest his political capital in this issue. He was now focused on greening the city and carbon reduction. I did not fault him for this. This was no longer a priority issue for the city.

As one program manager stated: "The conviction I come away with is that this is a sound, doable, and scalable program that requires the right circumstances and political leadership to push the right societal buttons. It wasn't our fortune to have either of these. That time had passed."

With an amazing team, we had taken this further than anyone had imagined possible and pioneered an effective new tool for urban disaster resiliency about which we all felt proud. On the one hand, I felt relieved not to have responsibility for continuing to shepherd this initiative further. While I had initially been recruited, along the way I owned the mission lock, stock, and barrel, and became personally invested in its success. I would not miss however, regularly waking up in the middle of the night thinking about the many challenges I encountered. On the other hand, I was sad that this journey was coming to an end for me. I would miss the many extraordinary people who modeled citizenship at its best, and the many sights and sounds served up by my newly expanded sense of New York City. The people and this city had touched a deep place in my soul.

But an unexpected thing happened on the way to singing my swan song. While the program was over for me, it was not over for these dozen community groups and government agencies. They now owned All Together Now, and they had come up with a Plan B. If the city was not ready for this initiative, *they* would be ready for the city, if and when the need arose. They formed into a loosely knit network that they called the "New York City Resilient Community Reserve Corps." They determined that between their community boards and organizations they served 15 percent of the city's residents. And because of their geographic distribution throughout the five boroughs, they were well positioned to train community organizations to be program managers as needed. They requested that I keep the program and tools on my web site so it could continue to be available. I gladly agreed.

Shortly after this development, I received an e-mail from a government official working for London's Office of Emergency Management. He had done an Internet search and was excited to discover the All Together Now program and tools on my web site. "This is the most robust disaster preparedness program I have found anywhere in the world," he wrote. "Given our recent round of terrorist incidents we are very keen to learn more about it." I responded that I would be happy to talk further and that he should feel free to use whatever parts of the program and tools might be helpful. I told him that All Together Now was now New York City's gift to the world.

While it was not New York City's time to scale up such an initiative, this five-year experiment had served as the proving ground for how to build disaster-resilient communities anywhere on the planet. With terrorism now a part of our world and the growing number of climate-change related disasters, more cities will need to help their residents develop disaster-resilient communities. Our research with All Together Now had shown that this was possible and could be achieved in a relatively short period of time at modest cost. And if the demand was there, the capacity could be built to bring it to scale quickly.

As useful as this social innovation might be to cities wishing to ensure the safety of their residents, for me this experiment was also about something else. It was a grand experiment on a canvas writ large, New York City, about our capacity to come together with our neighbors for the sake of ourselves and the common good. It was a grand experiment to see if community groups and local government agencies could rise above their individuation and differences and work together. It was a grand experiment to see if there could be individual healing of a collective trauma and fear of the future through the simple act of neighbors reaching out to one another and preparing themselves for that future. It was about "all *together* now," in its many different manifestations, becoming a believable statement of possibility for our future.

This experiment was successful. New York City passed the test with flying colors, a test that September 11, 2001, had uniquely initiated it to take on behalf of us all. I will always be grateful for having had the chance to contribute to the city that I had long loved and now deeply respected, as well.

CHAPTER 4: SOCIAL CHANGE 2.0 PRACTITIONER'S GUIDE

1. What is the potential for a public/private partnership in furthering your social change initiative?

2. What is your approach for forming strategic partnerships?

3. What communication protocols do you need to collaborate well with a strategic partner?

4. What is your plan for bringing diverse people into your social change initiative?

5. What is your strategy to help volunteers sustain their commitment to your social change initiative over time?

THE ARCHITECTURE OF TRANSFORMATIVE SOCIAL CHANGE:

DESIGN PRINCIPLES, PRACTICES, AND LESSONS LEARNED

THE ARCHITECTURE OF

TRANSFORMATIVE SOCIAL CHANGE:

DESIGN PRINCIPLES, PRACTICES,

AND LESSONS LEARNED

The people can shape buildings for themselves, and have done it for centuries, by using languages which I call pattern languages. A pattern language gives each person who uses it the power to create an infinite variety of new and unique buildings, just as his ordinary language gives him the power to create an infinite variety of sentences. Each pattern is a rule which defines what you have to do to generate that which it defines. Those who become master architects and builders keep practicing until they know exactly how to realize these patterns.
—Christopher Alexander, *The Timeless Way of Building*

Each of the four experiments described in Part One made a substantial contribution to the evolution of my thinking about the architecture needed to further what I have come to call transformative social change. As I analyzed the different initiatives again and again over time, a set of design principles and practices emerged. At first they were vague; I had difficulty articulating them. Eventually they came into clear enough focus that I could incorporate them into the transformative change architecture of new projects and observe the outcomes. I tweaked them during one project and built on what I learned in the next. When I had enough confidence that these principles and practices could be relied on to produce consistent results, I began teaching them to my colleagues and the students in my institute. This increased the number of social experiments and the depth of the learning.

Eventually these principles and practices coalesced into what architect Christopher Alexander calls a "pattern language." In this case the pattern language is not for an architect of buildings, but rather for an architect of transformative change in society, or a social architect. While I expect to be continually learning for the rest of my life, this social change architecture is now well enough established to share it. With our world facing so many daunting challenges, the time could not be more primed for this pattern language to enter the lexicon of social change.

- Chapter 5 offers empowerment practices that enable the adoption of new behaviors by individuals, groups and institutions.

- Chapter 6 puts forward the transformation craft capable of evolving a dysfunctional social system.

- Chapter 7 pulls back the curtain on the process of inventing and implementing transformative social innovations.

- Chapter 8 provides practices to accelerate social change through the multiplying power of synergy.

- Chapter 9 shows how to leverage and disseminate social innovations at larger levels of scale.

My goal in Part Two is to describe these patterns in enough detail that they can be applied to the social architecture of any transformative change initiative. To become an adept practitioner will take time and practice, but basic proficiency can be learned relatively quickly. As in the previous section, each chapter ends with questions to help those wishing to apply these principles and practices to a social change initiative.

CHAPTER 5

CREATING THE WORLD AS WE WISH IT:
THE PRACTICE OF EMPOWERMENT

Some men see things as they are and say, "Why?" I dream things that never were and say, "Why Not?"
    —George Bernard Shaw

As the plant springs from, and could not be without, the seed, so every act of a person springs from the hidden seeds of thought, and could not have appeared without them . . . A man's mind may be likened to a garden, which may be intelligently cultivated or allowed to run wild; but whether cultivated or neglected, it must and will bring forth.
    —James Allen, *As a Man Thinketh*

If you want to build a ship, don't drum up people together to collect wood and don't assign them tasks and work, but rather teach them to long for the endless immensity of the sea.
    —Antoine de Saint-Exupery

Social Change 2.0 is built on the fundamental premise that as human beings we can create our world as we wish it to be. Included in that premise is the belief that to devolve into a victim or cynic and complain about our fate or what is broken in society is to abnegate our elemental power as a human

139

being to right what is wrong in our world. To own our power requires a willingness to envision the world we wish and then bring it about. It is a path for those with the courage to dream and the willingness to act. Those who walk this path as practitioners must become adept in the practice of empowerment. This is the foundation of Social Change 2.0 and the subject of this chapter.

The practice of empowerment emerged from my personal exploration and quest to answer the question: What is possible for us as human beings? To understand the empowerment framework fully, it is helpful to understand this aspirational impulse and the experiences that helped shape these practices into a tool for social change. (Those readers who wish to skip this background can jump ahead to the section Pathology to Vision, on page 143.)

Changing the world has been the central organizing principle of my life ever since I was a young boy. I suspect I was partially influenced in my earlier years by reading a lot of *Superman* comic books. My parents thought this was a phase that I would outgrow, but they offered me the special gift of not throwing cold water on my fragile aspirations. They didn't impose their expectations on me, either—except for the clear expectation that I lead my life morally. At the time and into my early twenties, I saw this as a fault in their parenting, wishing they had given me more structure and guidance.

As I grew older I realized that by giving me the freedom to decide many things for myself at an early age, I was being taught how to become an independent thinker. As a result, I had no adolescent rebellion or need to stake out my independence. I understood that I was responsible for my life and what I would make of it. If I was to realize my potential and my dreams of a better world, I would need to seek out the knowledge necessary to do it. Seeking out this knowledge became my modus operandi.

I reached college and began asking more sophisticated questions about change. It was the late sixties and the notion of changing the world was in the air everywhere. But the form much of it took, social protest, did not appeal to me. I was grateful that there were people opposing misguided government policies, but it was not my path. I was interested in searching for proactive ways to further positive change.

I studied economics and business because I was interested in learning the art and science of bringing ideas to fruition in the world. I figured that I would not have much success changing the world unless I could manifest a better idea in society. One of the things that I found attractive about business craft was how quickly it could mobilize change in response to a shift in society. To stay competitive, business needs to be able to change its products or services and grow its intellectual capital. There is no other institution that I know of with this depth of experience and best practice in initiating effective change strategies. If I wished to be a practitioner of societal change, I concluded, I needed to be competent in business craft.

But business, as such, was not my passion. People were. The sorry state of our world has occurred because *people* have created it, or allowed someone else to do so. To change the world would require better alternatives and people willing to avail themselves of these alternatives. Learning how to create better alternatives and promote their widespread adoption was where I wished to focus my learning.

When I discovered management guru and philosopher Peter Drucker's description of the social entrepreneur, I found the change framework I was looking for. He describes this person as someone who "changes the performance capacity of society." I appreciated that he placed personal responsibility for the change on both the social entrepreneur and the members of society. In this world view there is no room for victims or people sitting on the sidelines. This was an epiphany for me.

I did an independent master's degree in what was being called at the time "human potential." Helping people develop their potential seemed like the natural starting point for helping the world develop its potential. I immersed myself in the study of what motivates people to grow, evolve, and achieve their highest goals. I wanted also to learn how to do this myself. I studied with different teachers offering personal and spiritual development training. I voraciously read the perennial wisdom teachings to learn about the various systems of thought developed and tested over time. And I read about people who implemented innovations that evolved society in some distinct way in order to learn about their techniques and ways of thinking.

The red thread running though this learning and self-development quest, although I never articulated it that way at the time, was the search for replicable design principles to accelerate human and societal potential. I was bushwhacking the path of a social architect. Interestingly, the sensibility of an architect was something I had received from my father. Although he had encouraged me to walk my own path, paradoxically, he was modeling it for me.

My father was an architect. His area of expertise—in fact, his sole focus— was designing glass installations for large office buildings; my mother worked by his side as his business partner. One important building that he worked on was the United Nations. Years after he had completed his contribution to it, the amazing structure came to have great significance to me because of the First Earth Run and the Hopi prophesy in which it played a role. As a young boy I would go into his office and see blueprints sprawled all over his architect's desk and wonder how he got all that glass into those big buildings. The substance itself fascinated me. It was fragile enough that it could easily be shattered and yet strong enough to withstand large gusts of wind; it could serve as a wall but could allow light to pass through it, too; and it was created through an alchemical transformation—the application of heat to the simple element of sand.

My task would not be the architectural challenge of installing glass in large office buildings, but the social architectural challenge of installing large transformational change into society. As a social architect I would work with a substance even more fragile than glass: people's dreams. I do find it miraculous how many clues are laid out on our paths when we have the eyes to see them, usually in hindsight.

One such clue that I could not miss was when my wife-to-be, Gail, entered my life in 1980 and we discovered we had the same aspirations both to help people realize more of their potential as human beings and to make the world better. Gail had previously expressed this impulse through serving in the Peace Corps and I had just completed organizing the Olympic Torch Relay. When we found ourselves both attracted to a vague idea just beginning to emerge in the culture, the notion of empowerment, we decided to pay attention.

The word was being used in many different contexts, from personal growth, to business, to work with the disenfranchised members of society. We felt the concept of empowerment perfectly described our philosophy of life, which we defined as taking responsibility to create our life and the world around us the way we wished it to be. Figuring out how to help people do that would be our work. It was wonderful to discover both my calling and the partner I had been seeking throughout my life in the same moment.

We called our first venture the Empowerment Workshop. It was a radical shift from the personal growth going on at that time, which was focused on healing the past and solving personal problems. Our goal was to help people *learn how to dream*, and equally important, to manifest their dreams. No one had done anything quite like this before. We developed a three-and-a-half-day personal growth experience that proved successful in helping people make meaningful and significant changes. Soon the word got out about this new methodology for personal growth and many people started attending the workshop. When enough of them asked us for help in applying the methodology to empowering people in their organizations and communities, we developed a second workshop that we called Art of Empowerment: A Professional Training in Facilitating Human Potential.

This workshop, too, became quite popular, and we began offering it throughout the United States, Europe, and Asia. A wide diversity of people attended, including senior business leaders and human resource practitioners interested in empowering people within their organizations, nonprofit and government leaders wishing to empower citizens to adopt new behaviors around key societal issues, community organizers wishing to empower the disenfranchised, as well as a variety of professionals wishing to bring the empowerment methodology into their work, including life and executive coaches, organizational development trainers, educators from kindergarten to graduate school, health-care practitioners, therapists, and various other change agents and representatives of the helping professions.

Over the years an extraordinary learning community—a global empowerment laboratory—evolved. Gail and I wrote a book called *Empowerment: The Art of Creating Your Life As You Want It*. The writing process brought further refinement to our model and the book's success as a bestseller attracted yet more people to our trainings. Along the way, I created the Empowerment Institute explicitly to apply our methodology to societal and organizational empowerment issues, and Gail and I developed a certification program.

The rest of this chapter explains the empowerment framework (see Figure 5.1, page 144) that grew out of this research and which was embedded in the social change initiatives described in Part One.

SHIFT FROM PATHOLOGY TO VISION: WATERING THE SEEDS NOT THE WEEDS

What we place our attention on grows. This is a foundational premise of our empowerment work. We can look to the natural world for the embodiment of this premise, where what we water grows. As we attempt to bring about social change we need to ask ourselves whether we are watering the seeds or the weeds. If we focus a person's, organization's, community's, or society's attention on solving specific problems, they will gain insight into these and generate possible solutions. If we focus their attention on a vision of what they want, this will generate a different set of insights and possible means for achieving them. *In the former, outcomes will be defined by the parameters of the problem; in the later, by the parameters of people's imagination.*

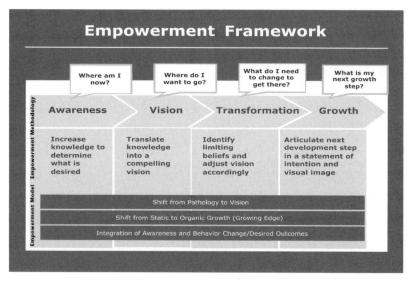

Figure 5.1

Problem solving as a way of thinking is well suited for the goal of discovering how to fix something that may be broken in an already designed system. When the goal, however, is to invent a new system or help people create a picture of what they wish for their future, we need a different type of thinking process. To reinvent our communities, organizations, and the world we need to help people learn the skills of visioning and bringing new possibilities into manifestation.

Shifting our focus in this way also helps motivate us to take action. We are much more inspired to take action when we think about a vision of possibility that excites us than when facing a problem that enervates us. Being human, we would rather not spend time thinking about our problems. Using the analogy of nature, one of my primary teachers in studying change, when planting a garden we can focus on removing rocks, roots, and weeds, or we can focus on the flowers or vegetables that will soon be thriving there. One focus makes the process laborious, the other engaging. We still need to remove the rocks, but when we are focused on a bountiful garden the work to get there is just part of bringing about our vision.

This part of the empowerment model can be summarized as a shift from focusing on pathology, or what is wrong and how to fix it; to focusing on a vision, or what we want and how to create it. *As practitioners of social change, one of the most consequential choices we make is where we focus people's attention. It determines both the outcome we will achieve and the level of participation.*

The design of the First Earth Run used this key foundational premise. The vision guiding the endeavor was to unite humanity in common cause for a more peaceful planet. The means was to experience our human connectedness and create possibilities for cooperation in and among communities and countries around the world. Our motto was "Relaying fire around the world to light the spirit of cooperation." Our hope was that this experience would transform some of the fears that cause people to protect themselves from those who are different. This vision pulled people toward it and generated significantly greater participation and media attention than the protest demonstrations, as important as they were, about avoiding a nuclear war. One approach focused on a vision of possibility and our hopes for the future, the other on the existing pathology and our fears.

This communication was embodied in the evocative and positive symbol of a torch of peace encircling the entire world with light, showing us we all share the common fate of living together on one small planet. Bringing together the world's people and political leaders in various forms of cooperation, from day-long ceasefires between warring parties, to symbolic acts of cooperation between groups with generations of antipathy toward one another, gave further impetus to the belief that we have the means to bring a peaceful future into reality. Chapter 1 recounts some of the specific positive outcomes that occurred as a result of planting and watering these seeds of possibility.

An example of the impact on people by making this shift from pathology to vision is illustrated by marketing research done by a large New York public relations agency. The firm created two 30-second commercials for a client who provided food to starving children in Africa. One showed a starving, emaciated, and sad child. The other a well-nourished and happy child. They wished to see which would generate the most donations from viewers for the organization. They assumed it would be the starving child, because it would tug on people's heartstrings, but were greatly surprised to discover that it was actually the fed and happy child by a three-to-one ratio. One image appealed to people's negative emotions of guilt, pity, and sadness; the other to their positive emotions of hope, optimism, and faith in humanity. While appeals to negative emotions as a call to action will get a response from people, they are not nearly as powerful or sustainable over time as appealing to our positive emotions.

Another example of the power of vision over pathology can be seen in the story related by a participant in one of my transformative leadership trainings. At the beginning of each training people describe their projects and the outcomes they wish to achieve. One woman described a grassroots organization she had created to oppose designating Maine as a storage site for spent nuclear waste. Given how relevant this issue was to people's safety she was befuddled by the modest show of support she was receiving. In passing, she mentioned that the name of her organization was "Citizens Against Nuclear Trash" or CANT. I made the simple suggestion that if she wished to increase her chance of recruiting people she should consider renaming the initiative to something more positive. Several months later she sent me a thank-you note. She had renamed her group "Clean Maine" and was amazed how much easier she found it to attract volunteers and raise money.

Since social change requires people to participate, each element of the change strategy needs to be designed to attract people. In the case of my community-based behavior-change work, this applied to the program name, the name of each action, how that action was described, the image that illustrated it, the assessment of the behavior or issue, how people were invited by neighbors, and the information meeting design. Each needed to create a pull toward something positive and enjoyable.

In crafting the appeals for our sustainable lifestyle program it was about:

- adopting sustainable lifestyle practices for the sake of our children's future,

- getting to know your neighbors,

- and creating a sense of community.

In the neighborhood program it was:

- making the block safer, healthier, and more livable,

- getting to know your neighbors,

- and building a sense of community.

With the disaster resiliency program it focused on:

- ensuring your safety (and that of your family, if relevant) through being prepared for an emergency,

- having the support of a community in case of an emergency,

- and getting to know your neighbors.

Diving a little deeper we can see another example of speaking to a positive vision rather than from avoidance of a negative outcome. In the neighborhood program (as representative of all the programs) potential actions to be taken are described in the "livability assessment" the team fills out at the beginning of each topic meeting. Each possible action the team considers taking is evaluated on a scale of 1 to 5. The higher the number, the closer the block is to that description. A number 1 or 2 would indicate an area where action would be warranted.

Here are examples of two assessment questions from the "Health and Safety" topic area:

- "Motorists in my neighborhood obey the speed limit and are respectful of the safety of pedestrians and cyclists."

- "My neighborhood feels safe and people look out for one another's well-being."

Again, we used a positive vision in helping people assess a possible outcome they might wish.

Positive visions pull people toward them; negative visions push people away from them.

A SHIFT FROM STATIC TO ORGANIC GROWTH: THE GROWING EDGE

When Gail and I created our Empowerment Workshop we searched for a model of personal growth that could be self-sustaining. Since our desire to help people realize their full potential as human beings could not happen in one workshop, we needed to offer them a strong boost onto this path along with a growth framework and tools they could use on an ongoing basis. The existing models either focused on helping a person heal the past or get to a predetermined destination. If the models were backward facing, they attempted to heal the wounds of our childhood or some dysfunction we might have acquired along our life path. There were many excellent workshops, trainings, and therapies developed with this goal in mind. But after the person healed the wound, then what?

If they were forward looking they attempted to help people accomplish some predetermined personal, work, or spiritual goal. Whatever the desired outcome, there was a specific destination. Before people got to the goal they would often feel inadequate and judge themselves against those who had already arrived at this destination they idealized. Once they got there, they would look around and wonder if that was all there was. What did they do now?

Both healing the past and striving for a predetermined destination in the future tended to leave people feeling empty at the end of the journey. There was a momentary sense of accomplishment, but then it was over. There was nothing that kept people moving toward the realization of more of their human potential. This approach to personal growth was static.

So we kept searching for an approach that was more dynamic, a growth model that could help people not just heal the past or accomplish a specific goal in the future, but could motivate them to stay on this journey throughout their entire life. We were seeking an approach to growth that helped a person continuously further their evolution as a human being toward more of their potential. The notion of *personal evolution* provided a breakthrough in our thinking. It allowed us to gain a new reference point, the multibillion year evolutionary experience of our planet, and in particular one of its most extraordinary accomplishments—the self-sustaining natural world. What could we learn from the natural world's model of growth that could be applied to human beings? What design elements could be extrapolated?

As we spent time thinking about this, the most obviously transferable design element was the quality of aliveness. This was a universal property of growth. If something is alive it is always growing. There is always the next shoot, bud, or "growing edge." A tree is a good example. If you look at the shoots on a branch that are just coming into existence this is where the tree is most vital. It is where the tree's life force is the strongest. It is where there is the greatest degree of aliveness.

These growing edges have several distinct properties. They are fragile and vulnerable, without any bark protecting them against the elements. They are soft and have the green color of new life. They are unique to that branch of the tree. While all trees share the same process of growth, each branch looks different depending on the unique circumstances and stage of its growth. There is no "right" growing edge for a tree. There certainly is no way to say one growing edge is better than another or one branch should be like another branch. The only meaningful criterion is the quality of the tree's aliveness. If a tree is fully alive it is always growing and has many growing edges. If there are no new growing edges coming into existence, then the tree is atrophying and moving toward death.

I found the parallels between nature's growth process and our human growth process very compelling. We have the most vitality and aliveness in the parts of our life where we are bringing something new into existence. That is where we are filled with excitement and brimming with energy; on the contrary, in the areas of our life where we are not growing we have limited or no energy. These areas tend to stagnate or atrophy. The aliveness generated by the growing edge has an innate wisdom about it. Gail and I hoped that this profound design achievement of our planet's evolution—the growing edge—might also propel people in their evolution as well. In short, we hoped that it would provide the underpinning for a self-sustaining growth model.

We chose to create the Empowerment Workshop around the two design principles we felt could enable self-sustaining growth. *The power of a vision to attract (like the sun)* and *the aliveness of the growing edge to energize (like a tree or a plant)*. Our work as facilitators would be to help people discover their deepest aspirations and shape them into coherent visions of possibility. Then we would help them identify each vision's growing edge and ground it with a specific statement of intention and visualization. Like the DNA blueprint encoded in nature's seeds, the intention statement and image would provide the specific instruction for how this mental seed should grow. The workshop would promote growth in all the areas of a person's life in order to enable balance and wholeness as a human being. The areas we addressed were relationships, work, body, money, sexuality, emotions, and spirituality.

Workshop participants completely took to this approach. It made sense to them intuitively and for the nearly four days of the workshop they were fully engaged designing their lives and crafting their growing edges. From the new job, to the new relationship, to the new body, to the new outlook on life, people got clear about what they wanted and developed their next growth step to bring it into reality. People were willing to risk evoking their dreams knowing that we would help ground them on the growing edge. The aspiration of the vision and pragmatism of the growing edge proved to be a powerful combination in helping people consciously create and evolve their life.

It was very inspiring for Gail and me to lead these trainings. Over the years we have had the opportunity of working with many thousands of people. We have been touched by their courage to dream and the energy they found in the growing edge. What moved us the most, though, were the letters they sent us afterward, in some cases many years later, sharing the impact this experience has had on their lives. Christiane Northrop, a medical doctor and pioneering author of a number of bestselling books contributing to women's health, wrote to us about how the workshop helped her at a formative stage of her career development, giving her the foundation of self-trust she needed to co-create her famous clinic. John Mackey, founder and CEO of Whole Foods Market and business innovator, wrote us almost two decades after participating in the workshop about its lasting value.

Ultimately people from all over the world wrote about positive changes in living situations, job satisfaction, professional stature, income, relationships, health, and just about any area of life you can imagine. We heard from so many that we started a newsletter so that others could be inspired by their stories as well.

In our follow-up research with many of the people who participated in the workshop, the common denominator for those who manifested their dreams and continued to recreate their lives was *their willingness to diligently work their growing edges*. By no means did all the people who went through the workshop continue to use the empowerment tools, but those who did, like gardeners who continue to cultivate their garden, were able to achieve self-sustaining growth. We now train others to lead the Empowerment Workshop not only as a foundational tool for personal development, but social change as well. Later in the book I will share how it is being used to empower disenfranchised women in Afghanistan and accelerate the healing process between the Hutu and Tutsi in Rwanda. For now, here is a much lighter story about the popularization of the growing edge concept.

One of the participants in my transformative leadership training, quite engaged but surprisingly discreet about what he did, came up to me after the training and asked if I would be willing to do an empowerment training for the band he managed. They were working on an album and feeling constricted creatively. I said I was open to doing this and asked him the name of the band. He responded "Aerosmith," and then waited for my reaction, which was—nothing. A blank face. Truth to tell, I had basically stopped following popular music after the Beatles broke up. He offered me a look of bemused amazement.

To make a long and fascinating story short, it was a wonderful experience. I loved the guys. They were committed to growing and were vulnerable in the way the growing edge allows people to be. They shared how this growth model, in contrast to the previous personal development work they had done, inspired them to see their lives in a new way and create them anew. They got the breakthrough they were looking for and the big song on their next album, one of their greatest hits ever, was "Livin' on the Edge."

BRINGING THE GROWING EDGE INTO SOCIAL CHANGE

It wasn't long before I began using the growing edge model in my work with organizations and communities. It became my primary tool for sleuthing out where the energy for change was most readily available. I would ask the simple question: What is this organization's next growing edge? or What is this neighborhood's next growing edge? or What is this community's next growing edge? When I found the edge, or more accurately facilitated the group or institution to find its edge, people were inevitably enlivened and excited to participate in a change process.

This process got more complicated when working at a societal change level. It was not always easy to discern what the receptivity for a particular change looked like until I invested some time exploring the issue. I have often been *over* the edge and have had to wait for society to catch up. Sometimes this as been as long as ten years, as in the case of the First Earth Run.

While being over the growing edge is frustrating for the change agent who is pushing the boulder uphill, for society it can set up the conditions for the desired change to be brought forward more easily at a later time. Those on the vanguard of a new way of thinking about an issue can find one another, test their ideas, and get feedback. Those designing prototypes for a particular change strategy can build and refine them before the demand is so great that they get pulled into service before they are ready. The very act of stretching people's sense of the possible can also accelerate its take-up in society.

In my work with the Dutch Ministry of Environment in the early 1990s I had the opportunity to work with visionary government environmental leader Paul de Jongh. He is one of the pioneers of national "green plans." A green plan is an environmental roadmap with specific and measurable environmental targets. Unfortunately, they are rare in government, because committing to measurable goals makes a politician vulnerable to criticism if he or she falls short. That made the Dutch Green Plan all the more impressive. And it was the first national green plan developed anywhere in the world.

To help achieve the Green Plan's environmental goals in the consumer sector of society, Paul chose to use our sustainable lifestyle program. Being part of the Dutch Green Plan allowed me to observe from a close vantage point the process of setting national environmental targets. I observed that this type of goal setting was a function of the perceived readiness, or, if you will, the growing edge of the country for this type of change. Too far ahead and you can't get people to believe it is possible and you get a lot of push back. Not enough of a stretch and people believe it will not have any real impact on the issue, and are not motivated to participate.

When Paul and his team began developing their targets, the need for environmental change far exceeded the political will available to support it. Finding the growing edge was a most challenging process. The Ministry of Environment ended up setting goals that were not as ambitious as the environmental community wanted or the science demanded. In spite of this, the Dutch government that set these goals still received severe criticism from the opposition party and business community because they believed achieving even these modest goals would damage the economy. Partially as a result of this criticism, that government was voted out of power in the next election. The new, more conservative party taking power soon found itself in a predicament. The environmental goals set by the previous administration paradoxically had been so internalized by the country that public opinion forced the new government to set even *more* ambitious environmental goals or face the consequences of being voted out of power.

Einstein states that a mind stretched never returns to its original shape. An essential part of the change process is discovering and testing the readiness of a culture for this mental stretch. Approaching it as a growing edge offers breathing room for the process to unfold organically as people and institutions acclimate to the change. This requires that the goals be set around a society's or an institution's current ability to accept them and not statically as if they were the final word on the subject. And it demands that they be reviewed regularly.

Goal setting on the growing edge is also important because it gets people into action. If they believe it is the right level of stretch, they are willing to engage. And once people have a specific target they shift into gear to accomplish it and invariably do. A local government association that helps cities reduce their carbon footprint, the International Council of Local Environmental Initiatives, observed that while it is hard to get a city to set a carbon reduction target, if they do set one, they consistently achieve it *before* the date set. And as soon as one city accomplishes this goal, others jump right in and do the same. When distance runner Roger Bannister broke the 4-minute mile, a previously unimaginable feat, others soon started repeating his accomplishment. By working skillfully with societal or community growing edges we have the means to accelerate the take-up of the desired change and the achievement of significant goals.

Working with citizens to achieve significant behavior change also requires skillful use of the growing edge. In the first version of the sustainable lifestyle program we designed the actions so that people could check them off after they did them. We discovered that many people would check off the action if they did some part of it and then not go back to it again. They were operating from a static-growth point of view. There was a place to get to, and they were either there or not. When they touched any part of the goal, they decided they were done and moved on to the next action.

I realized we needed to set up the actions not as checklists, which implies *done* or *not done* but rather as environmentally sustainable lifestyle *practices* that are ongoing. A practice is something that needs to be attended to on a regular basis. (Think athlete, dancer, and musician, among others.) This shift created a different orientation for program participants. They started operating from the point of view of the growing edge, although we did not use that term as such. They began to establish practices for their recycling, carbon reduction, or water conservation. This significantly increased their buy-in to the program and their performance.

An illustration of this shift from static to organic growth occurred with our sustainable lifestyle program in Portland, Oregon. Portland is a city known for its high level of environmental consciousness and the active participation of its citizens. It has one of the best recycling participation rates in the country. Just about everyone who participated in our program felt that he or she was were doing a good job of recycling. In fact, some felt this program was a waste of time because they were already doing everything.

As we probed below the surface of the belief that "I am already doing everything," we discovered three subbeliefs. "I recycle, therefore I do everything else." "I do these actions sometimes; therefore I do them all the time."

"I have knowledge about this issue, therefore I am taking action." When we pointed out these three beliefs in our information meetings and the importance of shifting from a "check it off the list" approach to environmental behavior change to "sustainable lifestyle practices," people got it. They were not interested in being self-congratulatory. They cared and they wanted to do the right thing, but had fallen into a static model of growth.

This shift had a powerful impact on their performance, particularly in the area of solid waste reduction. As people took full advantage of each of the actions, that is, viewed them as sustainable lifestyle practices to be constantly improved on, to their astonishment they found themselves averaging a 30 percent reduction *on top* of what they were already doing. When we reported this result to the city's solid waste agency, they too were astounded. The agency had reached a plateau in its solid waste diversion and in order to make further progress was now investing a lot of money and effort to get participation from the least committed people. This approach had not worked. When they saw our results, they agreed to expand our program and further encourage the participating population with incentives.

The growing edge is where the energy exists to further change.

INTEGRATION OF AWARENESS AND BEHAVIOR CHANGE

The final component of the empowerment model is about the process of achieving actual behavior change. Many change processes assume that if we are aware of something we should do, we will do it. The focus is on increasing our awareness or knowledge. While awareness increases our understanding about an issue, by itself it rarely leads to a change in behavior. If you need proof of this, think of all the things you know you should be doing, but aren't.

On the other hand, sometimes we set a goal for something we want, harness our will to achieve it, and then discover to our chagrin after we achieve it that it wasn't really what we wanted. This can be true of a material possession, a relationship, or a societal change. To avoid finding ourselves in this situation, we need to clarify, before we begin, what is important to us, what we value, and what we really want.

Combining a process for increasing awareness and helping people change behavior provides the best chance for long-term change. This process for behavior change, which I call the "empowerment methodology," has four steps, each associated with a question.

1. Awareness: Where am I now?

2. Vision: Where do I want to go?

3. Transformation: What do I need to change to get there?

4. Growth: What's my next step?

Awareness

To adopt a new behavior we need to start by understanding our current behavior. This awareness creates a baseline, and functions as a form of input for developing a vision of the change we wish to accomplish. In the sustainable lifestyle program, for instance, participants assess their current environmental practices in each topic area. For the neighborhood program, they assess the current status on their block around each of the program's livability actions.

The information meeting that precedes people's participation in any of these programs provides a foundation of basic awareness about the issue and helps people assess where they stand. For example, people are asked how prepared they are for specific emergencies or how well have they translated their environmental knowledge into specific sustainable lifestyle practices. When people begin active participation in the program this awareness process is repeated at the level of each action through a "Why Act" paragraph. The paragraph is written like a 15-second commercial and is designed to provide enough information for people to decide whether or not they wish to take that particular action.

Vision

With awareness of where we currently are on an issue, we can now better develop a vision of where we wish to go. The initial information meeting helps individuals create a vision for what they might get from participating in the program. This is reinforced in the team-building meeting in which the group creates a team vision and learns how to implement the program structure. The program's ability to attract someone to take and sustain action is a direct result of the power of their vision.

Adopting new lifestyle practices competes for time in people's busy lives and requires them to reprioritize. Without a compelling vision, life will overwhelm a tentative commitment. Helping participants develop a vision for what they want from the program provides them the motivation to sustain their commitment over time. To be compelling, the vision needs to touch deeply held values and aspirations, such as taking environmental actions for the sake of their children's future, improving their quality of life by getting to know their neighbors and improving the livability of their neighborhood, or taking emergency preparedness actions for the sake of their family's safety.

Visioning is also something we do with volunteers to help them get in touch with what they most wish for themselves out of their volunteer experience. This is often very personal. It could include developing more connectedness with their community or honing certain leadership qualities. During the First Earth Run, we did an exercise to help each person find his or her vision for participating. We assumed they wanted a more peaceful planet, but what did they want for *themselves?* What was the deeper personal growth opportunity? Because in most cases they were making little or no money, we knew we needed to help them connect with this deeper motivation in order to sustain their commitment and enthusiasm over months and in some cases years.

When I asked this question of myself, I discovered what mythologist Joseph Campbell calls the initiation of the warrior. He says "the cardinal initiation of the warrior is accomplishment." Being totally committed to something I believed could make a difference in the world was a defining moment in my life. For my own self-esteem, I needed to make this happen, no matter what it took. It ended up taking everything I had to give, but in return gave me something that was immeasurable—a profound sense of meaning in my life and a deep confidence in myself, on which I build every day. Only a vision that touches the deeper recesses of our being can keep us motivated through the inevitable challenges we face bringing change forward in the world.

Transformation

Once we have a compelling vision, a curious thing happens. All the reasons we can't make it happen begin visiting us unsolicited. I call these "limiting beliefs." The strength of a limiting belief is in direct proportion to the stretch of the vision. The greater the vision, the greater the intensity of resistance we often experience. This is natural and to be expected. We are envisioning something with which we may have no current experience in our life. As a result there is often internal pushback in terms of believing it is possible. If the vision is too far removed from our current belief about what is possible, the resistance will be so strong that we will call it fantasy and give up. That's where the growing edge comes in. It represents the next step that we believe is actually possible when it comes to manifesting our vision.

For leaders involved in social change, beliefs that might undermine their willingness to bring their vision forward could include: "I don't have the right skills or experience to make my vision happen; someone with more ability than me should do this." "The forces I need to change are much bigger than I am; I will never be able to make it happen." "It will take too much time." These limiting beliefs can undermine our enthusiasm and cause us not to proceed, or to do so timidly, which constrains our ability to make any real change. Given that social change, particularly transformational change, requires proactivity and passion, transforming these limiting beliefs is essential to keeping us on our path.

Often these limiting beliefs are a product of thinking in an "either/or" manner. *I can only do something one way or I should not consider doing it at all*, for instance. Transforming a limiting belief, or what I call creating a "turnaround," requires a more innovative way of thinking about the issue that often includes a "both/and" resolution. *This is true, and that is also true.* In many instances this type of thinking requires more imagination than the vision itself. A vision is based on "what" questions, so it allows us to think about a new possibility unconstrained by day-to-day reality. The turnaround to a limiting belief often requires us to address "how" questions and our deepest resistances. Creating a turnaround that we can believe in, a prerequisite for moving our vision forward wholeheartedly, requires us to dig deep for insights.

After we guide block leaders through a visioning exercise in our Livable Neighborhood Block Leadership Academy, they are excited by a new sense of possibility for themselves and their block. That is, until they start discovering their limiting beliefs. Then they start having doubts: doubts about their ability to lead, and about their neighbors' willingness to participate. Here are two examples of real limiting beliefs that came up for people in our Leadership Academy and how they turned them around.

Limiting Belief: "I don't have enough interpersonal communications skills and experience running meetings to be a good block leader. Someone with more experience should do this."

Turnaround: "My ability to be a good block leader comes from my desire to improve my quality of life and that of my neighbors. I carefully prepare myself by reading over the topic meeting guides and asking my teammates for support as I need it."

Limiting Belief: "I am afraid to reach out to my neighbors and risk rejection or offending them."

Turnaround: "Overcoming my fears and resistances is one of the opportunities provided to me by becoming a block leader. I take full advantage of this opportunity and make myself and block better as a result."

Our world is created from the beliefs we hold about it and our behaviors grow out of these beliefs. To create a world of our dreams requires us to identify and transform any beliefs that would prevent the realization of these dreams.

Growth

Helping volunteer block leaders assess their current abilities to deliver our program, create a vision for how they wish to improve their block and their leadership abilities, and transform any limiting beliefs that undermine moving this vision forward are all a prelude to this final step of the empowerment methodology: the articulation of their next growing edge crafted into an intention statement and visual image and a willingness to water this new seed regularly through mental attention. This final step is the enabler of the desired behavior change and the primary differentiator from awareness-oriented growth processes. (See Figure 5.2, page 160.)

Empowering our volunteer block leaders to work with their growing edges made all the difference in their effectiveness and their ability to sustain their commitment over time. Through our many community programs we learned early on that without a growth process like this, most volunteers succumb to the forces of inertia or the many competing demands for their time. To facilitate this growth process we trained our program managers to use the empowerment methodology in their skills training and follow-up coaching of volunteer leaders. And to support the ongoing growth of our program managers, we created a community of practice that we called a "master class."

The master class consisted of a two-hour conference call with eight to twelve program managers every month. Each person would share his or her growing edges for both the program and themselves. Working with the program's growing edges enabled them to develop their capabilities as social architects, and us to evolve our program strategies, methodologies, and tools on an ongoing basis.

We also vigorously supported the personal growth of our program managers. Community organizing with measurable goals around behavior change and public participation is very demanding work. It can be frustrating as volunteers make commitments and then change them. The master class was a lifeline for these dedicated change agents. Their growing edge issues focused on program management, work-life balance, time management, development as an empowerment trainer and coach, and leadership. As each program manager shared the vulnerability of his or her growing edge, others jumped in to help offer support. Because the program managers shared a common set of challenges, they were able to empathize with one another and offer valuable insights enabling real growth and significant leadership development to occur.

Empowerment provides the foundational design principle and practices for Social Change 2.0 because it offers an operating system to enable behavior change in society and among change leaders. But to transform our dysfunctional or marginally effective social systems so they can achieve the higher level of performance and social value our world needs from them, a complementary set of practices is required. I call this set of practices the craft of transformation. The next chapter takes us on a deep dive to see the application of this craft in action with a social system on the brink of collapse.

Figure 5.2—Techniques for Behavior Change

A WRITTEN INTENTION ABOUT THE GROWING EDGE
(NEW BEHAVIOR, BELIEF, OR OUTCOME)

1. *State it in the positive*—This sets the intention around what you actually want.
2. *Be succinct*—The more to the point, the easier to focus on it.
3. *Be specific*—Precision helps sharpen your intention.
4. *Be magnetic*—Use language that is motivational to you.
5. *State it in the present tense*—Keeps your intention real time.
6. *Include yourself in it*—This makes it personal.
7. *Make it about changes for you, not others*—Keeps the focus on what you need to change.

A VISUAL IMAGE ABOUT THE GROWING EDGE
(NEW BEHAVIOR, BELIEF, OR OUTCOME)

1. *Use a single image*—This helps you focus.
2. *Image should evoke feeling*—Feeling creates emotional buy-in.
3. *Include yourself in it*—This makes it personal.
4. *The image can be literal or a metaphor*—Use whichever best heightens emotion.
5. *Physically draw or describe the image*—Physicality makes it concrete.

TRANSFORMATION PROCESS

1. Regularly repeat statement of intention and visualize image to strengthen new belief or behavior.
2. Physically practice the new behavior to build confidence and strengthen ownership.
3. Identify and transform limiting beliefs to stay on the growing edge.
4. Interpret feedback and adjust growth strategy, intention, and image as necessary.
5. Celebrate accomplishments.

CHAPTER 5: SOCIAL CHANGE 2.0 PRACTITIONER'S GUIDE

1. What would a vision-oriented framing of your social change initiative look like?

2. What are the behaviors people need to adopt to achieve the objectives of your social change initiative?

3. What is your approach to help them adopt and continue to evolve these behaviors?

4. How are you supporting the personal development of the volunteers and staff involved in your social change initiative?

5. What are you doing to further your personal development as a social change agent?

CHAPTER 6

CHANGING THE GAME:
THE CRAFT OF TRANSFORMATION

It is not because things are difficult that we do not dare, it is because we do not dare that things are difficult.
—Seneca

You can never change things by fighting the existing reality. To change something, build a new model that makes the existing model obsolete.
—Buckminster Fuller

In the autumn of 2005 I received a phone call from Kathy Castro asking if I would be willing to work with a group of individuals whose social system was in turmoil and on the brink of breakdown. Unless the system could be fundamentally transformed to a higher level of functioning, Kathy reported, it was in danger of collapsing. All the key players would be in the same room for two days. Many of them viewed one another as adversaries and a few were barely on speaking terms. This, of course, was one of the reasons that the system was on the verge of breakdown.

Kathy was hoping that I would guide them through a training I had been delivering for fifteen years for leaders wishing to bring about transformative change in their organizations, communities, or larger social system.

None of the potential participants had ever done anything remotely "trans-formational," however, so there was a degree of skepticism about such a process.

Was I up for the challenge, she asked anxiously?

Absolutely.

The premise of the training, which I called "Changing the Game: The Craft of Transformative Leadership," is that if the current set of arrangements, rules, and social norms are causing a social system or organization to underperform or break down, we need to change them. But getting to a place that no one has ever been before is not easy without leaders skilled in guiding this type of journey. The purpose of the training was to build this guidance capacity—what I call transformative leadership—in the participants.

No one knew what to expect in such a fraught environment, least of all me as the facilitator. The one thing I did know, however, from leading many of these trainings was that the transformational tools were powerful and if these leaders were willing to invest in using them, they would work. But this was a big "if." They would need to be willing to lower their defenses, step out of their comfort zones, and partake in genuine growth. This is challenging enough for people who do not know one another and are actively seeking out this type of knowledge and growth. For the individuals involved in the story that follows, it would be an extremely high-stakes social experiment.

As I tell their story I will be sharing the architecture and tools of trans-formative change. Collectively these tools represent a transformational pattern language, or set of templates, that can be used with individuals, groups, organizations, and an entire social system. In this training we would work at each of these levels. I have placed these tools in an actual change context to provide insight into their sequencing and how they perform in real time.

HOPE IS BELIEVING IN SPITE OF THE EVIDENCE . . . AND THEN WATCHING THE EVIDENCE CHANGE

Kathy Castro is a director of the University of Rhode Island Sea Grant Program, which provides education to fishermen in a program comparable to the agricultural extension program that educates farmers. She is a dedicated environmental leader committed to the fishermen she works with and the vision of a sustainable fishery in Rhode Island. Her call to me had been prompted by the fact that different parts of Rhode Island's fishery were being overfished, and, because of the inability of the key stakeholders in the system to cooperate, were at risk of collapsing.

The leaders who would participate in this training each represented a key constituency associated with the fishery. There were leaders from commercial fishermen's associations who wished to have more or less unfettered access to the fish and who were living on the edge of economic survival, leaders from recreational fishermen's organizations who were angry that the commercial fisherman were not leaving any fish for them, leaders from the state environmental agency who regulated the type and amount of fish that can be caught and were in constant disputes and periodic litigation with the fishermen's associations, and leaders from major environmental groups who wished to save the fish. Theoretically Kathy's job was to help all these players cooperate for the common good of the fishery. More often, though, it felt to her as if she was simply trying to prevent them from causing bodily harm to one another.

She asked me to provide this training to improve their abilities as change agents within their own organizations and in their interactions with one another. Her not so hidden agenda was that it would help get them on the path of establishing a sustainable fishery. Normally I lead this two-day training for leaders who do not have anything in common beyond the desire to learn tools for transformative change. I had never led it for a group of leaders from different organizations that had contentious relationships with one another and were all part of the same system. This would provide a rare opportunity to put these transformational tools to a new test.

The training was held at the former Rhode Island country estate of industrialist W. Alton Jones, which had been converted into a serene retreat center with a lake, beautifully maintained grounds, and many hiking trails through the surrounding forested land. It was a picture-perfect spring day with flowers and trees coming into bloom. Kathy and her team had arrived the night before to help me set up the training room. It was a comfortable wood-paneled rustic room with plenty of windows looking out at the surrounding grounds and wooded areas. To create a sense of community, I arranged the chairs in a "U" shape so everyone could have eye contact with one another when they talked. I also took away the tables so they had no barriers between them. Here's how Kathy described the training.

The day finally arrived that I most dreaded and looked forward to. Would everyone think I had gone off the deep end bringing together sworn enemies to sit down at a two-day fisheries leadership training that was a bit off the beaten trail? What was transformative leadership anyway? Were we ready for it? Some had jumped at the opportunity, some had dragged their feet, and some I had to downright nag and work with the wind gods to blow a gale so they could not go out to sea. We were all there because we felt the need for change, of doing things another way. Many of the leaders were exhausted, beaten, and discouraged. I was simply frustrated that I didn't know how to help them.

I looked at each of them sitting around the room, partially wondering if they would ever talk to me again. There were leaders there from the Rhode Island Shellfishermen's Association, Rhode Island Lobstermen's Association, Ocean State Fishermen's Association, Commercial Fishermen's Association, Rhode Island Saltwater Anglers, Rhode Island Commercial Rod and Reel Angler's Association, East Coast Fishermen's Foundation, Atlantic Offshore Lobstermen's Association, and representatives from the Rhode Island Marine Fisheries Council and the North East Fisheries Management Council. The state managers from the Rhode Island Department of Environmental Management were there and we from Rhode Island Sea Grant Program.

Regardless of how everyone got there, I hoped they would each bring their best effort to the table and were prepared to listen, learn, and grow. But I was worried—was this too far out there for fishermen, government regulators, and hard core environmentalists? Was I being a "Kathy-anna"?

EMBARKING ON THE JOURNEY

To kick off Day One, Kathy shared her vision for the training and then introduced me as someone with a lot of expertise in developing leaders into change agents. She said she had gone though much effort and expense to create this experience for them. "So therefore," she concluded, "I want you all to be on your best behavior. That means no fighting in class."

Kathy, having raised the bar for participation in this training by saying that bodily altercations were out of bounds, turned the workshop over to me. I launched into the purpose and potential benefits. I told them they would be learning tools and strategies that would help them not only grow personally as leaders, but would also help them create transformative change in their organizations and the fishery. This was beyond business-as-usual leadership. It would ask them to become agents of positive change. That is, to envision and create their organizations and the fishery at a higher level of functioning. If they were successful using these transformational tools in their organizations, they could expect empowered people with a greater commitment, performing at a higher level of effectiveness, innovation, and satisfaction. If they succeeded in using them in the fishery, they would be on the path of creating a sustainable fishery. This was an ambitious two days and would ask a lot of them.

I then introduced a set of guidelines to help them get the most out of the training and give the most to it. I asked them to be open-minded; communicate honestly; commit themselves to their personal growth; and fully engage as a member of this learning and growth community. I asked if they were willing to practice these guidelines, and, fortunately, they all agreed. We had embarked on our journey.

SELF-AWARENESS AS A TRANSFORMATIVE LEADER

The architecture of the training would follow the four steps of the empowerment methodology with the goal of empowering the participants as transformative change leaders. This first exercise would help them gain greater self-awareness about their current abilities as a transformative leader. This would build the case for some of the learning ahead and provide input for creating their vision. I asked them to answer these six questions.

1. How committed am I to my personal development as a leader and how does this play out?

2. What are the qualities and skills needed to be a transformative leader?

3. Of these qualities which are my strengths and which do I need to develop further?

4. What obstacles do I need to overcome to implement transformative change in the arenas I wish to influence?

5. What skills and personal qualities do I need to transform these obstacles?

6. What am I willing to do to develop and implement these skills and personal qualities?

They shared their answers with a partner and then the entire group. They were quite forthcoming in sharing the obstacles and their views of one another.

"It's us versus them."

"The government agency managers just want to screw us."

"The scientists are wrong."

"Green groups just want to drive us out of business."

"Foxes are guarding the henhouse."

"Let's sue the ^&#%!"

"Fishermen are all greedy."

The honest communication guideline would not be a problem.

THE ART OF TRANSFORMATION

I explained that while it was not going to be easy to make the changes that were necessary for the fishery's survival, it *was* possible. I reminded them that they had agreed to the guideline of "open-mindedness." I then explained the empowerment model's shift from pathology to vision as a prelude to developing and enacting what I call "social transformation scenarios."

I explained that a transformation scenario requires us to envision a social outcome that does not yet exist. To succeed in this exercise, I said, we must go beyond conventional thinking to tap into our imagination and trust. Our imagination was required because we needed to invent both the future we desired and a way for people to get there. Trust was required in order to take the journey and believe in our fellow human beings' willingness to take it along with us.

Cultivating an attitude of hopefulness and possibility is essential when faced with large challenges, and so I took this moment to share a few quotes that speak to this attitude.

To be truly radical is to make hope possible, not despair convincing.
—Raymond Williams

Hope is not prognostication. It is an orientation of the spirit, an orientation of the heart.
—Vaclav Havel

Hope is believing in spite of the evidence and then watching the evidence change.
—Jim Wallis

I broke the community into four groups of six people, making sure each represented the different viewpoints in the room. I instructed them to create a transformation scenario that would represent a positive breakthrough around an issue related to fisheries. It could be modest or bold, local or regional or national. It needed to include who, what, where, and when. I then offered them an example and apologized for leading the witness.

- *Who*: commercial fishermen, recreational fisherman, government regulators, and environmental organizations

- *What*: creating and adopting a win-win model solution for a fishery

- *Where*: Rhode Island as a model for the country

- *When*: next two years

There was a lot of excitement in the room as each group was coming up with its own transformation scenario, the kind of energy that is released when people are invited to envision the future. Within fifteen minutes, each group had created its transformation scenario. I told them that the next part of the exercise was for each group to develop a five-to ten-minute skit showing how this actually came about. But there was one small twist. They would each enact the transformation scenario of another group. Because they were not overly invested in that scenario, this would free up their imaginations to invent innovative solutions. I told them they could use whatever was available in the room or outside as props, but they only had twenty minutes to prepare so they better get started.

This process completely freed them from their normal roles. Government regulators were playing the role of fishermen. Fishermen were playing the role of environmentalists. Environmentalists were playing the role of government regulators. Recreational fishermen and commercial fishermen were playing each other. People adopted the vocabulary, dress, and even the personality of the role they were playing. A few groups sent around "spies" to casually walk by other groups to see what they were doing and grab an idea or two. Not only were these individuals walking in one another's shoes, they were taking on one another's thinking processes. They were so far out of their comfort zones they could barely recognize themselves, and yet they were having a great time. Kathy had a stunned and bemused smile on her face as she watched all this take place.

Everyone had a great time acting out these transformation scenarios and role-playing one another. There was a lot of laughter, particularly when the personality quirks were incorporated into the role plays. Because people were given permission to step outside of the ways they were normally "allowed" to think by their organizations, and because they knew so much about the issues, they generated a number of plausible and convincing how-to solutions. Each group spontaneously built on the prior groups' solutions. As I observed those watching each scenario unfold, I noticed a degree of wonder in their eyes at the creativity enlivening the room, and the potential pathway for change that was being invented real time. A few rays of hope and possibility had quietly seeped into the space.

I then asked them to distill into a sentence what they observed that had allowed these transformation scenarios to "succeed." They came up with five sentences.

"It was us AND them."

"The goal was the same."

"We came to understand one another and therefore could learn from one another."

"We all participated together in generating the solutions."

"We all benefited when we worked together."

I told them that this process was an accelerated demonstration of how transformation can happen if we change the rules of the game. I then summarized what the new rules ought to include:

1. a compelling and transformative vision of possibility

2. a deadline for implementation of the vision to force action

3. action toward the vision to create solutions

4. enacting solutions to generate learning and evolve the solutions

5. inclusion of the key players to provide the expertise and influence needed for viable solutions

The participants had warmed up to one another and demonstrated a huge willingness to step out of their accustomed mental conditioning. They were also now beginning to wrap their minds around what transformation looked like in practical terms and what might be possible. We were off to a promising start.

TRANSFORMATIVE LEADERSHIP CORE BELIEFS

Our next work would be to examine the four core beliefs that influence an individual's ability to be an effective transformative leader. *A core belief is a fundamental attitude toward life. It is how we view ourselves and the world around us.* Core beliefs are like the operating system in our computer; they program our experience without our noticing. They come to us from our family, life experiences, religion, friends, colleagues, and culture. Once they are accepted by us, usually unconsciously, they manifest as our reality and we can't easily separate the belief about what is from what actually *is*. A core belief can, however, be changed if it is not serving us; it is a *belief* about our reality, not our permanent reality.

Self-Responsibility is the willingness to take personal responsibility to make change happen versus being a victim and blaming others. "How willing are you as a leader to take responsibility to help create the change you desire?"

Self-Esteem is confidence in your ability to be an effective leader of change. "How confident are you in your ability to be an effective change leader?"

Trust is the willingness to be open to others and their possibility for change. I asked: "How open are you to others and their possibility for change?"

Positive Attitude is the ability to look for what *can* work versus what can *not* in the change process. "How much do you look for the positive in the change process versus dwelling on the negative?"

I asked the participants to think about how they viewed themselves in relationship to each of these beliefs. I then explained the limiting belief (LB) and turnaround (TA) process, emphasizing that learning how to turn around a limiting belief would not only be important to them personally, but also when working with others as a leader. To make sure everyone understood, I offered a few examples of typical limiting beliefs for transformative change leaders along with some possible turnarounds. I suggested that if these were not their limiting beliefs they not take them on as my contribution to their leadership.

Self-Responsibility Limiting Beliefs and Turnarounds

LB: The problem is so intractable that my contribution won't make a difference, so why bother?

TA: Real change happens out of the commitment of the few. I am one of the few.

LB: Let someone with more authority or power do it.

TA: If they could have done it, they would have done it. I seize the moment and make change happen.

Self-Esteem Limiting Beliefs and Turnarounds

LB: Who am I to do this?

TA: If not me, who?

LB: The forces maintaining the status quo are much bigger than I am. I can't change them.

TA: The world is a function of our collective thinking. I am committed to changing my thinking and to changing the world, starting with me. Person by person I build a committed team and we make a difference.

Trust Limiting Beliefs and Turnarounds

LB: If I trust other leaders they will let me down and exploit me.

TA: I trust that human beings wish to act with integrity and honor their commitments. I model this in my own behavior and provide opportunities for others to do the same.

LB: I need to control every step along the way for it to work.

TA: I loosen up and allow others to contribute to the change process.

Positive Attitude Limiting Beliefs and Turnarounds

LB: The people in my organization will not change; they are too wedded to their complaints and stance as a victim.

TA: I create a compelling vision that excites them and encourages them to take the first step forward.

LB: If I take on more leadership responsibility, I will have to do it all alone.

TA: I will find colleagues to join with me because they see the possibilities and, like me, are motivated to achieve them.

It was time for those in the room to identify any limiting beliefs they held in each of these four areas and develop turnarounds. We concluded this exercise with everyone sharing one limiting belief and its accompanying turnaround with the group. Plenty of common themes emerged.

LB: "We will never be successful in getting all these different players to agree on anything."

TA: "We will never know until we have given it our best effort. I am willing to use these tools and give it my best effort."

LB: "This issue is doomed to adversarial relations and nothing constructive will be able to be accomplished."

TA: "It is, if I believe it. I change my belief and empower others to do the same."

LB: "My family life, income, and leisure time will suffer if I invest more time in trying to change things. Let someone else do it."

TA: "I will suffer if I don't do it. I go for it!"

LB: "I don't know how to be an effective transformative leader."
TA: "I educate myself and develop the skills I need."

Listening to their fellow leaders' limiting beliefs and turnarounds, and sharing their own, was pivotal in creating what I call an "empowered space," or an environment that creates the safety, trust, and courage needed for deep personal growth to occur. Acknowledging a limiting belief that was real to them and then daring to turn it around required them to peel away the outer veneer they normally show the world. They saw that when they did this, rather than being viewed as weak or somehow "less" by the others in the room, they were viewed as strong because of the courage it took to be vulnerable. When they each shared their struggles as a leader, the group's trust in one another deepened. All this strengthened the sense of safety they felt with the community and enhanced their willingness to participate at a more personal level.

In addition to creating an empowered space, hearing one another's limiting beliefs and turnarounds prompted people to look at themselves and their obstacles in new ways. It was freeing for the participants to see that having a limiting belief was entirely normal and didn't reflect a deficiency of any kind, and that in fact it was only what one *did* with the limiting belief that was important. Witnessing other people's turnarounds was uniformly inspiring, and gave these leaders new ways to think about their own current limiting beliefs and even those they might have in the future. And it helped everyone feel confident that change was actually possible.

With two feet firmly planted on the path, our next step would be to build on the work they had done so far and create compelling visions for themselves as leaders of transformative change. These would serve as the magnets that pulled them forward.

Crafting a Transformative Vision

In order to create a vision that truly inspires us, we need to open up our imaginations to new possibilities and our hearts to what compels us to be leaders. Most of the time our leadership is defined by others and the constraining influences of organizations and society. These definitions do not work when it comes to transformative leadership. The exercise we were about to embark on would require all in the room to free themselves from outside influences long enough to determine what they really wanted so they could chart their own course.

I told them that to be successful at doing this type of visioning they needed to focus on "what" answers, not "how" answers, and reassured them that a large part of this training consisted of teaching "how-to" skills, so they shouldn't worry that they'd be left with a castle in the sky. At the moment they were being asked to tap into their imagination and the deeper impulses that quickened their spirit in order to discover what would motivate them on their path of transformative leadership. Each person's answer would be unique. To get there they must give themselves permission to dream, and answer these seven questions.

1. In my highest vision what are the talents, gifts, qualities of my being and life experiences I wish to bring to my transformative leadership?

2. In my highest vision what are the values I wish to stand for as a transformative leader?

3. In my highest vision what do I most aspire to achieve as a transformative leader?

4. In my highest vision what do I do as a transformative leader to inspire others with a sense of possibility for their future?

5. In my highest vision what do I do as a transformative leader that enables others to succeed in achieving their personal visions?

6. In my highest vision what do I need for my transformative leadership to be personally fulfilling?

7. In my highest vision what will allow me to know I have succeeded as a transformative leader?

To stimulate this type of creativity it's helpful to access the right brain, which thinks in images and symbols. To do this I invited everyone to use pastels and art paper that I would provide. First they would respond to these questions with images and color; then they could flesh out their responses with words. So far I had not led them astray, so everyone grabbed for the pastels and art paper.

The fishermen, accustomed to working in a more intuitive way, immediately took to the process without any reservations. For the more analytical types in the room, there was a moment of pause. Would this work? Was it silly? Could they actually do this? Once a few gave it a try, the others joined in. Ultimately, they got into the drawing even more than the fishermen. It was as if they were now on vacation and it was time to play. Kathy was smiling from ear to ear as she watched the animation in the room.

After about twenty-five minutes, I told them to find a partner and share their visions with each other, and to do this with someone who they did not know very well. Again the intermingling of people with very different world views occurred, this time around their most intimate dreams of who they wished to be as a leader and what they most wished to contribute. After about twenty minutes of one-on-one sharing, I invited everybody to share with the entire group. Bravely people dove in.

"I have the courage to create real change and not accept the status quo."

"I commit myself to my personal development as a leader and helping those I lead do the same."

"I bring about genuine collaboration between people and organizations."

"I develop the next generation of sustainable fishery solutions for Rhode Island that serve as a model for the country."

"I take responsibility to reach out to my colleagues in this room and create a new way of working together based on respect and cooperation."

And on and on, until all twenty-five people had given voice to their visions. They listened to one another with admiration. It was obvious that they were all lifted by the aspiration now pulsating in the room. They had each taken a risk in order to give themselves fully to this process, and it showed. It was now time to help them put foundations underneath their visions.

MANIFESTING A TRANSFORMATIVE VISION IN THE WORLD

Over the past several decades of my transformational change work I have had the privilege of working with several thousand change leaders. Through the coaching of those who have been successful bringing their visions forward in the world and my own experience with large-scale change initiatives, I have discovered three practices that I believe are essential to the process of manifesting this type of vision in the world.

This is a different type of manifestation than creating change in our personal lives, where the only obstacle is ourselves—which is formidable enough. When we attempt to bring a vision of change into the world we have ourselves *and* the many entrenched people, organizations, and social systems attached to the status quo. Such a change must begin with a committed leader and a compelling vision that pulls him or her forward. The leader then needs to know how to cultivate the precious seed of his or her vision. The following three practices speak to this process.

Hold firm to impulse and let the form be flexible. The vision will need to change in different ways as it touches the real world. This is not unlike the way a seed trying to come through the soil needs to change direction to go around rocks and roots. To allow for this natural process, it is important that we not hold too tightly to the current form. Like the seed that follows its DNA-encoded impulse to see the light of day, we must allow ourselves to be guided by the impulse of our vision. The specific form is less important, and if we hold onto it too tightly, the process of manifestation becomes quite challenging, if not impossible. Imagine a seed deciding that the only way it can come into manifestation is to follow a very narrow path no matter what rocks or entangled roots it might encounter.

To hold firm to the impulse while remaining flexible requires that we understand the impulse of our vision and make sure it stays intact. The impulse represents the essence of the vision and, if we have really given ourselves permission to dream, emanates from the deepest place in our soul. Ghandi called this power *satyagraha* or soul force. This is where we get the passion needed to push through the inevitable challenges and resistances we encounter on the path to manifesting our vision in the world.

Holding firmly to the impulse allows the intelligence of the universe to conspire with us to bring it into manifestation. This process resembles the way the seed attracts the nutrients it needs from the soil in order to come into manifestation. The ideas that we use to describe this somewhat mysterious phenomenon in our culture are coincidence, synchronicity, and serendipity. Goethe speaks to this when he says: "Concerning all acts of initiative and creation, there is one elementary truth. The moment one definitely commits oneself, providence moves too. A whole stream of events issues from the decision, raising in one's favor all manner of unforeseen incidents, meetings and material assistance, which no man could have dreamt would have come his way."

I've had several very real experiences of holding firm to the impulse and letting the form be flexible. I shared two of them with the Rhode Island Fishery group.

When I was in my twenties, I was an aspiring marathon runner with a dream of running in the Olympics. I trained very hard for many years and, while achieving a respectable marathon time, fell far short of qualifying for the U.S. Olympic team. Even though I could not imagine how, I still secretly held the desire to participate in the Olympics. In 1980, because of my experience organizing the Bicentennial Torch Relay, I was invited by the Lake Placid Olympic Organizing Committee to organize the Olympic Torch Relay from Olympia, Greece to Lake Placid, New York.

As I pondered this extraordinary turn of events I got a deeper insight into the impulse I was nurturing. It was not really about athletic achievement, which was merely a means to the end I really desired. What I most wanted was to experience personally the unitive power of the Olympic spirit. Now I was the keeper of that Olympic spirit embodied in a flame and participating in the longest of all marathon runs—the Olympic torch relay. I had manifested my dream in a form way beyond anything I could possibly have imagined. It was a larger-than-life teaching to me about this principle.

I had another of these teachings sitting in the United Nations General Assembly Hall at the closing ceremony of the First Earth Run. When I initially envisioned this final event I saw the world's political leaders passing the torch of peace from one to the other in this hall. Although possible, it was hard to conceive how to get all these world leaders in the same building at the same time. But I was unwilling to let go of this idea of the torch, imbued with the intention of creating peace in our world, being passed from leader to leader. This powerful symbolic gesture felt too important to relinquish.

During the closing ceremony as I sat and listened to delegates from all over the world tell stories about how the flame had touched people in their country, I had an "aha" experience.

I realized that the political leaders, through the thousands of citizens of our world and through their support for this global endeavor, *had* passed the torch from one to another. And this did not need to happen within the confines of a U.N. building structure. The actual planet was the larger structure that held them and all of us. The people and leaders all cooperating in passing this torch of peace around the world *united the nations*.

Imagining both of these outcomes manifesting in the form I held them was a huge stretch, but it did give me something concrete to visualize. Beneath the surface of these visualizations was a deep yearning in my soul to experience and help bring into the world that which connects us all and transcends our differences, or what I have come to call a unitive consciousness. When I loosened up on what the form needed to look like and just rode the impulse, the way forward emerged. Being attuned to the natural support available from an intelligent universe has encouraged me to dream bigger and trust more.

Nurture the seed. Creating a vision instilled with our deepest yearning and aspiration is no small thing. Its manifestation will help us realize our unique calling and contribution to our world. To prevent this vision from losing its vitality and atrophying, we need to set up a regular time to nurture it. This means scheduling into our life regular time to ask the "how-to" questions. This can be once a week on Sundays from 3 to 5 PM, a day a month, or an evening or two a week. When we take time to reflect on our vision, questions naturally emerge: "What is my strategy to implement this vision?" "Who should I get to help me?" "How much money do I need?" "What is the best way to communicate the benefits of my vision to get the interest of the key people or organizations I need?" "What kind of management structure do I need?"

As we answer these questions, creating actions plans or proposals for funding, our pathway forward begins to clarify and this enables the "unforeseen incidents, meetings, and material assistance" to come to us. Eventually we have shaped our vision into a form that is ready to take into the world. This is the most demanding moment in the manifestation process as we confront the inherent pushback of those who don't understand what we are doing, think it won't work, don't think we are the right person to lead the effort . . . and the list goes on. How we respond to this barrage of resistance takes our measure as a transformative leader. This is when we need to move into the third practice.

Interpret feedback skillfully. Manifesting a transformative vision is very challenging. There are inevitably so many external barriers, along with our internal resistances, that it's easy to see why many of us give up. To move our vision forward we need to learn how to interpret the feedback we get skillfully. We need to keep asking "what is the growing edge?" and then make course corrections based on the insight we get. I've come up with what I call the 70-20-10 rule to help me in this process.

Seventy percent of the time the vision is not manifesting because of something we are doing or not doing. Two questions we can ask are: "Are we paying enough attention to the signals we are getting?" and "Are we actively soliciting and learning from the feedback?" Perhaps to increase people's confidence that our proposed change can indeed happen we need to bring in someone with more credibility to help us. Or maybe we need to sharpen the economic and social case of our proposal so it makes more sense to a financial supporter. Perhaps we need to present our ideas more coherently and dress up our presentation so it is more professional. Maybe we need to pull back a little. Perhaps we need more experience. When I first tried to organize the First Earth Run, I needed more experience before large institutions were willing to consider such a visionary idea.

Twenty percent of the time we need to work through a particular person or institution that has critical knowledge, credibility, or influence. To get the political buy-in needed to further emergency preparedness in New York City, I had to work with the Office of Emergency Management and modify the vision to meet their institutional needs. Similarly for the First Earth Run, in order to get the support of world leaders, I had to work with the United Nations and modify the vision to meet their institutional needs. (The initiative needed to further the goals of the United Nations International Year of Peace and the celebration of UNICEF's fortieth anniversary.) These adjustments were not hard to make, but without them these visions would either not have manifested or fallen far short of their potential.

Ten percent of the time it is about right timing. "To everything there is a season," goes the famous line from Ecclesiastes, and I have found it to be true that the rhythms of nature are eloquently instructive when we ponder issues of timing. The First Earth Run was conceived ten years before the world was ready for a global consciousness-raising event around the issue of peace and unity. I did not know that at the time, but based on feedback I soon realized that I needed to back off and gently let the idea incubate.

If you are working on a vision ahead of its time, you will discover this by the big gap between it and people's readiness for it. That doesn't mean you have to give up, but rather perfect your idea by building your prototype and accumulating more experience. Then when the time is right, you will be as ready as possible. With the Olympic Torch Relay credibility and leadership experience under my belt, when the time was right it was much easier to get UNICEF to partner with me on the First Earth Run.

CREATING A TRANSFORMATIVE LEADERSHIP GROWING EDGE

We were approaching the end of the afternoon's work at the W. Alton Jones retreat center. The energy in the room was still high even though it was late in the day. After reviewing the idea of a growing edge and how to craft it into an intention statement and image, I explained that we had one more critical piece of business to complete before breaking for dinner. Each person would come up with a statement of his or her growing edge. I offered four questions to assist them in the process of doing so.

1. Where are you now in terms of manifesting your transformative leadership vision?

2. What, if anything, do you need to change to manifest it and how will you implement this change? If the change required is because of your internal resistances, write down your limiting beliefs and do turnarounds.

3. What is your growing edge? Create it as an intention statement and a visual image.

4. Ask yourself if you believe it's possible. Adjust your intention statement as needed to get on the growing edge.

After about fifteen minutes, the participants had all prepared their growing edges. I then asked for several volunteers to share their growing edges and get help from me in tuning them up. This would help assure that they had found the right edge, with all the concomitant energy that releases; that they had articulated their intention statement crisply and powerfully; that their image was compelling so they were emotionally engaged; and finally that they felt a sense of ownership, so that the statement was more than just words on a piece of paper. Those willing to come in front of the room would also be making a contribution to the community. Through modeling this process others could observe how to work their own growing edge better, and would likely get vicarious learning because so many leadership issues are similar.

I was hoping that by now there was enough safety and trust in the room for a few brave people to be willing to go to this next level of self-disclosure. There usually are and this group was no exception. One example stands out.

The leader of a professional fishermen's association was struggling with the issue of time. He did not have enough of it to invest in helping change his organization, negotiate all the complex issues around fishery management, and be with his family—all on top of a very physically demanding full-time job as a fisherman.

His intention statement was: "I balance all the demands in my life." I asked how he felt when he said this. His respond was, "I'm kidding myself. There is no way this is going to happen." I then began asking questions to help him discover what he believed was possible and could get behind. Finding your growing edge means walking a fine line. You don't want to go *over* the edge, where you feel like throwing your hands up in the air, or *behind* the edge, where there's no energy or excitement to realize this vision. We kept peeling the layers until we got to something that hit a nerve. When I finally asked this rugged fisherman why he had taken on this leadership position with all the other demands in his life, he became quite emotional.

He said: "I really care about my struggling buddies who I fish with and I'm worried that they will be forced to go out of business because all of us in this room can't get our act together. I have another way I can make an income if this fishery goes belly up, but they have been doing this their entire life and have no place to turn, with families to feed. Our association does not have a lot of money to pay for lawyers. If I don't make this happen, we will likely get the short end of the stick and I will let them down. That is not acceptable to me."

We had finally gotten to the heart of the matter for him as a leader. After a little more work together, he came up with a new statement representing his growing edge: "I'm in too deep to turn back now. I commit myself to finding ways to work together better with those in this room so we can all meet our needs." His visual image was of everyone in the room on a fishing vessel far out at sea in stormy waters. The only way they were going to be able to navigate the ship safely back into the harbor was by all working together as a crew.

To complete this process, I asked this dedicated leader to choose one individual to share his intention statement and image with in order to help him ground and own it. He invited up one of the leaders of the state environmental agency that regulates the fishery. Earlier in the day they had enacted the transformation scenario together, role-playing each other quite humorously. Prior to this training, the two of them had barely spoken to each other. Now they looked each other in the eye and the fisherman shared his intention statement. It was a powerful moment of connection. The person from the state environmental agency gave him two thumbs-up and a big hug. I then asked the fisherman to look around the room and experience the group's support for his growing edge. The others, moved by his vulnerability, honesty, courage, and emotional investment in this issue, started clapping. The commitment level of this group had just gone up two notches.

It was time for dinner. The dining room overlooked a pond with a big apple tree abundant with pink blossoms. We were also treated to a beautiful sunset and a scrumptious fish meal complete with clam chowder and shrimp salad, of course. I kept a low profile about being a vegetarian and spent most of the meal eavesdropping on conversations that only eight hours earlier would have been unimaginable. After dinner in our final session of the day, we would begin wading into areas of great contention as we explored the practice of win-win negotiation. But for now these former adversaries were enjoying the well-deserved fruits of their labors.

WIN-WIN NEGOTIATION

When we reconvened, I told them that now that they were all chums, it was time to learn how to have conversations that could help them work together better as a crew and bring their ship safely to harbor. To achieve this type of outcome requires an ability to create *mutually satisfying*—or win-win—solutions. These require more imagination than compromise solutions, in which both parties are generally dissatisfied and often subtly undermine the agreement. And of course win-lose negotiations do nothing but put off the conflict for another day.

A good way to make the shift from win-lose to win-win thinking is to imagine sitting next to the person you are negotiating with on the same side of a table and placing the problematic issue on the other side. This helps begin the shift from competing with each other to using your joint creativity to find a solution.

I explained that we were going to do an exercise to practice this approach and asked them to pair up with someone who before this leadership training they might have labeled the "other." I gave each of these pairs a blank piece of paper. I then told them to imbue this piece of paper with a real outcome they desired for a fishery issue. Each person should stand up and face the other holding on to two corners of the paper, the paper forming a sort of bridge between the two people. At the end of the negotiation only one person could have the piece of paper. If it was destroyed, no one got to have it. They would have up to ten minutes to create a win-win solution. If after that time they had not come up with a solution, neither would get to have the paper, nor achieve their desired outcome. The exercise created a situation not dissimilar to the challenge they faced in the fishery. They had a limited amount of time to come to a mutually satisfactory solution or risk the collapse of the fishery and related businesses. When they were done they needed to answer two questions. What did you each learn? If you were to do this exercise over, what, if anything, would you do differently?"

The room was bristling with energy as they all came up with their best strategies for negotiation tempered by the fact that unless the other person also felt good, they would not succeed. This required a new way of thinking and relating to one another. Because they only had ten minutes, they literally were being asked to think on their feet, or fail.

There were eleven groups of two and one of three (with Kathy as the third). Of the twelve groups, only one did not reach a win-win solution.

This was another moment of truth for these emerging transformative leaders. They experienced what seemed like a fixed reality lend itself to time-bound creative solutions. It required a great leap of faith for people to trust that if they sacrificed today, they would ultimately benefit from it tomorrow. When they did so, more rays of hope and possibility entered the room, this time complemented in the late hour by the twinkling stars.

Day two would ask everyone to develop transformative strategies that could change the game around the issues that, prior to today had seemed intractable at worst and highly polarizing at best. At this moment however, it was time for bed.

Designing a Transformative Change Strategy

The next morning people arrived ready to work. A wonderful spirit of camaraderie filled the room; jokes and laugher abounded. I invited people to share how they were doing in an open forum before we launched into the day, and the general consensus was that people were feeling empowered by this process as leaders, but anxious about being able to transform their relationships with each other and create a viable win-win strategy for the fishery.

I told them they had just nailed the community's growing edge. Today's work would be the development of strategies that could get at that growing edge from different angles. I told them how inspired I was by the work they had done the day before and how it gave me hope for our planet. I acknowledged that what they were doing was bigger than the group in this room and the Rhode Island fishery, and that they were pioneers for fisheries across the country and around the world. With Kathy's network through the Sea Grant Program, it would be quite possible to disseminate their learning widely. Furthermore, there were many other environmental issues facing this same "tragedy of the commons" phenomenon, in which the pursuit of self-interests depletes a resource which then fails so that everyone suffers. These groups could also benefit if the individuals in this room were successful in creating a viable solution for a sustainable fishery.

But this could not happen with business-as-usual approaches to change, or it would have happened already. The type of change needed was transformational, and the tools they had learned and leadership development they had done the previous day comprised the first step on this path. Today they would take the second step: creating transformative change strategies. We could not have a more opportune moment for doing this with the whole system in the room right now, primed and ready. I encouraged them to seize this moment of energy and goodwill and I then walked them through the four principles for creating a transformative change strategy.

Create a positive vision of possibility. The classic approach in creating change strategies is to focus on getting rid of what we don't want. This approach negates the negative with an anti this or anti that orientation. It is painful to stay in this negative emotional state, and so eventually people either burn out or leave, out of self-protection. To be transformative we need to develop change strategies that are positive and inspiring, and that can attract people because they generate excitement, hope, and possibility.

Empower individuals to grow through participation in the transformative change strategy. For individuals to participate voluntarily in a social change strategy it needs to engage them personally. A positive vision is the first step in that it creates the pull. But meaningful opportunities to learn and grow must be provided to engage people fully in social change. This provides the extra motivation for them to invest their time over the long haul. If we want people to invest in social transformation, we need to invest in their personal growth.

Implement the transformative change strategy through social diffusion. Social science research tell us that the most effective way to further social change is to identify those receptive to this change, known as "early adopters," and help them to spread it. This is exactly 180 degrees away from the manner in which many social change strategies are designed. Their mantra is "don't preach to the choir," but rather go after the least receptive people. Unfortunately, this unreceptive population usually throws cold water on the social innovation, strengthening resistance to its further dissemination. The most successful diffusion of social change begins by preaching to the choir so they sing loud enough to attract people into the church, temple, or mosque. It then spreads outward from there.

Create a support system for individuals participating in the transformative change initiative. Individuals venturing forth to implement transformative change require support to be successful. Their enthusiasm gets diminished as they face those who oppose the change or are entrenched in habitual thinking and behavior patterns. Without a support system, it is hard to persevere against this resistance. But if we provide a support system of like-minded people who are also participating in the transformative change initiative, they can inspire and help one another to sustain their commitment. Support can include regularly scheduled peer-to-peer coaching, support groups, and online help for specific issues.

The next task was to create their own transformative change strategy. I walked them through five steps that would help them to do so, and I gave them thirty minutes to create it and an hour to partner with someone to give and get feedback.

TRANSFORMATIVE CHANGE STRATEGY EXERCISE

1. Create a positive vision of the transformative change you wish at the personal, organizational, and system levels.

2. Describe the new beliefs and behaviors that need to be adopted at each of these levels for your vision to manifest.

3. Describe the limiting beliefs inhibiting transformation at each of these levels and come up with possible turnarounds.

4. Describe what you will do specifically to bring about the adoption of these new beliefs and behaviors.

5. What is your next growing edge in implementing your transformative change strategy? Write it as an intention statement and create a visual image.

It was a sunny day and they all went outside to think and talk with their colleagues. Most of the pairs ended up in the comfortable Adirondack chairs surrounding the pond. I went outside to listen in on their conversations, and soon found myself acting like a bee, cross-pollinating one group's strategy with the next. This had not been planned and was able to occur only because all of the individuals were working to create complementary strategies for achieving the same collective vision of a sustainable fishery. This was a vision that everyone accepted intellectually, but, because of the bruises they had from bumping into one another so many times and the lack of any transformational practices, had been struggling to achieve. Now with more camaraderie and know-how, they were fitting together the important pieces of this difficult jigsaw puzzle.

As I told one pair about what another was doing, the workshop spontaneously morphed into small groups of four to eight people pulling their chairs around into tight circles to discuss and blend their transformative change strategies. Three viable strategies emerged out of these conversations.

The first strategy group focused on the transformation of the fishermen's associations from organizations where members sat around complaining about being victims, to gatherings of individuals who would take personal responsibility to develop win-win solutions in their working with other associations and government regulators. Each member of the association would be accountable for implementing a distinct part of the strategy so no one person was left holding the bag and burning out. To help their members grow into this, these leaders would provide a mini transformative leadership workshop to teach the basic principles and tools.

The second strategy group focused on the transformation of the Rhode Island Marine Fisheries Council, which consisted of fishermen, government regulators and environmental groups. Many of the people in this training were members of the council. Their vision was to transform it from a place of contentious relationships and bureaucratic procedures to one that worked with the principle of creating win-win solutions. To do this, these leaders would set up sessions away from the formal council meetings to teach current and new members transformative leadership practices. They would also use this time for the exchange of best practices so they could continue to grow and benefit from one another's experiences.

The third strategy group was interested in designing a sustainable fishery solution that would be able to get everyone's acceptance. They would do this by integrating the transformational tools they had learned with sustainable fishery best practices from around the world. They would regularly share their thinking with leaders in the larger group to get feedback on both the content of these best-practice models and the transformational tools they would use to help create the win-win solutions.

A great deal of very substantial work had been done and when we broke for lunch there was a palpable sense of accomplishment in the group. After lunch we would descend from this mountain top into the deepest part of the transformational journey. Those present would be asked to confront the fears, which, if transformed, could enable their desired changes to come into being, and, if left untended, could undermine them.

THE HERO'S JOURNEY

Joseph Campbell, the noted and late mythologist, calls the journey of all great quests to accomplish something of value and long-standing worth in our lives and the world the "hero's journey." (For a full discussion of the hero's journey I recommend Campbell's excellent book *The Hero With a Thousand Faces.*) George Lucas consulted with Joseph Campbell and built this archetypal hero's journey mythology into his *Star Wars* trilogy. Lucas's skillful integration of the archetypal-journey elements into his saga is one of the reasons that these movies are credited with having such a deep resonance for people. The leaders in this sun-filled meeting room in New England would now be asked to undertake the equivalent of Luke Skywalker's Jedi Knight training in the dark cave.

Campbell states that the hero's journey has six stages, or initiations. This training had moved them through the first three so far.

1. *The call*—Kathy's summons to which they responded.

2. *The awakening*—the change in their world views and the new skills they have acquired as transformative leaders.

3. *The journey*—their transformative leadership vision and the strategy they have created and committed to bringing into manifestation.

Now they were ready for the final three stages.

4. *The descent*—their willingness to face and transform the fears, which, if not addressed, would disable this vision and strategy from being brought into manifestation.

5. *The epiphany*—the insight they get from understanding their innermost, and often unconscious, fears.

6. *The ascent*—the hard-won self-knowledge and self-respect they will have acquired from transforming these fears and being able to sustain their commitment to the hero's journey.

They would repeat these six stages each time they accepted their next major challenge as transformative leaders. This was the journey on which they were now embarked as leaders.

THE DEEP DIVE: FEAR TRANSFORMATION

To succeed in the descent is one of the most challenging parts of the hero's journey because it requires the courage to face self. For some, this is more demanding than confronting the challenges of the world. It takes *inner* courage, which is harder to come by for leaders because it requires a commitment to ongoing self-development.

To prepare everybody for their own deep dive, I provided them with a personal example from the First Earth Run. In the early stages of that adventure I was constantly experiencing resistance. Many people believed such an undertaking was not possible, a response that was certainly to be expected. But I also experienced personal rejection and was repeatedly called naïve. The latter was hurtful to my pride and even more so to my spirit. My deepest fear had been putting my dream before the world and being rejected and called naïve. I knew I had to transform this fear or risk a slow erosion of my energy for moving this initiative forward.

My original intention statement was, "I accept feedback with an open stance, and listen." My image was palms open to receive. My limiting belief was, "No way. If they put down this vision or me I will get defensive, and, in defense, become adversarial and call them cynical. I don't have the temperament to accept criticism passively." My turnaround and new intention statement was, "I trust in my vision and the impulse propelling it into the world. I actively solicit feedback so I can improve this endeavor and have compassion for those not open to new possibilities."

This process of stepping toward my fear and transforming it not only helped me sustain my commitment to this venture, but also improve it as I applied people's constructive feedback.

I then read them a poem that never fails to impress me with its wisdom.

Risk

To laugh is to risk appearing the fool.
To weep is to risk being called sentimental.
To reach out to another is to risk involvement.
To expose feelings is to risk showing your true self.
To place your ideas before the crowd is to risk being called naïve.
To love is to risk not being loved in return.
To live is to risk dying.
To hope is to risk despair.
To try is to risk failure.
But risks must be taken, because the greatest risk in life
is to risk nothing.
The people who risk nothing, do nothing, have nothing, are nothing and become nothing.
They may avoid suffering and sorrow, but they simply cannot learn to feel, and change, and grow, and love and live...
Chained by their servitude, they are slaves;
they've forfeited their freedom.
Only the people who risk are truly free.

Author Unknown

I encouraged these change-agents-in-training to be "truly free" by having the courage to discover and transform their innermost fears. These might include the fear of rejection, loss of economic security, not feeling competent or capable, failure, or being gobbled up by work so that their personal lives suffered. Once they had identified their core fear they were to draw a picture and write down words about how the fear made them feel. Then they were to ask themselves what the fear had to teach them and why they had created it in their life. And finally they were to learn the lesson this fear had to teach them and let it go.

Now that they knew what it was they didn't want, what was it that they *did* want? It was then time to create a vision of how they wished it to be. I asked everyone to draw a picture of this vision and to write down the words that described how it made them feel. Once they had their picture and words they were to translate this vision into an intention statement and an image that represented their next growing edge, transforming any limiting beliefs and adjusting the intention statement accordingly.

The process asked them to go to a deep level of self-discovery. It was by far the most personal work they had done in the workshop. By now they had trust in me, the transformational processes, and one another, and were willing without reservation to do this final deep dive. We had built an empowered space and they were taking full advantage of it. As a result, they came out the other side of this self-discovery process with some very important insights and a transformation strategy.

The group's next task was to share their fear and growing edge intention statements, and then synthesize these into the dominant fears and the strategies used to transform them. This allowed everyone to take comfort in the knowledge that their fears were not isolated and to benefit from the collective thinking on how to transform them.

Five dominant fears, and concomitant transformational strategies, emerged.

Fear: I will burn out from this work.
Transformation Strategy: I help my organization create a positive vision of change and trust that they will want to make it happen.

Fear: I will go out of business and not be able to feed my family.
Transformation Strategy: I help make our fishery sustainable so I can stay in business.

Fear: I will not persevere to bring about the needed changes, and give up.
Transformation Strategy: I turn to my colleagues in this room for inspiration and support to stay on my path.

Fear: I will give up my dream of being a self-employed fisherman, and sell out.
Transformation Strategy: I follow my vision wherever it takes me and trust this journey will lead me in the right direction.

Fear: I will be rejected by the members of my organization if I say we are working with these other groups.
Transformation Strategy: That is the risk I am willing to take to bring about my vision and create the transformation needed to create a sustainable fishery and sustainable livelihoods.

THE END OF ONE JOURNEY... AND THE BEGINNING OF THE NEXT

It was now time to bring this journey to an end. I asked everyone to choose a buddy and commit to a once-a-month check-in over the next three months to support one another with their leadership growing edges. Getting support for these growing edges during this embryonic period of time was essential to securing the growth they had accomplished during the workshop. I also asked them to set up formal support groups for the three strategy groups and agree on regular times to meet and discuss the implementation of their transformative strategies.

Before closing the workshop everyone shared their major learning and the commitment they were willing to make going forward. While these statements were deeply personal to the individuals, the themes are universal. Here are a few:

"Problems can be clarified and roadblocks are not permanent.
We can change the world. I commit to staying on the front line
and helping to create a sustainable fishery."

"I learned the importance of staying open-minded. I commit myself
to walking my path as a transformative change leader."

"Being a leader doesn't have to lead to burnout. I commit myself to transforming my organization and helping it create a positive vision."

"I have a better understanding of this community and it is trustworthy. I am committed to working with these new tools and this community."

"It is easier to stay focused and listen to everyone's opinion than to fight. I commit myself to finding and creating win-win solutions."

"We don't need to be enemies. I commit myself to being a meaningful part of the solution."

The twenty-five participants left confident that they had the tools to help forge a more cooperative relationship among all the constituents of the Rhode Island fishery. They had seen one another with new eyes, and had faith that everyone in the room was a person who could be trusted to act with integrity and who wanted the best for the fisheries. And they had each experienced some sort of personal transformation. But could all the goodwill and good intentions produce the desired results? Two and a half years later Kathy gave me an update.

There has been so much positive activity that has come out of the training I don't know where to begin describing the effect it has had on these guys and me. They're so empowered it's crazy. This training has changed many of their lives and the whole way everyone now interacts with one another on this issue. They now have a vision rather than pathology orientation and can identify and transform their limiting beliefs.

Lobstermen have joined forces with the environmental groups and are now addressing the issue of pesticides in the ocean. There are now roundtables set up in the format of the workshop for exchange of best practices and the strengthening of our community. And we are making great strides in creating a unifying vision. The Commercial Fisheries Research Foundation was created out of the work we did at the training. Its purpose is to encourage the use of collaborative research and foster cooperation among all the organizations associated with Rhode Island's fisheries. They recently got a 1.3-million dollar grant from the Southern New England Cooperative Research

Institute. With it they hired as executive director one of the leaders in our training who is using the practices he learned.

All of this has led to the Rhode Island fishery becoming a role model throughout the country. As for me, I have been invited and funded by the Sand County Foundation to take this knowledge of how to empower fishery stakeholder groups toward a sustainable fishery to Europe and Africa.

Chris Brown, president of the Commercial Fishermen's Association and a major opinion leader in this community, was equally clear about the positive developments in the Rhode Island fishery and fishing community.

After the training I needed to look in the mirror at myself and our Commercial Fishermen's Association. We lacked finesse, were too confrontational, and had not known how to change any of this. We had fished down our fishery to the point where we were almost out of business and had nearly destroyed this hallowed ground. This was an honest moment for me and it hurt.

With that insight I set out to create change, working with the tools I learned in the training of leading from vision, vulnerability, win-win solutions and working with the early adopters who were ready to change. I invited myself to the recreational fishermen's association and honestly told them what we had done to the fishery. I learned that if you wish to disarm someone, drag yourself through the coals. They are now my fast friends. The same has happened with the other fishermen associations and among our Rhode Island Marine Fisheries Council members. Our battles are now not with each other but with the challenges of designing strategies to help our fishery be sustainable.

We have created major transformations. We have moved from fishermen being forced by government regulation to change to being proactive as stewards of the fishery. We have shifted from hunting the ocean to cultivating it. The only way your quota goes up is if the resource goes up. It gives you so much it is grossly irresponsible to do anything but help it succeed. We have stepped back from near total failure to unimaginable success at every level. We are now actually viewed, trusted, and appreciated by the politicians as conservationists and sought out by groups from other parts of the country! We have gone from almost complete collapse of our industry and livelihoods to making a difference for the Atlantic Ocean. How many people can say they have had a positive impact on the Atlantic Ocean?

To change the game requires a social system primed for transformation and willing leaders. And willingness is relative. The story of the Rhode Island fishery shows that placed in a certain environment and guided through a transformational experience, this willingness can be significantly increased. My experience working with many leaders, and certainly reinforced by the experience described in this chapter, is that the vast majority are willing to embrace this type of change if skillfully guided through it. That is not to say game-changing transformation is easy just because leaders are empowered with a vision and have transformational tools to help implement it. But without these, well-intentioned individuals trying to create transformational change are apt to feel like Sisyphus, condemned perennially to push the boulder up the hill only to have it roll back down again. The good news is that we can choose another option. I invite you to experiment with these tools. (See Figure 6.1, page 196.) Practice makes perfect.

The next chapter addresses another essential component of the Social Change 2.0 framework—the process by which we develop social innovations, not unlike those described in this and previous chapters, which are capable of changing the game.

Figure 6.1—Summary of Transformational Tools

TRANSFORMATIONAL TOOL	PURPOSE	DESCRIPTION/PAGE IN CHAPTER
Empowering the Space	Creates environment of safety, trust, and courage needed for deep personal growth to occur.	Workshop seating, page 167 Guidelines, page 165 Limiting belief group process, pages 171–174 Growing edge facilitation, pages 181–183 Open forum, pages 184–185 Exercise sequence to build trust in the growth process, entire chapter
Transformative Leadership Self-Awareness	Provides insight into transformative leadership development needs.	Pages 167–168
Social Transformation Scenario Building	Provides experience of possibility and means for social transformation.	Pages 168–171
Transformative Leadership Core Beliefs	Helps leader identify core beliefs as a change agent and transform those undermining effectiveness. Creates new social norm for leadership vulnerability from weakness to strength.	Pages 171–174
Transformative Leadership Vision	Helps leader develop a compelling personal vision as a change agent.	Pages 174–176
Manifesting a Transformative Vision	Enables successful implementation of leadership vision.	Pages 176–181
Creating a Transformative Leadership Growing Edge	Helps leader successfully identify growing edge and create intention statement and visual image.	Page 181
Growing Edge Facilitation	Tunes up growing edge, deepens ownership, provides modeling of an effective intention statement and vicarious learning for group.	Pages 181–183
Win-Win Negotiation	Enables joint creativity to develop a sustainable solution.	Pages 183–184
Designing a Transformative Change Strategy	Provides the principles and process for developing a transformative change strategy.	Pages 184–188
The Deep Dive: Fear Transformation (Hero's Journey)	Creates universal context and helps leader transform fears undermining implementation of change strategy.	Pages 188–192
Support System	Provides support to sustain leader's growth.	Page 192
Learning and Growth Synthesis	Enables insight into personal learning, anchors long-term commitment, and demonstrates the efficacy of overall transformational experience.	Pages 192–193

CHAPTER 6: SOCIAL CHANGE 2.0 PRACTITIONER'S GUIDE

1. What transformative leadership skills do you need to further your social change initiative?

2. Of these, which are your strengths and which do you need to develop further?

3. What is your transformative change strategy?

4. What obstacles must you overcome to implement your strategy and how will you overcome them?

5. What is your next growing edge as a transformative change leader? State as an intention and visual image.

IMPROVING THE PERFORMANCE CAPACITY OF SOCIETY: DESIGNING AND IMPLEMENTING A TRANSFORMATIVE SOCIAL INNOVATION

To take a sport analogy, some people may choose to change the disposition of players on the pitch or to redesign the playing field, but a few rare individuals work to change the rules of the game—or even the game itself. There is a bit of the game changer in most social entrepreneurs.
—John Elkington and Pamela Hartigan,
*The Power of Unreasonable People:
How Social Entrepreneurs Create Markets That
Change the World*

One key test of a social entrepreneur is they are totally on top of "how to" questions. The idealist by contrast will tell you what Xanadu is going to look like. Pleasure domes, etc.—but they can't tell you how the sewage is going to work in Xanadu once you get there and they certainly can't tell you how you will get there.
—Bill Drayton, Founder and CEO of Ashoka

When I examine myself and my methods of thought . . . the gift of imagination has meant more to me than my talent for absorbing absolute knowledge. Knowledge is limited. Imagination encircles the world.
—Albert Einstein

We have a lot of agreement about what our world should look like and the basic changes we need to make in order to move us in the envisioned direction. Those who doubt this just need to look at the countless hefty documents produced annually by the United Nations and nonprofits around the world. The severe stress on our ecological and social systems has also created an unprecedented readiness for these ideas to be accepted by society. The rub comes when these ideas bump up against the entrenched patterns of thought and practice in our current social systems.

Our great challenge as a species is to improve the performance capacity of these social systems before they collapse. This will require nothing less than social innovations capable of changing the game in multiple systems and the requisite transformational skills to accomplish this task. I call these transformative social innovations. The last chapter looked at the suite of transformational skills we will need; this one looks at the process of inventing, constructing, and implementing this type of social innovation.

Creating and manifesting a transformative social innovation bridges art, science, and craft. It requires the aesthetic sensibility of the artisan to be open to inspiration, the precise knowledge of the architect to design it, and the business acumen of the entrepreneur to bring it into the world. While each transformative social innovation has its own unique characteristics, they all involve these three phases: *social creativity*—conceiving of the social transformation idea; *social architecture*—designing the social transformation program, vehicle or platform; and *social entrepreneurship*—financing, managing, and marketing the social innovation.

THE PRACTICE OF CULTIVATING SOCIAL CREATIVITY

Whenever I lead a visioning exercise in a community or a transformative leadership training, I am amazed by people's social inventiveness. All I do is give people permission to vision, ask questions that stimulate their imagination, and create the safe and structured environment to help them bring these visions into form. They take over from there and run with it. This has taught me that the social creativity needed to invent the world anew is widely available to us.

In the transformative leadership training with the fishermen this process started with the participants being asked a series of questions that invited them to envision the change they would like to see *without being responsible for how it would come about.* This gave them the freedom to open up their imaginations. They couldn't possibly envision these possibilities if they had to deal with how to implement them at the same time. Thinking about implementation would come later, after the idea had been conceived.

Writing down their vision was the first step in owning it. They then shared their vision with someone in the group, which required them to explain it, taking them one step further down the ownership path. Taking them yet further, they were requested to share their vision in the larger community. Hearing the visions of their peers gave everyone the courage to own their own at a deeper level still, and helped establish having a vision as a new social norm in the community.

We were now ready to begin work on the how-to stage. I asked each person to follow a four-step process of creating a statement of intention and image that articulated their next growing edge. Those willing to come in front of the room and work with me modeled what it looks like to get a vision precisely on the growing edge and develop ownership in its realization. The rest of the workshop provided the personal growth and competencies in the core areas needed to implement their vision in the world successfully. By the end of this journey they were empowered with a vision for transformative change, an action plan, a support system, and motivation to carry it out.

In situations where there are similar visions, the process can go one step further if the dots between complementary ideas are connected. This enhances each person's vision and furthers the possibility for manifestation. This is what I did when I connected the various transformative strategies of the fishermen and divided them into three different working groups.

The fishermen story shows that the social creativity needed for transforming a social system is in plentiful supply and can be significantly accelerated. It also shows that the onus for transformative change is as much on those who view themselves as change leaders to create the transformational architecture, as it is on the people in the social system to come up with the ideas. Since this transformational architecture can be easily replicated and the facilitation and coaching skills easily transferred, far more possibilities exist than we have heretofore realized for releasing greater social creativity within a social system.

Another dimension of social creativity, one level up, is stimulating the imagination of change leaders in their role as social architects of the structures for transformation. In my case, this would be the transformative leadership training program I described in the last chapter and the other social innovations in Part One. I stimulate my social creativity by reading books on history, business, and philosophy in search of design principles, methodologies, strategies, and philosophies used to bring about change. Some I can use in their own right, others I need to combine with another change strategy. And some open up a whole new pattern language for thinking about social change. In the course of my research I have come across three transformative social innovations that have had a major influence on my thinking as a social architect.

Ever since I was an Olympic hopeful in my early twenties I have been inspired by the transformative social innovation of the ancient Olympic Games. The Games were created in 776 BC to transform the aggressive energy of young men from war making to athletic competition. The creators did not stop there. They required that all Greek city-states that wished to participate end hostilities for the duration of the competition. They called this truce an *ekecheiria*. The *ekecheiria* allowed time for the heated tempers of politicians and armies to cool down and gave political leaders the breathing room to invent more creative solutions for resolving their differences. In more than a few cases, hostilities that ceased during the games did not continue afterward.

How amazing to create a social innovation that could transform warrior energy into athletic energy. *Someone literally created a better game than war.* What social entrepreneur came up with this idea? How was it sold to the political leadership throughout Greece? What resistance did it meet and how was this transformed? What motivated city-states to honor this agreement? What can we learn from this social innovation about changing the game?

Twenty-eight hundred years later this social innovation is still alive and well, except, instead of bringing Greek city-states together, it now brings the entire world together. For two weeks every two years, for the summer or winter games, the world is reminded of what we have in common rather than what separates us. For a brief window of time, this picture of our planet at its best is broadcast into homes in virtually every country in the world. We celebrate this ideal of unity in the Olympic torch relay, opening and closing ceremonies, and even some of the commercials. My wife, Gail, always has her handkerchief on hand for me when we watch the Games together, as she has seen me moved to tears time and time again.

The Olympics have taught me many important lessons about what contributes to the power and longevity of a social innovation. They evoke an ideal for what we human beings look like when we put forward our best effort. They evoke an ideal of what our world looks like at its best. They are a teaching about setting a noble intention and inviting people and institutions to aspire toward it.

We can expand our thinking about the lessons of the Olympics further still by considering George Bernard Shaw's "why not" questions. If we can create a more peaceful planet for two weeks, why not create it for a longer time? If we can compete with those who are different from us, why not cooperate with them as well? If we can motivate people and political leaders by appealing to their pride in their country, why not motivate them by appealing to pride in their planet? If we can inspire and uplift billions of television viewers by this unitive vision of possibility, why not take this further and engage people directly to help create it? These "why not" questions directly informed my vision for the First Earth Run social innovation and have influenced every innovation I have designed since.

My social creativity has also been stimulated by Chinese sage Lao Tzu's and his 2,500 year-old classic the *Tao Te Ching*. It is a small treasure trove of wisdom on how to apply the laws of nature to societal change and leadership. It is a pattern language in its own right. R.L. Wing, a distinguished translator of and commentator on the *Tao Te Ching*, says Lao Tzu "was perhaps the world's first theoretical physicist. He devoted all of his intellectual energy to observing nature and its physical laws and to noting the interdependent relationship of all things. He saw a unified field of forces he called the *Tao*."

Wing continues, "Lao Tzu believed that the constant awareness of the patterns of nature will bring us insights into the parallel patterns in human behavior. Just as spring follows winter in nature, growth follows repression in society; just as too much gravity will collapse a star, too much possessiveness will collapse an idea. Our ideas become astute when they are based on this dynamic evolving reality, not wishful thinking. This allows us to be in harmony with the deeper trends in the evolution of society."

Understanding this counterbalance of forces in nature was the core insight that emboldened my confidence in believing the First Earth Run was possible back in 1983. It also helped me build my case to others about why the timing was right for such a seemingly improbable event to occur. The world was contracted and had a great need to expand. It was *ready* to move from separation and fear to cooperation and hope. I had to do my part to establish that the social innovation was indeed doable and that I had the necessary experience to lead it, but once that was accomplished, I got pulled into the powerful vacuum in the global psyche that was just waiting for something like this.

Ever since that experience I have used the design principle of contraction leading to expansion in all of my social innovations. I discern where the contraction is around a social issue, then look for what will enable the expansion and design an appropriate change platform to bring it about. I will talk more about this principle later in the chapter when describing the social system conditions necessary for a transformative social innovation to take root.

The *Tao Te Ching* also provides me a blueprint for how to observe the laws of nature and the evolution of the universe in search of relevant design principles. Observing how a plant grows in nature pointed me to the growing edge, which is foundational to my work with personal, organizational, and societal growth. Observing how a spider plant can easily replicate by cloning itself multiple times was a model we used in designing the EcoTeam replication process. Learning how ants accomplish complex social tasks through local interactions among worker ants rather than guidance by a centralized leadership source was a design principle in creating the distributed social learning model of the master class.

I replicated the evolutionary design principle of independent single-cell organisms evolving into multicellular organisms in order to carry out more complex tasks with the EcoTeam system. Individuals on their own may struggle to perform the complex task of greening their lifestyles, but when they join an EcoTeam, the exchange of information and the support system help them succeed. I have also worked with this principle in helping cities—Philadelphia, New York, and Portland, among others—evolve to a higher level of functioning by bringing together individual organizations working on a similar goal. In the next chapter I will describe practices for cooperation and collaboration that can enable complex social tasks to be accomplished quicker and at a higher quality.

We can look to other thinkers in the lineage of Lao Tzu for instruction and inspiration. Janine Benyus, a biologist and author of the book *Biomimicry*, uses nature's design principles to help businesses develop more environmentally sustainable products. She studies, for example, how electrons in a leaf cell convert sunlight to energy in a trillionth of a second, or how a spider manufactures a waterproof fiber five times stronger than steel. She then works with a business to help replicate these inventions in nature. I asked Janine if she had applied her biomimicry learning principles to social innovation. She said she hadn't yet and we agreed to start a dialogue.

Ori Brafman and Rod Beckstrom have applied their observations of nature to social systems. In their insightful book *The Starfish and the Spider* they note: "If you cut off a spider's head it dies, but if you cut off a starfish's leg it grows a new one, and that leg can grow into an entirely new starfish. Traditional top-down organizations are like spiders but now starfish organizations are changing the face of the world." The starfish teaches how a self-organizing system can work and provides insight into the success of the Internet 2.0 "many-to-many" strategies. In providing knowledge to EcoTeams on how to self-replicate I was using a "many-to-many" principle. Developing social innovations that can disseminate through self-organization is fundamental for large-scale diffusion, and I am always scanning the world in search of successful applications.

The story of the founding of America is another source of inspiration for me, and I find Thomas Jefferson, in particular, a most remarkable teacher. Unlike the other founders, who were primarily concerned with getting out from under the yoke of oppressive English rule, Jefferson's social creativity led him to propose a bold new vision for governance. He imagined a democratic form of government, "we the people," that provided the opportunity for individuals to pursue their individual dreams of "life, liberty and the pursuit of happiness." Collectively, these ideals ultimately came to be called the "American Dream." Jefferson had an aspiriational vision that, like the Olympic ideal, lifted people's sights well beyond the shores of America.

Respected British historian Felipe Fernandez-Armesto described just how visionary and courageous America's idea of democracy was at the time. "Democracy as we know it today—a system of representative government elected by universal or near universal suffrage—was really an American invention. Attempts to trace it from the ancient Greek system of the same name or from the French Revolution are misleadingly romantic. While democracy was growing within America in the late eighteenth and early nineteenth centuries, almost everyone in Europe was against it. Even advocates of popular sovereignty hesitated to recommend a system Plato and Aristotle had condemned."

The American democratic form of government was a transformative social innovation that changed the game of governance and is still viable more than two centuries later because it was skillfully designed by Jefferson and the other framers of the U.S. Constitution to evolve with the times. "Some men look at constitutions with sanctimonious reverence and deem them like the Ark of the Covenant too sacred to be touched," said Jefferson, "but laws and institutions must go hand in hand with the progress of the human mind." By Peter Drucker's definition of a social entrepreneur as someone who improves the performance capacity of society, Jefferson qualifies as one of America's first social entrepreneurs; and America qualifies as one of the world's great transformative social innovations.

Jefferson had a deep faith in people. For him, "we the people" was not just a political platitude; he believed in people as the ultimate source, arbiter, and promoter of social good. He said, "I consider the people who constitute a society or a nation as the source of all authority in that nation." And, "Were it left to me to decide whether we should have a government without newspapers, or newspapers with government, I should not hesitate a moment to prefer the latter . . . but I should mean that every man be capable of reading them."

Of all the things that have inspired me about Jefferson, it is his belief in "we the people" to do the right thing that offers me the most comfort. My experience has been that if I look for and draw out the best in people, they will find it within themselves and wish to prove my faith warranted through their deeds. This was what Jefferson did, and Americans have been aspiring to live up to his faith in them ever since. Faith that one's fellow human beings can be trusted to take responsibility for the common good is the ultimate social innovation that is America and the bedrock on which I have made my stand as a social innovator. I have had ample opportunity to test this belief all over the world and have not been disappointed. It is from this experience that I draw my hope for our civilization, and I am grateful to Jefferson for being a role model.

While few of us may achieve the same level of impact on society as Thomas Jefferson, Lao Tzu, or the unknown visionary creator of the Olympics, we can all tap into the same fountain from which these social innovations sprang—our social creativity. We move next to translating this social creativity into the design of social innovations.

DESIGNING THE ARCHITECTURE OF A TRANSFORMATIVE SOCIAL INNOVATION

A social innovation that changes the game transforms the established thinking and conventions in the current social system to help it evolve to a higher level of performance and social value. It must meet four conditions to be a game changer.

A strong need for transformation in the social system. The social system needs to be ready. In empowerment terms, the social innovation needs to be on society's growing edge. At the time of the First Earth Run, the world was on the verge of a nuclear war and looking for a better alternative than the threat of mutually assured destruction. When we initiated the sustainable lifestyle program, there was a growing awareness that we were reaching the limits of the Earth's carrying capacity and we needed to conserve natural resources or risk crashing our life support system. In Philadelphia, the crime, drugs, and blight in its inner city had not only seriously eroded these neighborhoods but the urban flight was putting the city at risk of losing its tax base and breaking down. And for New York City in the wake of 9/11, the need for security, healing, and community was at the top of people's and politicians' agendas.

Capacity to transform and evolve the current beliefs and behaviors of people in the social system. For the First Earth Run, the transformation was from fear and separation to hope and cooperation. For the sustainable lifestyle program, the transformation was from wasteful to resource-efficient lifestyles. For the inner-city neighborhood program in Philadelphia, the transformation was from feeling powerlessness to alter neighborhood living conditions to being in control. And for the disaster-resilient community program in New York City, the transformation was from isolation and fear to connectedness and preparedness.

Participation of the key players in the social system working in common cause. For the First Earth Run it was citizens, national political leaders, and the media coming to together to show we are a global community with a common aspiration for a peaceful world. For the sustainable lifestyle program it was citizens, neighbors, and local governments joined to create a more environmentally sustainable community and planet. For the neighborhood program, it was residents, their block, and the city working cooperatively to improve the living conditions on the participating blocks. And for the emergency preparedness program, it was neighbors helping neighbors in partnership with community groups and their city to create disaster-resilient buildings and blocks.

A repeatable solution capable of being brought to scale. Each of these four social innovations was designed as a repeatable solution with a dissemination strategy. With the First Earth Run, the replicability was based on a handbook and training describing how to plan the event, and an outreach strategy to recruit organizers from the community to country level. With the community-based behavior-change programs, the repeatable solution was a workbook of actions and peer support system designed to work for any household and cultural context, with trained community organizers to disseminate the programs.

Based on the readiness in a culture for the particular social innovation some spread widely, others less widely, but each helped change the game by transforming the established thinking and conventions in the targeted social system and helping it evolve to a higher level of performance and social value. I have provided detailed blueprints for these social innovations in Part One and the undergirding design principles in Part Two, but what follows is the invisible meta-architecture that won people's hearts and minds. These are the elements that enable the aspiration, inspiration, and hope that is essential if a social innovation is not only to take root, but to take wing and soar.

Creating Aspiration: Symbols and Ideals

In 1976 I began my journey as a social architect by organizing a fifty-state, 9,000-mile torch relay to celebrate the U.S. Bicentennial. It was post-Vietnam War America and the country's self-esteem was in a state of extreme disrepair.

I felt we needed something grand and inspirational to remind us of who we are as Americans and of the ideals on which our country was founded. The event combined the archetype of fire, which symbolizes aspiration, with the American ideal of trying to create a better world. Unfiltered by ideology, this fifty-one-day symbolic event touched people in a profound way. All along the route people were cheering and teary-eyed. It opened their hearts, uplifted them, and reminded them of what was good about America. The fire was alchemical. Seeing the torch effectively transformed people from their ordinary state of consciousness to a higher state. Unwittingly, I had discovered the power of an archetypal symbol aligned with an aspirational ideal.

I continued on this symbolic path organizing the Olympic Torch Relay in 1980. To further enhance the power of this event we petitioned the International Olympic Committee to allow us to modify the runner selection process. We requested that, as in the ancient Olympic Games, where athletes were selected based on both athletic prowess and their embodiment of the Greek ideal of the whole person, we choose torch runners based on their qualification as a whole person—fit in body, mind, and spirit. The committee agreed and we created a nationwide contest to select the runners

This aspirational ideal motivated 8,000 people to apply for the fifty-two slots—one for each state, Lake Placid, and the District of Columbia. Continuing down this aspirational path we invited these fifty-two runners to select the final torch runner who would light the stadium cauldron that would open the Olympics. This selection was to be based on who, over the course of the relay, they felt best exemplified the whole-person ideal. This so motivated our media partner, ABC TV, that they decided to broadcast this process with much pomp and ceremony on their prime-time *Wide World of Sports* program.

At the Olympic Games these fifty-two runners were invited to serve as an honor guard for the medal ceremony each night on frozen Mirror Lake. They stood in two columns with torches held high, providing a transcendent light in the nighttime sky as each athlete passed through on the way up to the medal podium. These Olympic torch bearers became as popular at the Olympic Games as the athletes, and I believe it is because they represented, whether the spectators could have articulated it or not, the aspirational ideal of the common person. We had raised the level of the game through the transformative power of a symbol aligned with an ideal.

By the time of the First Earth Run I had become a student of the symbolic. Here the task was to tap into the deep aspirational ideal rooted within the human psyche to live in peace with one's fellow human beings. It is an aspirational ideal that has existed ever since the very first war was introduced on this planet, and it has been passed down from generation to generation, predominantly by women. This ideal was explicitly imbued into the fire by Grandmother Caroline and amplified by the Hopi mythology that the event represented a great turning toward peace on our planet.

It was not surprising why people responded to the First Earth Run at such a deep level in every culture. We had combined the symbol of aspiration—fire, with the most profound aspirational ideal on the planet—peace.

And infused both symbol and ideal with the Hopi prophecy of hope for our future at a moment when the world was on the precipice of a nuclear war.

The behavior-change programs, while not able to achieve the emotional lift of a symbolic event using the archetype of fire, were nevertheless designed to be aspirational. The sustainable lifestyle program appealed to people's aspiration to do the right thing for the planet and future generations. The livable neighborhood and disaster preparedness programs appealed to people's aspiration to be a good neighbor and work for the common good. These aspirational ideals provided the lift for people to invest their time in something larger than themselves.

One of the most interesting pieces of data from our research on the sustainable lifestyle program was that saving money was never listed as the first motivation for why people chose to participate. It was always a secondary benefit. What universally motivated people was the aspirational ideal of doing the right thing for the planet and future generations.

When designing a social innovation we need to think about what we are aspiring to achieve. Most social innovators are moved by ideals. If we weren't, it's not likely we would invest so much time into programs and causes that have modest or no financial benefits to us. If an ideal motivates us, it will likely motivate others. We need to let others know about it by making it a prominent part of how we tell the story of our social innovation.

Creating Inspiration: Thinking Big

The level of transformation needed to prevent our various social and ecological systems from breaking down will not happen through incremental changes. We need to think about change at a much larger scale when contemplating the transformation of a social system. This is what is needed, and fortunately there is a significant side benefit. People are inspired by big ideas. John Kennedy's commitment to land a person on the moon was a big idea that inspired a generation.

In our time, however, we need more than passive inspiration and simple support for big ideas. We need people to put their shoulder to the wheel. To do this, they need to be inspired by the idea in which they are investing. We are wise to subscribe to architect Daniel Burnham's injunction. "Make no little plans. They have no magic to stir men's blood and probably themselves will not be realized. Make big plans. Aim high in hope and work. Remembering that a noble, logical diagram once recorded will not die."

For some reason, thinking big has never been a problem for me. I am always drawn to what is just on the horizon, but not yet easily seen. A transformative social innovator and Lieutenant Colonel in the U.S. Army, Jim Channon, once called me an evolutionary scout; I think it is a fitting description. The way I know if my idea is big enough either in scale, transformational impact, or both, is when skeptics call it naïve. It is a sure sign that I am pushing the boundary of conventional thinking. Because I have gained some credibility from being able to act effectively on a large scale, the skeptics do give me the benefit of the doubt more and more these days. But learning how to think big must now become more commonplace given the challenges we face. It is one of our planetary growing edges.

The First Earth Run was able to inspire people precisely because it was a big idea with a powerful ambition. People at that moment in time on the planet were open to thinking out of the box because the world was so stuck in the box with its mutually assured destruction "peace" strategy. People were also inspired by the First Earth Run because it was a daring social experiment. It provided multiple experiences that stretched our imaginations into new realms and planted these seeds of possibility all over the planet for immediate and future use.

It enabled humanity to experience itself being connected by and encircled in light. It highlighted all across the planet the many acts of cooperation among individuals, community groups, political leaders, and countries acting on behalf of the common good. It showcased the possibility of an aspirational ideal creating momentary peace in war zones comparable to the *ekecheiria* of the ancient Olympics. It showed the power of the media as a positive force for planetary good through broadcasting these multiple experiences into the world's living rooms for eighty-six days. And these "possibility seeds" are continuing to bear fruit and be replanted by those who carry this aspirational ideal for humanity. I will share more about this in Part Three.

The Global Action Plan for the Earth social innovation was another big idea, as indicated by its name. It was designed to put in motion a process that could help transform environmental behavior patterns in the high consumption countries of the world. Like the First Earth Run, it was a highly ambitious goal just on the borderline of what was perceived to be possible.

While the practicality of it engaged people, it was the ambition level that inspired them. Being part of a global endeavor made people feel important, and connected, and as if they were in the vanguard of a worldwide sustainable lifestyle movement—which they were. They knew that they had counterparts living halfway around the globe who were meeting in EcoTeams going through the exact same transformational process.

The practice of thinking big grows out of the discipline of seeking vision, not pathology, and trying to ascertain the growing edge. It requires a willingness to ask big questions, and then to go on a journey to answer them, trusting that a path forward will unfold. It requires commitment to stay the course through the many twists and turns of this journey into the unknown. It demands self-confidence to face the resistances and pushback of those afraid to let go of their known reality. Finally, it requires a genuine willingness to learn from feedback and keep making the needed course corrections. I like the way Einstein describes this endeavor. "One should not pursue goals that are easily achieved. One must develop an instinct for what one can just barely achieve through one's greatest efforts."

Creating Hope: A Whole Solution

To engage people wholeheartedly in a social innovation they need to believe it is more than just "the good fight." They need to believe that if successful, it has the potential to create the transformation needed to solve an important social problem or meet an unmet social need. And a viable solution needs to be able to solve the *whole* problem, not just part of the problem. If people do not believe that the social innovation can solve the whole problem, they will be unwilling to invest their time and their hearts.

Whole solutions do not just appear out of the blue. They take time, tenacity, and rigorous thinking. The process begins by identifying the major questions the social innovation needs to answer in order to be successful. Then it goes through a painstaking testing process to answer these questions. Like a scientific experiment, it needs to generate and test hypotheses, discarding those that don't work along the way and carefully working with those that do until consistent results are achieved.

With the sustainable lifestyle program the very first question I needed to answer was what would it take to get people to participate. I discovered, through asking people, that they wanted to know what to do, which were the important actions, how to do them, and that they made a difference. Addressing these questions became the criteria for designing the solution. The first three questions were manageable and I could answer them based on my empowerment work, but the fourth question—"Do my actions make a difference?"—was much harder to answer. I knew that if I did not come up with a plausible answer to this question, the endeavor would not be solving the problem at hand. It would not be a whole solution and if people participated it would not be wholeheartedly.

Attempting to genuinely answer this question led me on quite an adventure. It required that we create a feedback system to help people see their drop filling the bucket, rather than being a drop in the bucket. That in turn required that we collect hard data. Then we needed to tally up that information at a household level to help people see the difference they were making. But to answer that question at the next level with integrity required me get out of my comfort zone. It required that we look at the larger issue of household resource use in the industrialized countries in the world. This was a critical sustainability leverage point, as discussed earlier in the book, and became the impetus for creating the Global Action Plan for the Earth initiative.

Finally we had all the elements in place to address this question in a complete fashion. By no means were we suggesting that we would create change on a global scale, but we did have a case we could now make. If people chose to participate in creating a more sustainable lifestyle, given the leverage this represented, it might be possible to move the dial around sustainability on the planet; we were in enough high-consumption countries to make this happen. We were now on a path that had the possibility to change the game. Whether we would or not was unknown, but a plausible possibility now existed. We had created a whole solution.

Developing a whole solution is a very laborious process, requiring multiple iterations just to get the basics right, not to mention taking it to scale. To sustain our commitment we need to feel that the solution we are developing is worth this investment of time and energy. What allows me to make such a long-term investment is the belief that the social innovation I am developing has the possibility to change the game. I may not know the precise path, but trust that if I diligently commit myself to putting all the elements in place necessary to create a whole solution, the way forward will reveal itself. This is the path of the social entrepreneur.

IMPLEMENTING A TRANSFORMATIVE SOCIAL INNOVATION: THE PATH OF THE SOCIAL ENTREPRENEUR

So far this chapter has been looking at the process of inventing and designing a transformative social innovation. But behind each social innovation is a person convincing skeptical investors to back it, managing the project through its multiple ups and downs, and marketing it to an often skeptical world. This is the social entrepreneur. A social entrepreneur needs to be part innovator, part business person, and part evangelist.

The path a social entrepreneur walks is defined by three stages, each of which requires increasingly more competence. The first stage is the development and testing of the social innovation *prototype* to achieve a proof of concept. The second is the *demonstration* of the prototype with a larger and more diverse audience to determine if the social innovation is capable of going to scale. And the third stage is taking the social innovation to *scale* to further the desired social change.

An example of these three stages was my evolution in the torch relay event as a social innovation using symbols and ideals to transform societal beliefs and behaviors. The Bicentennial Torch Relay was the prototype stage in which I learned how to work with the transformative power of a symbol and ideal, and manage the complex logistics of the event. The demonstration stage was the Olympic Torch Relay. Again I worked with the transformative power of aligning a symbol and ideal and the complex logistics of the event. But I was now working internationally with the worldwide media covering every step of our journey. The First Earth Run was the final stage—going to scale. It required taking all the knowledge and experience gained in the previous two stages and applying them on a global scale with the participation of sixty-two countries and much more complex logistics, media, politics, and aspiration.

The major responsibility of the social entrepreneur in the prototype stage is raising the money to fund the development and testing of the social innovation. Since the idea is unproven, this is a high-risk investment. Generally funding comes from one's own savings, and from friends, family, or foundations specializing in startup social innovations. The types of foundations or philanthropists who invest at this startup stage are much like venture capitalists. They are willing to invest in high-risk ventures in the hope that they can achieve a major return on investment, except in this case, they are looking for a social return on their investment. They place their bet based on their perception of the social innovation's ability to change the game and the social entrepreneur's competence.

To get this type of funding from a foundation or sophisticated investor the social entrepreneur needs to develop a proposal that convincingly makes the case for this social innovation's potential to change the game.

Each funder has specific guidelines for what they want in a proposal but there are several components that are always required: a description of society's need and how the social innovation will address it, the target audience for the pilot and how this audience will be engaged, an explanation on how the social change will be measured, the qualifications of the person or team, and the budget.

The clearer a social entrepreneur is on the essential questions the prototype needs to test, the easier it will be to convince an investor that it is well conceived and worthy of investment. The focus needs to be on the mission-critical questions. For the sustainable lifestyle program the questions we wished to test in the prototype were: Would people participate? Would they adopt environmentally sustainable lifestyle practices? Would they sustain these practices over time? It took a few years to definitively answer these questions. With a proof of concept, the social innovation can then move to the demonstration phase.

In this phase the prototype is tested on a larger playing field with more people and greater diversity. The goal of this phase is to see if the social innovation has the potential to be brought to scale. In the case of the sustainable lifestyle program the main question was: What is the best approach to disseminate this program widely? Because there are more variables to be tested in this phase, it can take many twists and turns and as a result is usually the wildest ride.

This was the case for me attempting to find the appropriate outreach model for our sustainable lifestyle program. First I created an ad hoc network of community organizers based on people who had approached me to disseminate the program.

It was a "let many flowers bloom" approach. Because of the sophistication of this social innovation, without know-how the program quality fell off quickly. Moreover, these community organizers ended up competing with each other for funding, and with limited management experience their organizations floundered. After about eighteen months of watching this mayhem, I realized it was not working and it was driving me crazy to be in the middle of it.

My solution was to manage the program outreach directly by offering it to local governments and recruiting local staff to implement it. This allowed me both to control the program quality and test a business model that could be replicated. I sold the first of these to Portland, Oregon, as the official demonstration site. This demonstration phase taught me that there was a need in local government for this type of program. I could recruit, train, and manage staff to implement it. And the economics could enable a sustainable business model to be established.

With this knowledge I then moved into the scaling-up stage. The main question to test was how to scale up this social innovation within a community. Since it was a sophisticated social innovation and still very much a work-in-progress, to further its potential I would need those I worked with in each community to be more than just staff. I would need them to be partners willing to collaborate with me at every level, from design to financing. These individuals were well positioned to be collaborators because to carry out these tasks they were constantly putting the program through its paces and observing its needs; and they had working relationships with all the local government partners. But being a collaborator on a transformative social innovation required a far more sophisticated skill set than community organizing. What I was asking of them required the skills of a social entrepreneur. Either I had to clone myself, or I needed to build their capacity as social entrepreneurs.

I opted to build their capacity and developed a training program that included many of the elements of my transformative leadership training, combined with skill building in program architecture design; putting together public and private financing; management techniques; and dissemination frameworks. I followed that up with one-on-one coaching and a peer support system. They did not all make the transition from staff to collaborator, but many did. Over time we worked together continuously to evolve each of these core social entrepreneurial competencies. As a result of this community of social entrepreneurs, we were able to build an effective sustainable lifestyle campaign model which we disseminated widely.

It was encouraging to see how much potential social entrepreneurial talent exists in those who would not normally view themselves in this way, and how this talent can be systematically developed using the practices I have been describing in this book. To bring social innovations to scale at the order of magnitude needed to influence societal transformation requires a large talent pool of social entrepreneurs. The good news is that this talent pool is ready, willing, and, with some training and hard work, able.

A SOCIAL ENTREPRENEURSHIP MOVEMENT IS BORN

"There is what can only be called a movement springing up in our midst that could make an enormous difference in our country," says David Gergen, advisor to four U.S. presidents and a CNN political pundit in the fall 2008 issue of the *Stanford Social Innovation Review*. He continued, "Social entrepreneurs remind me of the Civil Rights movement because they share the same idealism and could almost have as big an impact on the country over time."

As society's problems have continued to increase, so has the need for solutions. Social entrepreneurship has stepped into this vacuum and it has rapidly grown in prominence in recent years with an ever-increasing number of organizations, foundations, and universities supporting it. The pioneer and elder statesman of this field is Bill Drayton, founder of Ashoka, a peer support group for social entrepreneurs with game-changing ideas from around the world. Drayton penetrates to the essence of the social entrepreneur when he says, "for some reason deep in their personality, they know from the time they are little that they are in this world to change it in a fundamental way."

In his book *How to Change the World: Social Entrepreneurs and the Power of New Ideas*, David Bornstein describes their process. "A social entrepreneur is an obsessive individual who sees a problem and envisions a new solution, who takes the initiative to act on that vision, who gathers resources and builds an organization to protect and market the vision, who provides the energy and sustained focus to overcome the inevitable resistance and keep improving, strengthening, and broadening that vision until what was once a marginal idea has become a new norm." He goes on to say, "For every one thousand people who are creative, altruistic and energetic, there is probably only one who fits these criteria of a social entrepreneur."

Given the scale of change required to pull our planet back from the brink we need a social entrepreneurship revolution. To do this we need to increase the percentage of people who walk this path from one in a thousand to ten or even a hundred in a thousand. How do we change the game of social entrepreneurship so it attracts more than just the most obsessive and intrepid individuals in society? The ground is being laid.

High-profile people and the attention the media and prominent institutions are paying to them have conferred a cool status on social entrepreneurship. Bill and Melinda Gates and Bono were honored by *Time* magazine as "People of the Year" in 2005 for their social entrepreneurial activities. There are now full-blown social entrepreneurial heroes who have won the Nobel Prize for their social innovations, including Al Gore for his film *An Inconvenient Truth*, which has dramatically raised humanity's awareness of the imminent threat of climate change, and Muhammad

Yunus of Bangladesh, for developing and scaling micro lending in developing countries. Bill Clinton's Global Initiative brings successful social entrepreneurs from around the world to New York every September to help them cross-pollinate their ideas and to increase the support for their work.

Social entrepreneurship prizes are offered each year by *Fast Company* Magazine and the Skoll Foundation. A half-dozen well-endowed foundations exist with the exclusive mandate to bring capital to social entrepreneurial ventures. There are over thirty universities offering courses and master's degrees in social entrepreneurship with some 350 faculty members actively teaching and researching the subject. Two popular conferences for social entrepreneurs take place at Harvard and Oxford each year. Stanford University has a quarterly journal devoted exclusively to the field of social innovation.

But even with this burgeoning media interest, managerial knowledge, and financial support, I have not seen much attention placed on the social entrepreneur's core strategic mission, or what Bill Drayton calls "changing the pattern in the field" and what I call changing the game. This capability seems to be viewed as a *black box*—a device, system, or object where there is no knowledge of its internal workings. I believe that opening the black box on how to design and disseminate transformative social innovations is a key leverage point for taking the field of social entrepreneurship to scale and the growing edge of this movement. (See Figure 7.1, pages 220–221.)

Social innovations that are skillfully designed to be game changers and brought to scale significantly increase their potential to attract financial support. These types of investments are the sweet spot for social venture funders and can expand the available funding pool as more foundations, government agencies, and social benefit businesses see the opportunity for social return on investment. With adequate financing, potentially game-changing social innovations have the greatest chance to move through robust prototype and demonstration phases and go to scale more quickly and effectively.

Increasing the number of social entrepreneurs taking their game changing social innovations to scale is the quickest way to attract the best and brightest talent to this field. Highly talented people want to be where the action is and where they see they can make the biggest difference. Increasing the number of talented social entrepreneurs in the game will increase both the quantity and quality of social innovations generated. With more successful social innovation models to build on there is greater chance for cross-pollination, creating new hybrids and producing even more social value. This is a virtuous cycle.

Think about this: If one of the twenty-first century's big new ideas for changing the world is social entrepreneurship, then taking it to scale could be a game changer for our planet. Building the capacity of social entrepreneurs to create transformative social innovations initiates this virtuous cycle. This is a strategic lever that this book is working.

In the next chapter we look at how to accelerate the pace and quality of social change through synergy, specifically, the competencies of bringing people and organizations together to achieve results they could not produce alone.

Figure 7.1—Opening the Black Box:
Anatomy of a Transformative Social Innovation—
The Sustainable Lifestyle Program

SOCIAL INNOVATION PHASE	ACTIVITY	RESULTS
Social Creativity	Invent a strategy to address the rapid deterioration of planet's ecosystem and our life-support system.	Developed Earth Day "Agenda for Green Decade" and determined unsustainable consumption practices in industrialized countries is a high leverage point for intervention. Later confirmed by U.N. "Agenda 21" report.
Social Creativity	Research barriers to people being willing to take proenvironment actions.	Identification of four barriers that need to be addressed to engage people.
Social Creativity	Research Empowerment Workshop and behavior-change methodology as possible templates.	Identification of templates for creating a modularized and structured behavior-change program with measurable goals, feedback, and community support.
Social Architecture	Design sustainable lifestyle program. Engage participants through *aspirational ideal* of doing the right thing for our children's future and planet.	A structured, six-module behavior-change program with recipe format for actions, concrete personal goals, self-directed meeting guides, feedback system, and EcoTeam peer support for motivation and accountability.
Social Architecture	*Prototype* program with 200 households to determine if it can achieve substantive and measurable behavior change.	Households on average reduced annual solid waste by 40%, water by 32%, energy by 17%, vehicle miles traveled by 8%, CO_2 by 15%, and achieved financial savings of $255. Comparable results ultimately achieved with 20,000 program participants.

(continued)

(Figure 7.1, continued)

SOCIAL INNOVATION PHASE	ACTIVITY	RESULTS
Social Architecture	Conduct longitudinal studies to determine if behavior changes are sustained over time.	Seven studies confirm behavior changes are sustained and 53% of participants transfer practices to their workplace.
Social Architecture	Design a replicable approach for engaging program participants within a community.	A block-based neighbor-to-neighbor strategy based on self-replication and social diffusion principles. Achieved a 25% recruitment rate.
Social Architecture	Design *whole solution* to address issue of unsustainable consumption. Engage participants through *thinking big* and possibility of *game changer*.	Developed international outreach strategy, Global Action Plan for the Earth. Disseminated sustainable lifestyle program to 22 high consumption countries.
Social Entrepreneurship	Design an effective management and financing strategy for a community-based behavior-change program.	Developed Sustainable Lifestyle Campaign under service contracts with local governments.
Social Entrepreneurship	*Demonstrate* the Sustainable Lifestyle Campaign community-based behavior-change model.	Portland Sustainable Lifestyle Campaign under contract with city of Portland, Oregon, from 1996–2001.
Social Entrepreneurship	*Scale* up the Sustainable Lifestyle Campaign model.	Cadre of social entrepreneurs in diverse community types developed robust Sustainable Lifestyle Campaign model. Disseminated to 200+ communities worldwide.

CHAPTER 7: SOCIAL CHANGE 2.0 PRACTITIONER'S GUIDE

1. What does changing the game in your arena of social change look like?

2. What would allow your social innovation to be a game changer?

3. What are the success metrics for each of its three stages—prototype, demonstration, and scale-up?

4. How could you integrate aspiration and inspiration into the architecture of your transformative social innovation?

5. What is required for your transformative social innovation to be a whole solution?

CHAPTER 8

SYNERGY AS THE ACCELERATOR OF

SOCIAL CHANGE:

THE ART OF BUILDING A UNITIVE FIELD

We must all hang together, or assuredly we will all hang separately.
—Benjamin Franklin

Synergy is the highest activity of life. It creates new untapped alternatives through valuing and taking advantage of the differences between people.
—Stephen Covey

Given the rapidly increasing breakdowns in our social and ecological systems, achieving transformative change in a timely manner is of the essence. Science has observed how our Earth progressed from single-cell organisms to multicellular organisms when a more complex system was required for the evolution of organic life. We must now consciously do the same for the evolution of human life. To create effective solutions to our societal problems, we must move from working as solo entities (whether individual or institutional) to working as partners and collaborators so that greater social value can be achieved in a shorter time.

The individual approach to change pervades every corner of the social change universe. Political parties fight one another tooth and nail and very little gets done. National, state, and local governments exist in a hierarchical system and rarely work collaboratively to solve social problems. Nonprofit organizations compete with one another for the same dollars, and constituents and often work at cross-purposes. Local government agencies work in silos, each competing for a share of the city budget and each reaching out to residents of their community with their individual messages and programs. Governments, nonprofits, and businesses engage in endless rounds of recrimination that neutralize one another's efforts, poison the change process, and turn off citizens. Neighbors don't help one another solve problems that could easily be addressed by working together. And individual citizens struggle on their own to try and adopt the socially beneficial behaviors asked of them by local governments and nonprofits. It doesn't have to be this way.

People are much more effective at solving common problems when working together. Groups and organizations working jointly for the common good in a community achieve results none could achieve alone. Cities working across their silos of individual agencies achieve much better results, more cost effectively. And countries cooperating are substantially more effective at solving the big global problems than those who act unilaterally. But while this type of cooperation happens from time to time, it is hardly the norm. For it to become a strategic lever for social change, we as a human community need to develop a new competency. From a social evolution point of view, our growing edge is to develop that competency. *We need to move from a single-cell social organism to a multicellular social organism.* While making this evolutionary leap is no easy task, staring into the abyss is a strong motivator.

The societal benefit we can expect from making this leap is the ability to transform our faltering or dysfunctional social systems much more rapidly and with far greater quality. By effectively working together we can achieve the force multiplier of synergy. Synergy is defined as "the working together of two or more people, organizations, or things that produce a result greater than the sum of their individual capabilities or effects."

I experienced the force multiplier of synergy working in collaboration with the Office of Emergency Management and Citizens for New York City when introducing disaster preparedness to the residents of New York. On my own I could not have achieved much, but working together we produced a higher-quality product and disseminated it significantly faster than any single organization working on its own could have done.

Synergy comes from combining talents in such a way that something new and more powerful emerges. A high-performing basketball team is a clear demonstration of synergy. I used to marvel watching Michael Jordan facilitate this process on his team. In basketball parlance, synergy translates as teamwork. Jordan said, "Talent wins games, but teamwork wins championships." The result, in his case, was six NBA championships. His team, the Chicago Bulls, could not have won these championships without Michael Jordan, but he could not have won them without his team performing at a very high level of synergy.

To create this synergy Jordan built what I call a "unitive field." In physics the term *field* is defined as "an area or region within which a force exerts an influence at every point." A unitive field is created when a force is exerted that brings people into a state of synergy to achieve a specific outcome. In Jordan's case, the force that built the unitive field was a set of practices for performing as an intelligent team, as modeled by him and with the NBA championship the desired outcome. A unitive field can be built around any type of outcome.

The first time I observed the power of a unitive field was in the early days of facilitating the Empowerment Workshop. Gail and I requested that participants commit themselves not only to their own personal growth but to that of the others in the group as well. We told them that much of the growth that occurred would be as a result of one another. Committing themselves to one another created a strong aspiration in the community toward growth. People were no longer on a personal growth journey by themselves, they were a *growth community*. We provided multiple points of contact through one-on-one and small- and large-group processes. Each time someone had the courage to transform a limiting belief or go to his or her growing edge, others were there supporting and cheering.

We had built a unitive field. All members of the group accelerated both the pace and the quality of their growth. They made personal breakthroughs they could not have done on their own. The community, using a distinct set of practices, had become a "force exerting an influence at every point" that enabled the unitive field to be built around personal growth. This same phenomenon was what contributed to the rapid transformation of the fishermen in just two days.

While the outcome produced by synergy is extraordinary, building a unitive field to create it is rather straightforward. The first requirement is a *connection* among people that establishes a meaningful relationship. The second is *cooperation* around a clearly defined common goal. And the third is *collaboration*, which enables individual talents to be multiplied. EcoTeams were designed with these three principles in mind, and the successful ones all demonstrated the power of a unitive field.

EcoTeams: A Unitive Field in Action

An EcoTeam fosters connection among people. Whether living on the same block, working together in the same organization, or as members of a faith community, people want more connection. Because of the structure of our society today many people are isolated, and many feel alienated. Robert Putnam, Harvard social scientist, describes this phenomenon in his book *Bowling Alone*. Drawing on the Roper Social and Political Trends research that surveys America's changing behavior over the past twenty-five years, Putnam states that "we have become increasingly disconnected from family, friends, neighbors, and social structures, whether they are the PTA, church, recreational clubs, political parties, or bowling leagues." He goes on to say, "Our shrinking access to the social capital that is a reward of community activity and community sharing is a serious threat to our civic and personal health."

One place where the lack of social capital is most apparent is where we live—our neighborhoods. As I have shared throughout this book, people rarely know their neighbors and, if they do, the relationships are apt to be superficial. This is not a situation that most people like, but they don't know what to do about it. That explains the warm reception received by EcoTeam leaders who knocked on their neighbors' doors and invited them to their homes. For many who did this, it was a transformational experience. They had been embarrassed to live next to someone for such a long time and never share more than a nod or a passing word; now there was the possibility of gratifying connection.

At the information meetings people would be asked to share personal experiences of environmental actions they had taken and how taking those actions had made them feel. This is not something most people usually talk about, and very few people were easily in touch with how doing an action made them feel. But they were willing to try. They talked about taking environmental actions to serve as a positive role model for their children. They talked about their fears for the planet, and their desire to contribute to a solution. They shared how it was one of the few things they could do every day that gave them a sense of meaning in their life. This deep level of sharing allowed others to get in touch with what motivated them or might motivate them in the future. And it allowed the people in the room to connect with the speaker, their *neighbor*. It was this *connectivity* as much as the practical environmental benefits of the program that caused 75 percent of the attendees to agree to participating in the four-month long program.

Once they were on an EcoTeam the group members served as a support system for one another. They motivated one another to follow through with the commitments they made to take action and provided hands-on support in helping one another take the actions. For example, some of the actions, such as weather-stripping a window intimidated those who were not that handy and the more technically minded volunteered to help. The team also exchanged information and resources—where to buy compact florescent light bulbs more cheaply, for instance, and the names of trustworthy local service providers. They might also divide up tasks to save one another time. Someone might purchase these energy-saving light bulbs on behalf of the team, while another might organize carpooling opportunities. Yet another might identify a community-supported agriculture farm and receive deliveries of fresh vegetables for distribution to the team. It was neighbor-to-neighbor *cooperation* that allowed people to accomplish these things.

As the team completed the program many took the action of starting more EcoTeams on their block or an adjoining block. This *collaboration* required a blending of talents to achieve a task that no individual member of the team could easily accomplish alone. It required neighbor-to-neighbor outreach, hosting an information meeting in someone's home, developing a format for the meeting, having team members share their experience, facilitating the meeting, and following up to make sure the new team or teams actually formed. All these tasks required planning, coordination, and management to make sure everything was getting done. Because of the groundwork established through the connection of team members and their experience of cooperation, most teams were successfully able to start at least one other team.

Collaboration also took other forms. Some teams would lobby for city services—such as curbside recycling, bike lanes, or better public transit that would make taking certain individual actions easier. They would divide up the responsibilities for speaking with local government officials, getting in touch with other EcoTeams to bolster their case, writing proposals, speaking at city council meetings, and even volunteering for the city environmental committee. This high level of collaboration enabled changes in environmental policy that could not have been accomplished by any one individual or in some cases any one EcoTeam.

Let's now look at how the unitive practices of connection, cooperation, and collaboration can be used to further social change.

CONNECTION PRINCIPLES, PRACTICES, AND LESSONS LEARNED

Providing opportunities for people to connect is the first step in building a unitive field. It is the simplest thing to do but the hardest step to take. Many of us are shy. Many of us are fearful of revealing anything too personal about ourselves. Sometimes we don't know how. Other times we try, fumble the opportunity, and then retreat back into the safety of our known world. For these reasons, all but the most extroverted among us often choose to defend ourselves from the possibility of embarrassment, disappointment, or rejection. For those of us in the role of change agent we must learn how to connect people if we wish them to sustain their commitment over time. Along with a meaningful cause, which is a given, it is the person-to-person connections that keep people motivated and engaged. In my various social change initiatives I have used six practices to create connections with and among people.

Make a request to participate in social change. The very first step is to connect personally with people and invite them to participate in the social change initiative. Often people are willing to do things for the greater good but they sit on the sidelines because no one has asked them to join in. There are a lot of potential contributors to social change ready and willing who are just waiting to be invited to play. We need to connect with these people and connect them to the larger needs in society.

This is the foundation of the neighbor-to-neighbor outreach process. We find potential EcoTeam leaders and request that they invite neighbors to their home to start a team. They then reach out to their neighbors and request that they come to a meeting in their home. At this information meeting the facilitator makes a request for the neighbors in attendance to create an EcoTeam. At the EcoTeam meetings the topic leader requests that team members report on the actions they will take. At the next meeting the topic leader requests that team members share what they accomplished and what support, if any, they might need to take any actions they did not accomplish. At each stage someone is connecting one-on-one with another person and making a request for that person to participate in social change.

And we should not be afraid to make bold requests. People are ready to play a bigger game if someone is willing to invite them. I have requested stodgy, bureaucratic city agencies to work collaboratively with one another and neighborhood groups, and more often than not, they have agreed. During the First Earth Run, we even requested that archenemies in both Nicaragua and Northern Ireland stop fighting for the duration of the time the torch of peace was in their country. Remarkably, they did!

A request is as powerful as our integrity sharing it. People relate to the sincere intentions and motives of another person. When they say "yes" to a request, it is because they have connected in some way with the person making it.

Share meaningful life information with one another. As human beings we want to know what is really going on in the lives of others around us. When someone shares at a personal level it creates an opening for a relationship to be established. When you invite people to connect, make it count. Have them answer deep and meaningful questions about themselves.

A process I have found very helpful in establishing a meaningful connection with another person is exchanging life stories with a particular emphasis on experiences and people that have forged one's character, view of the world, and path in life. To do this well requires two to three hours of uninterrupted time. These are the questions.

1. What have been the major life experiences that have shaped me?

2. How have I learned and grown from these experiences?

3. What have been my major accomplishments in life?

4. What have been my most courageous acts in my work and personal life?

5. What are the qualities I most value about myself?

6. What are the qualities I most value in each of the members of my family?

7. What am I most passionate about in life? Why?

These questions go below the surface and require a level of connection not normally experienced among people working together for social change. Individuals who take the time to answer them honestly, and listen to another's answers with full attention, usually feel that a heartfelt bond has been created.

Connect people around shared aspirations. We are much more alike than we are different. We all want community. We all want to live in safe, healthy neighborhoods. We all want the best for our children and loved ones. The meta-architecture of a transformative social innovation is designed around these universal ideals. One of the many benefits of an aspirational ideal is that it connects people around a commonly held value or experience—caring for the environment for the sake of our children, for example, or making life better on the street where we live, or creating a more peaceful planet.

Invite people to talk about the hopes and dreams they share in common. During the information meeting for the livable neighborhood program, neighbors share what they most love and value about their block and what they would most love it to be like. In twenty minutes they gain more insight into what is important for their neighbors than in twenty years of casually talking to one another on the street. This connection around one another's aspirations provides motivation to work together for these common goals.

Share authentically. At each topic meeting in the behavior-change programs there is time set aside for people to share about what challenges they faced, how they handled them, and what support they might wish from the group. This is a very powerful part of the meeting because it allows people to be real with one another about where they might be struggling.

With EcoTeams, for example, a team member might talk about a teenager who takes exceedingly long showers and frustrates her best-laid plans to achieve her water-conservation goal; a spouse who will not participate in the program in spite of a variety of subtle or not so subtle threats; or the challenge of finding time to take the environmental actions while leading a very busy life. It requires vulnerability to share our challenges with others and receive support. Creating formal opportunities to have these types of authentic conversations is what enables meaningful connections to be sustained over time, not to mention achieving the desired behavior changes.

Provide opportunities for people to be seen at their best. As human beings we all have a need to be seen, valued, and affirmed. When we feel respected and cared about we are willing to let down our defenses and open up to one another. To deepen the connections among people we need to create opportunities for people to be seen at their best. In my empowerment and leadership trainings I always ask the community to acknowledge others' courage for vulnerably sharing their growing edge in front of the group.

An exercise I do in many groups to connect the community is ask three of the life story questions. What is your most meaningful accomplishment? What is your most courageous act? What are the qualities you most love and value about yourself? I tell people that modesty is not acceptable; they need to allow themselves to be seen at their best. People's answers to these questions are always moving. The exercise only takes a few minutes per person, but the collective humanity shared creates a lasting connection among people.

Create opportunities for social connection. "All work and no play makes Jack a dull boy" is a saying my wife repeats regularly. Fortunately for me, I am trainable and take heed. In the arena of social change, "all work and no play" also has much relevance. Social time is how we bond. And when we bond we commit ourselves.

We always recommend that people have potluck dinners with no work agenda before an EcoTeam meeting. This provides time to enjoy one another on a purely personal level. When working with a team of people, office or birthday parties are great for building this personal connection. It is simple to arrange these gatherings, but we often let opportunities fall by the wayside because we are so busy changing the world. Remember: It is the social lubrication that motivates us to work just a little bit harder and go that extra mile. The "social" part of social change is the hidden secret right in front of our eyes.

COOPERATION PRINCIPLES, PRACTICES, AND LESSONS LEARNED

To change the world we must cooperate with others, but rarely do we think about *how* until we have a key relationship breakdown. Then we must scramble to stitch the relationship back together again, often at a lower quality, because of the deterioration of mutual trust. Or we blame the other person as the cause of the problem and write him or her off as not worth the effort. So many social change projects needlessly fall apart or perform at a low level relative to their potential because of limited skills in this area. There are many places to learn negotiation and team-building skills, but where do we learn cooperation skills? The assumption is we just decide to cooperate and it somehow happens magically; unfortunately, this is rarely the case.

Helping social change agents build competency in cooperation skills has been a major focus of my work for decades. Because cooperation is the foundation of peace building, it was an explicit goal of the First Earth Run. One of our slogans was "Relaying Fire Around the World to Light the Spirit of Cooperation." We attempted to accomplish this through our What's Working in the World program, the subtitle of which was "An Olympics of Cooperation." Each community the torch passed through was requested to identify the five most successful local self-help projects that either embodied or fostered cooperation among people or organizations. The head of state or mayor then honored these winners with a beautiful *Olympics of Cooperation* medal on a blue ribbon inscribed with the United Nations and First Earth Run logos. Our intention was to help communities and countries identify, highlight, and disseminate best practices for cooperation.

Whatever value this program may have offered the world, it turned out to be a personal research project for me on cooperation best practices. I continued to build on this learning in each of the subsequent social change initiatives in which I was involved. This next section represents the fruit of this learning on four levels: between individuals, among members of a small group, between organizations, and internationally.

Interpersonal Cooperation: Creating a Foundational Relationship

This is the building block for all the other levels of cooperation. Any dynamic relationship includes differences of opinion, heated discussions, and misunderstandings. Any one of these can lead to bruised feelings and a desire to pull back from the relationship. This comes with the territory of human beings working together to bring something new into the world. When disagreements or misunderstandings occur we have two choices. We can sweep our negative feelings under the rug as if nothing happened or we can talk about them. Having a difficult conversation is a choice many avoid because it is uncomfortable and most of us don't know how to do it. But avoiding this conversation will cause the relationship to lose vitality, deteriorate, or dissolve. To avoid this and maximize the potential for cooperation, we need to apply four practices.

Establish a formal agreement in advance to have difficult conversations when necessary. When I am establishing a relationship with a key partner on a project, I request that we develop a joint vision for what we wish to achieve and how we wish to work together. In the "how we wish to work together" part I describe the quality of the communication I would like as open and honest. In order to achieve this I request the other person to tell me if something I do bothers him or her so I can adjust my behavior. And I ask permission to do the same. The person inevitably accepts this request, usually with gratitude that we have made something like this explicit. The operating assumption of our relationship becomes *unless we hear otherwise everything is fine.*

This puts the onus on both of us to be accountable for the quality and workability of our relationship. This requires us to both pay attention to what we are feeling and be willing to communicate anything we may be harboring that is undermining the relationship. Are we feeling resentful or angry about something the other person said, did, or did not do? Are we concerned that something we said or did may have offended the other person? Have we heard something about this person that is bothering us? Making these types of communications is not easy, but it is essential if we wish to maintain a high-quality working relationship.

In spite of making the commitment to full disclosure, one person may still be afraid to risk this type of communication. The assumption that everything is fine unless we hear otherwise may not be playing out in actual fact. If we notice something is askew in the way the other person is acting, we need to be proactive and take the initiative to talk about it. Whoever has the most emotional awareness in the relationship at any moment in time needs to take a leadership role for bringing up and helping resolve any communication breakdowns that may have occurred. Over time this leadership responsibility can come to be shared equally.

In a communication breakdown take personal responsibility for your contribution to it. A typical communication in which one person blames the other for a mistake might go like this: "Your screwup caused the problem. You should have known better." The other person replies, "It was you who should have seen this coming. If you had done a better job managing this project we never would have gotten into this mess." A blaming conversation can also include some choice expletives.

The consequence of such a communication is that both people can harden into positions of self-righteousness and avoid talking about difficult subjects that might lead to heated exchanges again in the future. This polarizes the relationship, erodes the quality of cooperation, and undermines the potential for the achievement of substantive outcomes. Unfortunately, for lack of good communication skills many relationships deteriorate into this state.

Here's how an alternative communication might look when one person redirects the trajectory of the conversation by taking responsibility for his or her contribution to the situation. The person in blame mode says, "Your screwup caused the problem. You should have known better." The more skillful person can respond, saying, "I want to do a good job and I feel really bad about this situation. I clearly missed the signals. When you communicate your displeasure with me I feel even worse. I made a mistake and I apologize. I would welcome suggestions you might have to help me improve in the future."

Rather than responding in kind to the attack, the person takes responsibility to share how the communication makes him or her feel; owns his or her contribution to the problem by acknowledging a mistake; and demonstrates humility by requesting feedback. This creates an opening for the other person to understand the impact of their harsh communication style and hopefully modify it in the future; and to consider reciprocating in kind by also taking responsibility for his or her own contribution to the problem. Moreover, it short-circuits the potential for the recriminatory communication to escalate. Demonstrating this level of self-responsibility and vulnerability enables a clean resolution to an issue and lays the foundation for a healthy relationship going forward.

Resolve chronic issues by developing a win-win solution. If a communication breakdown keeps occurring then it is likely that the issue is more systemic. Perhaps there are assumptions about how two people are working together that need to be re-examined. Perhaps there is something in the power dynamic that is off-putting to one of the individuals. Perhaps there is an elephant in the room that people have been dancing around. It is great to be able to resolve communication breakdowns cleanly when they occur, but if the same issue keeps coming up, then it needs to be addressed at the root level. To achieve a lasting solution requires both parties engage in a win-win negotiation.

The premise of a win-win negotiation is that both parties feel good about the outcome. The process requires that both people share what they really want around the issue in dispute, and then work together to make sure both achieve it. For this type of negotiation to succeed each person needs to be vulnerable in sharing real needs, and willing to trust the good intentions of the other person. To get to this level of truth will often require peeling through several layers of the onion. But when we get there with another person, not only have we resolved the issue at hand, but we have deepened the relationship so both people are motivated to contribute at the highest level.

Create a regular process time to check in. One of the ways to keep the relationship functioning at a high level without requiring a serious intervention is to establish a formal process before each meeting, or every few meetings, just to check in. The time can be used to discuss little or large things that might need to be aired about either the relationship or the project. If there is nothing going on, then both parties can jump right into work, but if there is something nagging, this allows it to be nipped in the bud before it rises to the level of a problem.

The concern sometimes voiced about a process check-in is that it might evolve into a longer conversation that takes time away from doing the real work. The alternative, of course, is a hidden agenda that derails the work even more. To avoid either occurrence it is important to place a time limit on check-ins of no more than fifteen minutes. If, after that period, it is determined that the process communication requires more time, then a separate conversation can be scheduled offline.

Small Group Cooperation:
Creating a High-Performance Team
to Achieve Behavior Change

My interest in small group cooperation has grown out of the need in society for certain prosocial behaviors to be adopted by citizens. I discovered early on that a peer support group was a critical success factor in motivating people to change. But to achieve the gold standard of behavior change required that the group operate at a high level of performance. Learning how to transform a small group into a high-performance team capable of achieving substantive and measurable behavior change has been quite a journey. The more than 5,000 EcoTeams with whom I have had the privilege to work have been my teachers. The following five practices are results from this learning.

Create the right size group. The size of the group is very important. Too small and there are not enough energy and diversity of ideas. Too large and there is not enough time for each person to fully participate in the meeting. The ideal size for a team being used as a support group for behavior change is eight to twelve people. This allows each person a chance to personally share his or her accomplishments and needs and to get support from the group. This size also allows for groups to bond socially, as it is small enough for people to form personal relationships with each of the other people.

Build the group into a team. The first meeting needs to be devoted to building the group into a team. The most effective way is to ask each person what they want as the outcome for participating, and to combine these statements into a group purpose statement. If all members see a piece of that team purpose statement reflecting their personal vision, they can own it. This can be done in about fifteen or twenty minutes and is the quickest and most efficient way we have found for bonding the team.

The next step is for the group to divide up leadership responsibilities so everyone involved is invested in the process. This can be done by having a different host/facilitator for each meeting. This distributes the responsibility and ownership for the team's success among the different members. This also increases the pleasure of participation for everyone because they get to visit one another's homes and experience a diversity of meeting styles and hospitality.

In addition, it is helpful to have someone take on the formal role as team leader with the explicit responsibility of looking out for the overall performance of the team. This person has the job of making sure the team is performing well against the goals they have set, and if there is a problem, of getting the team back on track.

Establish a group process protocol. The primary rationale for individuals to choose to participate in a support group is that it will help them accomplish their goals better than on their own. The more effectively a team functions the truer this will be. Part of this functionality comes from the design of carefully crafted meeting agendas. But the other part comes from having an effective process in place to address any breakdowns in the group's performance.

It is important to explain the group process protocol during the first meeting. I have found it effective to have a group check-in at the start of the gathering of up to ten minutes to air any issues and to see how the group is performing. Are people coming on time to the meetings? If not, what can be done either to renegotiate the starting time or motivate any latecomers to prioritize this as important. Are people taking the actions they told the group they would? If not, why not? How can the group help someone who's having difficulty be more successful in the future? Is the meeting following the agenda or veering off in many different directions? If so, how does the group wish to handle this?

During this first meeting it is also important to establish coaching guidelines for these communications; otherwise there is a good chance they won't happen, or they'll be poorly done, causing hurt feelings. The coaching process provides a means for the effective delivery of feedback. It starts by asking individuals on the team if they are open to both offering and receiving coaching from teammates when they see a breakdown in an agreement either the team or an individual has made. Assuming people agree, which they generally do, then we need to ask people to share what type of feedback works best for them.

A regular time to check in and agreed-on guidelines for making difficult communications create the foundation for a team to achieve high-quality results.

Structure meetings to produce tangible outcomes. To get a group of people to achieve substantive results in a short amount of time requires structure. Underneath the softer process elements is the meeting skeleton. Like the skeleton in our bodies, this is what holds the meeting together. Each EcoTeam meeting has a structured agenda with time allotments for each agenda item and a script for the facilitator. Some meeting elements may run longer, others shorter, and the facilitator will inevitably improvise on the script. But this clear structure enables the facilitator to know exactly what has to be accomplished and how to get it done.

The elements for a ninety-minute EcoTeam topic meeting include: an inspirational start; sharing of actions taken since the previous meeting with support from the team as needed; a hands-on demonstration of possible actions people could take in the next topic area; sharing of individual action plans for their next topic with a request for support; check-in on team performance with interventions as needed; setup of support calls between the meetings by the facilitator to make sure teammates are on track; review of next steps; and acknowledgment of the team's accomplishments.

The opposite of this, which I have seen in teams that do not produce tangible behavior change, is what I have come to call pseudo empowerment. In this situation, the meeting facilitator and group prefer not to structure the meeting or hold individuals or the team accountable for doing the things they say they will do. Empowerment by this definition is a hands-off affair. Inevitably this approach quickly devolves into a discussion group or salon rather than a high-performing team committed to achieving the tangible behavior change of its members. At the end of the meetings people have not accomplished what they set out to and leave with a sense of dissatisfaction. Rather than being empowered by this approach, they often feel despondent, having spent so much time with nothing tangible to show for it.

The way to avoid this is by carefully establishing the value and rationale behind each element of the meeting agenda so that people understand why it's important to the outcomes the individual and group wish to achieve. This careful explanation helps the team appreciate the meeting design so that if and when someone wishes to deviate from the structure, the group has enough knowledge to make a clear-headed decision.

Demonstrate an expectation of success. The intangible of a high-performing team is the expectation of the person who initiates it—the team leader. My experience has been that the higher the expectation a team leader places on a team, the higher the expectation the team places on itself and the better the results it achieves. This was the intangible that Michael Jordan brought to the Chicago Bulls.

A team leader needs to demonstrate an expectation of success by asking the team to take its investment of time seriously. That is, to do the things they say they'll do. That's why the group check-in and commitment to mutual accountability are the team's backbone. When members of a team do not do what they say they will do, it's essential that the team leader intervene even though he or she may be tempted to think: "It's not the end of the world, I'll let it slide." If the team leader doesn't speak up, the lack of accountability will quickly spread throughout the team, become the new social norm, and precipitate a downward spiral in performance.

Equally important, an effective team leader should be constantly looking for opportunities to affirm excellent performance, belief in the team, and the importance of the goal. The combination of nipping poor habits in the bud and reinforcing positive achievements keeps a team on track to achieve outstanding results.

Organizational Cooperation: Forging Strategic Partnerships

The work to improve society is so enormous that no one organization can get very far on its own. A strategic partnership that combines the strengths of two organizations can achieve synergy and speed up the desired social change. But forging such a partnership is a demanding process. It requires the alignment of each organization's needs, mission, and competencies. It necessitates the development of an agreement around project management, decision-making responsibilities, and financial expenditures. Two different cultures must learn how to work together. As a result of these challenges, it is not surprising that very few organizations choose to create strategic partnerships.

But given the ever-increasing social problems we face and the limited resources available to tackle them, it is no longer an option not to work together. We must learn the skills for forging strategic partnerships that achieve a high level of organizational cooperation. As a social entrepreneur I have had to learn these skills through trial and error. In the process, I have identified four practices for forging successful strategic partnerships that further social change.

Identify strategic partners who provide mission critical assets you do not possess. The mission-critical assets I looked for in the various initiatives I have discussed were established networks to speed up the dissemination of the social innovation; a respected imprimatur to raise its credibility level; and resources—financial or human—to invest in it. It did not take me long to discover that public institutions with a comparable social mission provided the best place to find these assets. The rub is that these institutions are generally not looking for social innovations and are risk averse. So the social innovation needs to be successfully prototyped and provide a substantial benefit before a public institution will consider it. In the case of my community-based programs it was their ability to achieve measurable behavior change that attracted the attention of government agencies.

With a clear value proposition established, the next step is to find people in these institutions who have the vision and the credibility to champion a new idea. Although visionaries in government are not in abundant supply they do exist, as exemplified by people like Jim Grant in UNICEF, Molly Olson in the President's Council on Sustainable Development, Paul de Jongh in the Dutch Environmental Ministry, Mike Lindberg in Portland, Shirley Kitchen in Philadelphia, and Alan Leidner in New York City. They can be sleuthed out by asking a few simple questions. Who are the people bringing new ideas into these public institutions? Are they respected by their peers or isolated because they have a polarizing effect? What is their track record? It is important to find not just a receptive person, but the right person with the skill and passion to be an effective champion of the idea.

Once they are identified it is important to enroll them as the prime mover of the project in the political environments in which they operate. Sometimes they will want to hand this responsibility off to the social entrepreneur, but it is they who best know how to maneuver through the change-resistant conservative bureaucratic systems. If they have accepted the roll as the prime mover in their culture, it is wise to follow their guidance. The advice I received from Annie Grunwald and Alan Leidner when working with the city of New York was invaluable. They were seasoned trail guides and I was grateful for their navigational acumen.

Here's an interesting postscript on the unique synergy potential between a social entrepreneur and a public institution. The positive response they received from their participation in the First Earth Run so pleased UNICEF that they decided to develop their own in-house social innovations. To undertake this development they hired the UNICEF project manager assigned to the First Earth Run, assuming because of his association with the project he could become a social innovator. But he was a project manager and did not have the temperament or creativity of the social entrepreneur. For eighteen months he tried to invent something comparable to the First Earth Run before UNICEF closed down the project.

The moral of this story is that for social entrepreneurs with a proven social innovation there is fertile ground for forming strategic partnerships with public institutions. And for visionary government leaders who wish to increase the social value and profile of their institution, cultivating a relationship with an accomplished social entrepreneur is a time- and cost-effective way to go.

But this is only one type of strategic partnership that can be formed. It is important to bring in other partners who are playing in the same field if they provide complementary assets. This both strengthens the initiative and avoids a wasteful competition for resources and the attention of the public. An example of this type of partnership was my relationship with Citizens for New York City. Their network and on-the-ground organizing capabilities were the critical resources we needed to break through in New York City.

Working with socially responsible corporations provides another type of potential strategic partnership. Corporations can bring many assets to a project, including finances, people, and advertising. Companies who make these types of investments are rewarded by customer patronage, employee loyalty, and the attraction of top talent who wish to be associated with an organization that is making a difference in the world.

It is important when forming partnerships with business that the project not lose its social change integrity and be transformed into a corporate advertising campaign. This will not serve either party. If the integrity of the social change is lost, the company will get a backlash that undermines their brand in the marketplace, and the credibility of the social entrepreneur will be compromised for any future projects they may wish to pursue. To avoid this, both parties need to be clearly aligned around the desired social outcome and put that as the top priority. It is certainly appropriate for the corporation to receive recognition, but this needs to be done in a discreet manner. We formed many of these types of strategic partnerships in our sustainable lifestyle campaigns and using these guidelines they proved successful for both parties.

Create a visioning process. The immediate benefits to each organization from a strategic partnership are usually quite obvious or the conversation would never begin. But it is a missed opportunity for the strategic partnership if it stays just at this level. To achieve its potential for synergy, a visioning process is required to bring to the surface the expectations, needs, and opportunities for both organizations and their principals.

When UNICEF initially became a strategic partner with the First Earth Run it was based solely on their being a recipient of funds raised through the event. I knew there was substantially more potential for this partnership and suggested we engage in a visioning process to see what might be possible. UNICEF agreed and discovered that having a major association with the First Earth Run could generate goodwill with the political leaders and citizens in the developing world whose cooperation they needed to implement their development agenda. They also realized that the event could raise the profile of the UNICEF brand in developed countries, which would assist in future fund-raising efforts. And finally, they saw that the association would increase employee morale and retention, a major challenge given the high burnout rate in development work.

As a result of this visioning process, UNICEF decided to increase its association with the First Earth Run significantly. Not only did they agree to using their clout as a U.N. agency to encourage the participation of various heads of state, but they used their field offices and staff around the world to assist in the event organizing. In New York they provided an entire floor of their offices with staff support and access to all their global communications capabilities to organize the event.

The visioning process should also identify the learning and growth desires for the principal individuals in the project. What do members want out of their investment of time to further their own development? The more satisfaction each person gets through being able to grow and contribute, the more invested he or she becomes and the more the project benefits. A project can often be designed to provide these developmental opportunities. For example, during the visioning process with UNICEF, Gail shared her passion for traveling internationally and learning about different cultures. Knowing of this passion and the gift she had for cross-cultural communication, I encouraged her to become our international director, and UNICEF supported her by providing access to their cross-cultural experts and international briefing documents. Gail was thus able to take a natural strength of hers to an even higher level of proficiency, an outcome that she found extremely gratifying.

A vision is always in need of recalibration based on feedback received from interacting with the world. This was all the more so with the First Earth Run, given the logistical complexities and geopolitical challenges inherent in an endeavor of this magnitude. We were constantly weathering storms and making course corrections. This type of experience deepens trust in one another's judgments and builds ownership of the vision. When we hit an unexpected financial storm with our sponsor backing out at the last minute, I was not surprised that Jim Grant was right there to put up UNICEF funds. This was just one more storm to weather, albeit a large one, and we had been at the helm of this ship together too long for him to let it sink. When a vision is owned by both partners, the commitment each brings to its success is just one more dimension of the synergy.

Establish a detailed written agreement and communication protocol for addressing issues in the relationship. Strategic partners need to spend time up front clearly delineating roles, responsibilities, finances, and decision-making authority. Even when this is done well, which it often is not, given the dynamic nature of these endeavors, there will always be gray areas that come up with no agreed-on procedure in place. This might include areas where missions unexpectedly conflict or unanticipated changes occur and opinions differ on strategy adjustments. A high-functioning strategic partnership requires a good process for communication. This is where the protocols for one-on-one and small-group communication described previously fit in. Creating regular check-in time during meetings will nip any potential problems in the bud.

An example of one of these gray areas came up in my partnership with the New York City Office of Emergency Management, which has a policy of supporting anyone with special needs to participate in public events they hold. They put this in the flier advertising our capacity-building training. I didn't think anything of this at the time, as I knew the Red Cross building we were using was wheelchair enabled. A very committed hearing-impaired couple from Staten Island wished to do outreach to this community and therefore wanted to participate in our capacity-building training. We immediately realized that this was a special opportunity, as it was difficult to find organizers for such a hard-to-reach population.

We discovered, however, that for them to participate in the training required us to hire two sign language interpreters. Their fees were surprisingly expensive and we did not have any money to cover this in our budget, which was already overstretched. We asked OEM to cover this expense since it was their stated policy to work with those with special needs and the flier had included this fact based on their request. Unfortunately, they had no budget for this expense either and believed it was our responsibility. It was a gray area and we had a genuine difference of opinion.

As fate would have it, Annie Grunwald, with whom I had built this initiative from the beginning and developed an excellent communication process, had left to take another job. Since I did not really know the person with whom I was having this disagreement and we had not established any communication protocol, the conversation got bogged down. In the end I took on the expense, but the friction generated through this dispute for a time dampened our relationship with OEM. From this experience I learned that I need to reach out and proactively establish a communication protocol when a new person comes on to a project. Failure to do this puts the strategic partnership at risk.

Carefully align with a partner around the key metrics for evaluating a project's success. When I began working with the city of Portland, Oregon, to deliver our sustainable lifestyle campaign I was not skillful in articulating how best to define success. Because this was our first sustainable lifestyle campaign I was most interested in the two criteria necessary for long-term success: our EcoTeam recruitment rates on a block and the ability to get teams to self-replicate. My partner in the city, accustomed to a more straightforward framework of fee-for-service contracts, was interested in an easily quantifiable way to measure success: the number of EcoTeams formed.

I had no problem with this and proposed a goal of forming sixty teams in one year. In spite of my team's best efforts we only formed forty-eight, or 80 percent of our goal. I had fallen into the classic visionary's mistake of over promising and under delivering. In spite of my best efforts to convince our project partner to be less concerned with the numbers and more with the process, which had been successful, she was dissatisfied.

In spite of the mismatch of expectations around the criteria for measuring success the city of Portland wished to continue the partnership. Chastened by my underperformance relative to the quantifiable goal we had set the year before, I requested we meet to align our expectations and work together more synergistically going forward. As a result they were willing to provide us access to their networks for recruiting EcoTeam team leaders and take ownership for the goal we set. We renewed our commitment to the sixty EcoTeam goal, and now they were a committed partner helping us to achieve it—which we did.

This experience taught me the importance of taking the time to align with a strategic partner around the metrics for evaluating a project's success and making sure the partner is fully on board to help achieve it. With two heads now on the line, the chances of keeping mine intact significantly improved along with the results we could achieve.

International Cooperation:
Learning From the Diversity in Unity

Breakdowns in the international financial system and the threats of climate change and terrorism have forced the world to unify in common cause. This is not easy on a planet where each country has been accustomed to operating autonomously and the consequences of not cooperating have been minimal. But effective international cooperation is no longer optional. Failure to learn how to work together puts every country at risk. The First Earth Run, with the participation of more than sixty countries united by a common vision, can offer some insight on how to go about such a learning exercise.

We had divided up the world into sixteen regions and it was Gail's job to recruit organizers for each of them. After an intensive effort that took a year, she had succeeded in recruiting these sixteen people. We invited them to a beautiful conference center in the countryside not far from Woodstock, New York, for a workshop on how to recruit country organizers and train them in the First Earth Run organizing methodology. Gail was leading the meeting, so I got to mix in with the group and observe their interactions. I assumed since everyone had signed on for the peaceful planet vision they would see things pretty much the same way, and we would just need to work out the strategies and techniques for communicating the organizing process. I was quite surprised, however, by the degree of friction I observed between people. So I started paying closer attention to these clashes and discovered they were not actually on a personal level, but rather on the level of world views embodied in their cultures.

They were all united around the big idea of the First Earth Run as a global intervention to reduce the threat of nuclear war and further peace on the planet. Everyone recognized the archetypal power of the torch relay fire ritual. And everyone loved that this event was dedicated to creating a better world for our children with any proceeds raised donated to UNICEF. But people did not see eye to eye when it came to implementing the event in their respective countries or regions of the world.

The Japanese representative wanted things organized more formally. The African representatives wanted to stress spontaneity. Our colleague from

India wanted to accentuate the spiritual underpinning of the event. The European representatives wanted to stress the intellectual aspects of the strategies for cooperation. The Americans wished to stress the more idealistic aspects. Each person saw the world through his or her cultural lens and tried to shape the First Earth Run to reflect this world view. It was an enlightening moment for me. There was so much to learn from these differences, but rather than learning we were having cultural clashes.

After a day of observing these culture clashes I shared with the group what I had been observing. Putting into words what everyone had been experiencing seemed to bring a measure of relief in the room. Because we certainly were not making any headway around the agenda, we decided to try an experiment. I asked the participants to share with the group how they would like to organize the First Earth Run in their country. Their job was to listen with an open mind and look for ideas that they could take back to their own culture. Whenever they observed themselves getting judgmental, they were to note down what assumption they had about the world that was being confronted, and then go *toward* this new approach and imagine how they might adapt it to their own country.

This process allowed all to observe the unconscious cultural biases influencing their world views. After discussing what we observed in small groups, we moved the discussion to the large group. The exercise proved transformative. We came to realize that while we all thought of ourselves as independent thinkers, we were, in fact, significantly influenced by our cultures. As a consequence we were not availing ourselves of the remarkable opportunity the First Earth Run provided to expand our view of the world and pool our cultural resources to create something greater than any of us could achieve on our own. We were a microcosm of what the planet needed to learn and what the First Earth Run was attempting to teach.

We decided we needed to walk our talk, so to speak. For the rest of the training we continued the practice of observing our reactions to what each person was saying, and when we noticed resistance, going toward what was different rather than pulling back. We took on the mantle of cultural anthropologists being offered a remarkable opportunity to unearth new ideas that we could then cross-pollinate around the globe.

We unearthed much. We learned, for example, that Tanzania has a national unification torch relay tradition. Every year a torch is relayed from the top of Mount Kilimanjaro through each community as a way to bring the country together. Many of our organizers decided to offer this unifying theme to their country or region of the world. We learned about a solemn ceremony that takes place each year in Hiroshima, Japan. The entire city honors those who died as a result of the nuclear bomb blast, and prays for world peace. Many of our organizers added this ritual of honoring those who lost their lives in war and praying for world peace to the events they would promote in their part of the world. A few decided to blend these two ideas together.

It was enlightening to open ourselves to different ideas, practices, and world views. Not only did it enrich each person, but it strengthened the overall effectiveness of our global endeavor. We are so much smarter together than separately. Learning from one another's cultures is the key to unlocking our collective global intelligence. And we need to harness this collective intelligence to address the daunting issues we face as a human community. The silver lining of these global challenges is that they require us to learn from the diversity in our unity, and take our next evolutionary step on the path to becoming an interconnected planetary species.

COLLABORATION PRINCIPLES, PRACTICES, AND LESSONS LEARNED

This next section describes three different types of collaboration, each with the goal of achieving creative breakthroughs that bring about new social solutions. Each of these approaches attempts to accomplish this outcome through creating synergy among the participants. The first approach is creating a high-powered thinking partnership among two or three people. The second is through eliciting the genius embedded in a group operating at its full potential. And the third is a combination of these two.

Creating a Thinking Partnership:
Multiplying One Another's Intelligence
to Achieve Creative Breakthroughs

Every initiative I have described in this book has been developed through a robust collaboration that blended complementary strengths with the goal of achieving creative breakthroughs. In some cases I sought out people, in some cases they sought me out, and other times the people came with the territory. Each person brought different talents, competencies, and experiences, but the one thing each relationship had in common was that we needed to learn how to collaborate in a creative manner to design and/or implement a social innovation. In each case we were navigating uncharted territory. As the prime mover of the social innovation it fell on me to facili-tate this process and elicit my collaborators' core talents and creativity through the creation of a thinking partnership. The next section describes the process I developed to do this and its application in building the sus-tainable lifestyle campaign in Portland, Oregon.

Learn about one another at a more profound level. To achieve the type of synergy needed for creative breakthroughs requires knowing the other person beyond the exchange of biography details. I have found that to build a strong foundation for the thinking partnership there are three important topics to discuss.

The first is *our view of the social change process* and how we came to hold it. This is not something that is at the top of most people's minds so I usu-ally take the initiative to explain mine. I start by sharing how my back-ground as a designer of transformation tools has informed me. In particular, I discuss my belief that the onus for social change rests more on the change agent's skill level than on the individuals they wish to see change. I talk about the fact that most people are willing to do the right thing if provided effective tools and support, and that empowering individuals to participate directly in the social change process is critical to changing a social system. I also talk about how the First Earth Run was a defining experience in my life, and the lessons it taught me about dreaming big and what is possible in our world.

I then attempt to elicit the influences that have shaped my partner's world view about social change. As my partner speaks I am listening for common experiences that can create a shortcut to our values and a shared vocabulary we can use in working together. I am eager to learn about expe-riences or strategies that can be complementary to my areas of competency. I am also interested in my partner's degree of self-knowledge. That is, how much his or her life is informed by self-reflection. I have found it much easier to work with someone who brings self-awareness to a close working collaboration.

The second area of exchange is around *our thinking styles*. Here I am looking to compare the basic way we each think through an issue so we can identify areas for maximizing synergy. This can either be as a result of thinking in a similar way, so we can go deeper, or thinking differently, so we use each other's minds to bring fresh insights. Again, I usually take the initiative. I explain that I am a big-picture thinker, and that as a social architect I need to begin any thinking exercise by scoping out a picture of what success looks like—the end game. I then like to think about strategies and tactics that can be used to achieve that end game. Finally I move into design, implementation, and iterative learning.

Throughout each of these stages I like to work with a partner to rigorously think through an idea until we have identified a plausible path forward. The process entails identifying key questions we need to answer, building on each other's ideas for answering these questions and challenging any unexamined assumptions and conventions that might limit our options.

While this is not usually something most people have considered they can usually extemporaneously describe their thinking preference and process. As the facilitator I am paying close attention to how their minds work. Some people naturally think strategically and rigorously about an issue. Others don't have the temperament for this and are more interested in designing operational- or tactical-level solutions. Still others are not interested in spending a lot of time thinking things through and want to jump right into the fray and see what happens. They use the ready, fire, aim approach. Having this conversation before we begin brings more awareness to our respective ways of thinking and allows us to build on each other's strengths.

The final area of exchange is around our *aspirations and passion for the particular initiative.* Why are we each motivated to do this work and how does it move our soul? This is the fuel that feeds the creative fire of the relationship. Again, this level of conversation may be new for a partner and I generally need to model it. I often will share that ever since I was a young boy my passion has been changing the world and making a difference with my life. I talk about the unitive impulse that has moved me throughout my social change work of bringing people and groups together to improve the human condition.

Making our deeper motivations explicit enables bonding to occur at a more profound level and creates synergy around our collective aspirations.

Use the empowerment methodology as a transformational framework for the collaboration. Using a transformational process enables the collaboration to perform at a high level of effectiveness. Its foundation is the creation of a joint vision to serve as the collaboration's North Star. I generally use the following four questions or some variation thereon depending on the nature of the collaboration.

What do we wish our collaboration to accomplish?

What is the creative breakthrough we need to achieve?

What are the measurable outcomes?

What do we each want personally from our collaboration?

The process of co-creating a vision jumpstarts our thinking partnership and allows us to develop joint ownership of the initiative. I then introduce the transformational tools of limiting beliefs and turnarounds, and the growing edge, which we apply to this vision. Throughout the project we return to these tools to tune up our project and our personal growing edges.

Develop a communication protocol for managing challenges and breakdowns. A dynamic co-creative process tends to generate heat. The final step in laying the groundwork for a successful thinking partnership is creating an interpersonal communication protocol. I explain the procedure described in the interpersonal cooperation section and we agree to a regular time for process check-ins.

Forging a Thinking Partnership in Portland

Over the years I have had the opportunity to use these three practices many times. On shorter projects or less intensive collaborations I use them more informally. But on long-term projects they are the bedrock on which I build the collaboration. The major collaborations described in this book have benefited from these practices, but one in particular stands out because of the unprecedented nature of the creative breakthrough required.

In the fall of 1996 we received our first contract to create a sustainable lifestyle campaign from the city of Portland, Oregon. While we had successfully tested most of the community-organizing tools, we had never done so in a systematic way before. Although this was the next incremental step on the long journey I had been on with the sustainable lifestyle program, one might better call this a quantum leap. To get to this next level would require a creative breakthrough with no precedent in community organizing. We needed to invent *a self-organizing and replicable strategy for disseminating environmental behavior change communitywide.* I was most fortunate to find two individuals perfectly suited to this pioneering endeavor. Over the next several years the three of us would develop a vibrant thinking partnership.

Michael Dowd was a former evangelical minister who had developed a green ministry based on the work of theologian Thomas Berry and the story of evolution. I had met Michael many years earlier in one of my transformative leadership trainings. After the training he came up and offered me a suggestion for how I might phrase several questions to be more in alignment with Thomas Berry's thinking. I opened my training book to look at the particular questions Michael was referring to and before I could say anything he had graciously written in his preferred words. I loved his passion and commitment to his beliefs. If anybody could sell EcoTeams, about which he was passionate both as an environmental imperative and an evolutionary act, it was Michael.

I met Llyn Peabody when she came to interview for the job of program manager in Portland. Within minutes, she had transformed the conversation into an exploration of the deepest issues facing humanity and the world. She asked me profound questions about my motivation and vision. I loved the way her mind worked. It was creative, facile, deep, systemic, and practical. She loved to design transformative structures and processes. She was passionate about the environment, could articulate her ideas with the best of them, and was able to move easily among the different circles of people that made up Portland's many subcultures.

If Michael was the assertive, active, and goal-oriented archetypal male, Llyn was the imaginative, grounded, and process-orientated archetypal female. They were a perfect counterpoint to each other and represented the exact set of skills we needed to be successful. Our synergy would be built around Michael's salesmanship, Llyn's ability to create and ground our process structures, and my knowledge of social architecture. For our respective strengths to become more than the sum of their parts we needed to achieve a high level of collaboration.

We started our collaboration with the visioning process described previously. We wished to create a self-organizing behavior-change model that was scalable. The creative breakthrough we needed to achieve this was a consistent way for people to start an EcoTeam on their block and for that team to replicate itself. To use a nature metaphor, we wished to plant a seed in a variety of different types of soil, have it take root, and when it matured, self-propagate. The measurable outcome we wished was the formation of sixty EcoTeams over the next twelve months. What we wanted personally was the satisfaction of working on something that was on the cutting edge of social change, and support for our individual development through this creative process.

While we had set the goal of forming 60 EcoTeams to accommodate the need of the city for a metric, our larger objective was a community-organizing model breakthrough. This, however, would take much longer than a year to design and test. It takes time to recruit and train team leaders, for them to start teams on their block, for these teams to complete the program and then start new teams. It takes even more time to see if this process will continue on the block or surrounding neighborhood. We projected it would take about eighteen months to go through this full cycle.

This learning process would require us to assess our experiences with each team rigorously, and make adjustments in real time based on identifying the right variable or combination of variables to tweak. We isolated seven success factors: the team leader, invitation script, training of the team leader, neighbor-to-neighbor outreach process, information meeting design, final team meeting when the team decides if it will replicate, and the support process enabling that team to start a new team. It would take each of us operating at a high level of collaboration to develop best practices for each of these success factors.

Through the exchange of our life stories we discovered we each had a passion for evolutionary science and particularly the critical junctures when breakthroughs were achieved that moved life to the next level. We would often think of ourselves as conscious evolutionary agents on the threshold of a breakthrough to a higher-order solution in nature. Thinking about ourselves this way got us quite jazzed. We would regularly have two- to three-hour creative mind melds looking for clues from evolutionary history and nature's best practices on self-replication to expand our thinking on how to start and replicate teams. We asked ourselves questions like: What was the catalyst and biological process that enabled single-cell organisms to evolve into multicellular organisms? What could we learn from the wide variety of ways that nature spreads it seeds? How does nature create new ecological niches?

The thinking partnership flowed effortlessly from high-level theorizing to practical design to execution to debriefing and back again. We constantly invented new techniques and procedures associated with each of the seven success factors. Michael and Llyn would test each one several times, and then we would have a rigorous debriefing session to determine whether to keep it intact, make adjustments, or discard it. If we kept it we would observe it in action for at least three months before we would qualify it as a best practice. We maintained this remarkable level of iterative creative collaboration around each of the seven success factors for more than three years. During this time we were also tuning up our relationship as needed, and we were supporting one another's growing edges.

Through this collaborative process we achieved the community-organizing breakthrough we sought. We were able to achieve an average recruitment rate of 25 percent of the households on the block joining the initial team. We were able to get most of these teams to start at least one more new team on their block or the surrounding blocks. On a number of these blocks, the team replication process continued until it included almost all the households.

Without the synergy Michael, Llyn, and I established through our thinking partnership, there was no way these outcomes would have been possible. We brought the best out in one another. While the three of us were fortunate to enjoy such a natural meshing of our thinking styles and abilities, in subsequent years I have applied what I learned with them on many different types of projects with many different types of people. In each case, the synergy achieved through the thinking partnership enabled creative breakthroughs that would never have been realized otherwise.

Eliciting the Group Genius Effect: Achieving the Full Potential of a Community

Collaboration within a group of talented people can allow synergy to go exponential because of the magnitude of concepts, bodies of knowledge, intelligence, and creativity available. Some have called this the *group genius effect*. Creativity expert Gail Taylor defines group genius as "the ability of a group working collaboratively and iteratively to put into place higher-order solutions." But getting at this is not easy. Groups consistently underperform against individuals or one-on-one collaborations because people want to fit in and not rock the boat. This results in what has come to be called groupthink, the output of which is pejoratively referred to as design by committee.

When I first learned about the group genius effect I was quite intrigued. I read all I could to see if anyone had developed a process that could help groups consistently perform at this level. I learned about a number of techniques to enhance creativity within a group, but I could not find any process that achieved the genius effect with any degree of consistency. It seemed that getting this to happen was a little bit like entering the flow state; you know it when you experience it, but it's hard to produce on demand. How could I resist the challenge of trying my hand at eliciting it on a reliable basis?

I had an opportunity to do just that when invited to lead my transformative leadership training for a group of government environmental policy makers and activists from the nonprofit community. They wanted to learn how to work collaboratively on sustainable development projects with businesses where there was often an adversarial relationship. I told the organizers of the training about the notions of building a unitive field and eliciting the group genius effect, and asked if they would like to try an experiment where we attempted to model this within the group. They enthusiastically agreed.

Toward the end of training, after the group was well connected, I explained that to create breakthrough solutions with those who hold diverse or even contrary points of view around sustainable development requires competency in cooperation skills. I asked how many people felt they had this competency. Out of the group of twenty-five leaders a few people tentatively raised their hands. I told them that rather than my offering my insights on cooperation we would learn about it by actually cooperating in an experience that built on each person's knowledge. The journey would be as important as the destination.

I explained that we would break up into four groups with each working on a particular type of cooperation—interpersonal, group, interorganizational, and international. They should choose the group that had the most interest for them. I then explained that to tap into the group genius each person would need to share without inhibition. Their contribution could be cognitive knowledge, direct experience, intuition, or feelings. There were no right or wrong answers, there was only each person offering an ingredient into the pot of the group's collective intelligence. To avail ourselves fully of the group genius each person would be asked to contribute even if only to add a nuance to what had already been said. That nuance might make the difference in discovering something new, cognitively or experientially. The process goal for each member of the group was to look for each person's gift and draw it out to the benefit of the group and that person.

We would use the Native American council format where whoever was inspired would pick up the talking stick and speak from the heart. Everyone

needed to listen deeply so they could learn what this person was really saying beneath the words. There was no cross-talk until everyone had gone.
When each person had gone once, those who wished could have a second
round. When this was complete the group would blend the contributions
and identify the main themes that had come out of the group sharing. As
they went through this blending process they should practice what they had
been learning. Each group would then translate these themes into a five-
minute skit to educate the rest of the community. I then invited them to tap
into their own wisdom and the evolutionary wisdom of the Earth around
cooperation and begin.

As I looked out at these four groups with chairs pulled together in small
circles, I could sense a palpable mind meld occurring. People were in deep
rapport with one another and their own intuitive knowing. They were respectful and solicitous of one another's contribution. Watching a group
made up of primarily environmental scientists and government policymakers, trained to learn through analyzing factual information, give themselves
permission to learn in such a multidimensional manner made this sight all
the more remarkable.

The skits reflected this rich learning process by portraying the cognitive,
emotional, and pragmatic dimensions of cooperation. In one skit the group
demonstrated how to invite people into a cooperative relationship by reaching out to each person in the larger community. Another skit showed two
groups each struggling to accomplish a task and then cooperating and much
more easily accomplishing it. After each skit the full community entered
into a dialogue with the group that had just performed in order to draw out
insights both about the content and the process they went through to get it.
After we did this with each of the groups we identified the common patterns that had emerged. Throughout this dialogue we used the process of
making sure each person contributed and looking for the gift each one
brought to the discussion.

Afterward I debriefed the process to see what everyone had learned. The
universal experience was amazement at the power and profundity of the
group. They appreciated how effective the process was at eliciting the group's
genius and helping them learn experientially about cooperation. On a more
personal level, they loved the way the nonlinear process allowed them to tap
into their own intuition and deep knowing. They valued that the focus was
looking for each person's gift and building on it. They liked that the skit demanded them to move to a high level of synthesis in order to communicate

their insights in an experiential manner, and that we continued this amalgamation of ideas with the whole group. We had built a unitive field around the topic of cooperation, which became a principal teaching on how to cooperate, and then multiplied this learning by tapping into the group genius. The group experience was synergy that had gone exponential.

I led this exercise numerous times after that training and each time it accomplished the same extraordinary results. After awhile, this experience raised another question for me: If the group genius of an ad hoc group of people can be elicited, what might be possible with an existing group with an actual need to collaborate? I did not have to look far to find guinea pigs for this experiment. They were on my doorstep.

Thinking Partnership Meets Group Genius: Multiplying a Community's Intelligence Over Time to Achieve Creative Breakthroughs

Because of our success with the sustainable lifestyle campaign in Portland within a relatively short period of time, six new cities signed on. We had two small West-Coast cities—Issaquah, Washington, and Bend, Oregon—with high levels of environmental awareness and an affluent middle class; two heartland cities—Columbus, Ohio, and Kansas City, Missouri—with limited environmental awareness and many pockets of low-income people; a Midwest college town—Madison, Wisconsin—an oasis of environmental awareness with a transient student population; and a large urban East-Coast city, Philadelphia, contending with urban blight and middle class flight to the suburbs.

To disseminate this social innovation successfully we would need to evolve Portland's best practices so they could be adapted to the unique circumstances of each of these communities. But instead of three people in a thinking partnership we now had a group of fourteen, each bringing different skill sets and backgrounds to our common endeavor. This presented a great opportunity to take the work Llyn, Michael, and I had done to the next level, but it also presented a distinct challenge to get a group of this size and diversity to collaborate effectively.

To take advantage of this opportunity I invited everyone to a two-day retreat at our office in Woodstock, New York, to explore how best to develop our potential as a collaborative group. This first day was focused on their personal leadership development as community organizers, and on creating a transformational framework for our collaboration. I began by explaining the empowerment model and then led them through visioning and limiting beliefs, culminating with each person identifying his or her leadership growing edge. They then divided up into pairs to help each other tune up and build ownership of their growing edges. This was also an opportunity to practice empowerment coaching, which was a core competency they needed to develop as a community organizer. I then modeled this coaching process with several people in front of the large group.

Their growing edge issues included learning specific community-organizing competencies, project management, time management, work-life balance and specific challenges they needed to address in their communities. As we discussed each of these issues in the large group, there was tremendous resonance because of their shared mission. By the end of the day we had become a committed growth community. The next day would be about transforming this growth community into a team capable of performing at a high level of collaboration.

We began day two by training people in the community-organizing model we had developed in Portland. The group determined that about 80 percent was directly relevant to their situation and the other 20 percent would require adaptation. I told them that I wanted to engage them as thinking partners to participate actively in this evolution. I then explained the process Michael, Llyn, and I had used to form our thinking partnership, and led the group through it.

We discovered that their dominant view of social change, not surprisingly, given that they were community organizers, was a belief in people's self-efficacy to effect societal improvement. We had a diversity of experiences to build on, including various types of community organizing, volunteer management, sales, event planning, coaching, training, and process design. Their dominant thinking styles were oriented around action learning and tactical design. We all shared the expected aspirations of wishing to make a difference with our lives and caring for the Earth, but it was a very rich process for each person to share this in his or her own words.

I then talked about the group genius effect and said that I would like to tap into this group's genius for how we could collaborate in an ongoing way to evolve our community-organizing model. I divided them into three smaller groups, explained the process, and set them to their task. Again this process performed its magic both in the quality of the ideas generated and the unitive field that got built. But unlike my prior uses of this process with ad hoc groups, we were able to put these ideas to immediate use in designing the structure for our collaboration.

We would create an ongoing community of practice, a master class, which would meet monthly via a two-hour teleconference. Its goal would be to discover best practices and support one another's growing edges. Each person would come to the master class ready to talk about an accomplishment large or small from the past month and his or her growing edge. We would practice the type of listening and communication techniques used in the group genius process. When the group discovered a potential best practice, several people would volunteer to work together offline to tune it up and test it in their communities. They would then report their results back to the group to evaluate. When we were satisfied that we had a best practice, the group who had worked on the practice would organize a separate call to teach it to others. We would also allocate ten minutes at the beginning of each class for a brief check-in on our group process.

The master class process proved very effective. In a relatively short period of time the communities were achieving results comparable to Portland's. But this was just the beginning. Through this dynamic collaboration process they kept evolving the community-organizing model and developing new applications. They created new best practices for recruiting team leaders, starting EcoTeams, and replicating teams. They discovered new ways to coach EcoTeams so they were able to increase their environmental resource savings per participating household. They developed effective ways for reaching low-income and non-English-speaking parts of the community. They also pioneered new applications for the community-organizing model. It was this body of best practices that allowed me to hit the ground running with our new programs in Philadelphia and New York City.

The master class combined the thinking partnership and group genius tools with a strong commitment to develop best practices and support for each individual's personal growth. This collaboration tool was a social innovation in its own right. The result was a group operating with a high level of synergy at its full potential and achieving significant creative breakthroughs over a sustained period of time.

This group was living proof for me of Margaret Mead's oft-quoted maxim with a twist. "Never doubt that a small group of committed people can change the world—indeed it's the only thing that ever has." The twist—this small group of people operated at its full social potential. Imagine the possibility for changing the world if more groups operated at this level. It staggers the imagination thinking about the potential in our midst when we know how to tap into it.

This chapter has described the unitive practices needed for building on one another's strengths to create results we cannot achieve on our own. We must develop competency in these practices if we hope to address the magnitude of today's societal challenges. (See Figures 8.1 to 8.3, pages 260–261, for a summary.) The problems are just too big to solve without collaborative solutions. Becoming proficient in these unitive practices also offers us another opportunity—one that is both personal and global and with implications that transcend any particular social change initiative. Being willing to connect and cooperate with those who are different from us in whatever way that might be—race, ethnicity, values, beliefs, or culture— is the accelerator not just of social change but of human evolution. I will speak more about this in the final chapter.

In the next chapter we look at the last core competency of Social Change 2.0, taking a social innovation to scale. This is a social innovator's crucible and final exam.

Figure 8.1

CONNECTION – UNITIVE PRACTICES

1. Invite people to participate in social change.
2. Share meaningful life information with one another.
3. Connect people around shared aspirations.
4. Communicate authentically.
5. Provide opportunities for people to be at their best.
6. Create opportunities for social connection.

Figure 8.2

COOPERATION – UNITIVE PRACTICES

INTERPERSONAL COOPERATION: CREATING A FOUNDATIONAL RELATIONSHIP

1. Establish a formal agreement in advance to have difficult conversations when necessary.
2. In a communication breakdown take personal responsibility for your contribution to it.
3. Resolve chronic issues by developing a win-win solution.
4. Create a regular process time to check in.

**SMALL GROUP COOPERATION:
CREATING A HIGH-PERFORMANCE TEAM TO ACHIEVE BEHAVIOR CHANGE**

1. Create the right size group.
2. Build the group into a team.
3. Establish a group process protocol.
4. Structure the meetings to produce tangible outcomes.
5. Demonstrate an expectation of success.

ORGANIZATIONAL COOPERATION: FORGING STRATEGIC PARTNERSHIPS

1. Identify strategic partners who provide mission-critical assets you do not possess.
2. Create a visioning process.
3. Establish a detailed written agreement and communication protocol for addressing issues.
4. Carefully align with a partner around the key metrics for evaluating a project's success.

INTERNATIONAL COOPERATION: LEARNING FROM DIVERSITY IN UNITY

1. Identify your cultural assumptions and world view.
2. Observe when you make negative judgments about another culture's world view.
3. Go toward these different approaches and views of the world.
4. Try them on and expand your personal experience of our planet's cultural diversity.

Figure 8.3

COLLABORATION – UNITIVE PRACTICES

CREATING A THINKING PARTNERSHIP:
MULTIPLYING EACH OTHER'S INTELLIGENCE TO ACHIEVE CREATIVE BREAKTHROUGHS

1. Learn about each other at a more profound level.
2. Use the empowerment methodology as a transformative framework for the collaboration.
3. Develop a communication protocol for managing challenges and breakdowns.

ELICITING THE GROUP GENIUS EFFECT: ACHIEVING THE FULL POTENTIAL OF A COMMUNITY

1. Use cognitive and intuitive approaches to learning in a small group.
2. Solicit feedback from all participants in creating a learning product.
3. Integrate learning by physically enacting and engaging in dialogue about it with others.
4. Continue using group genius practices in debriefing the learning process.

THINKING PARTNERSHIP MEETS GROUP GENIUS EFFECT:
MULTIPLYING A COMMUNITY'S INTELLIGENCE OVER TIME TO ACHIEVE CREATIVE BREAKTHROUGHS

1. Create a committed learning and growth community.
2. Use a practitioner master class to evolve a specific body of knowledge.
3. Develop criteria for rigorous testing of innovations by practitioners.
4. Generate and disseminate best practices to practitioner community.

CHAPTER 8: SOCIAL CHANGE 2.0 PRACTITIONER'S GUIDE

1. What is your strategy to develop the synergy potential of your social change initiative?

2. What are the unitive practices you need to deploy to create a greater connection among the key players in your initiative?

3. What are the unitive practices you need to deploy to create greater cooperation among the key groups or organizations in your initiative?

4. Where do you need a creative breakthrough for your social change initiative to realize its potential?

5. How might you use the collaboration tools described in this chapter to help achieve this creative breakthrough?

TAKING A SOCIAL INNOVATION TO SCALE:

THE LEVERAGE OF

DISPROPORTIONATE INFLUENCE

Contrary to conventional wisdom, mounting massive change is not about putting forth an equally massive effort; rather it is about conserving resources and cutting time by identifying and leveraging the factors of disproportionate influence.

—W. Chan Kim and Renee Mauborgne, *Blue Ocean Strategy*

Each spring I marvel at how effortlessly trees blossom without requiring a large-scale mobilization of resources to motivate them to grow leaves, and how plants effortlessly disseminate their seeds without requiring an infinite number of Johnny Appleseeds to come to their rescue. In early 1993 I found myself wondering if there might be a comparable elegant solution for disseminating social change. Given the ambition level of the change-the-world plan I was currently working on, if such a solution existed, I needed to find it quick.

In 1992 the U.N. conference on the environment had concluded that the development of sustainable consumption and production practices in the industrialized countries of the world was the single greatest solution to restore the planet's deteriorating ecosystem. Here it was a year later, and our sustainable lifestyle program had proved effective in helping households move from good intentions to the measurable adoption of resource-efficient lifestyle practices. Disseminating this program throughout the high-consumption countries of the world, and particularly America—the most profligate—could be a major linchpin for creating a sustainable planet. There was one large problem with this grand ambition, however. How does one disseminate a social innovation that requires more than a billion people around the globe to voluntarily adopt resource-efficient lifestyle practices?

THE PRACTICE OF INNOVATION DIFFUSION

You can't imagine how excited I was to come across a social science researcher that had built his entire career on the topic of how to disseminate innovations. In his seminal book *Diffusion of Innovation*, Everett Rogers, a professor at Stanford University, describes the specific manner in which successful innovations have diffused. These innovations are based on his research of 1,500 innovations over a fifty-year timeframe and include the introduction of new seed strains to farmers, new medicines to doctors, new family planning practices to developing world countries, and new technologies. Before discovering Rogers all I had come across on this subject were speculative theories and anecdotal stories, and, while intriguing, they were not a set of practices I could easily replicate and test. Rogers, on the other hand, describes a rigorously researched and proven pathway.

He divides up the population for a particular innovation into four groups. The first group he calls *early adopters*. These are people who have a high tolerance for experimentation and seek out innovations based on their interests. Early adopters represent about 15 percent of the population for that innovation. The next group he calls the *early majority*. They wait for the innovation to be proven and more accepted before they adopt it. They are mostly interested in belonging, and represent the next 35 percent of the population for the innovation. The next group he calls the *late majority*. They wait until the innovation is well established and participate because of necessity or to avoid social ostracism. They represent the next 35 percent. The final group he calls the *laggards*. They will never voluntarily accept the innovation and it is not worth spending time trying to convince them. They represent the last 15 percent.

Although this was interesting, what I found most compelling was his research on how to get people to participate and achieve a tipping point for an innovation. His research indicated that people respond best when approached by a peer, because this is someone they trust. Conversely they are apt to be resistant to the professional change agent because they feel this person is trying to sell them something. The peer with the most influence is someone who is viewed as an opinion leader in that particular community. When the innovation is adopted by approximately 15 percent of the population for it, whether that is farmers in a country, people on a block, or organizations in an industry—if it is capable of diffusing, and some plateau at this point—it hits a tipping point and begins spreading on its own momentum through word of mouth. It then diffuses into the later categories of adopters, and, depending on how well the change agent aids the communication process, can achieve the participation of up to 85 percent of the population for that innovation.

This research was revelatory for me and opened up a whole new way of thinking for how to design an outreach process. It told me that the focus needs to be on the people who actually want to hear the message, need the least convincing, and, in fact, may already be seeking out the innovation— the early adopters. The first early adopters to focus on are those viewed as opinion leaders because they have the most influence in convincing their peers. A strategy needs to be designed to help these early adopters get 15 percent of the universe of possible participants to adopt the social innovation. Mechanisms to aid the dissemination among the later categories of adopters then need to be developed.

This strategy boils down to the analogy of preaching to the choir, asking the choir to sing loud enough to get people into the church, and then encouraging and supporting these new churchgoers to become evangelists. Now this is an elegant solution. It is a sad irony that so many social change agents go about this dissemination process in exactly the opposite way and actually undermine their efforts.

The "don't preach to the choir, they're already convinced" approach has change agents trying to convince people who do not know or trust them and who are highly resistant or will never participate in the social innovation. If they do somehow succeed in convincing the laggards and members of the late majority to participate, these individuals who have a low tolerance for experimentation may throw cold water on the social innovation unless it is already perfected—which it rarely is in the beginning of the diffusion process. They will then tell others why it doesn't work and start a negative diffusion process. It is therefore not surprising that social change agents who use the "don't preach to the choir" approach to disseminating social change have a high level of burnout, often become quite cynical about the public, and feel the only option for change is command and control.

As I began reflecting on my experience with the First Earth Run I realized that the "preach to the choir" approach was exactly how the diffusion process occurred, even though at the time I was unaware of the mechanism causing it. Metaphorically and literally, we held the torch up high enough for people to see it, and the early adopters ran with it. Early-adopter country organizers came on board and spread the word to their peers, and then we hit a tipping point and it began rapidly diffusing through word of mouth to other countries. This was repeated at a community level in most of these countries. We sought out the support of two early-adopter heads of state to serve as opinion leaders—the presidents of the United States and the Soviet Union, Ronald Reagan and Mikhail Gorbachev. Once they accepted, aided by UNICEF's wide publicizing of this fact, most of the other national political leaders in the world came on board because they didn't want to be seen as not supporting a global peace-building initiative. The same thing occurred with the world's media once ABC became our television sponsor.

But the First Earth Run was a one-off high profile mythic event. How would the practice of diffusion work for a social innovation that was more mundane and required people to attend a seven-meeting program and change a lifetime of ingrained behavior patterns? How would we get it to work on a block where you quickly run out of early adopters? How would we get it to jump the boundaries of a community and diffuse to other communities? Ditto for countries with the added complexity of cultural differences? And finally, how might this social innovation be leveraged to effect systemic changes in communities and society at large around environmental sustainability?

This chapter describes my decade-long learning process of putting social diffusion through its paces around the issue of sustainable living on the planet. From what I have written already you are familiar with some of these outcomes. This chapter unpacks how we got there or didn't, as the case may be, and the lessons learned on this adventure. These lessons transcend this particular journey and can be adapted for the diffusion of most social innovations.

DESIGNING AND IMPLEMENTING A DIFFUSION STRATEGY

The block was where we decided to dig in our heels to master the diffusion process. The thinking was that if we could develop this competency on a block level we would have the foundation for scaling it up to the neighborhood, the community, and beyond. This section describes the key learnings that stand out as critical to a successful diffusion process at the block level.

Select an outreach strategy that supports the diffusion process. We had experimented with a number of platforms for diffusing EcoTeams including social networks, faith-based groups, workplaces, service clubs, and blocks. We had successfully formed EcoTeams using each of these platforms, but we landed on the block because it best met Rogers's conditions for diffusion. We had a captive audience of people living within close proximity capable of easily communicating with one another. Living on the same block meant that people had a natural peer-to-peer relationship that could be activated. A block was a replicable unit around which to do the organizing and therefore had the potential to be brought to scale communitywide. And the block offered us more benefits with which to attract people: environment plus getting to know your neighbors and improving the livability of the neighborhood.

Develop communication mechanisms to aid the diffusion process. Rogers's research indicated that an innovation must meet four criteria to be taken up by an early adopter: it must be compatible with his or her values; provide a discernible advantage over the current approach; be easy to implement; and be able to be test-driven without having to make a commitment.

Most people had the environmental, community, and livability values so that was easy. Our job would be to emphasize these values in our neighbor-to-neighbor outreach and information meeting. The relative advantage of the program over trying to make these environmental changes individually in a slapdash manner was evident, and so again we just needed to accentuate this benefit. The ease of implementation criteria was a bit more demanding, as the program would take time and commitment. Our strategy was to help people develop a vision in the information meetings around the value of an environmentally sustainable lifestyle so they would be willing to reprioritize their time commitments and then explain how this program, which used the support of a team, was the easiest way to achieve it. The test drive would occur at the information meeting, as people perused the workbook, experienced the EcoTeam group process, and met their potential teammates.

To enhance the peer-to-peer communication process we would have past EcoTeam participants from other blocks attend the information meeting. Along with talking about how the program helped them make the personal environmental changes they sought, we would ask them to speak about changes on their block such as carpooling to take their kids to sports activities, riding their bikes to work together, looking after one another's children, sharing tools, setting up a block repair shop for bicycles, enjoying potluck meals with their neighbors, and the improved quality of life through neighbors knowing and being able to count on one another for help if a need arose.

Identify potential partner organizations where team leaders might be found and develop benefits for the organizations' participation. Our primary approach for identifying team leaders was going through existing networks and organizations with compatible values. Because of the program's benefits, our natural allies were environmental groups and neighborhood associations. We appealed to environmental groups around both shared sustainability values and self-interest. We suggested that this program could be an offering they made to enhance the organization's value to their members. Moreover, because our work was complementary, we were happy to take their message to a much larger swath of the community. This could be done through the platform the program provided their members as leaders of EcoTeams; and through a local online resource directory describing the partner organization's environmental work that we made available to program participants.

We used a similar approach in appealing to neighborhood associations. We talked about our shared values of improving the quality of life in the neighborhood and the opportunity to attract more members to their organization. We described how once people had a relationship with their neighbors and a commitment to their block, they were predisposed to taking the next step and contributing to the overall livability of the neighborhood. We also told them that we would be happy to provide information about the neighborhood association and promote a follow-up meeting if they wished to have a representative speak to EcoTeam members. Of course if the EcoTeam was led by a member of the neighborhood association, then this could happen automatically. In addition we would promote their association through our online resource directory.

We also looked for team leaders in other networks including faith-based groups, businesses, nonprofits, and government agencies. Although these groups were not directly connected with the program's environmental or neighborhood benefits, there were other interests to which we could appeal. Faith-based groups were interested in the opportunity to help congregants fulfill their moral obligation to be better stewards of the Earth. The term they often used was "caring for creation." Business, government agencies, and nonprofit organizations were interested in increasing the environmental literacy of their employees and being good citizens through contributing to the community's environmental sustainability.

Most of the organizations we approached were interested and our program managers were invited to attend their meetings to make a presentation. We would use the basic talking points from the information meeting and identify team leader candidates. Our goal was not to close the deal on the spot, but rather to get a show of interest and then follow up with a one-on-one meeting. The purpose of the follow-up meeting was to explain the commitment, scope out the particulars of their block, and answer questions.

Whenever possible we would arrange the follow-up meeting in person. This investment of time was worth it to us because once a team leader was enrolled he or she became a core part of our outreach effort not only on his or her block but throughout multiple blocks in the neighborhood. The only way we could take this to scale in both a time- and cost-effective manner was through building a strong base of committed and effective volunteers.

Train and coach team leaders. Once a team leader was on board we invited him or her to participate in a two-and-a-half-hour training on an evening or weekend. We walked the leaders through the neighbor-to-neighbor outreach script and had them practice with one another until they were comfortable. We explained how to keep a record of what each neighbor said and how to do the follow-up calls confirming their attendance at the information meeting. If they felt a need for moral support we told them that our program manager or an experienced volunteer would walk with them for the first few houses until they got their sea legs.

We then guided them through the information meeting script and provided them a chance to practice with one another. We shared with them the major issues that might derail the meeting and interventions to prevent this from occurring. We stressed the importance of collecting the resource-saving results at the end of the program so we could communicate the value of this program to other neighbors and the larger community. Again we offered to have either a program manager or a volunteer attend their information meeting as a backup if they wished this support. To deepen their ownership of this endeavor, we helped them articulate a vision for what they wanted personally, for their block, for their community, and for the planet. They then translated this vision into a statement of intention and image.

A program manager or experienced EcoTeam volunteer provided follow-up coaching to support them in starting their EcoTeam, having a successful experience so they and their team were predisposed to starting new teams; and then in starting these new teams. When new team leaders understood the level of our commitment to their success, their energy and excitement blossomed, and they had the confidence to go for their goals full out.

Track results based on the diffusion model. Before finalizing the block-based outreach approach, we hired a market research firm to test how deeply our neighbor-to-neighbor multiple benefit script might penetrate into the population of these communities. As mentioned in Chapter 2, they did a random phone survey with people in four cities, with 43 percent surveyed saying they would be "very likely" to attend and 42 percent saying they would be "somewhat likely" to attend. From the point of view of Rogers's research, this survey told us that this set of benefits delivered in this peer-to-peer manner had the potential to get a positive response well into the late majority. These survey results reinforced my conviction to put our full weight behind this approach.

These numbers turned out to be remarkably predictive. In each of our communities when a neighbor invited another neighbor to attend an information meeting in their home, about 85 percent were interested. About half of that number actually came—the "very likely" category in the survey. Of those that attended, on average 75 percent joined the EcoTeam. As I have communicated previously, this came to the remarkable average recruitment rate across all of our communities of 25 percent—well into the early majority—of those people approached on a block! And we had already primed the rest of the early majority and late majority for participation on the next round of teams after their early-adopter neighbors had proven the program worked. That is why we were able to get EcoTeams to replicate to as many as 85 percent of the households on a block.

This level of diffusion certainly did not happen on every block. Some teams lacked the chemistry that keeps people feeling motivated, and they felt complete after the program. In other cases the EcoTeam did not follow the program structure and consequently people did not achieve good results and were not motivated to continue. Or there was too much going on in the lives of the people on the team and they did not have the time to start a new team. And in some cases, the other people living on the block were not predisposed to this social innovation for any number of reasons. But in more cases than not, the teams did move forward and the social innovation was able to diffuse. Getting environmental practices that have traditionally had a hard time breaking out of the early-adopter population to diffuse this widely was one of our major breakthroughs with the program.

USING THE MEDIA TO RAISE AWARENESS ABOUT A SOCIAL INNOVATION

As previously discussed, the media are not effective in changing behavior through awareness campaigns. They can be used, however, to raise awareness of a social innovation that is being diffused through a word-of-mouth strategy. Having community members already familiar with the social innovation when a neighbor knocks on their door makes them that much more receptive. This section looks at how we attracted the attention of the media so they might tell the EcoTeam story to a larger population than we could reach with one-to-one contact.

Create high profile EcoTeams to attract media interest and serve as role models. To get the media's attention, you need a news peg. One such news peg for us was high-profile people in the community participating on an EcoTeam. These people also serve as opinion leaders and role models for the community and so we would always attempt to get elected officials, prominent civic leaders, heads of the government agencies sponsoring the program, business leaders, and celebrities, when available, as part of the first round of teams. We dubbed these Turbo Teams because of the way they boosted media interest and motivated residents to participate. These high-profile people were interested in participating because, in addition to its being the right thing to do, they enjoy networking with their peers, serving as role models in their community, and having this attention.

Tell the story through its human-interest news angle. Because of the desire of media to find human interest and positive stories to tell about the environment, it was not hard to attract local and national media coverage. The standard approach was to follow a team by attending one or more meetings and reporting on the group process, team members' successes and challenges, and the sense of community that was built. Specific actions people were taking and their resource and money savings were also included. Usually a list of actions from the book was included as a sidebar so that readers could do them if they wished. My favorite headline from a story done by the *Kansas City Star*, which I have subsequently stolen and used as a pithy description of the EcoTeam diffusion process, was "Psst—Save the Planet, Pass it On."

In one case we formed a partnership with a media outlet to help promote the program. Local TV stations are always looking for ways to differentiate themselves in their market and almost all of them wish to provide community service. We established such a partnership with the NBC TV affiliate in Minneapolis, KARE 11. Their weatherman, Paul Douglas, a passionate environmentalist, inspired the station and drove this partnership. The plan was to create one or two stories a week of a couple of minutes each and broadcast them over a six-month period as part of his weather report. The concept, way ahead of its time, was "green makeover" meets "green idol" reality TV series.

The first story helped viewers appreciate the need for taking personal action. It showed images of the local landfill filling up, electric utility air pollution, and water going into the local wastewater treatment plant. A subsequent story showed a woman knocking on her neighbors' doors inviting them to attend an information meeting in her house later that week. It was very heartwarming to watch the connection being forged among neighbors. Another story filmed the neighborhood information meeting, where people shared why they cared about the environment and the actions they had already taken. They also filmed the close of the meeting when people committed themselves to spending the next four months taking actions to reduce their environmental footprint.

All this built the viewers' interest in this process and these specific people. What would happen in these meetings? Would they be successful? How exactly do you weather-strip your windows anyway? Several teams were covered so there was plenty of variety and enough content to fill up the story slots each week. This also created some friendly competition among the teams.

The crew did background stories on some of the more interesting people on the teams, the way NBC does cameos on the lives of Olympic athletes.

The heart of the series was following the team members. Viewers seemed to like watching people they felt like they now knew go through the process of making their lifestyles more environmentally sustainable. Team members were filmed taking actions in their homes or going to the store to buy supplies like weather stripping or compact florescent light bulbs. They were filmed in meetings telling their neighbors what actions they had taken and what actions they had not taken and why. The team would then brainstorm with that person to develop a solution. Each meeting concluded with people saying what they would do by the next meeting.

In the last meeting, people reported on the specific actions they had taken and the quantitative resource and financial savings they had achieved. They talked about what they had learned and what the experience meant to them. This was also when the team had to decide if they were willing to form more teams on their block. Each of the teams made this commitment and KARE 11 followed the process through the start of new teams.

The KARE 11 producer told me that if I had had to pay for the production and advertising time, the cost would have been about $500,000. I was duly impressed. When all was said and done, this green reality TV program achieved its goals of raising awareness for our program and getting great ratings and positive PR for our partner. There is no question that as a result of this intensive exposure for six months on a major TV station, there was a buzz about EcoTeams in Minneapolis, St. Paul, and the surrounding communities. But while it raised awareness about our program, which was great for door-to-door recruiting, it did not directly attract viewers to participate in any significant manner. I found this perplexing and always felt that we could have done a lot more with this opportunity.

Using Vision and Feedback to Inspire Participation and Build Momentum

With the perspective of many more years of experience I have come to see how the KARE 11 media opportunity could have been used more effectively. We did a good job capturing the *interest* of viewers, but we did not capture their *imagination* and mobilize them to participate in the campaign. What follows is a framework I have subsequently developed for cities wishing to implement a communitywide behavior-change campaign.

Create a compelling vision that captures the imagination of the community. The starting point for such an endeavor is communicating a vision in which people see themselves as part of something important that is making a difference in their community. The vision must show that the campaign has a big goal and needs their participation to realize it. It must show what success looks like at each of the three adopter milestones of 15, 50, and 85 percent. It should have a short and focused time frame so people feel a sense of urgency around achieving this goal; if it drags out too long it is hard to keep people's attention. The target I use is three years, focused on the early adopters in year one (15%), early majority in year two (35%), and late majority in year three (35%).

The vision should describe in concrete terms what can be expected at each of the milestones. For example, what would be the impact on water quality, water conservation, CO_2 emissions, air quality, road congestion, landfill space, recyclables collected, green business economic development, and community livability from a sustainable lifestyle campaign at 15, 50, and 85 percent participation levels? If there is a green dividend from reducing the need for expanding infrastructure—such as a landfill, water treatment plant, or new road—it should be communicated that these financial savings will be invested in community greening projects like creating bicycle lanes, parks, or more open space. Neighborhoods that have achieved a 25 percent or more reduction in their residential environmental footprint would be invited to participate on the city committee that prioritizes how these green investments are allocated.

This vision then must be translated into a persuasive and easily understood plan that shows how a community can get from here to there through the personal action of its citizens. It must also be emotionally engaging and appeal to people's need for meaning, purpose, and influence, by showing precisely how each citizen and block is making a difference, and how the community is serving as a role model within the state, country, and world. It must culminate with a passionate invitation to play, with clear instructions on how to take the next step (in the case of a sustainable lifestyle campaign initiative, for example, who to contact to become trained as a team leader). This type of robust vision goes a long way toward transforming the belief that undermines the participation of many people in social change: "I don't make a difference, so why bother?"

Disseminate the vision through the media and multiple community channels. The vision should be widely communicated to the media, like-minded community organizations (to display on their web sites), and opinion leaders (to e-mail to their networks). It should be communicated in video, audio, and print. With this foundation in place the next tier of communication media could include music videos, school poster and video contests, and text messages. The idea is to immerse every demographic in the community in this vision through every medium so everyone knows about it, understands it, and feels a civic duty to participate.

Develop a set of success metrics and provide ongoing feedback to sustain momentum. Once a compelling vision is widely communicated the next critical communication step is developing a robust feedback mechanism. When people participate in something they want to see that their efforts are making a difference. This is where the media channels of television, radio, newspapers and the Internet can play a huge role.

In political campaigns the metrics of success, short of winning, are the amount of money raised, the number of contributors, and performance in polls. This is how campaign momentum is generated and sustained. For a sustainable lifestyle campaign, the metrics of success are the number of households, blocks, and neighborhoods participating; the number of civic, faith-based groups, and businesses serving as outreach partners; the measurable resource savings and environmental improvement achieved; and these results described in relationship to the interim and overall goals of the campaign.

The Internet is the ideal vehicle for keeping track of these types of results because data can be easily entered by individuals and groups and automatically compiled. Geographic Information Systems complemented by Google Earth can visually show the households on a block that are participating in the campaign and compare participation levels between blocks. This allows people to see themselves in relationship to one another and provides motivation to participate in this communitywide endeavor. This information can then be uploaded to all the various media channels in the community for distribution.

An excellent way to inspire individual accomplishment is to display a leader board on the initiative's web site that highlights the top performances of households, blocks, and organizations throughout the community. This feedback mechanism multiplies the power of peer-to-peer motivation, à la

EcoTeams, exponentially. "Wow, you reduced your carbon footprint by 32 percent; I can stretch to get there." "Your block has 75 percent of the households participating! We should try to match that on our block." "Your organization has participation of 40 percent of its members and has collectively enabled three million pounds of carbon to be taken out of the atmosphere. We can do the same with our organization." Through the Internet people can also exchange ideas, problem solve, and reach out for advice from those who have achieved a high level of success.

To make this feedback more personal, each week the accomplishments of a household, block, or organization can be showcased through a two-minute video interview that is uploaded to YouTube and disseminated through all the communication channels that have been established for the campaign. This allows people to learn best practices and be inspired by real flesh-and-blood people with whom they can identify. It also helps to concretize the new social norm being diffused by the campaign, and inspires people to stretch so that their achievement might be recognized in this manner.

Create public recognition for achievement. A variation on the recognition theme is the creation of public events honoring outstanding achievement. Having the mayor periodically host a public ceremony honoring the achievements of individuals, blocks, and organizations adds more gravitas to their accomplishment. The high achievers are motivated to stretch to the next level both through the recognition and through their association with others of comparable accomplishment. The event can be videotaped with highlights communicated through the communication network. And of course the media should be invited to the event so they can communicate the story to the larger community. By this point, the local media should be highly engaged in the campaign because it is *the* story in the community that everyone is thinking and talking about. And this is an opportunity to honor the community's local heroes—true green idols, if you will.

Public recognition can also take place in a more localized grassroots manner. In Philadelphia, one block that had completed our Livable Neighborhood Program spontaneously posted a sign identifying it as a "livable neighborhood." This increased the pride of people living on the block and encouraged residents to sustain their commitment after the program because of the positive recognition they received from others coming into the neighborhood. It also attracted those living on the block that had not yet participated on the team. We shared this story with the city of Philadelphia, who then began to recognize, with an official sign, the achievement of blocks that had successfully gone through the program. This feedback model evolved into one of our more successful diffusion strategies.

Another form of localized public recognition used by blocks in our sustainable lifestyle campaigns was the provision of stickers to individual households completing the program. People were encouraged to display these "green household" stickers in their windows, thus increasing the visibility of the program and motivating others on the block to participate.

People are motivated by a compelling vision and feedback of results. The better we communicate the vision and provide feedback, the easier it will be to get people to participate and sustain their commitment. Said another way, our job as change agents is to create the bucket and then show the drops filling it.

LEVERAGING EARLY ADOPTERS TO ACHIEVE A SYSTEM LEVEL CHANGE

Diffusion of a social innovation, as we have seen, is about achieving a disproportionate outcome relative to our effort. Spending the time to build a relationship or to train and coach an early-adopter team leader often resulted in participation in the program by an entire block. Investing the energy to make sure one block had a successful experience could tip a whole neighborhood. But that is only part of the diffusion picture. Individuals and EcoTeams also helped leverage system level changes.

EcoTeams leverage policy change. We landed in Kansas City, Missouri, because of a visionary environmental leader, John Stufflebean, who ran the Environmental Services Division of the city. When we began working there in the late 1990s I would categorize it as an early-majority or even late-majority city around its environmental policies. A key indicator was that they did not have curbside recycling, at that time long a basic service of large cities. John wished to change this situation. John had participated on an EcoTeam and seen it transform his conservative neighbors into advocates for city services to help them reduce their environmental footprint. This experience gave John an idea for how he might leverage EcoTeams.

Kansas City, like many municipalities, had a citizen environmental advisory committee. The members of this committee were appointees of previous conservative administrations who did not share John's vision for positive environmental change and who constantly undermined his efforts. They had just recently thwarted his attempt to bring about curbside recycling, saying it was not a good use of taxpayer dollars and there was no demand to justify such an investment. While they could not create policy, they certainly could impede it. This is where John's idea came in. He would attempt to stage a quiet coup and replace this committee with EcoTeam members.

As the top environmental policy maker in the city, John approached the mayor and city council with a proposal to expand this advisory committee to include citizens with firsthand knowledge of the environmental needs of their fellow citizens. He made the case that for an environmental advisory committee to provide him good advice on policies that affect the lives of citizens, its members should be actively involved in using the environmental services his department provides. He told them that one of the city programs he was managing, and that they had been funding, was developing this type of engaged citizen, and he would draw on it for candidates to fill these new committee positions. He also requested permission to increase the responsibilities, influence, and time commitment of committee members so that they might play a bigger role in both developing environmental policy and advocating for it in the community.

John was granted permission to expand the committee from six to twelve people and increase its scope of responsibilities. He had already taken the temperature of various EcoTeam members and knew there was a strong desire to change the city's environmental policies. Given that EcoTeams were filled with the city's environmental early adopters and this was the next frontier, there were many who volunteered to serve on the committee. He narrowed down the finalists to twelve people. He chose six and asked the others to be on a waiting list, just in case any of the current members did not have time to take on the increased responsibilities.

These people were approved by the mayor and John was off to the races. He presented the committee with a comprehensive set of proposals and requested they whittle them down to the best ones, flesh them out, and develop recommendations. The existing committee members could not keep up with the time commitment required of them, not to mention the policy rigor, and surprise, surprise, John had to accept their resignations and replace them with EcoTeam members on the waiting list. Within a short period of time, John's shrewd strategy was in place. He had a committee empowered by the mayor and city council with the authority to shape environmental policy and advocate for it in the community. Because of their experiences on EcoTeams, the committee members knew exactly what policy changes were needed to support citizens in developing more environmentally sustainable lifestyle practices, and because they were walking their talk, could communicate their message with credibility.

They operated the committee like an EcoTeam and used all of their neighbor-to-neighbor recruitment training to excellent advantage. They competently and passionately articulated the need for these new environmental policies in meetings with the mayor and city council. In their now-formal role as designated representatives of the city, they reached out to EcoTeam members inviting them to offer comments on the proposals. They made sure to invite EcoTeam representatives from each city council member's district to share their stories during public meetings about these new environmental proposals.

The city council was impressed with this new and improved Environmental Advisory Committee and the way it worked with the city's Environmental Services Department. This was a type of advocacy the city council had not seen before. They were not being approached with the standard "build it and they will come" argument. Instead, this empowered Environmental Advisory Committee quickly and effectively showed that the demand already existed. This was very compelling, and it wasn't long before the city had curbside recycling and was on the path to becoming more environmentally sustainable.

John and his Environmental Advisory Committee, a.k.a. Super EcoTeam, showed risk-adverse policymakers in the Show Me state exactly how people would come if they built it. He had leveraged the disproportionate influence of a few to create a system level change.

EcoTeams leverage demand for a green economy. The local economy was another area where we noticed the disproportionate influence of a relatively small percentage of a community's population. As households went through the sustainable lifestyle program they wanted green goods and services to implement the actions they wished to take. They wanted organic and locally grown food, green cleaning products, compact florescent light bulbs, and products that were recyclable and produced with less packaging. They wanted to purchase energy-efficient appliances, fuel-efficient cars, solar hot water, and photovoltaic electricity systems. They wanted green sources of power from their electric utilities, energy audits, triple-pane windows and better insulation for their homes. This placed a demand on local businesses to begin providing these goods and services. As friends and neighbors of the early adopters saw them making these green purchases or observed these products in their homes, they too, began adopting some of these practices, which further increased demand.

After observing this phenomenon occur spontaneously in a number of neighborhoods, we made building demand for a local green economy a core part of our sustainable lifestyle campaigns. Our program managers or committed EcoTeam members explained to local businesses the various good and services promoted by the program so they could stock them or make them available. We provided suggestions on how to advertise the green features that would be of most interest to EcoTeam members. We also provided local businesses with a list of features that they could communicate to their suppliers, which would increase the desirability of their products. The list included such items as reducing the product packaging and increasing its recyclability or re-use potential.

To attract EcoTeam members we encouraged merchants to offer discounts, have a section in their store which linked the green goods to the specific actions in the book, put in bike racks for green customers, and allow notices to be posted of upcoming information meetings and other local environmental activities. We then promoted these stores at our information meetings and online. As a result of our intention to engage with local businesses in this way, many of them, in both the United States and Europe, chose to participate which in turn helped build demand for a local green economy.

In this case the ripple went way beyond the community and into the larger economy. Savvy companies looking to understand future trends heard from these local businesses what EcoTeams required to purchase their products. Unlike the focus groups these companies regularly run, which indicate someone's *intent* to purchase, EcoTeams were making *actual purchasing decisions* based on very specific product features. A number of companies, including the large multinational Unilever, became enamored with EcoTeams as a source of market intelligence. Market trends are not a small thing for these companies, as it can take several years and hundreds of millions of dollars to gear up and make adjustments in their manufacturing facilities and marketing.

These companies began interacting with EcoTeam members and the local businesses to get insight on what products to produce, and how to make and package them. EcoTeams, in the role as trendsetters, were now having an influence on what products were being offered into the larger marketplace far beyond their communities. And these companies were sending the first signals to the larger economic system about the product features needed to attract the newly emerging green consumer and stay competitive in the marketplace.

As amplifiers of sustainable consumption practices we found ourselves influencing sustainable production through the demand side of the economic equation. It was most wondrous how this opportunity circled back to my original strategy for addressing the unsustainable patterns of consumption and production in the industrialized countries. It was also a perfect marriage of the empowerment mantra of *holding firm to the impulse and letting the form be flexible* and the diffusion mantra of *leveraging disproportionate influence.*

LEVERAGING OPINION LEADERS TO JUMP GEOGRAPHIC AND CULTURAL BOUNDARIES

What I most appreciate about Rogers's diffusion research is that it allows us to work much smarter. Trying to get a social innovation adopted through going after all and sundry will wear down even the most committed of us rather quickly. Working smarter translates into looking for situations that meet Rogers's preconditions for diffusion. The starting point is identifying early-adopter opinion leaders for the social innovation we are introducing.

Sometimes we can get lucky and an opinion leader who is an early adopter for this social innovation finds us. In this case, our job is to orchestrate the diffusion process so it has the best chance of success. If we are not fortunate enough to have such an opinion leader come to us, we need to seek him or her out in the community through which we wish to diffuse our social innovation. To diffuse the sustainable lifestyle campaign beyond Portland and the sustainable lifestyle program beyond America and not burn to a crisp, I needed to find opinion leaders to help me. I was lucky in both cases.

Opinion leadership and diffusion through an early-adopter network. Public Technology Inc. is the innovation arm of the National League of Cities and National Association of Counties. Its members represent the largest and most innovative cities and counties in the United States and it attracts local government leaders who wish to improve their performance in serving the public. The meetings of Public Technology Inc. provide welcome opportunities for these early-adopter leaders to exchange ideas and inspiration with like-minded peers. As good fortune would have it, Mike Lindberg, as former chair of their Energy Task Force and Commissioner of Public Utilities in cutting-edge Portland, was viewed in this community as an opinion leader for green innovations. And he was most willing and excited to share our Portland success with this group.

The situation could not have been more primed for diffusion. We would be describing a social innovation to a group of early adopters who were looking for new ideas and who had budgets to invest. We had a proven and repeatable solution that performed better than existing methods for engaging citizens and changing behavior. Mike Lindberg was a trusted peer and opinion leader for this type of social innovation. Through the regular meetings held by this group as part of Public Technology Inc., we would have a way to aid ongoing word-of-mouth communication. All that was missing was for this group of early adopters to be able to observe and experience the social innovation in person without any risk.

Our plan was simple. Mike reached out to the chair of the upcoming meeting and told him about the success we were having with the sustainable lifestyle campaign in Portland, and as a result we were invited to make a formal presentation to the group. If the group was interested, we would invite them to Portland to kick the tires. They were interested, did go to Portland, and, as I have described previously, we came out the other end with our first wave of recruits. As good results started getting fed back to this group, more cities signed on.

We had leveraged Mike's and Portland's stature as opinion leaders by carefully orchestrating the conditions needed for the diffusion of our social innovation. This allowed me to work smarter rather than harder and live to see another day.

Opinion leadership and diffusion across cultures. I learned during the First Earth Run that the diffusion of a social innovation originating in America and traveling to Europe can be difficult. European countries wish to protect themselves from what they view as American cultural imperialism. "Invented in America" is a reason *not* to participate in something for many European countries. But Europe was where the sustainability early adopters were located, so if I wished to disseminate the program outside of

America, I would need to find an opinion leader *country* as the launching point.

The natural choice was the Netherlands, with a government highly respected for its "Green Plan." It is a quintessential early-adopter country and eagerly seeks out new ideas to disseminate throughout Europe and the world. It has played this role from its earliest days as one of the world's largest trading countries. The citizenry have deeply embraced green values and are called by some the first "postmaterialist" country. It is a small and therefore manageable country for testing the scaling up of a social innovation. Its size also makes the Netherlands nonthreatening to other European countries. Since everyone speaks English and often three other languages it is a perfect intermediary between America and the rest of Europe. And it was my good fortune to have friendships with several people who had the interest and capacity to build a successful program.

Paul de Jongh, the lead architect of the Dutch Green Plan, was searching for new policy instruments to help the government reach and promote change in the residential sector of society. They could not achieve their measurable environmental goals without effecting change in this sector and they had bumped up against the limits of their standard tools of regulation and tax policy.

One aim of the Green Plan was to use the country as a role model to demonstrate best practices for sustainability. This is how, as a small country, they could leverage their environmental innovations and influence change globally. To do this they established a group, of which Paul was a member, which sought out these best practices. Paul was an opinion leader in both the Netherlands and Europe, with substantial credibility in the circles in which we would need to travel.

Bessie Schadee had been organizing our Art of Empowerment training program in Wassenaar, near The Hague, for three years. As a result she had developed a high level of competency in communicating the subtle ideas of empowerment to business, social-change, and government leaders throughout the Netherlands and Europe. She was also an environmental opinion leader who had been asked to run as a national Green Party candidate and had an extensive network of influential people throughout the country. Bessie would be an excellent person to help us adapt this social innovation to the Dutch culture while maintaining the empowerment framework integrity.

Peter Van Luttervelt had participated in a number of our empowerment training programs and was a committed and active practitioner. He had a

strong background as a social entrepreneur with excellent marketing instincts. He, like me, was always reading books on business and looking for
strategies that could be applied to social change. We had excellent chemistry
and enjoyed hanging out together scheming up change-the-world strategies.
I could see myself working closely with Peter to evolve this social innovation for use within the fertile soil of the Netherlands.

Paul, Bessie, and Peter all signed on. Paul provided the seed financing to
get the program going. Bessie served as chair of Global Action Plan (GAP)
Netherlands and was responsible for translating and adapting the program.
And Peter became the national director with whom I worked on program
and financing innovations.

Because I traveled to the Netherlands twice a year to lead empowerment
trainings and because it was so accessible from other countries, it became
the natural site for international gatherings to exchange best practices
among the growing number of countries that were coming on board. Bessie
hosted these at her nationally respected conference center, the Narwal, and
we combined these events with field trips to observe how the program was
taking root across the country. Again with Paul's help, the Dutch Environmental Ministry invested in an international capacity-building training to
accelerate the speed and quality of this diffusion to other countries. Our
team from the United States, in cooperation with the Dutch team, transferred our sustainable lifestyle campaign best practices to these early-
adopter European countries.

But the Netherlands had more to offer than just serving as a diffusion
point. Being a small, well-organized country with a populace highly educated on the issue of sustainability enabled the EcoTeam seed to be planted
in very fertile soil. Global Action Plan Netherlands became the top-funded
nongovernmental organization, supported by both the Dutch Ministries of
Environment and Finance, which allowed it to service the entire country. To
assist in program diffusion, the organization established strategic partnerships with many of the country's leading national nonprofits and all the
major municipalities. To validate the effectiveness of the program they established a rigorous national data-collection process with participants providing the actual energy and water savings as recorded by their household
meters. They also participated in a two-year longitudinal study funded by
the Dutch government and conducted by University of Leiden, the outcome
of which, as stated earlier, was that the program was "unsurpassed in changing behavior." And the term EcoTeam became a household name.

Global Action Plan Netherlands had taken this program to scale in its native country in a way I could only dream of in the United States.

With the Netherlands now serving as a national role model and the social innovation well advanced in the United States, our country organizer from Sweden, Marilyn Mehlemann, stepped forward to help promote and solidify the program's international diffusion. She developed a startup program to help new countries through the adaptation process, and to provide basic training in the empowerment principles and community-organizing strategy. She expanded our international best practice exchanges to twice yearly, and organized them to maximize each new country's learning and each experienced country's ability to collaborate. Her diligent commitment to quality assurance and best practice exchange enabled this now completely internationalized program to diffuse successfully to twenty-two countries throughout Western and Eastern Europe, the former Soviet Union, and Asia. And it is still growing!

LEVERAGING A SOCIAL INNOVATION THROUGH THE REINVENTION PROCESS

With this social innovation spreading throughout the United States and around the world, another dimension of Everett Rogers's research became evident. Rogers called it "reinvention." He said that as a social innovation diffuses it starts to be reinvented for different circumstances and uses. In the case of our sustainable lifestyle campaign this was not just one social innovation, but a whole series of seamlessly integrated innovations that included the workbook program, peer support group model, neighborhood delivery platform, measurement and feedback system, social learning and growth processes, campaign management structure, and financing mechanisms. Over time many of these elements found themselves in very different configurations from those I had originally conceived for them.

Some of this reinvention I initiated, and some of it was initiated by our GAP international network. But much of it was initiated by people who had participated in the program or learned about it at conferences, research web sites, and through professional publications.

The sustainable lifestyle program model was reinvented by local and state governments, electric utilities, and environmental nonprofits as new programs to address behavior change. The peer support group and self-directed meeting guides were reinvented for use in a discussion group format by several organizations addressing topics such as sustainable living, global warming, and voluntary simplicity. And several state environmental grant programs reinvented their guidelines to include measurable behavior change as the key performance metric for a project being selected and against which it would be evaluated.

The reinvention of a social innovation is a mysterious process that one cannot plan for, but it can be as important as its initial application. It is important not to lose sight of the forest of social change while attempting to plant a grove of trees in a particular section.

THE STARS IN ALIGNMENT

We were able to scale up EcoTeams on many blocks and neighborhoods in cities throughout the United States and around the world, and leverage them to effect systemic change at the public policy and economic levels. We were able to take the program to scale nationally in the Netherlands, and enjoyed the participation of the majority of high-consumption countries. We helped establish in the culture the notion of an environmentally sustainable lifestyle and the concomitant practices this entails. And the social technology through reinvention diffused far and wide. (See Figure 9.1, page 288, for a summary of the diffusion principles that enabled these results.) One thing, however, that eluded us was being able to take the program fully to scale in a specific community, which I define as the participation of between 25 and 85 percent of the residents.

I discovered on my decade-long journey with this and other behavior-change programs that for this to occur the stars need to be in alignment. To take a transformative social innovation to scale in a community, the stars in question include: a social issue in which a large majority of people are eager to participate; a proven social innovation capable of being brought to scale; an early-adopter community which takes pride in leading the charge for that issue; an effective management team well connected in the community; local elected officials and community opinion leaders actively supporting it; a strong foundation of strategic partner organizations willing to reach out to their members; financing or a team of volunteers fully committed for at least three years; and a good working knowledge of diffusion research to maximize the efficiency and acceleration of the social change.

It is not easy to find (or create) all of these elements at hand in a single community at a particular moment in time. But knowing what we need for success and how to bring it about allows us to be ready for those times when the stars do come into alignment. And I believe that time has now come, not just at a community level, but worldwide. I have not seen anything like this before in my lifetime.

By humanity being brought to its knees financially and ecologically, a hardened set of beliefs that have held our communities and world hostage are cracking open. Combine this with the extraordinary opening for change brought about by Barack Obama and the vision and skills he brings to enable synergy between Social Change 1.0 and 2.0 (see Figure 9.2, page 290, for a summary of the 2.0 action principles), and we find ourselves with circumstances ripe for profound transformation to occur—a type of transformation that can allow us to make an evolutionary leap.

Those of us who identify ourselves as change agents are being given a once-in-a-lifetime opportunity. But as the biblical saying goes—"to whom much is given, shall much be required." We need to be prepared to take full advantage of this fortuitous alignment of the stars. The final section of this book directly addresses this challenge and opportunity.

Figure 9.1

PRINCIPLES FOR TAKING A SOCIAL INNOVATION TO SCALE

POPULATIONS FOR A SOCIAL INNOVATION

1. Early Adopters (first 15%)—Have high tolerance for experimentation and seek out the new. At 15% can achieve a tipping point where the innovation can diffuse on its own momentum.
2. Early Majority (next 35%)—Wait for the social innovation to be proved and wish to fit in.
3. Late Majority (next 35%)—Participate out of necessity or fear of social ostracism.
4. Laggards (final 15%)—Will not participate in innovation.

FOUR CRITERIA FOR A SOCIAL INNOVATION TO DIFFUSE

1. Compatible with a person's values.
2. A discernible advantage over a person's current approach to addressing the issue.
3. Easy to implement.
4. Testable without requiring a commitment.

DESIGN AND IMPLEMENTATION OF A SOCIAL DIFFUSION STRATEGY

1. Incorporate four criteria into diffusion strategy.
2. Develop mechanism for early and later adopters to communicate innovation to their peers.
3. Train and coach change agents in using these communication mechanisms.
4. Identify early-adopter organizations and develop specific benefits to attract them.
5. Measure results of diffusion strategy and make adjustments as needed to achieve goal.

USE OF VISION AND FEEDBACK TO INSPIRE PARTICIPATION AND BUILD MOMENTUM

1. Create a compelling vision that captures people's imagination.
2. Disseminate vision through media and multiple community channels.
3. Develop success metrics and provide feedback through media and community channels.
4. Create public recognition of participants for achievement of goals.

LEVERAGE OF A SOCIAL INNOVATION

1. Look for opportunities to use the social innovation for systemic level change.
2. Identify early-adopter opinion leaders in early-adopter networks to diffuse social innovation.
3. Support the reinvention of the social innovation for different platforms and contexts.

CHAPTER 9: SOCIAL CHANGE 2.0 PRACTITIONER'S GUIDE

1. What is the diffusion strategy for your social change initiative?

2. Who are the early-adopter networks and organizations for your social change initiative and what specific benefits will appeal to each of them?

3. Who are the opinion leaders within these organization and networks and how will you reach them?

4. What tools and training are needed to assist change agents in communicating to their peer groups about your social change initiative?

5. What is your media strategy for building awareness about your social change initiative so those approached to participate are already primed?

Figure 9.2—Social Change 2.0 Action Principles

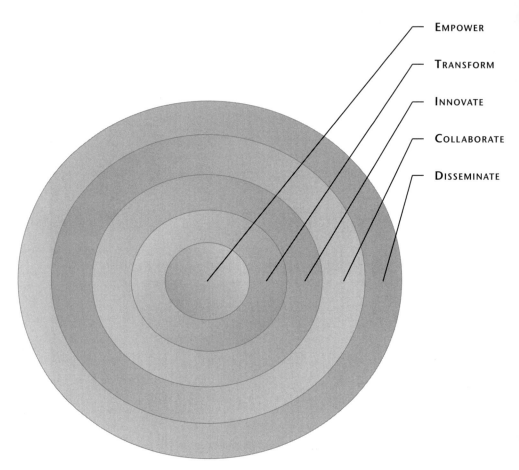

PART THREE

REINVENTING OUR WORLD:

THREE TRANSFORMATIVE SOCIAL INNOVATIONS TO CHANGE THE GAME

REINVENTING OUR WORLD:

THREE TRANSFORMATIVE SOCIAL INNOVATIONS

TO CHANGE THE GAME

As I look out across the planet there are so many things we need to do to make our world better. I have been personally drawn, however, to three leverage points to help us make the profound transformation that is now so primed to happen. We need leadership capable of facilitating large-scale transformative change. We need to address the climate change issue or face an inhospitable planet for humankind into the foreseeable future. And we need to tackle the last taboo and biggest blight on humanity's moral development—war, the choice to kill our fellow human beings as a way to resolve our differences.

These are gateway issues, each of which opens the possibility for addressing a host of other societal needs inextricably connected with them. Mitigating climate change will not only enable us to survive on this planet, but is a primary driver for building the twenty-first century green economy and investing financial resources in developing countries. It is also a planetary rite of passage for humanity, providing us the opportunity to come together to solve our first truly global survival challenge. The capabilities we gain can be used to tackle many other planetary issues that affect the future of the human condition.

But we will have a difficult time avoiding the worst effects of climate change and acclimating to what cannot be averted, not to mention addressing the many other problems encroaching on humanity, including chronic poverty, when the United States alone invests half of its discretionary federal budget on military spending. Only 1 percent of this amount could cover the entire annual budget of the United Nations, which struggles financially each year to carry out its worldwide humanitarian work.

We are being boxed into a corner where we have to transform our dysfunctional behavior as a human species if we wish to have the resources needed both to survive and to help all of us and this planet to thrive. And to bring about these large-scale transformations we need leadership schooled in the competencies of transformative change and social entrepreneurship. With our planet on the line and with such a propitious opening for positive change available to us as the world strives to reinvent itself, this is not the time for change leaders to be foundering. We all need to be playing at our best.

This final section provides three specific transformative change blueprints for addressing these issues using the Social Change 2.0 framework. Each of these social innovations is the next turn in the spiral of the transformational work I have been writing about in this book and to which I have dedicated the past three decades of my life.

- Chapter 10, "Building Leadership Capacity to Change the World" describes a school for transformative social change based on the five principles and practices described in Chapters 5 through 9.

- Chapter 11, "Empowering a Climate Change Movement" grows out of my work with EcoTeams and community-based behavior-change campaigns described in Chapters 2 through 4.

- Chapter 12, "Transforming the Paradigm of War," builds on the First Earth Run experience described in Chapter 1 and the unitive field practices in Chapter 8.

Each of these initiatives is designed as a game changer. That is, each has the potential to change the pattern in the field around the particular issue it addresses. Each of these initiatives can serve as a transformative social change blueprint for comparable endeavors. Each is an example of Social Change 2.0 in action to help solidify the ideas of this book. And each is a building block in the cathedral of a reinvented world that so many of us have devoted our lives to constructing.

BUILDING LEADERSHIP CAPACITY

TO CHANGE THE WORLD:

A SCHOOL FOR

TRANSFORMATIVE SOCIAL CHANGE

The core of the matter is always about changing the behavior of people. In highly successful change efforts the central challenge is not strategy, not systems, but changing people's behavior—what people do and the need for significant shifts in what people do.
  —John Kotter and Dan Cohen, *The Heart of Change*

Nothing is more important and more abiding than the wisdom required to transform customers. The transformation economy represents the very engine of growth that will create more than enough jobs to supplant slowdowns in the lower-echelon economic sectors.
  —Joseph Pine and James H. Gilmore, *The Experience Economy*

*D*elamater Inn, Rhinebeck, New York. As you look around the sun-filled conference room there is a most improbable mixture of people sitting side by side explaining their reasons for being there. Women from Afghanistan, Rwanda, South Africa, and Darfur wish to start movements to empower disenfranchised women in their countries. A hip-hop performance artist and community activist wishes to empower young women leaders from marginalized communities throughout the United States to become more effective at furthering social change. A senior program officer for the World Bank is wishing to empower community groups in Paraguay to deliver health care services to young mothers.

The senior vice president of a large healthcare system wishes to empower physician leaders to facilitate a cultural transformation in their ten hospitals by instituting preventative health practices. The chairman of a marketing consultancy working with global brands wishes to help his clients develop new business strategies based on corporate social engagement. The executive director of a national training organization wants to build the capacity of community development organizations in transformative change leadership. The CEO of a life sciences consultancy wants to develop the full potential of his people to enhance their organization's intellectual capital and value to society.

Also in the room are social entrepreneurs who wish to empower people living with AIDS in Mali, West Africa; battered women living in shelters in Louisville, Kentucky; men and women living on the street in San Francisco; unwed mothers living in the South Bronx; and seniors living in assisted-care facilities. Elementary and high school teachers who wish to empower students to increase their academic performance by transforming self-defeating attitudes are here, too.

When the introductions are complete there is silence; a sense of awe fills the space. We have all been touched and inspired by the extraordinary diversity of people gathered together and their collective aspiration to make a difference in the world. Finally Gail and I speak. "Welcome to Empowerment Institute's school for transformative social change. We deeply honor each of you for your courage to imagine a better possibility for our world and your commitment to make it real. And in case you are wondering how it is that such a wide swath of society has come together in the same room, it is because this is the world in need of change."

CREATING A SCHOOL FOR TRANSFORMATIVE SOCIAL CHANGE

The inspiration for our school grew out of several decades of conversations with the many change agents I met while mounting my various initiatives. I always made a point of spending time with them to learn what they were doing, both for my own edification and in search of best practices. I was inevitably inspired to hear about other people's ideas for changing the world and to feel the passion they brought to their endeavors, but as I asked probing questions, I often found these committed individuals lacking a rigorously thought-out strategy. Their initiatives tended to be improvised, reactionary, and short term. I was therefore not surprised that so many of these change leaders were frustrated by the lack of traction they were getting and often at their wits' end having invested huge amounts of time and in some cases a sizable portion of their life savings.

They frequently began their initiatives with great enthusiasm and intuitively pieced together a strategy. As they moved it into the culture they wished to change, it met the inevitable resistances that are part of any process of transformation. Not knowing how to work with this resistance, many of their initiatives fell apart or were stopped in their tracks. Those change agents with strong wills and good entrepreneurial skills made adjustments and persevered. But these adjustments were generally to lower their expectations about what might be possible for the people, organization, or system they wished to change. Some adopted the belief that "this is just the way it is" and defaulted to providing information or training without any accountability for measurable behavior or culture change. And some chose to blame the intransigence of "the system," having swallowed the bitter pill of cynicism.

This didn't have to be their experience. As I have said many times in this book, most people and institutions are ready and willing to change if provided a vision of a better way and the tools to make the change. *It is we change leaders who must rise to the challenge of becoming more skillful in helping people achieve their desired outcomes.* Over time I came to realize that empowering change leaders and social entrepreneurs to be more effective was a strategic leverage point for transforming society. Given my predisposition and skills in transformational change, I knew I could make a contribution, and embarked on this journey.

My first effort, an example of which I described in Chapter 6 with the story on the Rhode Island fishery, was to develop a training on transformative leadership. It helped leaders articulate a vision of the transformative change they wished to bring about and provided them with the skills to assist in its manifestation. After leading this training for a number of years I came to realize that, although it was an important step, it was not taking change agents far enough to effect the scale and speed of societal change that I knew was possible. Leaders left with transformational vision and skills but they did not have a transformational product with which to implement their desired change.

Combining these two capabilities in a single training was the obvious next step. But this would require a very different design. It would take time to develop a transformational product; this could not be done over a weekend. It would require people to develop mastery; this would demand a serious commitment. To be willing to make this commitment they needed to believe they could come away with a transformational product that would help them achieve their social change objective. I knew from my years of experience that only transformative change products capable of achieving measurable behavior change can provide that assurance.

Not only was this the right next step for me, it also felt like the natural evolution of the joint empowerment work Gail and I had been pioneering for two decades. I shared this vision with my partner in crime and asked if she would be willing to team up with me. "Count me in," she said, without batting an eye, and we were ready to embark on another great life adventure together.

What emerged was part master training on transformative change leadership, part incubator for developing transformative social innovations, and part business school for social entrepreneurs. We called it a school for transformative social change. Its hallmark would be helping change leaders and social entrepreneurs deliver products that achieve the gold standard of transformation—measurable behavior change. We would build the school around five core principles.

Whole-system solutions. One of the defining characteristics of our school would be to approach social change in a holistic manner. We cannot reinvent our world if we have great social innovations that empower people to make the necessary changes around a vital issue needed for humanity's survival and evolution, such as climate change, but only marginally functional organizations implementing them. It will be most frustrating to create a transformative social innovation that empowers the homeless to reenter society if there is insufficient support to get back on their feet because the human services system is dysfunctional.

Our institute would be committed to developing transformative change competencies at each of the three levels needed to implement a whole-system solution: the personal, organizational, and systemic. Minimally this would provide an opportunity for the organic diffusion of world views and strategies among people implementing change initiatives at each of these levels. And for those who were ready, we could help them design and implement a whole-system solution.

Diversity. Another principle of our school would be diversity in all its forms. To change the world we would need to have the world reflected in our institute. Having a diverse learning community would also maximize its synergy potential by allowing everyone to become a teacher. To accomplish this would require us to attract change agents from different racial, cultural, economic, and institutional backgrounds working to bring about transformative change in multiple sectors of society. Given Gail's passion for racial and cultural diversity she was excited to take on the challenge of recruiting, and, as needed, raising the money to help subsidize participation for change agents who had the goods but not the money. I was excited to work on a wide spectrum of issues with change agents from many types of institutions and sectors of society.

Transformational pattern language. The school would be based on the pattern language notion or concept of templates discussed in Part Two. This would save people the time and frustration involved in designing a transformational product from whole cloth, and allow them to focus on the more pressing social entrepreneurship and marketing issues. It would also provide change agents with the basic building blocks to evolve their social change initiatives continually as demand or opportunity required. These patterns would include our turnkey programs: the Empowerment Workshop and its derivative twelve-session Empowerment Life Coaching program, the Empowering Organization and Transformative Leadership trainings, and the various community-based behavior-change programs. It would also include a core empowerment template that could be applied to any area of content.

Transformational product. One of the pillars of our institute would be assuring that people graduated with a high-quality transformational product. To help people focus on the specific type of transformative change they wished to further and help us better guide them we would ask: "Whom do you wish to empower to do what?" Depending on their answer, we would propose that they either use one of our turnkey empowerment products or our empowerment template for creating a new transformational product. We would accept people on the latter path only if they had substantive content expertise and the entrepreneurial temperament to sustain the ups and downs of bringing a new transformational product into the world. If they did not, we would encourage them to begin by using one of our proven transformational products.

Competency in behavior change. To be able to use their transformational product effectively would require competence in the empowerment behavior-change methodology. This would demand both skill as an empowerment facilitator and the credibility of their own experience of personal transformation from doing this work themselves. To achieve this level of competence and confidence would entail an initial three-and-a-half-day training to learn the basic empowerment facilitation skills, followed by between forty-five and sixty-five hours of practice over the next six months delivering their product with coaching supervision and master classes; and a final four-and-a-half-day training in which to debrief their learning experience, learn how to market their transformative product or develop a social diffusion strategy, and participate in the Empowerment Workshop so they could be walking their talk. If they met these criteria, we would certify them as an empowerment practitioner.

In 2002 we launched the Empowerment Institute with sixteen people. Since then hundreds of change leaders and social entrepreneurs from all over the world have attended. The quality of these people and the transformation they have implemented in every sector of society has been remarkable. The rest of this chapter describes some of them and how they are transforming the world. We start this journey at the place where all social change must begin and the foundation on which our school is built—the empowered individual.

PERSONAL EMPOWERMENT: THE FOUNDATION OF SOCIAL CHANGE

Personal empowerment is the basis of all social change. As we become more self-aware and achieve greater personal fulfillment we become more compassionate, caring, and tolerant human beings. This inevitably ripples out to our families, organizations, communities, and society at large. A Sufi story by Indries Shah illustrates this basic principle of social change.

A dervish was sitting by the roadside when a haughty courtier with his retinue, riding past in the opposite direction, struck him with a cane, shouting: "Out of the way, you miserable wretch!"

When they had swept past, the dervish rose and called after them: "May you attain all that you desire in the world, even up to its highest ranks!"

A bystander, much impressed by this scene, approached the devout man and said to him: "Please tell me whether you were motivated by generosity of spirit, or because the desires of the world will undoubtedly corrupt that man even more."

"O man of bright countenance," said the dervish, "has it not occurred to you that I said what I did because people who attain their real desires would not need to ride about striking dervishes."

Empowerment as a value in society has proliferated to the point where the term is now used in common parlance around the world. When Gail and I began our empowerment work three decades ago this idea was so new that most languages had no comparable word, much less an understanding of its meaning. And in America it was *the* cutting edge. That's how relatively new this idea is in our world. Although there is still a long way to go before it is practiced widely, we are definitely now on the path where its value is appreciated. This is a big deal for our world. We need to heal our wounds, transform our limiting beliefs, and enrich our impoverished visions of possibility if we wish to change the conditions that have created our current world. Otherwise they will keep showing up in our children, parents, teachers, politicians, business leaders, clergy, and social change agents. For our planet to evolve, we the people living on it need to evolve. This is a prerequisite for any lasting transformative change.

Gail and I have had the privilege of being on the front lines helping diffuse the idea and practices of empowerment into the world through our Empowerment Workshop. This has provided us profound insights into the human condition. It has helped us see how fundamentally similar we all are no matter what our culture or socioeconomic background. It has shown us how easy it is to pick up limiting beliefs along our journey, which then translate into behaviors that cause us endless amounts of pain and hold back our potential. And it has proved to us time and time again how willing we are to change these circumstances and begin moving toward our dreams if provided a safe and nurturing environment, transformative tools, and the guidance of a skilled personal empowerment facilitator.

Once we created our Empowerment Institute we decided it was time to invite others to lead this workshop. We needed to let it grow and take wing to places on the planet Gail and I would never take it in person. It also needed to realize its potential as a tool for social change. First, to help empower those within disenfranchised sectors of our society to realize their potential and break the cycle of dysfunctional behaviors embedded in these cultures and passed on from generation to generation. And second, to empower change agents so they could operate from a deeper level of self-knowledge and personal power. This not only would make them more credible because they were walking their talk, but significantly increase their effectiveness in manifesting their social change vision through being able to transform the self-generated obstacles on their path.

We redesigned this intensive three-and-a half-day weekend format into eight four-hour modules to make its delivery more flexible and better able to fit into more niches. It could now be delivered over two consecutive weekends, eight weekly four-hour sessions, one long intensive weekend, or as separate modules that could be mixed and matched. We also adapted it into a life-coaching program that could be delivered in twelve one-hour sessions in tandem with exercises from our book.

We have been amazed by how many different places this transformational tool has been able to take root and how quickly it has been able to diffuse through a culture. The following four stories offer some insights into the multifaceted impact of personal empowerment on social change—and they provide a large dose of inspiration, as well.

Creating a Women's Empowerment Movement in Afghanistan

Shqipe Malushi came to the United States from Serbia as a young woman, having survived the war in Kosovo. Shortly after her arrival, a devastating car accident almost crippled her, but she was able, after many surgeries and with much determination, to walk again. Sometime after that she was diagnosed with cancer. More surgeries. More survival.

When we met her she was running a woman's organization that supported Bosnian war refugees in rebuilding their lives. She was burned out, utterly exhausted by the huge effort it took to help these traumatized women move forward in their lives. She came to us seeking transformative tools that would help her work better with these women.

Shqipe instantly soaked up all the tools and coaching we offered her. Before long, she had healed her traumatic past and jumped into a new vision for her life as an empowerment life coach. Within a short time she saw the Bosnian immigrant women go through a transformation similar to the one she had experienced. After repeated success with the many women who came to her organization, she began thinking about how to take this program to other women suffering from the ravages of war. Shqipe, not being one to think small, hatched a very large vision. She would take the life-coaching program to the place on our planet where women had been most brutalized and traumatized by war—Afghanistan—to help them rebuild their lives.

But there were a few details to work out. For starters she would need to get to Afghanistan, learn a new language, and acclimate to a country that was still at war. After she got over those hurdles she would need to figure out how to introduce a transformational program that was extremely innovative, even by American standards, into a culture that just a couple of years earlier had stoned women to death for attending school or not wearing a veil. She would be working with women so traumatized by the Taliban rule that they suffered from deep depression and residual fear even after these severe restrictions had been lifted.

When Shqipe shared her vision with Gail and me we didn't know what to think. We were deeply inspired by it and by her courage, but felt it was an extremely daunting venture and were concerned for her safety. Shqipe was wishing to go where angels feared to tread. We raised many questions with her. Would women be willing to participate? If so, could this transformational approach work in a culture where they were so downtrodden and systematically disenfranchised? And if she did succeed in empowering them, might this threaten their spouses and put them at risk of physical harm? How would those religious and civic leaders wishing to maintain a fundamentalist culture view Shqipe and this approach to change? Might she herself be in danger?

No matter what questions we threw at Shqipe, she had the perennial response of the committed agent of change. "If not me, then who? If not now, then when?" She was determined; for her it was not a question of whether, but rather how, she would succeed. She told us that she was not afraid, that she had survived so many life-threatening challenges in her life that she knew how to live by her wits. She said that she had waited her whole life for a moment when she could make a real difference and this was it. No matter the obstacles, she was going to seize this opportunity.

It wasn't long before she had convinced the U.S. Agency for International Development and a German aid organization, GTZ, to hire her to lead community development workshops for women in Afghanistan. While this was not her long-term vision, it allowed her to get to Afghanistan and sleuth out a way to hatch her empowerment strategy. We offered her our blessings and told her we would supply however many of our empowerment books she needed and support her in any way we could. After Shqipe had been in Afghanistan about six months, she sent us an e-mail reporting on her progress.

> As women attend my community development workshops I identify those I feel might be open to life coaching and who have a reasonable command of English. I invite them to meet in my room in the early mornings and evenings before and after work to go through the empowerment life-coaching program. It has taken off and I am working around the clock! Since I don't have time to stretch the program into twelve weeks, we agreed to do it in twelve days. I know that weeks are necessary to thoroughly process this information, but since these women have been so completely shut down they are thirsty for empowerment. They have forgotten how it feels to be human, laugh, feel pleasure, and feel alive. They are so traumatized and under so many cultural pressures it's like they have a time bomb ticking inside of themselves.
>
> Each client arrives at my door exactly on time for their sessions. This is unheard of, as Afghans are never on time and often don't show up and don't call. They carefully prepare their homework, and use the hour as the most precious time in their day. I am able to do coaching in such a simple way in both English and Dari. I wait patiently for them to understand the concept in English, and then I ask them to translate it into Dari. Boom it works.
>
> Afghanistan is unlike any place in the world. These women are burning in the bottom of hell. But the one bright spot in their lives is the empowerment life coaching. Each coaching session is so deep and moving for me as I see their faces and hearts transform. When

they leave my room, I see hope in their eyes. It is a miracle. This makes being here worthwhile. I have never felt more valuable as a human being than doing this empowerment work in Afghanistan.

One of the women Shqipe coached was Shiama Khinjani. During the Taliban regime, Shiama personally supported her entire extended family by holding a girls' school in her house, which put her life at risk. She describes her experience of receiving coaching from Shqipe.

This coaching brought lots of changes in my life. Before the life coaching I felt sad, hurt, powerless, useless, loveless, small, and fearful. During the Taliban time I suffered from losing my father, a job I loved, the opportunity to continue my studies, and the great violence against women in my country. I had lost all my hope.

At first I didn't know if this coaching would be very effective. I just wanted to keep myself busy with something new. But after a few sessions, I noticed something marvelous. I started feeling confidence, power, and happiness coming back into my life. Hope started growing in my heart. I started loving myself and loving life. For the first time I realized how beautiful life is. I decided to wake up, to go further, to reach my goals, and to make my dreams come true. In my coaching sessions I created a vision for my life. I believe it and I will do it. It made me hopeful. It allowed me to start living again with dreams and joy.

I am currently working with several projects with women civil servants and I would like to do this coaching with them. These women are amongst the most deprived and powerless because they don't speak up in their own behalf for fear of losing their jobs. I have already started to practice life coaching with both my sisters and my mother. The results are amazing.

Within a year Shqipe had taken over 100 women through the empowerment life-coaching program and they were creating a real buzz in the aid community. The leaders of these aid organizations, seeing all these empowered women, wondered what was going on. All roads led to Shqipe. When they approached her and asked what she was doing, she told them, "I am running an underground railroad for women. Except in this case it is not helping women find freedom through leaving a place, it is helping them find freedom within themselves." They were impressed and asked how they could help. She told them the best way would be to increase the ranks of empowerment life coaches and workshop trainers by providing scholarship financing for Afghan women to attend the Empowerment Institute in the United States. They agreed and asked Shqipe to develop a proposal.

Again Shqipe, not lacking for vision, developed a plan for building a women's empowerment movement with the goal of empowering women to improve their lives, economic status, and the larger society. She would carefully select from among the women she had coached, those with the most potential to be effective. They would need to be willing to bring the empowerment work to a particular sector of society or region of the country. Her job would be to coordinate this effort within Afghanistan and with us. The aid organization GTZ agreed to this proposal. So far we have certified eight Afghan empowerment trainers and coaches, including Shaima.

One is empowering women in the eastern provinces—the most desolate and isolated region of Afghanistan. Her vision is to "bring strength and a new vision to these women." Another is working with female elementary school teachers in Kabul, helping them to infuse their teaching with empowerment principles. We helped them translate our book into Dari so they could spread these principles to other teachers throughout the country.

Another life coach has begun working with nurses and doctors. She believes that people are getting sick from the extreme trauma in Afghanistan, and observes that the medicines they are given often don't help. She is using empowerment life coaching to provide these healers with what she calls "a deeper and more sustainable healing model."

Another is leading the Empowerment Workshop for community development leaders. One of the women who participated in her workshop developed a vision for enhancing the status of women, was elected as a national legislator, and helped pass one of the country's first laws providing rights to women.

Another workshop trainer, Robina Bangash, a gender advisor for the Aga Khan Foundation, is helping transform the role of women and the cultural conditions disempowering them. She describes how her own act of personal empowerment was able to influence the rights and opportunities of women in one of Afghanistan's most backward regions.

I participated in a Community Shura Councils' conference where elected leaders come together from different villages to share their development plans with one another. In keeping with this region's conservative cultural traditions women and men were to sit in two different rooms. Men would do the talking and deciding and women would listen. I decided to take a big risk. Just before the conference was to start I requested a meeting with the governor of the province to discuss the design. He accepted my request. As I prepared for this meeting, so many negative thoughts and limiting beliefs started going through my mind and I was constantly turning them around and looking toward possibilities.

When I finally met with him I was clear what I needed to say. I recommended that in order to get the most value out of this conference it would be important to hear directly from women. I said that they played an important role in community development and without their insights it would be difficult to make informed decisions. To be able to make this contribution they would need to sit in the same room with the local elected leaders and be able to directly express their views. After graciously hearing my recommendation, the governor said he would be willing to call a special meeting with the religious leaders whose approval would be needed to break with this custom. He asked if I would be willing to share my recommendation directly with them. I said of course. To my amazement, they agreed!

We called in the women, who actively participated and made presentations in front of eighty-five political and religious leaders, and the governor—all male, of course. The governor was so moved by what they had to say that he encouraged them to visit his office whenever they needed help. Nothing like this had ever occurred before in this part of the country. This was a revolutionary change. Within three hours we had brought women into the mainstream of society.

The empowerment ripples continue to spread throughout Afghanistan as each year we train more Afghan facilitators to bolster the ranks. Collectively they have now trained over 3,000 women in the tools of empowerment. This all began because of the unwavering determination of an empowered woman with a compelling vision. If this level of personal and societal transformation is possible in one of the most repressive parts of our planet with women who have been disenfranchised for centuries, what is possible under more favorable conditions? With fearless people like Shqipe Malushi, effective personal transformation tools, and commitment, we can only begin to imagine.

A New Tool for Post-Conflict Reconciliation: Transforming a Culture from the Inside Out in Rwanda

Immaculee Iligabiza lost her entire family in the Rwandan genocide. In her moving bestseller, *Left to Tell*, she shares the extraordinary story of how she and seven other women lived in a small bathroom for three months, trapped by the constant threat of death. Her story of faith throughout this ordeal is a testament to the remarkable resiliency of the human spirit. Immaculee wanted to use the platform her book provided to, in her words, "help the people in my country transcend their old wounds and hatred and learn to live together again." She came to the Empowerment Institute looking for tools to help her achieve this transformational vision.

Her hope was that this healing process—which might take decades as older generations died off, or not occur at all because the recriminations were passed down from generation to generation—could be significantly accelerated through an explicit transformational process. The idea was to invite Hutu and Tutsi women to go through the Empowerment Workshop *together*. We would begin with women, because they are a culture's early adopters for healing and community building, and therefore the most receptive to this type of transformation. We would be testing whether an experience of shared humanity at the level of one's fears, wounds, and dreams might allow these women to connect in a way that transcended their animosities; and whether the empowerment tools could allow them to heal and transform deeply held pain, anger, or shame.

Immaculee invited two fellow Rwandans living in the United States to join her on her mission. Consolatie Uwera, a recent immigrant to the United States, would lead the workshop in Rwanda on one of her regular trips back. Claire Umubyeyi, who works in the United Nations on peace building issues, would test out the workshop with Rwandan immigrants in the United States.

The journey to transform their country took an unexpected turn for all three of them as they discovered that they needed to go through their own personal transformation around pain, anger, and fear before they could help others. They soon found themselves embodying Ghandi's oft-quoted words of wisdom as they became the change they sought for the world. It was from this strong foundation of personal healing and growth that they then took this empowerment tool to other Rwandan women.

Consalatie was able to organize the Empowerment Workshop for six Hutu and six Tutsi women in Rwanda. "When the Hutu and Tutsi women started the workshop," she explained, "they had deep anger toward each other instilled in them by our culture. They came out of it understanding that they shared a common journey as human beings. They not only were able to accept each other, but committed to working together for the healing of our country."

Claire led the workshop for Rwandan women living in New York City. "The women attending my workshop had been torn apart by the conflicts in our country," she said. "The workshop helped them move beyond the past and the burden it carries in preventing self-love and tolerance and begin creating a better future for themselves. But it went beyond just helping these women develop their potential, it also furthered the type of healing our country needs to rebuild our dignity." She continued, "Given my work at the United Nations with conflict prevention, I have introduced this approach of personal empowerment as an innovative new tool for peace building in Rwanda and other postconflict settings where deep ethnic or racial animosity exists."

Consolatie, Clair, Immaculee, and the other women who went through these empowerment workshops give us hope that below the surface of even the most horrific tragedy there is the possibility for transformation. This possibility begins each time we step forward and open up to our potential. And with dedicated change leadership and skill in using transformative tools, it can go even further. Rwanda has been one of the planet's teachers of the worst of what is possible among human beings. Perhaps it might also be a teacher, with the help of these three women, for the best of what is possible on our planet as people learn how to transform themselves and their country from the inside out.

Retrieving People from the Margins of Society: Empowering the Homeless in San Francisco

The Empowerment Workshop was put to another demanding test when a visionary Californian called on its tools and methodology in an effort to retrieve people living on the margins of our society. Shelly Roder, who runs a homeless shelter in the Tenderloin District of San Francisco, shares her story of leading the workshop for homeless men and women, and her efforts to offer them dignity and new possibilities.

> I work with the homeless population in San Francisco. Most of the participants are people who depend on professional help—social workers, psychiatrists, counselors, case managers—to deal with daily life. Rarely in these interactions are they given the opportunity to envision life in a different way. Rather, these "rehabilitative" sessions tend to focus on the problem areas of life, thereby reinforcing the self-limiting beliefs characteristic of individuals living under extreme conditions of poverty. "I am a failure," "I am psychotic," "I am an addict," "I make bad decisions," "I am worth as much as I own, which is nothing."
>
> The workshop offered the participants a radically different approach—time to imagine a different reality, therefore motivating them to make behavior changes by working with these tools. They were excited to have an opportunity to dream—to envision the way they would like life to be—and then to be provided a methodology that could enable them to manifest these dreams.
>
> The bravery and humility shown to me by the participants was inspiring. As we worked with the exercises, two participants started to identify the deep sense of shame they feel for their poverty, specifically for living on government assistance.
>
> Once this stuff was out and we could work to transform these beliefs, participants left the experience with a recovered sense of dignity, despite the fact that they were returning to their shelter or hotel room. This taught me at a profound level that the starting point for social transformation is personal transformation.
>
> A by-product of the workshops was the camaraderie experienced by the groups. The workshop built a strong sense of connection, something that is often absent from the lives of people who are homeless. The groups have continued to meet with each other for ongoing connection and support. I am now working to get this nascent group of empowered residents in the homeless community more actively involved in helping the larger community by adapting their personal empowerment skills to the work of neighborhood

transformation. And I am trying to make the system they deal with better able to support their newfound sense of empowerment.

Shelley took empowerment into the heart of one of America's most pathologically oriented communities. This community of people is deprived of many things, but one of its greatest losses is a sense of hope. Opening up the possibility of hope is the beginning point in the transformation of people mired in pathology and who feel trapped in the system. The next critical step is helping them build a positive vision for their life and providing the tools and support necessary to achieve the vision. How else could we expect someone to change?

An effective personal empowerment process, while light-years better than providing band-aids, is not enough, though. It then requires knowledge of how to help change a system that is not designed to empower. Homeless people by themselves cannot do this. Their main job is to heal, transform, and reenter society. It is for change agents like Shelley who are willing to challenge the assumptions of this system to further this transformational process. Like a Russian doll with many little dolls nested inside it, the empowerment process continues to repeat itself.

As change agents we empower ourselves to find a better way. We then learn how to empower others. As we experience greater levels of success empowering others, we are willing to engage more directly with the system itself. Based on our success, early adopters in the system are willing to have a conversation about a better way. We then co-create a vision of this better way and begin testing it within the system. As we demonstrate success, more people become interested and we expand to the next level of scale. This is a long journey, but if we persevere and keep practicing the empowerment process we can retrieve people from the margins of society and the system they need to reenter it.

Getting to the Root of Social Change: Empowering Unwed Mothers in the Bronx

There are few higher-leverage interventions for transforming a multitude of social ills than helping inner-city unwed mothers gain control of their lives. Young women out of wedlock raising children while they themselves are still children will perpetuate more of the same. As with the homeless, this is an issue that requires a transformative change process to break the cycle of disempowerment. Ijeoma Ude, a community organizer in New York City and herself an unwed teenage mother in her youth, has taken on this task. She defines her mission as "addressing societal problems at their root by integrating personal transformation with social justice." She participated in our Empowerment Institute to learn how to lead the Empowerment Workshop for inner-city unwed teenage mothers. She describes her experience.

> In my workshop I had thirteen young, single mothers who lived in a home together and ranged in age from 11 to 19. They kept saying, "I'm glad we're doing this" and told the program coordinator in between sessions: "Thank you for getting us this workshop. It's good. It's different from anything we've ever taken." They loved the "letting go" exercise and really got into creating release rituals. Afterward some of their comments were: "I feel so much lighter"; "I didn't realize I had so much anger in me"; "That was fun." They loved the self-love lecture and really got it. They really liked the fear guided exercise. Most of them focused on family. Some of their comments were: "I need to learn to accept my mother more"; "I want to be stronger in myself so I don't keep letting myself get manipulated into having sex."
>
> The workshop was totally accessible and applicable to their lives. It helped these young women address and transform limiting beliefs that had been passed on to them from generation to generation, and create new positive visions for their life. I will continue to lead this workshop for unwed teenage mothers in other under-resourced communities around the city because it is one of the few tools I have come across that gets at the root of social change.

As Ijeoma identified, unless we can help an unwed teenage mother address and transform her root limiting beliefs, these beliefs will continue to manifest as dysfunctional behaviors and be passed on to her children. To change an endemic societal problem like this requires an intervention at its source—the belief system of those people in that social system. To do this requires personal transformation. This is not a luxury but a necessity.

What I value about Ijeoma's work is that while the battles are raging over the best way to transform the social welfare system, a necessary undertaking for sure, she is transforming it from the ground up. She has invested her time in empowering those people trapped in the system that have not known how to get out. As society learns how to invest in more people like Ijeoma it will find itself with a win-win-win situation. People in the system will be liberated from generations of disempowerment. We will attract more transformationally oriented people like Ijeoma who wish to participate in something that produces real results and is personally gratifying. And lasting, cost-effective systemic social change will be achieved through the personal transformation of the people in that social system.

Personal Empowerment Tools: A Societal Game Changer

Each of these stories demonstrates the vast potential for social change available to us by learning how to work more skillfully with the wounded cultures and dysfunctional systems all across our planet. This is not about working harder, but smarter. It is not about investing more money to solve these problems, but investing less and using it much more intelligently. Not only will this free up the vast amounts of financial resources currently invested in poorly performing change strategies, but it will aid in the creation of robust societies by enabling so many more people to become fully contributing members. And it will significantly accelerate the time it takes to accomplish this change.

A big part of the social change agenda in the twenty-first century will be making one of the truly innovative social innovations of the twentieth century—personal empowerment tools, of which the Empowerment Workshop is just one—a new best practice for how social change is implemented. To achieve this will require building the capacity of a new cadre of change agents in multiple sectors of society. This is eminently doable, and its accomplishment will be one of the planet's most significant game changers.

THE EMPOWERING ORGANIZATION: CHANGING BEHAVIOR AND DEVELOPING TALENT

There are two primary ways to increase the performance capacity of society: advancing solutions to social problems and unmet social needs; and increasing the efficacy of societal institutions. We have been focusing a lot on the former. It's now time to look at the latter.

In today's "knowledge economy," an institution is relevant in society based on its intellectual capital—its stock of beneficial ideas and practices. And those institutions capable of increasing their intellectual capital, whether non-profit, for profit, or governmental, will offer the most value to society. For society to evolve, its institutions must evolve. And for its institutions to evolve, the people who work in them must be operating at their full potential. Previously I have shared tools to increase the potential of both individuals and groups. In this section we will look at how to do this within an organization.

In *The Only Sustainable Edge*, authors and respected management consultants John Hagel and John Brown offer their insights on just how important this is to an organization's future. "The primary role of an organization in today's society should be to accelerate the capability building of its members so they can create more value. Institutions that can do the most effective job of building capability will create and capture value—the rest will inevitably fall by the wayside."

So how are organizations doing at developing the capabilities of their people? According to the research of Tom Peters, former management consultant for McKinsey and Company and author of the mega bestseller *In Search of Excellence*, they are not doing very well. He says, "people in most organizations spend no more than six minutes a day working on improvement. That is a ratio of self-development to work of .01 percent. This will catch up with those organizations as they are out-competed by those with more robust efforts to develop people." According to Gallup studies, approximately 75 percent of employees in organizations are not intellectually or emotionally engaged at work because of marginally functional or outright dysfunctional organizational cultures. And organizations have just barely tapped the potential of the 25 percent of their employees who *are* engaged.

For an organization to bring value to society and stay relevant in the twenty-first century, it will need to attract, develop, and retain talented people. This will necessitate the creation of a very different culture and set of capabilities than exists today in all but an extremely small number of organizations. Building this capacity, which I call an "Empowering Organization," has been a facet of my work for several decades, and a track of the Empowerment Institute, as well. I led a train-the-trainer application of this behavior-change and talent-development model for American Express—an organization with a strong commitment to growing its people and a long history, through its employee volunteer programs and philanthropy, of corporate social responsibility. Bob Franco, vice president of their Global Talent Division, tells his story.

A key challenge in institutions is how to move individuals to higher levels of performance, specifically when it involves building partnerships within complex organizational systems. Our team—whose mission is to build and improve talent within the company on a worldwide basis—had been working under circumstances that prevented our ability to achieve this including lack of access to critical information and key partners, a politicized environment, and limited skills.

My team went through an intense, personalized transformational learning experience using the empowering organization process and tools. This helped us separate the circumstance around us charged with a disempowering "pathology," and helped us focus our own personal accountability toward what we can accomplish and what we are ultimately capable of attaining. After a deep assessment of our organizational culture and challenges, this process enabled us to build our consulting skills and leverage our collective talent.

The outcome was significant, measurable, and sustainable behavior change within our team, a clearly defined value proposition based on our new capability to develop talent within our organization, and an ability to be successful despite any organizational barriers. The process moved us away from the crippling power of "problems" to a new power—one inside us, one focused on what we want to create. Through this work, our team now has daily practices focusing on their vision. We are empowered!

Creating a Learning and Growth Culture

To enable this group to adopt new behaviors and develop their talent first required the establishment of a learning and growth culture. Many organizational change interventions assume that this learning and growth capacity is inherent within the culture. It rarely is, and as a result the organization's ability to achieve the desired behavior change is inhibited.

Using the analogy of nature, for new seeds to take root they need fertile soil. In an organizational context, this fertile soil is a learning and growth culture. To create this type of culture requires a set of practices be in place that enable individuals to feel safe and trusting enough to risk true growth.

The six practices, which are built into the empowerment framework, are experienced during the training and then transferred to the workplace.

1. **Self-Responsibility:** Individuals take responsibility to have their job, team, organization the way they wish it.

2. **Authentic Communication:** Individual communication is open, honest, and transparent.

3. **Trust:** Individuals feel safe enough to try out new behaviors and take risks.

4. **Learning and Growing:** Individuals are encouraged to work on the real behaviors they need to change.

5. **Interpersonal Process Skills:** Protocols and skills are learned to resolve interpersonal issues.

6. **Caring:** Leadership demonstrates tangible concern for individuals.

The Transformational Process

With this foundation for behavior change in place, the empowerment framework provides the transformation strategy culminating with each individual working on his or her growing edge grounded with an intention statement and a visual image.

Let's go back and follow Bob through this process. As a result of a guided exercise around his core beliefs, he identified self-responsibility as the issue he wished to work on. Specifically, he wanted to move from being a victim within his organization to creating a different possibility for himself and his team.

First Bob went through a *self-awareness* exercise. He discovered that he was just going through the motions, having lost a lot of passion for his internal consulting and leadership. As he went through the *visioning exercise,* he saw the very real possibility that he and his team could develop a behavior change and talent development skill set that could more effectively serve their internal clients. He realized that rather than feeling held back by the organization, he could change his circumstances by increasing the capability of his team.

However, when Bob came down from the mountaintop he saw that to achieve this would not be easy. Were he and his team up to learning these new skills? Would his clients be receptive? He then went through a *transformation* exercise in which he identified and turned around the limiting beliefs that might get in the way of a new way of working with colleagues and clients.

His *growing edge* was believing in his team and being willing to engage in this capability-building process. As team members revealed their own growing edges, it became clear that in contrast to the past, when Bob needed to lift everyone by the force of his vision and will (a draining proposition at best), they were developing the ability to do this on their own.

He translated his growing edge into this intention statement: "I help my team build our consulting skills and leverage our collective talent to create results. I lead and am led by an empowering team who knows what it wants and gets it!"

The process enabled Bob and his team to adopt new behaviors and develop transformational capabilities that furthered their individual aspirations, the needs of the group, and the organization. This mutuality strengthened everyone's commitment, enabling greater sustainability for the behavior changes and the implementation of their new capabilities over the long term. And the learning and growth culture that was now established, assisted by these transformational tools and a robust support system, provided the foundation for people's ongoing development.

Any organization that wishes to increase its value to society, and ultimately its longevity, must learn how to develop the talent of its people. And as Bob and his team have shown, it is quite achievable with benefits for all. If enough organizations did what was in their own self-interest and grew their people, it would significantly increase the performance capacity of society. With the huge challenges our world now faces, we cannot afford for our societal institutions to be operating at anything less than their full potential. This is the low-hanging fruit of social change and we must pick it.

A WHOLE SYSTEM TRANSFORMATION: EMPOWERMENT MEETS PUBLIC EDUCATION

Our final area of exploration is what I call whole-system transformation. This is the ability to evolve a social system to a higher level of performance. This section describes such a transformation by applying the practice of empowerment to all the key elements of the education system: students, teachers, parents, administration, the teacher culture, and the very process of learning and teaching.

In spite of decades of research into best practices in teaching techniques and classroom design, there is one question at the very core of the learning experience that has not received much attention. How can we empower students to take more personal responsibility for their learning? In the current education culture, the onus is always on the teacher to make his or her teaching or the subject matter more compelling. When students are not learning, it is the teacher's job to find a better way to convey the material. If this does not work then the last alternative is to discipline the students. This makes teaching an endless and thankless task that often leads to teacher burnout and a high rate of attrition when talented individuals leave the profession.

In 2004 a visionary administrator, Jane Ebaugh, from the Rhinebeck, New York, public school system, was curious to see if our empowerment model might add value to the traditional way education was practiced. She had participated in one of our empowerment trainings; now she and a few teachers decided to come to our Empowerment Institute. She quickly saw the impact empowerment work could have in the schools, and so she encouraged more teachers to experiment with it, who in turn encouraged still more of their colleagues. We have now worked with some thirty Rhinebeck educators who teach from kindergarten to high school, representing approximately 20 percent of that town's public school system.

When I first began working with them I did not appreciate the impact the empowerment principles customized into a classroom-specific transformational curriculum would have on the traditional teaching model and on them as teachers. I soon discovered that it is impossible to apply these principles without affecting the assumptions in the system in which they are being employed. What follows are four stories of transformation in the classroom and beyond.

A Sixth Grade Science Class Discovers the Growing Edge

Debra Breger integrated the empowerment tools into her sixth grade science class and explains their impact on her students' academic performance, on how she conducts her class, and on her as a teacher.

> I helped students learn about the growing edge by observing a cactus plant. We discussed all of the different characteristics of a growing edge. I then asked them to think about what we could translate from watching growth in the natural world to growth in our own lives. We

then talked about the growing edge of our learning community—our classroom. I explained how self-responsibility is a macronutrient for human growth. I then helped them discover where they are around their learning and how they wished it to be. We then discussed what habits or emotions got in the way of their learning.

We concluded with what they needed to do differently. What change is needed to increase their learning over the next quarter in science class? What are they willing to practice and work on? What will this look, feel, and sound like? Each student wrote "I am responsible for my own learning. What I attend to grows. I will take responsibility to _____."

Each Monday and at the start of every class I would ask them to open their notebooks and read these statements to themselves. To revise them if needed and share with a new partner in the class about how they are doing. I kept a record of each student's growing edge to support their efforts. This is very teachable to a class of sixth graders. Science class is a perfect laboratory for them to experiment and practice with their own learning. This also started changes in the classroom, including more student independence, interactive collaborative work, and student choice.

As a result of the empowerment learning strategy with its focus on vision, transformation of limiting beliefs that undermine their learning, and growing edges around specific new behaviors, students have improved their academic performance and interest in learning. The atmosphere in the classroom is much more dynamic. Aside from using the methodology with my students I used it for myself as a teacher. I created a vision for my classroom and my teaching and brought it into reality. It now embodies my values and my true being. My classroom is a different place to be.

Debra creatively integrated the empowerment process skills into her existing curriculum. This helped increase the crossover effect of the learning and made it much easier for her to teach. Not surprisingly, she discovered that when students took greater responsibility for their learning, both their academic performance and their motivation improved. She also saw her own motivation improve when she applied the tools to her own teaching. She created an inspiring vision of her classroom and herself in it. She envisioned the values she wanted to convey, the quality of teaching she wished to embody, and what she wanted her classroom to feel like for the students. No one had ever encouraged Debra to dream as a teacher. She is now living her dream on a daily basis.

Changing "I Can't" to "I Can" for Students and Teachers

Vicki Hoener teaches languages skills to 8- to 11-year-olds with various learning challenges. She describes her experience applying the empowerment tools to create attitudinal and behavioral shifts in her students. Like Debra, she discovered it is hard to teach empowerment without its having a personal impact. "My goal was to change students 'I can't' attitude about learning," commented Vicki, "and along the way, while helping my students change, I noticed I changed as well." She shares her story.

> After a great deal of thought on how best to teach the salient features of the growing edge model while maintaining sound pedagogical practices, I created a fable called "The Gopher Who Discovered Growing Edges." The fable presented the model simply and clearly, using key vocabulary terms which students understood, internalized, and applied to their own growing edges.
>
> This format was enormously successful. My students loved the fable so much they decided to write their own growing edge fables, which were incredible. Integrating reading and writing with process work met my need to use every minute of time with my students as "teaching time."
>
> I was amazed by how introspective and insightful my students were. They figured out where they needed to make changes. Academically it included being able to focus better in class, write longer sentences, and read more fluently. Socially it was around being picked on by peers and siblings as well as being embarrassed to ask for help in class.
>
> When I first started this work with my students I thought I did not know the right questions to ask, but then I started paying more attention to their needs and the right guiding questions flowed like water. I was amazed that I could do this. The more I practiced the more natural it became. This new approach affected my teaching as well. I no longer focused on problems and orchestrating solutions.

Instead, I spent my time guiding students to find solutions that worked for them.

I did a session spontaneously when one of my students came to me in tears about an issue centered around her ability to listen and learn in her fourth grade classroom. I listened carefully, and asked her questions which led to a vision, identification of limiting beliefs, and a growing edge. She wrote the growing edge on a card so she could keep it with her when she went into her class.

The next day an unbelievable thing happened. She came to see me and asked if we could do another "session with the cards." I was floored! This time the issue was that she keeps forgetting her planner at home (with all of her homework in it) and wanted help in figuring out how to remember to bring it to school. This process is so simple and powerful that even a 9-year-old can recognize it and ask for it by name as in "the session with the cards!" This is so exciting!

The empowerment process, however, goes beyond just empowering students; it also has had an impact on how I engage with my fellow teachers. At a committee meeting that usually consists of talking about student problems I brought their "growing edge" notebooks and turned the conversations into opportunities to discuss positive solutions. For every negative that came up (student doesn't complete homework, daydreams in class, etc.) there was a growing edge addressing that very issue! Focusing on how students were taking personal responsibility for their learning transformed the whole tenor of the meeting.

This empowered me to take more responsibility to effect change in the school environment, which can be somewhat negative and divisive. This was the hardest and most prickly area for me to work on. I started changing this system by beginning with myself. Rather than just ignoring the part of the culture which affected me, which is how I had been operating, I decided to put myself out there and focus on solutions. Colleagues noticed and responded in a positive way. I have replaced inaction with positive action. Focusing on my vision changed things for my students and me!

A parent of one of her students noticed all the positive things happening, too. Inspired by Vicki's vision, competence, and commitment, he offered her a $10,000 grant to spend on the school any way she wished. *That* is empowerment in action.

Empowering the Very Young

Jennifer Hammond King, who teaches reading to first- and second-graders, shares how even very young children take to the practice of empowerment.

As part of my thirty-minute reading classes, I teach students the four steps of the empowerment methodology. Each child develops a vision of themselves as a reader and draws pictures to illustrate that vision. Two of my favorites were a second-grader who envisioned himself as a father reading a bedtime story to his children and a first-grader who envisioned himself hiding under a table and understanding the words his parents were spelling to each other in their conversation: "time for b-e-d."

One of the wonderful things about young children is that they have not had the time or need to clutter their minds with a lot of limiting beliefs. We discovered that the best way to work with limiting beliefs was to confront them as they came up during the course of our regular reading work. "Let's turn that around," became one of the favorite phrases of our classes.

Each student created a flower with petals that could be added to represent their learning growing edges. There was at least one petal for a reading or writing skill area and one for a learning behavior. The children loved the term "growing edges," and it was a great tool for us to talk about the individual strengths and needs of each student. On one occasion, a little first-grade girl forgot to bring her homework back to school. Another boy said to her, "Did you remember that homework was one of your growing edges?"

Jennifer helped me and the other teachers appreciate how ready very young children are to be more personally responsible for their learning. Whenever I come across an adult in one of my trainings who complains that the empowerment process is too complicated, I always use Jennifer's story about teaching the growing edge to first- and second-graders.

Empowering Parents With a Vision of Their Child's Education

Clare Dwyer, a special education teacher, discovered that her empowerment skills translated to working with parents as well. She describes how empowering them to help their children became an important part of her teaching.

> I invited one of my parents to create her vision for the outcome of her child's school career. I had a picture of a road and we began with the questions. "What would you like to see at the end of this road for your son?" "What do we need along the path to reach that goal?" This parent needed to face the reality that if her son is going to earn a degree, he would need to learn how to perform independently. We worked on her growing edge of needing to allow her child to feel and express frustration and not succumb to it.
>
> With another set of parents I learned that to be effective using this model you need a strong inviting question to redirect a challenging situation. This couple began arguing about each other's parenting skills and the lack of appropriate guidance and consequences regarding their child. Before things became too heated, I invited them each to share how they would like their evenings to look with their child. We created a vision they both could support. I believe for the first time they heard each other.
>
> I left that night feeling I had made a positive difference in both of these families' lives, one that would help not only their children, but the parents too. It was a very satisfying experience.

Clare skillfully closed the loop with her students' learning by empowering parents to become actively engaged and more sympathetic to the challenges their children faced. By empowering parents to work through their own limiting beliefs and address their growing edges for how best to contribute to their child's education, Clare addressed the whole learning system, thereby tremendously increasing the likelihood of a positive outcome for all.

Transforming the Education Paradigm

Shifting the responsibility for the students' learning from the teacher to the student was a huge and dramatic change. The need for this change was not something I immediately understood. I was just doing my empowerment thing by asking teachers what they did when students didn't learn what they wanted to teach them. For the most part they answered sheepishly that they basically just told students to study harder. When I asked them if they had ever tried to discover and change the beliefs undermining their students' learning, they look puzzled and said they wouldn't begin to know how. When I asked them how accountable the students were for their own learning, the teachers looked at me with a blank stare.

As I continued to probe deeper, I saw that the teachers felt overburdened with accountability for student learning. Other than finding better ways to teach the material, they had no real tools for helping children when they did not learn. In addition, their self-esteem was often tied up in being "the teacher." Who were they as teachers if the students became more accountable for their learning? What would this look like in the classroom? How would they feel about themselves? There were many issues that needed to be looked at and many changes to consider.

The empowerment methodology was able to transform the educational paradigm of these teachers for the most pragmatic of all reasons—when students owned their own learning they improved academically and socially, and made the teachers' jobs not just easier, but more dynamic.

Once the empowerment process was learned it was used on an ongoing basis. Teachers did a simple visioning exercise before starting a new teaching unit, and, when students encountered a learning block, they worked with them on their growing edges. If the student needed extra help the teacher could provide it or encourage the person to work with another student. Bringing other students into the learning and growth process both provided a richer support system for students and expanded the resources available to assist each student's learning process.

The empowerment model worked at all the age levels from kindergarten to high school. The way it was taught varied according to the grade level, but the simple and profound notion of empowering students to envision and take personal responsibility for their learning worked at any age. It also empowered the larger educational community of fellow teachers and parents to play more constructive roles in a student's learning.

This enhanced the learning process and allowed everyone to come away invigorated. The practice of empowerment is now diffusing throughout the school system with its principles formally written into the district's teaching philosophy. There is still more to be done in Rhinebeck, but this new approach to learning is now firmly established in the teaching culture and is on its diffusion path.

This inspiring story of a whole-system transformation around one of America's central challenges—the education of its children—is very hopeful. It says we can improve the performance capacity of the educational system through a relatively modest, albeit seemingly radical, idea—empowering students to become accountable for their learning and for adopting the behaviors that enable it. Rhinebeck's story is yet another illustration of how we can change the game—in this case, the basic assumptions of the teaching and learning process—by bringing a transformational approach into the equation. This allows us to work smarter, not harder—which is always a good thing.

The common themes of each story in this chapter have been the need in the world for strategies that can change the game; the universality and efficacy of the empowerment tools across a wide swath of societal issues in furthering this type of transformative change; and the readiness of change leaders to engage. This journey continues in the next chapter where we explore putting these tools to a test where failure is not an option—global warming.

CHAPTER 10: SOCIAL CHANGE 2.0 PRACTITIONER'S GUIDE

1. Whom do you need to empower to do what to further your social change initiative?

2. How will you empower these individuals?

3. How will you build the capacity of the people working on your social change initiative to be effective agents of transformative change?

4. How will your social change initiative transform the system in which it resides so it is capable of supporting it and other comparable initiatives?

5. If you wish to design or expand an existing curriculum on social change, how will it help students implement a behavior change strategy to further their social change initiative and facilitate their personal growth as change agents?

EMPOWERING A CLIMATE CHANGE MOVEMENT:

LOW CARBON DIET

AND THE COOL COMMUNITY

If there is no action to reverse the growth of greenhouse gas emissions before 2012, that's too late. What we do in the next few years will determine our future.
— Rajendra Pachauri, Climate Scientist,
Head of U.N. Intergovernmental Panel on Climate Change,
Nobel Peace Prize Winner

We are in imminent peril. We have at most 10 years. Not 10 years to decide upon action, but 10 years to alter fundamentally the trajectory of global greenhouse emissions and take significant action to reduce them. If not, we will hit a critical tipping point after which it becomes impractical to make further changes. We are then locked into disastrous effects including major coastal flooding and droughts.
— Jim Hansen, NASA's Chief Climate Scientist,
Speech in 2008

In the view of climate scientists around the world—and many others—it is imperative that our civilization's central organizing project become the transformation of our adverse impact on the climate system before we reach an irreversible tipping point. To accomplish this transformation requires boldness, innovation, and speed unlike anything humanity has ever encountered. In the face of this crisis, people and institutions around the world are rallying like never before to find real solutions. But the large-scale solutions many are pinning their hopes on—renewable energy and new technologies—will take a decade at best, or, many predict, several decades to scale up. Much more time than scientists tell us we have.

There is, however, one solution that has the potential to bring about significant large-scale carbon reduction in the short term and buy us some critically needed time for these other approaches to scale up: *household energy conservation in America*. America represents a quarter of the planet's carbon footprint, and half of it comes from the fossil fuel energy we use to power our homes and cars. Empowering citizens to reduce their carbon footprint will not only slow the deterioration of our climate system, but also help create a carbon-literate society desirous of bold government climate policies and demand for the low carbon products and services on which much of the U.S. economic future is being built. Moreover, this will send a message to other countries that as Americans we are ready to reduce our high carbon-emitting lifestyles for the sake of the planet, allowing us once again to be a member in good standing of the global community and a source of inspiration for other countries, such as China and India, to up their ante.

The good news is that there is an unprecedented readiness among Americans to take personal action on the issue of global warming. A 2007 Yale University study indicated that 75 percent of Americans recognize that their own behavior can help reduce global warming, and 81 percent believe it is their responsibility to do something about it. Furthermore, making these changes is not demanding, and will increase people's quality of life and save them money. And one more piece of good news: We have spent the past two decades figuring out how to do this and by now you should be able to as well.

This chapter applies this knowledge to the issue of empowering individuals and communities to reduce their carbon footprint, in particular, through the use of the Low Carbon Diet behavior-change program and the Cool Community campaign for taking the program to scale. It ends by taking a look at the social, environmental, and economic dividends a community can expect—in addition to the not-too-shabby benefit of helping secure a future for humankind—from going on this journey. But this journey needs to go back before it can go forward.

LOW CARBON DIET: AN IDEA WHOSE TIME HAS COME

The city of Portland, Oregon, kept wishing to push the envelope, as is its accustomed mode of operation. By the year 2000 we had formed more than 200 neighborhood-based EcoTeams. The local government leadership had demonstrable proof that the program worked, and now wanted to experiment further with this tool. Mike Lindberg had procured a small grant from a regional foundation for extension of the program. Susan Anderson, the director of Sustainable Development for the city and a major program advocate since the very beginning, asked if I would consider using the grant to create a program addressing global warming.

Portland was the first city in America to develop a climate action plan in 1993 and they were aggressively engaged in lowering the government's carbon footprint. She was interested to see if the EcoTeam behavior-change approach might help them engage citizens in this issue as well. While Portland is a progressive city, it was still seven years before Al Gore's Academy Award winning documentary, *An Inconvenient Truth*, would help raise America's awareness about this issue, and before the U.N. Intergovernmental Panel on Climate Change would publish research that demonstrated unequivocally that human beings were the principal cause of global warming and at imminent risk of creating a planet inhospitable to human life. In October of 2007, Al Gore and the IPCC would share the Nobel Peace Prize for their work in this area.

There was local government advocacy for addressing the issue of global warming in many cities through an effort called Cities for Climate Protection, sponsored by the International Council for Local Environmental Initiatives. This effort inspired many local governments to take on climate change by making their own municipal operations more energy efficient. This was a relatively simple sell since doing so also saved them a lot of money. But, no city had attempted to help its residents lower their carbon footprint in any serious way. In accordance with its plan's goal of reducing carbon emissions 10 percent, Portland was looking to see if the EcoTeam model could get a 10 percent reduction per participating household.

I was intrigued by this opportunity, but wondered if people would be willing to take on an issue that seemed so big and out of their immediate control. Up until then, whatever widespread education and outreach efforts there had been around the issue were principally focused on energy efficiency. Addressing global warming was seen as a bit too complicated to sell in its own right, so it was described as an "added value" to energy efficiency. This, in fact, had been the way our sustainable lifestyle program had described it. I knew we would easily meet the 10 percent goal if we could get people to participate in this program, since we were already getting a 15 percent reduction through our sustainable lifestyle program.

I decided to give it a try. Susan offered me the support of her department's energy expert, Michael Armstrong, who was smart and creative and relished the opportunity to help pioneer something like this. We identified all the actions in our sustainable lifestyle program that had a CO_2 impact and could realistically be measured. I knew there was a carbon footprint for each of the actions in the program that used fossil fuel, but until I dug in I was not aware of just how much opportunity there was to reduce it. This was a much more interesting process to me than just saving energy and some money, or even than doing the right thing; I now felt like I was saving the planet. I wondered if others would feel the same way.

The actual actions were quite simple to take. Some required changes of habits, like turning off lights. Others required making our mechanical systems more efficient, like tuning up our furnaces or cars. Still others required a one-time change, like paying our local utility a small monthly fee to provide us electricity from renewal energy rather than fossil fuels. None of these things was difficult to do, but they wouldn't get on a priority list, unless people thought they were important.

Building on Michael's technical expertise we began developing a carbon footprint number for each of these actions. It was fascinating and a bit shocking to see every aspect of my daily use of energy through the lens of how much CO_2 it released into the atmosphere.

Coming up with these numbers, though, was not easy. There were so many assumptions we had to make to establish a carbon reduction number for each action. For example, we discovered that a full dishwasher load is much more efficient than washing dishes by hand, but that a small load is not. So how many dishwasher loads might we project for the average family over the course of a year? What is the carbon reduction difference between average use and this more efficient use? We had to immerse ourselves in studying the daily inefficient usage of an average household compared with more efficient usage. Believe it or not, companies that make these appliances have this type of information.

Once we figured all this out we could get the energy usage and finally the carbon footprint. This was certainly based on much extrapolation and was as much art as science. But even though the actual numbers might be off by as much 20 percent on a case-by-case basis, relatively speaking, this type of feedback would help people become aware of the carbon footprint reduction opportunity in each aspect of their daily lifestyle. At the time, we were the first to do this type of carbon footprint exercise. Now, fortunately, there are many more people doing it.

Our next task was to create a carbon calculator to help participants identify their current carbon footprint. If you were going to reduce your carbon footprint you needed to know where you were starting this journey. We approached some colleagues at the consulting firm ICF who had developed the U.S. Environmental Protection Agency's carbon calculator, and with the financial support of the EPA they helped us construct a Portland-specific calculator. This was becoming such an interesting experiment that we had no trouble attracting backing.

Participants used this online calculator by entering their annual electricity and oil or propane usage, miles driven, and miles per gallon for each car in their household, among other things. Once they gathered this information, it only took a few minutes to enter it into the calculator and get their annual household carbon footprint. (Carbon calculators have now proliferated over the Internet and at last count there were over a hundred versions available.) The hard part would be getting people to take action based on this knowledge. Here is where the EcoTeam model would be tested.

Knowing that so many people in Portland pride themselves on what they had already done, we decided to create a rating system from 1 to 10 depending on their footprint. A rating of 1 would represent a footprint of over 80,000 pounds of carbon used annually, with 10 being carbon neutral. This would allow people to start at a level that reflected all of their previous conservation efforts.

Measuring one's carbon footprint also allowed people to set very specific carbon reduction goals. They could easily ascertain, for instance, how many pounds they needed to reduce in order to go, say, from level 4 to level 5. They could also compare themselves against others in a friendly competition. Because everything was measurable it was much more interesting than just doing green actions. How many pounds can you lose in what period of time? Thus came the perfect name, *Low Carbon Diet: A 30 Day Program to Lose 5,000 Pounds*. This was starting to be fun.

I had no idea what to expect, but as always I hoped for the best. People chuckled when they saw the book title. This was a good sign. Within a few months we had started seven neighborhood teams. To my amazement, we increased our neighbor-to-neighbor recruitment rate from 25 to 43 percent. Tackling this issue directly was very appealing for people in this environmentally conscious community. We had tapped into a pent-up desire to be part of the solution rather than the problem.

The program itself also exceeded our expectations. Households from the participating EcoTeams reduced their annual emissions by 6,700 pounds. And they more than doubled the 10 percent reduction goal the city had set, with an average carbon footprint decrease of 22 percent.

People liked the program and found it to be user friendly. They liked the community-building aspect and the way it set up a challenge. John Wadsworth described how the program helped him to get his daughter involved and make changes she would never have otherwise. "It's a pretty cool thing to know your carbon footprint. Bringing my daughter, age nine, to one meeting helped her get on board for a five-minute shower. This inspired me to look into solar hot water, which in the normal course of things I wouldn't have done."

It was very encouraging to see how ready the residents of Portland were at a time when the world felt like a very different place. In an environmentally aware city like Portland, people naturally saw this as the next important issue to take on and so were quite enthusiastic. Susan and I had approached this project with a modest expectation and so we were thrilled with the results. This was proof beyond doubt that a program like this could work.

We approached the city for funding to expand the pilot. While it provided the city bragging rights in the local government climate change community, the initiative was not a budget priority. There was no political will to take it on at a community level at that point in time.

But this social experiment had registered indelibly in my mind. I knew there would be a time when American communities would need to help citizens reduce their carbon footprint. When it came, I would be ready. Fortunately for our planet, that time has now come, and none too soon.

In 2006 I could see the tide was turning on the issue of global warming. It was time to make Low Carbon Diet available to a wider audience. I updated and expanded the book to include new actions on food, and on starting EcoTeams in workplaces, neighborhoods, social networks, faith-based groups, and communities, thus allowing people to run with the outreach aspects of the program on their own. The expanded book made its debut in the fall of 2006. Since then it has been quite a ride. It won the Independent Publishers 2007 "Most Likely to Save the Planet" book award and tapped into the huge groundswell of demand for personal and community action on global warming that was stimulated by Al Gore's documentary.

In December 2006 the *Christian Science Monitor* published a seminal story about this emerging grassroots movement and the role of Low Carbon Diet as a tool supporting it. Written by Moises Velasquez-Manoff, it was widely passed around the Internet because it helped people see and understand the growing momentum behind personal carbon reduction that was taking shape in America. He writes:

> The timing for a book offering day-to-day solutions to an overwhelming global problem couldn't be better. Gore's group, The Climate Project, which recently began training 1,000 volunteers to give his now-famous slide show, is handing out copies of the book at the end of the session. Many environmental and religious groups are also recommending the book to their members such as the Regeneration Project, a San Francisco-based interfaith ministry, which has linked to the book on its main page. Indeed, preceding and perhaps contributing to the demand for Low Carbon Diet is a remarkable prior effort by The Regeneration Project and its Interfaith Power and Light national network. The organizations showed *An Inconvenient Truth* to 4,000 congregations nationwide, reaching an estimated 500,000 people. After seeing the movie, audience members around the country asked what, exactly, they could do about global warming.

Velasquez-Manoff goes on to ask "whether the book is a beneficiary of, or a contributor to, this grassroots movement." What I experienced was one of those moments that come along rarely where the forces perfectly align to support change. This confluence was a result of the U.N. Intergovernmental Panel on Climate Change scientific consensus reports on the peril the planet is facing; Al Gore's highly effective communication of these risks in his movie; grassroots organizations stepping up to the challenge and recognizing that empowering people to take personal action is one of the most important solutions available; and the availability of the Low Carbon Diet and Cool Community-Organizing tools.

The rest of this chapter tells the story of this growing grassroots movement, and of how these transformative tools are helping it change the game around global warming one household and community at a time. We begin by taking a closer look at this diverse movement of environmental organizations, local government agencies, community and faith-based groups, businesses, and activist citizens.

An Inconvenient Truth Finds a Convenient Solution

Along with the immense gratitude so many people felt toward Al Gore for raising our collective consciousness about the threat of global warming came some criticism that he did not spend enough time helping people understand their unique contribution to climate change as individuals and what they could do to mitigate it; the problem came across as out of our control. While this may be fair criticism, it was not his primary aim to tell us precisely how to solve this problem. That is a tall order. His job was to tell us, the blissfully unaware passengers on the Titanic, that we are about to hit an iceberg and sink unless we dramatically change course.

Many have taken heed of his warning and are developing ways to help humanity make the necessary course correction as rapidly as possible. Al Gore is among the most prominent of these, advising the Obama administration on how America can take a leadership role on global warming and advocating for a shift to a 100 percent renewal energy system in ten years. But one of his less visible roles is as a thought leader shaping a strategic way of thinking about the process of change around this issue. It is in this role that he provides an answer to the question posed to him about what we can do as individuals, and as Americans. He offers a strategy that both empowers and holds us accountable as individuals.

"When people take personal action on global warming," Gore explains, "it leads inevitably to their desire to have changes in policies. They begin communicating with their representatives at the local, state, and national level. They say 'Look, I've made these changes in my life and I want you to work for changes in policy.' They are linked together. And when enough American citizens become part of this new critical mass and the U.S. changes policy, then it becomes much more likely that China will make the changes it has to make. We're all in this together." What I like about his thinking from a social change point of view is that it is a whole-system approach and therefore capable of generating the synergy we need to accelerate transformative change within the limited time available to us.

What I find unusual and noteworthy coming from a person who has spent his career as a policymaker is his understanding of personal action as a strategic lever that can work both the demand and the supply side of the equation. Many people who spend their time formulating public policy tend to undervalue the importance of personal action—the demand side of the equation. This is mostly because they are not familiar with how to build demand for change of this nature and scale up personal action; and so, rather than trying to crack that nut, which is a hard nut to crack indeed, they stick with what they know. In this context, that would be passing global warming legislation that provides subsidies and tax incentives to homeowners for taking actions like putting solar panels on their roofs, insulating their homes better, or buying new energy-efficient automobiles. But people need to be motivated to want to make these purchases and to adopt low carbon lifestyle practices. As the old maxim goes, you can lead a horse to water but you can't make him drink. A supply of policy solutions without demand for them will not get us across the finish line.

But Gore goes further than just encouraging personal action; he recognizes that people who are invested in this issue as individuals, when mobilized, can be remarkably effective advocates for supply side solutions. They know exactly what policies will help them lead a low carbon lifestyle. Carbon-literate and committed citizens become a true force for policy change when they can say to a political leader, "I am doing my part, but need your help to go further. These are the specific things that will help me. And by the way, most of the people in my neighborhood have made similar behavior changes and are also very eager to see these policies adopted." What political leader would not be motivated to vote for a more aggressive climate change policy knowing that they will be rewarded by their constituents?

The wider and deeper the constituencies of people who have taken personal action, the stronger the impetus available for policy change. As Gore noted, "They are linked together." This was John Stufflebean's brilliance in Kansas City, Missouri. When EcoTeam members advocated for environmental policy change, after having taken personal action, and made it clear that there were many more people like them, they encouraged conservative city council members to vote for policies they might not have otherwise.

To help further this personal action and policy advocacy strategy Al Gore created The Climate Project and personally trained 1,000 community leaders from all across America to present his slide show. In return for the training, each agreed to make at least ten community presentations. This is where Low Carbon Diet came in. He gave the book to all his trainees so that they would have a resource for the personal action part of his strategy, and invited me to offer a teletraining for those who wished to apply it in their communities.

To take full advantage of this seminar I realized that participants would need more than the book and some tips on how to organize their communities; they would also need the community-organizing tools we had developed over the past two decades. This was clearly a teachable moment in America for these empowerment tools, so we posted them on our web site as an open source social technology and encouraged people to use and modify them as they wished.

The seminar attracted the early-adopter grassroots organizers within his cadre of trainees and they spread the Low Carbon Diet and these community empowerment tools far and wide. When the full story of Al Gore's many contributions to helping get America on a low carbon path is told, one of the important credits he deserves is helping spawn this community empowerment movement committed to furthering personal action. I am very grateful for his leadership and the opportunity he provided me to share our work with his community.

Empowering a Movement

I posted the times I would be leading this seminar on our web site and requested that Al Gore's trainees register so we knew how many to expect and who was on the call. Because we were posting this in a public space, it would be awkward to say this was only for The Climate Project trainees, so we allowed anyone who might come across this posting to attend. Since the only advertising was by The Climate Project to their trainees, we didn't really expect anyone else. That proved to be an erroneous assumption. News of this free training for community organizers and other individuals wishing to address climate change spread rapidly among the many grassroots networks around the country. There was such a paucity of resources other than carbon calculators and checklists on web sites, and such a pent-up demand for taking action stimulated by *An Inconvenient Truth*, that when a proven approach to household behavior change and community organizing became available, we found ourselves inundated with interest.

As of this writing I have given this seminar twenty-one times and trained more than 600 individuals from environmental, faith-based and community groups, local governments, and large and small businesses; university and high school student environmental leaders and unaffiliated citizen activists have participated as well. People have come from thirty-six states and over three hundred cities and towns across America. The largest interest has come from California with forty-eight cities participating, followed by New York with forty-two, Massachusetts with thirty-nine, Washington with thirteen and Oregon with ten. There have also been participants from Canada, Australia, United Kingdom, the Netherlands, Germany, and Japan.

The teletraining format consists of people introducing themselves and their community and briefly describing how they wish to apply the program. Eve Baer, who organizes these seminars for Empowerment Institute, chooses a representative sample of about five people to introduce themselves. This introduction process allows these change agents, who are often working in isolation, to experience the wide diversity of committed people like themselves who are part of this climate change movement. To further enhance this connection, Eve sends everyone a list of all the attendees on the call, their community-organizing background (which they send us when they register) and e-mail addresses. This allows them to get a better sense of one another and follow up to exchange ideas with those applying the program in similar venues.

After this introduction I present what I call the Cool Community slide show. This is posted on our web site and participants view it as I go through each of the slides. It begins by making the case for the need to achieve rapid carbon reduction based on the urgency communicated by climate scientists. I then explain how conservation at the household level is the low hanging fruit, makes up half of America's footprint, and buys us time for the longer-term solutions to kick in. I briefly talk about the five Social Change 2.0 design principles so that they have an understanding of the operating system embedded in the tools and can make future adaptations in their organizing strategy based on them. I then describe our behavior-change and community-organizing research with the sustainable lifestyle campaigns to build their knowledge of and confidence in the model they are about to use. Finally, I explain the design of the Low Carbon Diet, and the tools and strategy for taking it to scale.

I tell participants that this slide presentation is itself one of the community-organizing tools in that it allows them to make the case for an effective residential carbon reduction program to key community stakeholders, and they should feel free to customize it as they see fit for such presentations. I then take questions, which vary from requesting more technical knowledge on how to implement one or more of the tools, to asking for additional strategies for getting started.

I conclude with an exercise, in which I offer consultation on the community-organizing plans of three represented cities based on a template we provide in advance of the call and which they subsequently submit to us. The template asks them to answer seven questions:

1. Who is your target population?

2. How will you engage them in the program?

3. What is your carbon reduction goal through engaging this population?

4. By when do you wish to achieve this carbon reduction goal?

5. What do you see as your greatest challenges in implementing this program and how are you addressing them?

6. What questions would you like to have answered to help you implement your strategy?

7. What is your next step in implementing your strategy?

This is when the seminar comes alive for people because we have real people with real strategies in real communities with real problems to solve. Based on the slide presentation, we also have a community-organizing framework on which to build. These interactions provide me an opportunity to share some of the experience we have acquired over these many years and help both the person I am speaking to and the others on the call to see how all this works on the ground. Based on the feedback we get from people, they leave this training inspired by one another, hopeful that there is a practical and immediate way to begin addressing global warming, and empowered with concrete tools and a strategy for taking action in their communities.

On a personal level it is very gratifying to share the fruits of all these years of trial and error with such receptive people from all over the country and world. What a difference it makes when an idea's time has come.

Although pushing a boulder up a mountain is a good upper-body workout, it certainly is more fun when it is poised to go down the other side on its own momentum. Although we are not at that point yet, it seems to me, based on the large number of competent and committed people attending these seminars, that we are edging ever so close.

Instead of Cursing the Dark Light a Candle: One Person Making a Difference

Wes Sanders was a participant in one of my very first teletrainings and a leader in the national Interfaith Power and Light initiative, which promotes the use of the Low Carbon Diet in the faith community. As of this writing he has personally started fifty-four EcoTeams which have reduced their carbon footprint by an average of 23 percent. Wes is a great inspiration to me and one of the real heroes of this personal action movement. He personifies the spirit, motivation, and no-nonsense approach of this special breed of change agent who has stepped forward to light a candle in the dark. Here is his story in his own words.

I became very concerned about the climate crisis in the 1980s, while still the artistic director of the company I founded in 1978, the Underground Railway Theater. If Jim Hansen and the other IPCC scientists were right, and it is becoming clearer and clearer that they are—all other social and political issues are moot: If we don't deal successfully with this one, there will still be a planet, but we won't be on it. My artistic staff of writers, actors, designers, and directors tried to raise the global warming alarm through our plays, developing an art form called the "eco-cabaret," but art turned out to be too indirect for the urgency of this issue. I felt strongly the need for direct action, and had become impatient with symbolic gestures that produced no tangible effects.

So I retired early and moved to Vermont and became a volunteer-activist on climate change. Once here I spent five to six years trying to get my fellow citizens to cut their carbon emissions through a nonprofit loosely connected with city government, which used a web site calculator with suggestions for changes in energy behavior. But, like every other strategy for behavior change I had encountered, it was something one did alone, and it was a one-shot deal; there was no means for following up on the changes people pledged to make.

Finally, in frustration, I decided to spend the summer of 2006 finding, or creating, if necessary, an approach that would get people engaged in real change. I stumbled on a faded photocopy of a climate change program that had been piloted in Portland, Oregon, based on the EcoTeam concept. As it happened, I had gone through the predecessor of this program with the co-op where I lived with seven other families in Cambridge, Massachusetts. I knew this approach had worked in getting my community to change their behavior: We set up compost bins and made soil in them, which we used in a garden; we replaced all our toilets with a low-flow model, etc. What had worked in the EcoTeam approach was the peer accountability, sense of solidarity, and group creativity of the other members of the community, combined with the generous amount of time allotted in the program for entrenched behaviors to get changed.

When I found a contact number for the Empowerment Institute on the photocopy, I inquired; this was August of 2006. It turned out that an updated version of the Low Carbon Diet was just getting ready to be printed. I ordered the first copies, scheduled two showings of Al Gore's *An Inconvenient Truth* at my church in Burlington, and followed up immediately, while the audience was in full awareness of the urgency about the climate crisis, and formed two EcoTeams at each showing.

This is essentially the scenario I have followed since: a film or talk to get everyone on the same page emotionally and conceptually, followed by a nuts-and-bolts workshop on how the Low Carbon Diet program works, with Q and A interspersed and lots of anecdotes from EcoTeam experiences, and then "closing the deal" on the spot; that is forming the EcoTeams with those present, and asking (politely) why those who don't raise their hands to join haven't done so. Usually other members of the group come up with answers that convince these people to join after all. A Methodist came up to me after one of these sessions and, with a knowing smile, said, "You're an evangelist!" So be it. My Southern Baptist grandmother always hoped I would end up a preacher.

The format I prefer and generally am allowed to use now in churches is giving the Sunday sermon from the "bully pulpit," then following up immediately after the service with the workshop. When I am organizing in town energy or sustainability committees, the sermon is a talk, with a little less emphasis on the stewardship of the earth and more talk about our grandchildren's futures. I always find out as much as I can about the audience beforehand, and frame the talk accordingly.

If the EcoTeam is going to complete the Low Carbon Diet program successfully (at least 5,000 pounds reduced per household), all the members of the team need to be in the room when I give the talk and workshop. When I have used the "train the trainer" approach, I find there is generally too much dissipation of the message, in addition to the fact that the initiator/facilitator is a friend or colleague of the other participants (rather than an outsider like myself) and therefore is diffident about insisting on the discipline that is required if the process is to get results. Calculating and recording the numbers, for example, often gets slighted in this situation, because the facilitator does not want to appear to be a martinet. This is not always true: When the facilitator is a highly effective individual, they can manage very well.

Vermont Interfaith Power and Light offers a pro bono energy audit to communities of faith, done by a former professional on our board who submits a report of recommendations to the church about energy conservation in its buildings. I often use these contacts, following up with an EcoTeam presentation, to get the congregation on board as well, in their own use of energy at home and on the road. I am sometimes invited to regional conferences of some denominations, Congregational/United Church of Christ and Episcopalian are two examples, as well as statewide environmental organizations such as the Sustainable Energy Resource Group. These are networking opportunities: Following my presentation to interested church leaders or activists at these conferences, I get called in to do my dog-and-pony show.

I don't have any goals that are expressible in numbers. I just form as many EcoTeams as I have the opportunity to, mostly in Vermont. Occasionally I am able to identify high achievers in EcoTeams I am facilitating whom I can convince to begin and run

EcoTeams of their own. I helped to initiate a citywide Low Carbon Diet initiative launched by the mayor of a Vermont town on Earth Day 2008, with less than impressive results so far: This has been approached to date as a "train the trainer" exercise, with all of the weaknesses outlined above in such an approach. The challenge is to scale up this program.

Wes is an exemplar of what can be done by a single dedicated individual. Importantly, he also describes the challenge and dilemma of a solo citizen activist in attempting to take this program to scale in a community. To get to this next level requires an approach that is very different from getting more dedicated and effective people like Wes willing to start EcoTeams on an ad hoc basis.

What is needed is a whole-system solution that includes the participation by all of a given community's institutions, including local government, faith-based and civic groups, neighborhood and block associations, businesses and schools, and having them reach out to their constituencies and members to start EcoTeams. This shifts the community-organizing strategy from ad hoc and retail to systematic and wholesale, providing a plausible path forward for achieving an ambitious carbon reduction goal. It provides the labor pool needed to reach out to people and the synergy to grow the community's intellectual capital around community organizing for household carbon reduction. Based on my experience with the teletrainings, this broad swath of organizations are primed to participate.

Approaching household carbon reduction (which represents between 50 and 90 percent of a community's carbon footprint, with the high end in most communities) in this manner provides the possibility for creating a game changer for those cities where the community is aware and there is political skin in the game. Given that 935 cities representing eighty-five million citizens (28% of Americans), as of this writing, have signed the U.S. Conference of Mayor's pledge to "strive to meet or beat the Kyoto Protocol targets in their communities of 7 percent reduction from 1990 levels by 2012," and only a few have achieved this modest goal, there are many potential candidates looking for a cost-effective solution that can achieve substantial carbon reductions in a short period of time. And if enough of these cities choose to play, it will be a game changer for this issue both in America and around the world.

I call this whole-system solution a Cool Community campaign. This next section describes the tools and strategy involved in such a campaign, and an early-adopter city, region, and state who have thrown their hat in the ring to prove it is possible to scale up household carbon reduction and bring Americans onto the field of play.

A COOL COMMUNITY CAMPAIGN: TAKING THE LOW CARBON DIET TO SCALE

The purpose of a Cool Community campaign is to empower residents through local organizations across all sectors to reduce their carbon footprint by 25 percent through participation in the Low Carbon Diet. The goal is to engage between 25 and 85 percent of the citizenry over a three-year period. This time frame is short enough to keep the pressure on and people's attention and long enough to allow for an effective diffusion strategy. This allows the early-adopter communities, which signed the U.S. Conference of Mayors agreement on a wing and a prayer, to substantially exceed their current carbon reduction goal while building the demand for local green economies and a constituency for the bold climate change policies needed. We start by looking at a tool to engage members of the community in this undertaking.

Global Warming Café: Creating Emotional Engagement and Translating it Into Action

The first step of a Cool Community campaign is to enroll as many community organizations as possible as partners and diffusion points. Once partner organizations are enrolled, the challenge in getting a wholesale approach to work is designing a recruitment tool for them that is easy to use, does not demand great expertise on the topic of global warming, and has the potential to start multiple teams at one time. We had solved a similar problem on a smaller scale in our sustainable lifestyle program through our block-based, peer-to-peer recruitment process for forming and replicating EcoTeams. This overcame the need for a charismatic enroller, thus enabling the process to be scalable. The design challenge here would be to apply a peer-to-peer approach with much larger numbers of people.

As a matter of course I am always looking for social innovations that I might be able to repurpose for the various issues I am addressing. I experienced one such social innovation I liked very much and tucked it away in the back of my mind for future use. Called "The World Café," its purpose is to accelerate the formation of intellectual capital by tapping into the collective intelligence of a group of people through a series of guided small-group conversations. It can work with groups as small as twenty people and as large as several hundred. It was created by two dear friends, management consultants Juanita Brown and David Issacs. Their critically acclaimed book describing this tool, *The World Café: Shaping Our Future Through Conversations That Matter*, has made a major contribution to the field of large-group processes.

The guidelines for a successful World Café process, as described by Juanita and David, are as follows:

1. Groups of four to six people sit together. The café is most interesting and effective when people sit with those they do not know.

2. Once the World Café begins the facilitator presents the questions to be explored.

3. For centuries indigenous peoples have used a talking stick to encourage mutual support and deep listening. Use a pen from the table or a symbolic object to pass around the table to each person. When you hold this object, it's your turn to speak and answer the question. No one should interrupt the person. Those listening are encouraged to write, draw, or doodle on the paper tablecloths as others talk. Once everyone has spoken then general discussion is encouraged.

4. You move in rounds of conversation to different tables to cross-pollinate ideas—carrying key insights, themes, and questions to each new conversation. Patterns emerge, additional perspectives surface, and surprising combinations of insight and creativity reveal themselves. The café facilitator lets people know when to move to the next table.

5. Each table chooses one person to act as host and agree to stay at the same table to welcome each round of guests. When the new guests are seated, the host briefly shares the high points of the last

conversation and then encourages the guests, using the talking object, to link and connect ideas coming from their own table. As each person shares, the others continue to record and or draw key ideas and new connections on paper tablecloths.

6. As part of the final round the host asks, "What's at the center of our conversation?" and invites people to "listen into the middle" for the deeper themes and larger patterns so they can access the collective wisdom.

7. These insights are shared in the larger group, and if possible, visually recorded for the larger community to observe.

Juanita, along with another friend involved in the World Café work, Tom Hurley, and I would periodically talk to support one another in our various endeavors. In one of our conversations I told them I was interested in developing a large-group enrollment process for the Low Carbon Diet. I was keen to see if we might be able to combine the World Café tool with our EcoTeam recruitment event. I told them our challenge was not making the case that we had a problem; Al Gore had already done that with his movie. In fact he had done this so well that people left feeling a sense of foreboding doom. This is part of the nature of accepting reality. To empower people to take effective action, which was our goal, we would need to help them first address and transform the fears they were feeling, and then help them gain a measure of control by becoming part of the global warming solution.

What I knew from our large-group empowerment processes is that much of the healing and transformation occurs as a result of people's interaction with one another in the group. I also knew from our information events that enrolling people on EcoTeams is most effectively done by their peers. If the new social norm is to reduce our carbon footprint to minimize our impact on global warming, the people most able to influence the take-up of this new set of behaviors are our peers. What I appreciated about the World Café process was how it enabled highly engaging peer-to-peer conversations. We would need to use these conversations in such a way that people could both process their feelings and move to concrete action to reduce their carbon footprint. This would require people to shift from intellectual knowledge, detachment, or avoidance of the issue, to emotional engagement. If we got this right, we would have a transformative tool that could create real lift to this emerging movement.

Collaborating with Juanita and Tom was as good as it gets for me. They each combine strategic thinking and heart, informed by a unitive way of addressing change. This would also be a good modeling of the synergy that can and needs to be created by blending complementary social innovations—in this case, the World Café large-group engagement process, EcoTeam information and recruitment event, and Low Carbon Diet behavior-change program. We called this hybrid social innovation a "Global Warming Café" and defined its purpose this way: "To help people bear witness to the fact that life as we have known it on this planet is imperiled with global warming and based on that to provide them an opportunity to process their fears and hopes for the future. And then become part of the global warming solution through taking personal action in their household and larger community."

We designed the process in both a two- and four-hour format and recommended the latter to get the full benefit. It would begin as soon as people entered the room through the projection of slides that connected people with the diversity of our planet's people, cultures, and natural beauty, interspersed with images of Earth from space. These images served to remind everyone of the common ground of our shared humanity, now at risk. The images would continue to be projected during the World Café process, subliminally building a unitive field experience to inform and inspire people as they engaged in conversation with one another.

The World Café guidelines would be explained and people would then be immersed for the next two hours in answering two questions.

"What are my fears for myself, my family, my community, and my planet's future inhabitants around global warming?"

"What provides me hope that we can successfully address global warming?"

People would move from table to table four times, first doing two rounds on fears and then two on hopes. Depending on the number of individuals participating, they would interact with as many as twenty different people. Each table would have a host who at the end of the process would synthesize and report on the fears and hopes of the people who were at that table. A graphic facilitator would record the group's fears and hopes on large butcher block paper displayed on one of the walls in the room.

This would be followed by a presentation of the slide show I described earlier in this chapter, to inform people that there was a proven community-based behavior-change strategy for taking effective personal action with the potential to be brought to scale community by community across the nation. The goal of this part of the Global Warming Café was to help people move from feeling like victims of forces outside their control to feeling hopeful that there is a way of concretely addressing this issue.

To avail ourselves of the power of peer-to-peer diffusion, after the slide show, we would, if available, have several people who had participated on Low Carbon Diet EcoTeams describe the concrete carbon reduction results they achieved and their experience of social connectivity from participating on a team with neighbors, friends, co-workers, or members of a faith community. This would be followed by a question-and-answer period. Questions could be directed to any of the EcoTeam members or to the Global Warming Café facilitator.

We would then have people participate in a final World Café process around making a personal commitment to action. We would encourage participants at a minimum to consider participating on an EcoTeam; and then consider volunteering for the Cool Community campaign or championing ideas to help their organization, workplace, child's school, local government, or businesses, lower its carbon footprint. The latter commitment provided an opportunity to spawn social innovations to address carbon reduction and create openings for synergy.

We would "close the deal," to use Wes's term, by asking people to raise their hands if they planned to participate on an EcoTeam. From our past experience we expected that most people would make this commitment, and having one's personal commitment witnessed by peers created the motivation for them to follow through. We would then invite people to share the ideas they were willing to champion and record them next to the hopes and fears, all the while encouraging cross-pollination where possible. We would conclude by getting interested people organized into EcoTeams and collecting names of volunteers wishing to participate in the Cool Community campaign.

An opportunity soon came along for testing out the Global Warming Café in my own backyard. Gail, being the enthusiastic and environmentally conscious person that she is, had organized an EcoTeam of our friends as soon as the new version of the *Low Carbon Diet* was published. Our EcoTeam was completing the program just as I was putting the finishing touches on the Global Warming Café. I asked the team if they would be interested in being guinea pigs and helping me prototype this new tool. They were enthusiastic and we set a date two months out to give it a try in our very own community of Woodstock, New York.

This would be an interesting experiment on several counts. A lot of progressive former New Yorkers make their homes in Woodstock and the surrounding area, but I would not characterize the town as an early adopter for environmental issues. Testing it here would provide a good gauge for the level of demand for taking action on this issue that existed beyond the bright green communities. I was also intrigued to see how it would work to have an EcoTeam serve as the organizers for a Global Warming Café. This would be taking the process of EcoTeams replicating themselves quantum and was a model that could easily be scaled.

Before I proceed further I have a true confession to tell about my personal experience of doing the Low Carbon Diet. Gail and I assumed we would ace this program, given that we were leading a very green lifestyle. After all, we'd done so many of the actions in the sustainable lifestyle program, and thoroughly integrated them as a way of life. However, because I am always flying all over the planet telling people to lower their carbon footprint or promoting some other save-the-world idea, our household carbon footprint was not a pretty sight. When Gail and I calculated it on a scale of one to ten with ten being the best, carbon neutral, and one being the worst, 80,000 pounds or more, we scored a one—the worst!

Fortunately, there is a happy ending to this story. After accepting our fate as high carbon emitters we got down to business and got to level five by losing what we called the "hard pounds," or those lost through behavior and system changes. We insulated our roof, installed triple-pane windows, switched to renewable energy from our electric utility, and installed a solar hot water system, among other things. We then got to level ten by losing "soft pounds" through purchasing carbon offsets. Most of my team was also in need of a similar low carbon lifestyle makeover. My take-away from this experience: *A green lifestyle is not the same as a low carbon lifestyle.* And if my EcoTeam was the early-adopter crowd, what a vast opportunity we had to impact the American carbon footprint.

Anyway, our EcoTeam stepped up to the challenge. We got a local faith community, the Woodstock Jewish Congregation, to donate a room for seventy-five people. We persuaded our town board, a wonderful regional environmental organization called Sustainable Hudson Valley, and our state environmental agency to co-sponsor the event. We got food donated from local businesses. A member of our team created a flier that we distributed to various community groups. We got our local media to do stories encouraging people to come. Because we wished to make sure we had the food and space size right we requested that people RSVP.

To our delight and surprise, within about a week of our advertising, over a hundred people had signed up. We called the Woodstock Jewish Congregation and asked if we could get a larger room. They obliged and provided us a room for 150 people. Three weeks later we called back again for their next room upgrade to 200 plus people, which was their congregation room.

When the dust had settled, 225 people attended from throughout the mid-Hudson Valley region of New York. All attending committed to lowering their carbon footprint by least 5,000 pounds for a total commitment of over 1,000,000 pounds. We formed twelve EcoTeams on the spot with a commitment from people to form another eight teams when they went home. This comes to about a 70 percent recruitment rate. The New York State Department of Environmental Conservation sent a representative from the region who liked the format so much that she decided to organize Global Warming Cafés throughout the Hudson Valley region. The Woodstock Town Board was so motivated by this outpouring of citizen interest that they agreed to make the town carbon neutral and were featured in the *New York Times*.

To provide a little of the local color and a sense of how the event motivated our government officials—the personal action to policy change equation—I have excerpted comments by several of the government officials attending from an article written February 15, 2007 by Andrea Barrist Stern for our local newspaper, *The Woodstock Times*.

"I was impressed by the turnout and the format that had people speaking to strangers about their hopes and fears," said Kristin Marcell from the New York State Department of Environmental Conservation. "It created a sense of bonding . . . and had everyone on the same page in a way I hadn't seen before. We usually see the scientific side and this presented the emotional side, which is something we need to do."

Woodstock Environmental Commission chairwoman Mary Burke said her "general feeling" at Sunday's program was "Wow." She added, "It wasn't that I didn't think people were concerned, I just didn't think you'd reach them that easily."

Woodstock Town Board members Liz Simonson and Bill McKenna and Ulster County legislator Don Gregorius were among those present on Sunday.

Gregorius said he exchanged cards with a Putnam County legislator at Sunday's event because both are interested in seeing how the program might be useful at the county level.

Simonson related she was at one table with two young boys who found the prospect of reducing their carbon footprint "exciting" even as several middle aged participants were dejected about the possibilities. She said the boys' enthusiasm made her feel, "that I have to pick myself up, dust myself off and get moving."

The Global Warming Café activated the civic and political will to be part of the global warming solution. It also met the need people have to talk deeply and personally on this issue. Because the tool is easy to use and the procedure for using it is described in detail on our web site, many hundreds of Global Warming Cafés have now taken place throughout the United States and around the world involving all the sectors needed to scale up a Cool Community campaign.

I'll share one particularly promising application for the Global Warming Café from the corporate sector. The director of Corporate Social Responsibility for Nike, Sarah Severn, an early adopter within an early-adopter company on issues of environmental sustainability, asked me to lead a Global Warming Café for employees in their Beaverton, Oregon, headquarters. Within one hour of advertising the opportunity to attend the café, the event was filled at 100 people. Sarah's team found a larger room and opened it up to 150 people, which was also quickly filled.

They did it up right, turning the largest room in their Tiger Woods Conference Center into an Italian Café with ices, espresso coffee, and red and white checkered table clothes on each table along with a vase of freshly cut flowers. In addition to the employees from every part of the company who attended, there were interested community leaders and visitors from other companies who were attending a national sustainability conference Nike was hosting. Sarah had thought to include them so that the event could disseminate the program more widely. The slide show building the planetary unitive field used sports, of course, as the metaphor for our shared common humanity.

She got the president of the company, Charlie Denson, to kick off the café. He talked in a very heartfelt manner about how his children had motivated him to get involved in environmental issues and how excited he was to see so much interest among employees in taking personal action. We went through the café process, slide show, and then the action commitment. Four hours later all of the Nike employees attending committed themselves to participating on an EcoTeam; making changes to help the company lower its carbon footprint; and taking this program into their communities as part of their corporate volunteer program. And three of the companies represented—Hewlett-Packard, Harley-Davidson, and Schlumberger—agreed to put on Global Warming Cafés for their employees.

Within a short period of time, Nike had sixteen EcoTeams working on reducing their personal carbon footprint and helping the corporation do the same. Some of the teams even developed "biggest loser" contests among themselves. And with the active support and encouragement of the company, many employees have now taken the Low Carbon Diet into their communities and shared it widely throughout the company.

With the Global Warming Café tool we had cracked the code on how to engage larger numbers of people in participating on EcoTeams. We saw that it could be effectively used by any group from an EcoTeam to a large corporation, and everything in between. We also saw that it was capable of bringing the civic, public, and private sectors of a community together. We were on our way.

Carbon Reduction and EcoTeam Participation Tracker: Helping a Community Keep Score and Manage Results

One more tool was required to take this program to scale at a community level. We would need a web-based means to measure results so people could see that a Cool Community campaign was achieving its goals. It would also need to be self-organizing so partner organizations did not have to keep track manually of EcoTeams formed and their carbon reductions. This was essential to building momentum for people's ongoing involvement and making the participation of organizations more manageable. I spoke in chapter nine of the use for such a tool, and it is one I had wanted to build forever. But to do this right would be beyond the means of many communities.

I had the good fortune of finding a strategic partner with a compatible mission and the resources to build this tool to these specifications. Joe Laur, a friend and colleague, had just left his private practice as a sustainability consultant to become the director of content for a new startup, Greenopolis, a green living portal. He reached out to me and asked if I would be interested in having my various environmental behavior-change programs as part of this web site. It was a natural fit and we decided to work together. The sustainable lifestyle program content would be sprinkled throughout the site, providing users information on green living. We would also put our carbon calculator and Low Carbon Diet action plan on the site, with the encouragement for people to form EcoTeams.

But my real interest was developing a carbon and participation tacking tool to support the grassroots climate change movement that was building around Low Carbon Diet and the Cool Community campaign. I asked Joe if he was interested. He was, and six months later we had built it. Over time the focus of Greenopolis shifted so we made the tool available directly to Cool Community campaigns who have continued to refine it.

With the Low Carbon Diet behavior-change program, the Global Warming Café community engagement tool, and now the Carbon and Participation Tracking tool, the "hardware" of this movement was in place. The final element was to flesh out the "software," or the detailed strategic implementation plan, for bringing this program to scale communitywide.

The Cool Community Strategy: Bringing It All Together

I had created multiple versions of these types of strategies over the past couple of decades and got a little wiser each time about the conditions that needed to be in place for this to occur. This issue was primed and the tools were tested and ready to go. Given early-adopter communities with political will there was as good a chance as I had ever seen for scaling up a communitywide behavior-change initiative. But no matter how ready the tools were, and how primed communities and the timing in the world were, a venture of this sort was not for the faint of heart. Success would be hard won, so my job was to do my best to make sure those who wished to go on this journey knew what they were getting in to and had the staying power.

I would tell communities that embarking on this adventure brought to mind Winston Churchill's definition of democracy. He was fond of saying that "democracy was the worst form of government except for everything else." In a similar vein I would tell these communities that trying to bring a Cool Community campaign to scale was the hardest thing they could do to reduce their carbon footprint except for everything else. If they were still interested I would share the following strategy and help them in any way I could. The strategy employs eight key steps.

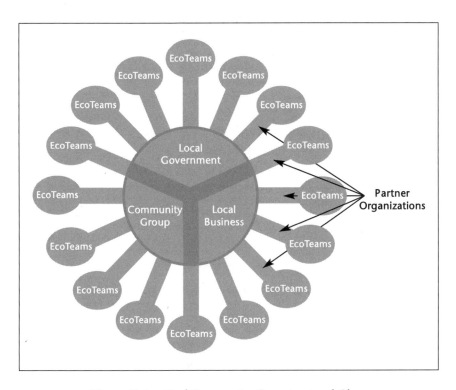

Figure 11.1—Cool Community Organizational Chart

1. **Form a core organizing team.** A Cool Community campaign can be initiated by a community group, business, or local government. (See Figure 11.1 for the Cool Community organizational chart.) All three sectors should be represented on the organizing committee to network within their peer groups and help model this initiative as a whole-system solution. Given that the heavy lifting for the campaign is delegated to partner organizations forming EcoTeams, the bulk of the responsibilities for the organizing team are around recruiting and supporting partners and overall coordination. Consequently, a campaign can be managed initially by one full-time equivalent staff position. As the campaign grows more help might be needed. Because the campaign is a set of discreet tasks, this coordination function can be split up among different members of the core

team so that no one individual or organization is overloaded. With many hands making light work, this initiative can be implemented in a cost-effective manner.

2. **Identify the carbon footprint of the residential sector and set a carbon reduction goal.** As the management mantra goes: You can't change what you can't measure. While communities are now starting to measure their carbon footprints, very few organize their data from a household point of view. As a result, residents of the community do not understand their collective carbon contribution. When communities crunch these numbers they discover that if they do not have any major business or industry, the household carbon footprint is around 90 percent of the overall community footprint. For communities with a lot of industry, the household carbon footprint it is at least 50 percent.

   I recommend using 25 percent as the average carbon reduction goal for participating households. Based on our initial results this is quite achievable, and, with good participation, will allow the community to make a substantial dent in their footprint.

3. **Create a three-year plan with quarterly benchmarks.** Here is an example of how the organizing would work in a city of 100,000 people. With 2.5 people per household on average, this equates to 40,000 households. The campaign's maximum participation target is 85 percent, or 34,000 households. With an average of eight households per EcoTeam, 85 percent of the households represent 4,250 EcoTeams. To achieve this number requires the participation of approximately eighty-five local campaign partners, each forming fifty EcoTeams over a three-year period of time.

   For a Cool Community campaign to achieve this ambitious goal they will need clearly articulated benchmarks. I recommend that this plan consist of twelve waves rolled out every three months over a three-year period of time. Year one the goal is to get the early adopters on board, representing 15 percent of the community. The goal for year two is the participation of the early majority, representing the next 35 percent of the community. The year three goal is to engage the late majority, or the last 35 percent of the community. The laggard population of 15 percent will never participate and are not worth investing the time to recruit. They will eventually be brought along through renewable energy sources and new technologies being brought to scale. While a Cool Community campaign may plateau well before the late majority, unless it sets its sights high it will have no chance to get there.

Given how few feasible opportunities exist in the short term for substantive carbon reduction in a community and the magnitude of this crisis, my view is that if we can we must.

4. **Identify partner organizations.** The community-organizing strategy is based on leveraging existing networks. Campaign organizers need to identify potential partners capable of forming fifty EcoTeams over a three-year period—or between fifteen and twenty EcoTeams a year. Depending on the turnout this could be accomplished by one to three Global Warming Cafés a year. Partner organizations without the ability to form fifty teams can collaborate in co-hosting Global Warming Cafés. Local elected officials will already have connections with most of the organizations in a community.

5. **Host a recruitment event to enroll partner organizations.** Because local government has the authority—and in some states will soon have the statutory obligation—to help a community reduce its carbon footprint, it is a key player in implementing a campaign. The mayor or the equivalent top elected official, as the spokesperson for the municipality, invites partner organizations to a special invitation-only event. With the organizing team, the mayor shares the vision and strategy for implementing the campaign. Partner organizations are invited to participate and commit to forming fifty EcoTeams over three years or smaller number based on their size. The municipality also participates as a partner organization and forms a high-profile Turbo Team of local elected officials to serve as a role model.

6. **Build capacity of partner organizations.** A big learning from my work with communities is how important it is that the organizers know what they are doing. Otherwise they go down unnecessary dead ends that undermine the goodwill of volunteers, and the campaign eventually flounders. People's discretionary volunteer time is limited. To attract and retain the most talented people in partner organizations, the campaign needs to be well conceived and effectively executed. This is all the more essential given its ambitious carbon reduction and participation goals.

To accomplish this level of effectiveness requires a capacity building training for participating partner organizations. The training should include teaching partner organizations the campaign's social change framework; how to publicize and host Global Warming Cafés; how to keep track of results online; and basic transformative leadership skills so they can address the inevitable resistances to change in their organizations. At its conclusion a peer support system should be established consisting of buddies, master classes, and coaching. I have described this support system framework in some detail in previous chapters.

7. *Mobilize students and businesses to strengthen outreach.* The bigger the labor pool the easier it is to mount a Cool Community campaign as this allows for more people to help in forming EcoTeams. Two excellent and often underused community resources for this are students and corporate volunteers.

For high school and college students global warming is their issue and no one has more moral authority than they do, because it is their future at risk. The perfect role for students is starting neighborhood-based EcoTeams among the people not reached through partner organizations. Students can do this as volunteers or, if their school wishes to play an active role in the campaign, it can organize this as a service-learning program and provide students credit for their participation. An added value to the Cool Community campaign is it is building the capacity of the next generation of environmental and community leaders in a sophisticated community-organizing and behavior-change skill set. We call this program the Cool Community Corps.

As Nike demonstrated, the Low Carbon Diet is attractive to companies because it helps employees reduce their carbon footprint and take that knowledge back to the company and out into the community. The company increases employee loyalty through doing the right thing for the planet, has carbon-literate and emotionally engaged employees to help in their internal carbon reduction activities, and generates goodwill and an enhanced image locally. Corporate volunteers can play many roles in the campaign, from participating in neighborhood organizing, to taking on various campaign leadership roles, to enrolling other companies as partners.

We call this program Cool Corporate Citizen and it is representative of an emerging and very positive new trend in business: the evolution from corporate social responsibility—"I minimize the harm that I do"—

to corporate social engagement—"I maximize the good that I do." Along with Nike, two other pioneering Cool Corporate Citizens are Seventh Generation and Green Mountain Coffee Roasters—two of Vermont's finest.

8. *Engage media and partner organizations to promote campaign successes.* To keep people motivated and bring the campaign to life, it needs to be kept in front of people regularly. Local newspapers, TV, and radio stations should be encouraged to do regular feature stories about EcoTeam and partner organization successes. Given the huge number of community members and organizations involved, this will be a major media attraction.

A less sophisticated but highly effective way to tell the ongoing story of the campaign and showcase its successes is to have someone on the organizing team with media and video skills interviewing various participants. These down-home interviews could include EcoTeam members, partner organization volunteers, the mayor, and city council members talking about the things they did, large and small, that week to make a difference in furthering the campaign. These two-minute interviews would then get posted on YouTube and sent to partner organizations to disseminate.

A number of communities have signed on to take this journey. Their first task was to prototype the program with at least a hundred households so they knew what it was all about and would be credible taking it to this next stage. Going from a hundred households to many thousands is a large chasm to cross, for sure, but with eyes open and proof of concept these communities are well positioned to enroll the partner organizations they need. I have chosen three stories to represent those communities embarked on this journey. I honor them for having gotten this far, and am hopeful that they will succeed and serve as role models for the many communities who will need to follow in their footsteps.

Davis, California:
A Local Government Steps Up to the Plate

Mitch Sears, the sustainability director and person responsible for addressing climate change for the city of Davis, California, attended our Cool

Community teletraining to learn how to set up a pilot program and, if successful, develop a full-scale Cool Community campaign. The City had set an aggressive goal of reducing the community's carbon footprint 80 percent by 2050 with equally impressive interim targets to get there. After much research they determined that a Cool Community campaign offered them one of the best possibilities to achieve these goals.

Davis is a city of 65,000 people and describes itself as "a progressive, vigorous community noted for its small-town style, energy conservation, environmental programs, parks, preservation of trees, red double-decker London buses, bicycles, and the quality of its educational institutions." It is also internationally renowned for its sustainability and energy conservation practices.

From October 12, 2008, through November 10, 2008, the city organized 100 households to participate in Low Carbon Diet EcoTeams. Participation included the city council and staff; University of California, Davis, administrators, faculty, staff, and students; local businesses; and community members at large. Results were received from 65 percent of the households who reported reducing their carbon footprint an average of 5,516 pounds.

They are now gearing up to take this program to scale over a three-year period with the participation of 75 percent of the community's households. They will be working in close collaboration with a consortium of partner organizations, including the University of California, Davis, faith-based groups, community organizations, and the local schools. Davis has once again stepped up to the plate to demonstrate what is possible. The world will be watching with great anticipation.

Rochester, New York: Who Says One Person Can't Make a Difference?

Another community mounting a Cool Community campaign is Rochester, New York. Their aspiration is to be the "best midsized city in America." And their motto is, "Oh yes, we can!" Their can-do attitude has allowed them to receive many awards, including one from the U.S. Department of Housing and Urban Development for their "creative tools and processes which bridge the gap between residents and government." They got onto my radar screen a number of years ago for their pioneering citizen engagement program, "Neighbors Building Neighborhoods."

Bob Siegel, a Rochester resident, learned about the Low Carbon Diet at a Global Warming Café I led for a group of sustainability-oriented businesses and nonprofits. Bob approached me after the cafe and said that he would like to launch a Cool Community campaign in Rochester. I wished him well, as I always did, but did not expect much given the number of hurdles he would need to surmount to organize a campaign. Not an endeavor for the faint-hearted, this was all the more challenging as he did not have any backing or an organization to help him do this.

Six months later Bob had formed an organizing team and convinced the mayors of Rochester and surrounding communities to launch the "Low Carbon Diet Challenge." They organized 120 households into neighborhood, workplace, and faith-based EcoTeams, which achieved an average carbon footprint reduction of 10,828 pounds. Just as important was the enthusiastic and tangible support his organizing team garnered from local businesses, and university, civic, and government leaders who served as community role models by actively participating in EcoTeams.

Rochester's Low Carbon Diet Challenge culminated in a major celebration at City Hall in which Mayor Robert Duffy handed out awards to the program participants, saying, "I look forward to a future award ceremony honoring citizens who have participated in this program taking place at the Riverside Convention Center" (which can accommodate 20,000 people). At that same event, Bob Siegel offered up the next stage of his vision. "Our goal is to launch Cool Community campaigns throughout our region that reach at least 100,000 people and put Greater Rochester at the forefront of low carbon communities across the nation."

Given the drive and enthusiasm of Rochester's citizens and mayor, and the organizing skills of Bob Siegel and his team, this community is another serious contender. And a demonstration of what committed citizens can do if they take to heart Rochester's mantra, "Oh yes, we can!"

Cool Mass: Taking Cool Communities to Scale Statewide

By far the most ambitious Cool Community campaign effort is taking place in Massachusetts under the auspices of the state's largest climate change organization, Massachusetts Climate Action Network (MCAN). This is a coalition of locally organized groups promoting carbon reduction in homes and communities and leveraging their collective clout to encourage bold climate change policy at the state level. They have built a climate change movement second to none, which represents more than fifty cities and towns encompassing most of the state's population. And they are not only a potent force in Massachusetts, but their Climate Action Network (CAN) model has diffused nationally.

Susan Altman, the outreach manager responsible for supporting these local chapters, had attended our teletraining and said that she wished to scale up Cool Communities across the state when the time was right, but her goal for now was introducing the Low Carbon Diet to all of their chapters. Eighteen months later she and her Executive Director, Rob Garrity, contacted me. They said that thirty-two of their community chapters had collectively taken more than 1,000 households through the Low Carbon Diet program and achieved an average carbon reduction of 25 percent. Given this success and platform, they felt it was time to take the next step.

The state of Massachusetts has set the country's most ambitious carbon reduction goal of 10 to 25 percent below 1990 levels by 2020. Since 47 percent of the state's footprint comes from the residential sector, they must engage citizens to have any hope of achieving this ambitious target. To help the state achieve this goal, MCAN wished to scale up Cool Community campaigns and they invited me to join with them to build the capacity of the participating communities—an offer I relished. We created what we called Cool Mass—the first goal of which was 25-25-2012: Twenty-five percent of the households in the state (approximately 700,000) reducing their carbon footprint 25 percent by 2012. We would then move to 50 percent of the households by 2015 and 75 percent by 2020.

Rob and I launched Cool Mass at MCAN's annual conference at MIT in November 2008 in front of 350 climate change movers and shakers from across the state. There were representatives from citizen groups, local MCAN chapters, municipal and state government, and business. We announced our audacious goals for the campaign and stated that our intention for Cool Mass was to serve as a prototype for bold and timely carbon reduction action for states across America. We invoked the Massachusetts brand and invited those gathered to start the second American Revolution. Their response to this salvo was a loud and prolonged standing ovation.

After my talk, I led a workshop for communities interested in being selected as the first ten in Massachusetts to start the three-year adventure to get up to 85 percent of their residents through the Low Carbon Diet.

I invoked my usual Winston Churchill caveat about this being really hard to do. In spite of this injunction, fifty-nine people representing forty-five communities signed up to be considered for this adventure. Through a rigorous application process we selected our first wave of ten communities: Boston, Braintree, Brookline, Cohasset, Dedham, Hingham, Hull, Milton, Newton, and Winchester.

They ranged in size from 7,200 in Cohasset to 590,000 in Boston, for a total population of 955,000. One of the questions we asked them in the application was for their vision of Cool Mass. One of the participating communities, Hull, represented by the group Sustainable South Shore, captured its essence.

> While the goal of Cool Mass is ambitious, it is at the scale that stabilizing climate requires. If we are successful, the culture of our communities will be transformed. Beyond our town, however, Cool Mass creates a learning network among communities and ultimately a movement through which to set an example for the rest of our Commonwealth and our nation. In so doing, it shows the world that the American people are willing to provide positive leadership in reversing our past unsustainable resource use.

The citizens of Massachusetts, with their huge can-do attitude, spirit, and passion, have fired the first shot and are once again ready to lead an American Revolution—in this case by helping America become a model of citizen accountability for the creation of a livable planet.

THE COOL COMMUNITY DIVIDEND

The word "crisis" in Chinese is signified by two symbols, one for danger and one for opportunity. The danger for a city or town in attempting to scale up a Cool Community campaign is that it doesn't succeed. The opportunity provided by a Cool Community campaign is in a word—sustainability. This sustainability plays out in three very powerful ways. Environmental sustainability from increased natural resource conservation, economic sustainability through building demand for a green economy and the investment of energy efficiency savings in the community, and social sustainability through the generation of social capital among the EcoTeams and organizations that can be reinvested into building a more livable and re-silient community.

But beyond these immediate benefits, a Cool Community will generate the civic pride that can only come from rising to a great challenge. With this spirit a community can transform whatever dangers the twenty-first century may bring into opportunities.

And the dividend that accrues to humanity from successful Cool Com-munity campaigns occurring across America and the planet is, in a phrase—a rite of passage. The human species will have crossed a threshold by rising to the challenge of our time, smarter, more connected, and more empowered, with the capability of transforming whatever dangers the twenty-first cen-tury may bring our planet into opportunities.

One such planetary danger and opportunity confronting the human species and the final rite of passage to becoming a functioning civilization is transforming the paradigm of war. Chapter 12 explores this next frontier.

Chapter 11: Social Change 2.0 Practitioner's Guide

1. Because global warming requires all hands on deck, what role do you see yourself playing?

2. What role will your social change initiative play in addressing global warming?

3. How might you use the Social Change 2.0 framework to play a transformative role?

4. What is the synergy potential between your social change initiative and a Cool Community campaign taking place in your city or town?

5. What role might your social change initiative play in creating or supporting a Cool Community campaign?

TRANSFORMING THE PARADIGM OF WAR:

THE EMERGENCE OF A UNITIVE CONSCIOUSNESS

Nothing that I do will change the structure of the universe. But by raising my voice I can help the greatest of all causes—good will among humankind and peace on earth.
— Albert Einstein

The solutions to our world's major problems are attainable, but part of the reason why we haven't attained them is that we are facing our problems in the wrong way. We are so convinced the problems are intractable . . . that paralysis reigns . . . . We need to subdue our fears and cynicism.
—Jeffrey Sachs, The End of Poverty

As challenging as global warming is to wrap our minds around, there is growing consensus that we must act, and the question is not "if" but "how." There are, of course, huge consequences for humankind if we don't get it together soon, but we are at least now on the path. There is, however, another critical issue for humanity's evolution where there is no consensus, and which is a blight on our claim to be a civilized species. In this final chapter I wish to explore how we might create a shift around the paradigm of war. A paradigm shift is defined as "a major change in a thought pattern; a radical change in personal beliefs, complex systems or organizations, replacing the former way of thinking or organizing with a radically different way of thinking or organizing."

Might we be ready for a shift in the way we think about war? Might it be possible to move away from seeing it as an inevitable part of human nature that we must tolerate, and start recognizing it as an outdated behavioral anachronism, engaged in only by cultures on the fringes of modern civilization? Although we are not there at the moment, are there any signals indicating that this is on humanity's horizon? And if so, is there anything we can do to hasten the adoption of this new paradigm? These are questions I have been pondering ever since the First Earth Run, my first foray into changing our thought pattern about war.

The starting point in changing a pattern of thought is holding the belief in another possibility. Did I, in fact, honestly believe that transforming the paradigm of war was possible? If I couldn't convince myself, I would have a hard time convincing anyone else. Certainly there is limited evidence to back such a belief, and to the contrary, a great deal of evidence to prove the opposite. Unless I could turn this belief around, any effort I made would ultimately be a noble but futile exercise—like Don Quixote fighting a windmill. I have had my share of hard sells, so I am not afraid to take on big challenges, but I certainly wanted to increase my odds.

What I know about transformative change from my work with large organizations is that to increase the odds of being successful you need a "burning platform"—a need or event that provides an impetus and sense of urgency to change. In the classic movie *The Day the Earth Stood Still*, Klaatu, an alien from a more evolved species, has determined that humanity's behaviors are too destructive and Earth's life-support system too important to the galaxy to take a chance that we might destroy it. As a consequence, he has been sent to Earth to make a final determination if humankind is worth saving or if they should wipe us out with their sophisticated weaponry. The movie revolves around whether Klaatu can be convinced by representatives of humanity that we are willing and able to change our behavior. Humankind faced with a burning platform is forced to look at our destructive behaviors and either change them or ultimately be destroyed as a result of them.

We face a variation on that burning platform theme with climate change. Knowing that we must come together as a human community to address the climate threat that impacts everyone—north and south, east and west, poor and wealthy of every ideology—or face the slow and painful destruction of our species, has created a burning platform for change. The brilliant evolutionary thinker Teilhard de Chardin many years ago prophetically spoke of a moment like this. He said, "Without any doubt people today suffer and vegetate in isolation; they need a superior impulse to intervene and force them to pass beyond the level at which they feel immobilized, leading them to discover their profound affinities. The sense of Earth is the irresistible pressure which will come at the right moment to unite them in common passion."

Whether we will rise to this challenge is the central existential question of humanity's short stretch on this planet. With the superior impulse of our life-support system, Earth, in imminent peril, will we discover our "profound affinities" to help us change our behavior? None of us knows how this movie ends, but I do know that in order to tackle climate change, even with the best strategies we can muster, we need to discover our affinities and learn how to cooperate in ways that we have never had to before.

The climate crisis will force us to overcome our differences in a way that only one's survival instinct can. In times of war members of a battle unit who would hardly speak to one another under normal circumstances have to cooperate to save their own lives. With a growing need for all hands on deck to tackle climate change, fighting with one another will suddenly become an indulgence humanity can no longer afford.

But behavior change, even with a burning platform, does not happen by need alone. To galvanize the political will to transform the "us versus them" mentality into just "us," we need to believe that achieving this is possible. Otherwise we will cling to the reality we have always known, even when it means our demise as a species. It would not be the first time that this has occurred. Jared Diamond in his presciently useful book, *Collapse: How Societies Choose to Succeed or Fail*, describes these moments of choice for civilizations and how some seized them and others did not and died off.

What is important here is that we need to use this global teachable moment to turn ourselves away from our old ways. As the saying goes, a crisis is a terrible thing to waste. So what will it take both for our short-term survival and long-term evolution as a human species to transform the paradigm of war? We need to begin by delegitimizing the dysfunctional behavior of war, publically acknowledging that it is unacceptable for a civilized species—like slavery, cannibalism, and killing women and children. This behavior may still occur but it is taboo, and perpetrators will pay the price of being viewed by the rest of humanity as pariahs, the way the United States was viewed for starting the war in Iraq.

We then need to develop a new paradigm with enough power to attract us as a human species so we are willing to let go of that which pushes us away from one another. I believe this source of power is the development of a unitive consciousness that propels us to discover our profound affinities while at the same time respecting and learning from our differences. This needs to be complemented by a set of unitive practices, some of which I described in Chapter 8, to help us implement this new paradigm. When a unitive consciousness is preponderant on the planet, peace will be the by-product.

Finally, to get people to participate, we need to set a credible goal for the achievement of this evolutionary shift. War has existed as a tool for resolving our differences for the entire history of humankind. Changing this behavior and the belief underlying it is not something we can expect to do right away. How far into the future would we need to set this goal to open up the possibility of achieving it? The conclusion I came to from asking this question of many people was that this could be humanity's "stretch goal" for the twenty-first century. That is, by the end of the century it would be possible for humanity to have adopted a new code of human conduct on this planet. *Civilized countries and groups don't and won't kill one another to resolve their differences.*

This transformative change strategy needs to be seen from a long-term perspective. Like the stone masons of old who viewed building the great cathedrals of Europe as an undertaking that they might not see finished in their lifetimes, we, too, must understand that we may not live to see our work come to fruition. But like the patient stone masons, we can proceed with the knowledge that, once our foundations are laid, there will be many others to add future layers of bricks over time. I believe that the building of a unitive consciousness on this planet needs to be humanity's great work for the twenty-first century and our defining project as a species. If we achieve this, all the other problems humanity faces can be resolved. If we don't, we will limp along from problem to problem. The purpose of this final chapter is to describe practices to assist us on this journey, provide hope that it is already underway, and put out a call to transformative change leaders to help further it.

We will start by circling back to the launch of a cyber version of the First Earth Run in 2003 to seed a set of unitive practices around the planet. We then look at the Millennials who embody this unitive consciousness and the important role they are playing in furthering it. Finally, we will look at the unitive political leadership of Barack Obama and his influence on world culture. Throughout the chapter we will be looking at what we can do to bring unitive practices into our communities, organizations, and personal lives.

Hopi elder Grandmother Caroline told us to look for the signs of a "great turning," which could also be called this emergent unitive paradigm. She said the signs will be there if we know how to identify them. The signs I will share in this chapter indicate to me that that the first waves of this unitive consciousness have begun lapping on the shore. This should give heart to the many to take up or sustain this century's great work.

SEEDING THE UNITIVE IMPULSE: THE FIRST EARTH RUN GOES CYBER

As the Iraq war was heating up in 2003, many, many people were frustrated by how impotent they felt to stop it. The protests were of little avail and those opposed to the war felt utterly defeated. This despair and hopelessness in the country reminded me of the despair and hopelessness that prevailed here during the mid-1980s while we were stuck in a nuclear confrontation with Russia. Because of the deep sense of contraction that prevailed at that time, there was a pent-up need for expansion; the physics of change always creates a pull in the opposite direction. It was that need for expansion in the global psyche that allowed us to create the First Earth Run in 1986. In the pervasive despair over the Iraq War, I felt a similar opening for something transformative.

My days of running around the world with a torch of peace had come to an end, but not my desire to continue furthering the unitive impulse it represented. I did this by showing the First Earth Run video and telling its story at conferences and in my workshops. People would consistently come away inspired by the way the world had come together, touched by the sense of possibility the event conveyed, and hopeful that a more peaceful planet was perhaps possible. And they always asked what they could do to be effective in furthering this unitive impulse.

I began thinking about how this story had such a consistently positive impact on people who heard it and saw the video; and how it prompted them to want to take action in their own lives. Knowing that people are able to make behavior changes when they have a compelling vision and the tools to manifest it, I wondered what might happen if the First Earth Run story and the practices embodied in it were diffused widely across the Internet. I decided to do some "evolutionary scouting" to see what was possible. With the state of contraction caused by the Iraq war, the time was certainly right to seed a transformative change strategy.

I wrote the story of the First Earth Run and called it "A Dream for Our World." Chapter 1 of this book represents some of this account. I then plumbed the story for the key unitive practices that it embodied, and identified seven. I created each as a pattern language so people could build on these templates with their own unique acts of social creativity. Like the other programs I have discussed in this book, they were created as a menu of choices, with some quite simple and others requiring more commitment.

This overall strategy embodied the five design principles of Social Change 2.0. It *empowered* people to create the world they want by taking personal responsibility to bring it about, starting with their own lives and the people they knew. It was *transformative* by attempting to change the war paradigm. It was *unitive* in that it directly asked each person to go beyond that which separates him or her from other people. The whole initiative was imbued with the invitation that people develop *social innovations* that build on this unitive impulse. Finally, powered by the vast *diffusion* power of the Internet and its social networks, it had the possibility to go to scale because of the many people on the planet wishing to bring this consciousness into manifestation.

The seven practices disseminated were:

1. Hold the intention that it is possible to create a unitive consciousness on this planet that changes the paradigm of war.

2. Befriend those who are different from you.

3. Empower children to do the same.

4. Create artistic events that enable people to experience the unitive impulse.

5. Honor community initiatives that demonstrate and model the unitive practice of cooperation.

6. Contribute time and money to initiatives that are furthering this unitive impulse.

7. Pray for and visualize a world where people are living in harmony with one another and the Earth.

(The web link to these practices is www.empowermentinstitute.net/dream. It is also provided in the resource section on page 391.)

In the fall of 2003 I posted the "A Dream for Our World" story and seven practices along with the First Earth Run video, photo gallery, music, and art on our web site. I wrote a letter describing what I hoped to accomplish, and sent it and the link to the many people in my global network, encouraging them to share it widely with their networks, who in turn were requested to continue to ripple it out.

As I had sensed, it was a fertile time for this initiative. Based on web site traffic and the many e-mails I received, the story and practices spread quickly from network to network and involved several hundred thousand people around the world, and particularly in America, the Middle East, and Africa, where the war paradigm was still strongly held. In parts of the world where there was no violence or active war, people joined in common cause. The Hopi prophesy of the "great turning" that was being enabled by the First Earth Run provided a mythic dimension that further enhanced people's desire to participate. Years later thousands of people are still visiting the site as this story and set of practices continue to careen through cyberspace.

This evolutionary scouting showed me that the unitive consciousness pulse on this planet is strong and if people are provided tools they will act on it. For this consciousness to expand, people need to participate regularly in practices like the ones this initiative disseminated. And to sustain their commitment to these practices, people need to feel hopeful that the level of fundamental change they represent is possible. This is why Grandmother Caroline, in describing the "great turning," encouraged us to look for the "signs."

But these signs are usually hidden to an untrained eye constantly drawn in by the media's pathological focus on violence and the war *du jour*. They are patterns of change that move at a much slower pace, and to discern them requires us to move beyond information gathered solely with our eyes. It requires us to refine our instincts and intuitive responses to be able to perceive the larger influences and consequences of specific social phenomenon in the world. Cultivating this instinct helps us discover the signs at the origin of change.

In that light, let me close this section with two such signs. One of the seven practices, "the unitive impulse," is about creating artistic renderings of our universal aspiration to live in harmony with one another. This practice is most commonly expressed through art, and gets a special boost every two years when it is magnified during the opening ceremony of the Olympics. During the Opening Ceremony for the 2008 Beijing Olympics, witnessed by one-third of humanity, the unitive impulse was transmitted more powerfully, profoundly, and precisely than I had ever witnessed before.

The master choreographer of this event, Zhang Yimou, who also directed the remarkable movie *Hero*, built this awe-inspiring experience around the Chinese theme of *he* or peaceful harmony: the idea that conflict in the world foretells the desire for and ultimate culmination in peace. It is always our artists that feel the grand waves of human evolution before the rest of us become conscious of them. Was Zhang Yimou responding to a collective longing in humanity to experience this unitive impulse? And is our longing itself one of the signs of a great turning? I believe he was and it is. As they say in the East, when the student is ready, the teacher appears.

Another of the unitive practices, "befriending the other," has entered into the mainstream of our public education system. Once again we return to the Rhinebeck School System. Richard Zipp, the middle school psychologist, attended the Empowerment Institute and was inspired by the "A Dream for Our World" initiative. He applied the unitive practice of "befriending the other" to his work with eleven-year-olds. He describes his project and the very encouraging results he achieved.

> Let me give you a little taste of the workshop I do with all the sixth-graders called "Befriending the Other." It is designed to address issues of bullying, teasing, and other forms of social and emotional harassment. I do all of the empowerment work through writing classes with another teacher and it occurs over three consecutive days.
>
> Students reflect on questions, share in pairs, and then share in the larger group. On the first day the questions are "What are you afraid might happen if you reached out and befriended someone who is different from you?" and "What has been your experience when you or someone else befriended someone who was different?" Students commonly respond that they're afraid they'll lose their friends or that trouble will somehow come their way.
>
> The first day ends with an activity. I outline a box on the floor with tape and have all the students attempt to get into it. They fight to get into the middle, where it is fun and safe and they really do enjoy the challenge. When they act as individuals or small subgroups

with separate agendas, they can never get everyone in the box. The box becomes a metaphor for the social dynamics the students experience during middle school. Are you in the box or out? Were you pushed out? Did you reach out to others to invite them into the box? Did you cooperate to get everyone into the box?

Day two is all about creating a vision of a school community where respect and mutual consideration are the norms. I ask them to draw a picture of a tolerant community. We then develop a wall quilt of all the students' drawings and hang it in the hallway as a symbol and daily reminder of their vision and commitment.

Day three focuses on intention statements of the new behaviors the students wish to develop around befriending the other. In conjunction with the workshop, my colleague, Nancy, reinforces the empowerment work by having the students grow plants in the room. She talks about all the steps needed to grow healthy plants and connects that with the students' personal growing edges to create a tolerant and inclusive school community.

Typically after the workshop, some of the students seek us out and inform us of their actions to befriend other students. One student, Sally, told us she saw a student sitting by herself in the cafeteria. She told us she wanted to get outside of the box to befriend another girl who was not very popular. She mustered up the courage to ask this girl to join her table. She said it made her feel great and no one really minded. And that everyone at the table who knew about the box exercise appreciated her action. She said she is now excited to have a new friend. This has become a very common experience of many students.

A lot of students have also been forthcoming when they see someone not being treated the right way or being made fun of on the playground, in the hallway or at recess. Because of this workshop these students became tuned in to the needs of others, and advocate for students who are not as popular and don't have a lot of friends. Kids have come to me years later and told me they are now more assertive in helping others because we pulled out this behavior, gave it a name—"befriending the other," and reframed it as cool.

What most touches me about Richard's story was how ready these children were to shed the behavior of intolerance with something that seemed more real and meaningful—befriending the other. But this unitive practice is not limited to Richard's teaching or the Rhinebeck School System; it is part of a much larger trend around teaching tolerance in public education. There are now many curricula and many students across the country learning to befriend the other. When the students are ready, the teachers will appear. And when society is ready, the teaching will appear. Are we facing a teachable moment in our society for unitive practices? Given that public education is a barometer of society, this trend would certainly indicate we are. This next section helps us see the unitive consciousness groundswell that is building in this next generation.

PASSING THE TORCH TO THE WE GENERATION: A UNITIVE CONSCIOUSNESS AS THE NEW SOCIAL NORM

An inspirational story that shows the possibility and yearning in the world to come together, a set of practices that empower people to act on this yearning being disseminated around the Internet, and hopeful signs that a great turning has begun all show us that we may be ready for a paradigm shift around the issue of war. By themselves, however, they do not address the large reality gap around effectuating this transformative change, given the war paradigm world view that still deeply pervades the planet's power structures. How do we get the numbers and momentum needed to transform this paradigm?

This is where the "Millennials" come in. In the United States and many other countries they embody a unitive consciousness and are ready for action. They were born between 1978 and 2000 and represent almost a third of the United States and half of the world's population. And they are 21 percent larger in numbers than the baby boomers born between 1946 and 1964. In their seminal and very well-researched book about the Millennials, *Generation We*, authors Eric Greenberg and Karl Weber describe them as "a socially tolerant generation that consider themselves a part of planetary humankind, not divided by race, religion, or national boundaries, ready to accept differences in beliefs and values in exchange for progress, peace and a better life for all." I could not have defined a unitive consciousness any better.

Greenberg and Weber describe the Millennials' values as: hopeful, ready for change, self-aware, wired to the world, socially responsible, politically engaged, entrepreneurial, progressive, socially tolerant, and committed to green activism. Their values overlaid perfectly with Barack Obama's transformative and unitive political philosophy and this is why they, more than any other demographic, provided him the volunteers and voting bloc that helped him win. Given this experience of their collective power in combination with their commitment to social change, "Generation We," say Weber and Greenberg, "is ready to support a collective social movement focused on the greater good; and based on their numbers and sense of urgency, once such a movement emerges it is certain to be large, powerful and lasting."

Building a social movement capable of transforming the war paradigm is no small undertaking. Minimally it needs a compelling positive vision to attract people. My generation of baby boomers also wished to transform the paradigm of war, but all we had to replace it with was an *anti*war movement with a default position of peace. As a consequence, we unwittingly reverted to the thought pattern that props up war—intolerance of another world view—and created a more politically correct form, which we called the "culture wars." An antiwar belief system is just not powerful enough to transform the thought pattern underpinning the paradigm of war, in spite of our best intentions.

The Millennials, certainly in America, are a ways down the path to being able to transform the paradigm of war because their unitive consciousness is so antithetical to the belief system of intolerance, and because they are so passionately united in a generational mission to heal our planet. To go the rest of the way they need to articulate these values into a compelling unitive vision and develop a transformative change strategy capable of effecting behavior change. This is what Richard Zipp did, and it enabled his students, when faced with the choice either to accept experiences of intolerance or do something about them, to choose the latter.

To build this into a social movement will require many people like Richard to educate the young Millennials in the techniques of "befriending the other." It will also require the older Millennials to take up the torch and build the social innovations and institutions that enable the planet they've inherited to reflect their values. Because of the profound readiness for transformative change that is now so prevalent among the Millennials, this leadership is starting to proliferate.

But we don't need to wait for the Millennials to come into their own to take advantage of what they have to offer us. What can those of us born before 1978—representing two-thirds of America and half of the rest of the world—learn from them to help us evolve along the unitive path they are walking? And what are some of the best ways to learn from them?

I set out to answer these questions over one long Fourth of July weekend by attending the inaugural Rothbury Music Festival on the converted Double JJ Ranch in northern Michigan. It would be attended by some fifty thousand Millennials listening to more than eighty music acts performing at six venues. The Rothbury producer, AEG Live Madison House Presents, described one of the festival's goals as "bringing attention to climate change and clean energy alternatives." They invited me to participate in several of the environmental panels that would take place during the day to complement the evening musical entertainment. They also requested that I serve as a strategic partner to help them take the festival beyond just music and environmental awareness raising, to engaging fans and musicians in actual behavior change through the Low Carbon Diet.

One of the first things I noticed was the difference in sophistication between the social change strategies practiced by the Boomers and Millennials at the same age. Our strategies were vague and working against the system, whereas theirs are results oriented and working with the system. This is a function of the issues being addressed, but also the point of view from which they approach social change. Millennial environmental leader and one of Rothbury's youth organizers with whom I collaborated, Dan Worth, captures these distinctions in his Huffington Post blog entitled "From Woodstock to Rothbury: From Activism to Energy Independence." Describing the Millennials, he says:

> In many ways they represent the maturing of the Utopian visions created at Woodstock. They won't be wearing flowers in their hair, sporting tie-dyes, or touring on Magic Buses. Many of them may appear at your town and city meetings in button-down shirts and suits talking about financing schemes and payback periods. When you listen to them speak, you will hear the energy and idealism that was born forty years ago, tempered and refined by the long, difficult decades since, and empowered by both the fear of today's impending climate crisis and excitement over new, revolutionary solutions. And, yet again, it will be young people who will change the world!

Since Rothbury was being billed as "The Green Woodstock" and I live in Woodstock, in his blog Dan referred to me as the "official representative of Woodstock." Which was actually quite accurate, but perhaps not how he imagined, as shortly after the Woodstock Music

Festival in 1969, I had stopped following rock music. Gail, a music lover who considered me very cool for attending such an event, was eager for me to report back to her everything I learned, including the names of the musicians performing.

What was becoming clear was that my quest to learn from the Millennials had two parts: a conscious part, what I wanted to learn, and a cosmic part, what the Universe wanted me to learn. I've observed from past experience that when the cosmic part starts showing up I know I am in for an adventure and I should just enjoy the ride. *Of course* I would need to learn about the Millennials' music and musicians if I wished to learn about their culture. If someone wished to learn about me in the sixties, they would have had to learn about the influence of the Beatles.

I flew in Friday night for a 10 AM Saturday morning meeting, very early by rock music festival standards, to talk to some of the organizers I would be collaborating with over the next two days. I was driven to the site by a young woman working for the festival producers who was barely holding it together, having stayed up until the early morning hours rocking out. In spite of her sleep-deprived state she was most accommodating in answering my many questions about which bands to see. When she asked me about my musical tastes, I told her I liked music that had a positive message and was uplifting and mind expanding. She gave me a look that I roughly translated as, "Boy, have they ever imported a relic of the sixties," but to my delight she said that there was a whole genre devoted to this type of music and she told me which bands I should see.

I found this all very exciting. This would be the most fun I had had in an official save-the-planet capacity in quite a long time; perhaps another cosmic learning was in the making here. I also tucked away the insight of how comfortable this generation was with such a wide diversity of musical genres.

When I got onto the festival grounds I couldn't belief what I was seeing. I felt like I had walked into Ecotopia. The festival was organized as an eco-village to accommodate 50,000 residents for four days while producing close to zero waste and being as energy efficient as possible. All the food and drink concessions used compostable cups, silverware, and plates. There were 2,000 recycling/composting/waste bins spread throughout the festival grounds and no litter to be found. All the power generators for the stages, sound systems, and musical equipment ran on biodiesel fuel. Organic concessions and an on-site farmers' market supported local growers. All the staff were given one water bottle to refill and most of the festival goers also had their own water bottles. Staff coordinated flight arrivals to maximize carpooling among festival goers to the site. The festival participated in a carbon offset program for all site operations. And proceeds from the festival would be used to outfit the local high school with solar power.

There were futuristic geodesic domes housing the music venues and serendipity sculptures with various environmental messages all made from recycled materials. There were thousands of young people in a huge grassy field on their yoga mats being led through a vigorous workout with soft rock kirtan music in the background. Then there was Sherwood Forest, a wooded area with old pine trees and mythical art installations, which by day served as a place to cool out on hammocks and by night was lit up and turned it into a magical wonderland.

The festival organizers complemented the eco-village environment with a very clear intention to help everyone, including the musicians, get with the program of saving our planet. Shannon McNeely, who was responsible for organizing the environmental panels, was another Millennial who inspired me with her results-oriented mentality. She was extremely clear about her vision for Rothbury.

> This is not your parents' or your grandparents' festival. This is about empowering youth today to create the world they want to live in instead of just inheriting the mistakes of the past. The climate challenge we face today requires us all to participate in creating a sustainable future. We can make a huge difference, but we don't have any time left to lose at this point. It's up to us.

An example of her commitment to "it's up to us," all of us, can be seen in this excerpt from a letter she wrote to the participating musicians, encouraging them to do their part. No pedestals provided by this woman.

> One of the unique opportunities musicians have is to connect their fans with green solutions at concerts and through their web sites. One of the challenges green-conscious musicians face is doing this effectively. Rothbury aims to help! We want this festival to do more than just inspire. We want to empower fans to measurably reduce their carbon footprint and engage others to do the same. To help achieve this goal, we have developed a special project. We call it

Bands CAN (Climate Action Networks). Using the tool of Low Carbon Diet you can encourage your fans to create EcoTeams.

The musicians playing at Rothbury by design were among the most inspired and environmentally conscious artists in America, and were quite ready to take up Shannon's call to action. These musicians were eager to find ways to tell the climate change story better, serve as role models, and empower their fans to be part of the solution. Many of them were offsetting their carbon footprint on their tours and making as low an impact on the environment as possible. I got to meet a number of them through the environmental panel sessions, in which they also participated. I was touched by their sincerity and desire to do the right thing with their celebrity status. They showed me what it looks like for musicians to bring words and deeds together in service of the planet, yet another of the Millennial teachings.

One Millennial rocker, Brett Dennen, who *Rolling Stone Magazine* proclaimed one of "10 Artists to Watch in 2008," described his sense of responsibility in one of the panels this way: "As an artist we have the special privilege of having a microphone, and we need to use it for the good of the planet." Brett does that in many ways, including Love Speaks, an organization he founded that helps local nonprofit foundations in every town that he tours. He explains, "I think every show is an opportunity to make a difference in people's lives and communities. I'd love for people to know what's going on in their communities and hopefully, they may get involved."

And then there were the hundreds of volunteers who participated on the green team. They were stationed at each recycle/compost/waste station to educate people on which bin to use in accordance with the zero-waste policy of the festival. This was trickier than it sounds, given that all the paper goods and utensils were compostable. In fact, one of the musicians, Michael Franti, commented from stage on how challenged he was to know which bin to put his chewing gum in. When a musician is concerned about the recycling of his chewing gum, we have come a long way, and these Millennial volunteers, with their good cheer and very clear intention that people do the right thing, helped create a context in which we all, indeed, wanted to do the right thing.

And of course there were the tens of thousands of festival goers. They were in heaven in this green ecotopia environment. Great music, beautiful weather, green values, and a change-the-world ethic. I hosted the final wrap-up panel and honored the festival organizers and volunteers for creating what would be known henceforth as the greenest music festival in history and the gold standard against which future events would measure themselves. There were many thousands of fans strolling around the festival grounds within earshot of the loudspeakers. On hearing me offer this acknowledgment they broke out in spontaneous applause. This was the world they had all helped create over four days and they were very proud to be part of it.

I came away from this experience inspired by those who will be carrying the torch on the next leg of the journey for humanity. For the Millennials, a unitive consciousness was about both the respect they offered one another and the Earth, and the action they were taking to make this planet a better place for us all. If this is what we can look forward to with the Millennials in charge, I can't wait.

I close this chapter with a sign that needs very little substantiation for us to believe that the world is moving in the right direction. We will look at how Barack Obama has brought a unitive consciousness into politics and inspired many people around the world to believe that profound change is possible.

BARACK OBAMA:
THE EMERGENCE OF A UNITIVE APPROACH TO POLITICS

Gail came back from a fundraising event in New York City called "Broadway for Obama" in September, 2007, almost five months before then-Senator Obama would win the Iowa Caucus, raving to me about Barack Obama. She said, "David, this man represents everything you believe in about a unitive approach to social change. You have to hear him speak." With Gail's encouragement I started listening very carefully to his speeches and the unitive spirit that permeated them. It did not take me long to see that he was a different breed of politician from anyone I had ever seen or heard before.

The first result of this listening was the identification of a major limiting belief I had been holding. I had not thought it possible to be unitive in politics. What I saw in Barack Obama, however, was someone attempting to change the game of politics by displaying a unitive approach with other politicians, policy, and the public. Here was a person running for the highest political office in America with a highly sophisticated and transformative social change strategy. Wow! Now this was someone I could learn from. With gusto, I spent the next thirteen months studying his every move.

At every critical juncture in his campaign when his back was up against the wall, he chose to go unitive. No matter how many times he was asked by his advisers and goaded by the media to become adversarial, which Chicago politics had certainly taught him how to do, he refused. He raised the level of conversation above left versus right, or attack and parry, to the deeper human truth of tolerance and respect for another's point of view, all the more so when he disagreed with the person. His most commonly used refrain was "we can disagree without being disagreeable."

When he needed to tackle a potentially polarizing issue he went toward it. He honored its complexity by not offering us simple bromides but rather telling us honestly what we need to do to evolve as a culture. And he did so by accentuating that which unites us as human beings and appealing to our better nature. His speech on race at Constitution Hall in Philadelphia was a work of genius in this regard. He inspired a new sense of possibility in America that as a nation we can heal our past and create a new postracial country. It was a remarkable moment of unitive politics.

And he was able to take this unitive approach to the grassroots. One of the major reasons he was able to build such an extraordinarily effective political campaign was because he invited people to take ownership of it. He encouraged his supporters to help shape his transformative vision and he engaged in active dialogue with them. He empowered them to express their unique creativity through the political organizing process and offered tools and best practice exchanges to help them do so effectively. As a result he was able to bring more people than any other presidential candidate had ever done into the ranks of political organizing while at the same time preparing them for the larger social change journey ahead.

Through all this he was helping heal a political divisiveness that had been eating away at the American soul for decades. By modeling this unitive approach, the Millennials were activated, and many others who had been turned off by old-style politics began reclaiming their civic responsibility to engage in the political process.

The big question the media and political pundits kept asking was, "Is it possible actually to succeed with this approach to politics?" And of course there was that other not-so-small issue of running for president in America as a black man. For more than a year the world watched with bated breath to see if Barack Obama would resort to politics as usual and be discounted by voters because they did not think we were ready for an African-American president. He did not, we did not, and the rest is now history.

The election of Barack Obama as president was a remarkable achievement in America's long journey to heal our great wound of slavery. What was all the more remarkable was that he did this by respecting and even honoring the political process—but he approached it on his own unifying terms. If he had waged a politics-as-usual campaign, we would have won the battle for a progressive agenda but lost the war of a transformational politics to help us implement it. Barack Obama proved his mettle in so many ways, but his steadfast unitive vision was, I believe, the greatest achievement in his run for president. That, more than anything else, changed the game of how politics is played, and opened the door for a unitive consciousness to begin diffusing through society.

But up to this point it was his journey, and while many of us may have volunteered to get him elected or dug deep into our pockets to provide him the financing he needed, we were observers of a social phenomenon. For him to continue to work his political high art of helping America and the world transform from division and enmity to connection and cooperation, he is going to need all the help he can get. Being an experienced community organizer, he was wise enough to see this in advance and told us he needed our help. Here's how Barack Obama, as community-organizer-in-chief, has described our mission as citizens, change agents, and community organizers.

> Change doesn't come from Washington. Change comes to Washington. Change will not come if we wait for some other person or some other time. We are the ones we've been waiting for. This is our chance to answer that call. This is our moment. This is our time to promote the cause of peace; to reclaim the American Dream and reaffirm that fundamental truth—that out of many, we are one; that while we breathe, we hope, and where we are met with cynicism, and doubt, and those who tell us that we can't, we will respond with that timeless creed that sums up the spirit of a people: Yes We Can. And together we will change the world.

Now he needs us to step forward as partners to help change the world. This is something he referred to quite literally in many of his campaign speeches, and I believe he meant it quite literally. So what must we do to help our president—and ourselves—succeed with the ambitious transformative and unitive mission with which he has inspired us? We must be willing to dream boldly about what we truly want our communities, institutions, and world to be, and then we must create it. We must help those who would continue to divide us into the old and worn divisions of *us* versus *them* to see that there is a better way. And we must learn from the Millennials and practice a unitive consciousness in our lives, inspiring others by our example.

America has a unique role as the world's petri dish for social innovation. We have offered humanity the best and the worst. Whatever we do, we have a big footprint that will ripple across the planet. As we make our changes we should know that we are not acting parochially; our changes will spread. The world has a lot riding on a transformative and unitive leadership coming out of the United States. Perhaps this is why people took to the streets around the world to celebrate the election of Barack Obama as president of the United States. While they may not have been able to vote for him at the ballot box, clearly hundreds of millions of global citizens voted for him with their hearts and minds.

Let me end with a story told by Grammy-Award-winning singer Melissa Etheridge, which demonstrates the possibility of growing a unitive consciousness in America when, inspired by the example set by Barack Obama, a citizen steps forward to change the way the game is played.

> This is a message for my brothers and sisters who have fought so long and so hard for gay rights and liberty. We watched as our nation took a step in the right direction, against all odds, and elected Barack Obama as our next leader. Then we were jerked back into the last century as we watched our rights taken away by Proposition 8 in California. Still sore and angry we felt another slap in the face as the man we helped get elected seemingly invited a gay-hater to address the world at his inauguration.
>
> I hadn't heard of Pastor Rick Warren before all of this. When I heard the news, in its neat little sound bite form that we are so accustomed to, it painted the picture for me. This Pastor Rick must surely be one hate spouting, money grabbing, bad hair televangelist like all the others. Would I be boycotting the inauguration? Would we be marching again?
>
> Well, I have to tell you my friends, the universe has a sense of humor and indeed works in mysterious ways. As I was winding down the promotion for my Christmas album I had one more stop on the last night at a conference. I'd agreed to play a song I'd written with my friend Salman Ahmed, a Sufi Muslim from

Pakistan. The song is called "Ring the Bells," and it's a call for peace and unity in our world. Just the day before I'd received a call informing me that the keynote speaker at the conference was Pastor Rick Warren. I was stunned. My fight or flight instinct took over. Should I cancel? Then a calm voice inside me said, "Are you really about peace or not?"

I told my manager to reach out to Pastor Warren and say that in the spirit of unity I would like to talk to him. They gave him my phone number. On the day of the conference I received a call from Pastor Rick, and before I could say anything, he told me what a fan he was.

He had most of my albums from the very first one. What? This didn't sound like a gay hater, much less a preacher. He explained in very thoughtful words that as a Christian he believed in equal rights for everyone. He believed every loving relationship should have equal protection. He had struggled with Proposition 8 because he didn't want to see marriage redefined as anything other than between a man and a woman. He said he regretted his choice of words in his video message to his congregation about Proposition 8 when he mentioned pedophiles and those who commit incest. He said that in no way is that how he thought about gays. He invited me to his church; I invited him to my home to meet my wife and kids. He told me of his wife's struggle with breast cancer just a year before mine.

When we met later that night, he entered the room with open arms and an open heart. We agreed to build bridges to the future.

Brothers and sisters, the choice is ours now. We have the world's attention. We have the capability to create change, awesome change in this world, but before we change minds we must change hearts. Sure, there are plenty of hateful people who will always hold on to their bigotry like a child to a blanket. But there are also good people out there, Christian and otherwise, that are beginning to listen. They don't hate us, they fear change. Maybe in our anger, as we consider marches and boycotts, we can consider stretching out our hands. Maybe instead of marching on his church, we can show up en masse and volunteer for one of the many organizations affiliated with his church that work for HIV/AIDS causes all around the world.

Maybe if they get to know us, they won't fear us. I know, call me a dreamer, but I feel a new era is upon us. I will be attending the inauguration with my family and with hope in my heart. I know we are headed in the direction of marriage equality and equal protection for all families. Peace on earth, goodwill toward all men and women... and everyone in-between.

This is the unitive consciousness that is now being modeled by the president of the United States. If President Obama can do it with all the polarizing forces he faces, so can we. Melissa Etheridge just showed us how.

Are we ready as a human species to take this major step forward in our evolution? The signs are certainly pointing in the right direction and the conditions for fundamental change are as propitious as they could be. If ever there was a time, it is now. And who better than us, the first generations to set eyes on our beloved home from space, to further this great turning toward peace on earth? With the wind at our back, it is time to ride it.

CHAPTER 12: SOCIAL CHANGE 2.0 PRACTITIONER'S GUIDE

1. Who is the "other" for your social change initiative?

2. What could you do to reach out and befriend these people or organizations?

3. What unitive practices would assist you in this effort?

4. Who do you perceive as the "other" in your life in general?

5. What could you do to reach out and befriend these people?

OUR RESPONSIBILITY AND OPPORTUNITY

TO REINVENT THE WORLD

Again and again in history some people wake up. They have no ground in the crowd and they move to broader, deeper laws. They carry strange customs with them and demand room for bold and audacious action. The future speaks ruthlessly through them. They change the world.
　　　　　—Rainer Maria Rilke

Knowing is not enough. We must apply. Being willing is not enough; we must do.

　　　　　—Leonardo da Vinci

From runaway climate change that threatens the survival of humanity and the many life forms on Earth, to the many starving people and those just eking out an existence at the very edge of survival, to the desperation of our inner-city youth, to our patterns of thought that perpetuate a divided world, our planet is in need of a radical transformation that goes to the very root of our vision as human beings.

What could enable such a fundamental transformation is our innate longing as human beings to create a better world for ourselves and our children. This inherent desire for self-improvement is a key lever for human evolution because there are enormous possibilities to tap into it. But to access this potential requires transformative change leaders capable of calling forth our intrinsic aspiration. The intent of this book has been to help such leaders succeed in this enterprise.

At the Federal Convention of 1787, after three and a half months of deliberation over a constitution for the new United States, Benjamin Franklin was asked, "Well, doctor, what have we got, a republic or a monarchy?" "A republic," replied the doctor, "if you can keep it." The same could be said about our planet. Whether we get to keep it as a viable dwelling place for human habitation and evolution is up to us. To do this we must be able to change the game. Changing the game is not a spectator sport. It requires each of us to play a position on the team, and to play it with all of our heart and soul and mind. It requires nothing less than our very best and highest efforts.

Those of us alive on the planet at this moment in time have a special destiny in its evolution. We are the ones who must reinvent our world to sustain the fragile social experiment of human civilization. This is a momentous responsibility and enormous opportunity. As we accept this responsibility and seize this opportunity, we align our individual purpose with humanity's advancement. We become conscious actors in our planet's great evolutionary adventure. I wish you and all of us Godspeed on this epic journey.

ACKNOWLEDGMENTS

I always find it wondrous to observe the universe in action. Having worked on this book for three years (or, to be more accurate—most of my life), I handed off the manuscript to my editor on January 20, 2009, at the Woodstock Inaugural Ball, organized by Gail, of course, celebrating the election of Barack Obama as president of the United States. Throughout the most active phase of my writing, Barack Obama was reinventing politics. His vision and being were constant inspirations, and I offer my gratitude to him for what he stands for and the social change mantle he has taken on for our world.

I finished entering the edits to this book on Earth Day, April 22, 2009—again another remarkable synchronicity. So much meaning and fulfillment in my life has come from trying to help our planet sustain its bountiful blessings. What better day to hand off this book to the larger world. I offer my gratitude to our Earth for her beauty, endless wonders, and magnificence.

This book is possible because of the very good fortune I have had to collaborate with many extraordinarily talented and dedicated people over the past thirty years. The list could fill many pages but I wish to acknowledge several whose collaboration has been most influential: Eve Baer, Bob Bagar, Bob Barton, Lawrence Bloom, Michael Clark, Harlan Cleveland, Michael Dowd, Paul de Jongh, Danit Fried, Robert Gilman, Patty Goodwin, Jim Grant, Annie Grunwald, John Hadalski, George Kaufman, Shirley Kitchen, Alan Leidner, Mike Lindberg, Susan McDowell, Marilyn Mehlemann, Brooke Newell, Molly Olsen, Llyn Peabody, Bill Powers, Bessie Schadee, and Peter Van Luttervelt. To the many other colleagues whose names I did not mention, please accept my heartfelt appreciation and gratitude. This book represents our collective aspirations, learning, and achievements.

I wish to thank the great team that has helped produce this book: my star editor, Nan Satter, who has graced this book with her brilliant editing; Steve Busch, whose artistry can be seen in the book's cover and interior pages and who has brought this same aesthetic sensibility to so many of my projects over the years; Rachel Hockett, for her impeccable copyediting and proofing; Margo Baldwin and Peg O'Donnell of Chelsea Green Publishers, for their guidance, wisdom, and collaboration.

This book also greatly benefited from several friends and colleagues who read an early draft. I wish to thank my long-time thinking partner, Craig Hamilton, for his many incisive questions that helped me refine my thinking and for coming up with the title Social Change 2.0; my dear friends, Nathaniel Charny and Carla Goldstein, for their excellent suggestions and constant encouragement; John Winter, for both his enthusiastic feedback—so heartening to me as the first person to read the manuscript—and insights into how to build a Social Change 2.0 community of practice.

Finally I wish to thank my parents, Philip and Sylvia Gershon, for offering me the gifts of life, love, and support to pursue my passion for changing the world from a young age; and Gail Straub—my beloved wife, soul mate, friend, partner, collaborator *par excellence*, and co-adventurer in life—for her constant cheerleading, wise counsel, kindness, and love throughout the entire process of writing this book and our magnificent life together.

Empowerment Institute Resources

To learn about Social Change 2.0 activities including consulting, training programs, and partnership opportunities visit www.socialchange2.com.

Chapter 1
The World at the Brink: Creating a Better Game Than War

First Earth Run Video. This fifteen-minute inspirational video takes you on a journey around the world with the torch of peace as it engages with world leaders and citizens in over sixty countries. It is available for free download or purchase. Visit www.empowermentinstitute.net/dream

First Earth Run Photo Gallery. This 105-picture photo gallery captures some of the people young and old, political leaders, special moments and places among the sixty-two countries, twenty-five million people and forty-five heads of state that celebrated the torch of peace's journey around the world. It is an immersion in the feeling of the people as they participated in this creation of eighty-six days of peace on earth. Visit www.empowermentinstitute.net/dream.

A Dream for Our World, by David Gershon, High Point. This book expands on the story told in Chapter 1 and includes the seven unitive practices that grew out of it, photos, and communications from world leaders. Visit www.empowermentinstitute.net/dream for free download or to purchase the book.

What's Working in the World. These guidelines explain how to select and honor outstanding projects of cooperation solving local challenges in your community. Visit www.empowermentinstitute.net/dream.

CHAPTER 2
ENVIRONMENTALLY SUSTAINABLE LIFESTYLES IN AMERICA:
PSST—SAVE THE PLANET, PASS IT ON

Green Living Handbook: A 6 Step Program to Create an Environmentally Sustainable Lifestyle, by David Gershon, Empowerment Institute. The program focuses on solid waste reduction, water, energy, transportation efficiency, green purchasing, and empowering others. It can be done by single households or EcoTeams. To learn more or to purchase the book, visit www.empowermentinstitute.net/glh.

Sustainable Lifestyle Campaign. Using the *Green Living Handbook* as its behavior-change tool, the campaign helps a community conserve its natural resources and protect its environment through empowering residents to create more environmentally sustainable lifestyles. It can be implemented by local government, a community group, or a business. To learn more, visit www.empowermentinstitute.net/slc.

Journey for the Planet: A Kid's Five Week Adventure to Create an Earth Friendly Life, by David Gershon, Empowerment Institute. This is a children's sustainable lifestyle program. It can be done by children on their own or as part of a classroom or youth organization. A twenty-six-lesson teacher's curriculum is available to support the program. To learn more or to purchase these books, visit www.empowermentinstitute.net/journey.

Water Stewardship: A 30 Day Program to Protect and Conserve Our Water Resources, by David Gershon, Empowerment Institute. This program helps households develop practices to use water more efficiently and reduce pollutants emitted into local water bodies. It can be done by single households or EcoTeams. To learn more or to purchase the book, visit www.empowermentinstitute.net/wsp.

Water Stewardship Campaign. Using *Water Stewardship* as its behavior-change tool, the campaign helps a community or watershed conserve its water resources and reduce pollutants going into local water bodies through empowering residents to create water friendly lifestyle practices. It can be implemented by local government or a watershed organization. Visit www.empowermentinstitute.net/wsc.

Citizen Sustainability Assessment. This tool for creating a sustainable community strategy enables a municipality or community group to assess the effectiveness of government policies and programs from the point of view of residential resource conservation and environmental protection. To use this free web tool, visit www.empowermentinstitute.net/csa.

Chapter 3
Neighborhood Livability in Inner-City Philadelphia: Against the Odds

Livable Neighborhood: Making Life Better on the Street Where You Live, by David Gershon, Empowerment Institute. This program is divided into four topics: neighborhood health and safety, neighborhood beautification and greening, neighborhood resource sharing, and neighborhood community building. The program also explains how to create a block-based team. For more information or to purchase the book, visit www.empowermentinstitute.net/lnp.

Livable Neighborhood Campaign. Using *Livable Neighborhood* as its behavior-change tool, this campaign helps blocks improve their safety, health, and overall livability. It can be implemented by local government, a community group, neighborhood or block association. For more information, visit www.empowermentinstitute.net/lnc.

Chapter 4
Disaster-Resilient Communities in New York City: All Together Now

All Together Now: Neighbors Helping Neighbors Create a Disaster-Resilient Community, Empowerment Institute. This program helps individuals prepare for emergencies and create disaster-resilient blocks and buildings. It can be done by individuals or a team. The version of the book created for New York City is available for free download; visit www.empowermentinstitute.net/atn.

Becoming Resilient, Empowerment Institute. This is an abbreviated version of the *All Together Now* program designed for single households. The version of the program created for New York City is available for free download; visit www.empowermentinstitute.net/atn.

All Together Now Disaster-Resilient Community Campaign. Using the *All Together Now* and *Becoming Resilient* behavior-change tools, this campaign helps buildings or blocks become more disaster resilient. It can be implemented by local government, a community group, a building, or a block association. For more information, visit www.empowermentinstitute.net/atn.

All Together Now Video. This is a ten-minute inspirational video about the *All Together Now* program that took place in New York City. To view it, visit www.empowermentinstitute.net/atn.

All Together Now Community Organizer Materials. These are the materials for starting a building, block, and neighborhood level disaster-resilient community initiative. The materials created for New York City are available for free download; visit www.empowermentinstitute.net/atn.

CHAPTER 5
CREATING THE WORLD AS WE WISH IT:
THE PRACTICE OF EMPOWERMENT

Empowerment: The Art of Creating Your Life As You Want It, by David Gershon and Gail Straub, High Point. This book, considered a classic in the field of personal empowerment, guides readers through a self-transformation program to envision and create what they wish to achieve in seven key areas of life: relationships, sexuality, money, work, body, emotions, and spirituality. To purchase the book, visit www.empowermentinstitute.net/eb.

Empowerment Workshop, led by David Gershon and Gail Straub. The purpose of this training is to support individuals in creating their life as they most want it. The workshop focuses on seven areas of life—relationships, sexuality, money, work, body, emotions, and spirituality. To learn more, visit www.empowermentraining.com/ew.

Art of Empowerment: A Professional Training in Facilitating Human Potential, led by David Gershon and Gail Straub. This training provides the knowledge and skills to use the empowerment methodology in social change, educational, organizational, and therapeutic settings. To learn more, visit www.empowermentraining.com/aoe.

Empowerment Institute Certification Program, led by David Gershon and Gail Straub. The institute provides change leaders and social entrepreneurs with the training, coaching, and tools to integrate the Social Change 2.0 framework into their social change initiative. Participants can also become certified in leading one of Empowerment Institute's turnkey personal development programs—Empowerment Workshop and Empowerment Life Coaching; community transformation campaigns—Sustainable Lifestyle, Livable Neighborhood, Water Stewardship, Cool Community, or Disaster-Resilient Community; or organizational transformation—The Empowering Organization. For more information visit www.empowermentinstitute.net/ei.

CHAPTER 6
CHANGING THE GAME:
THE CRAFT OF TRANSFORMATION

Empowerment Institute Certification Program. See Chapter 5 in this resource section for a description of the Institute. For more information, visit www.empowermentinstitute.net/ei.

Changing the Game: The Craft of Transformative Leadership, led by David Gershon. This two-day training described in detail in Chapter 6 is customized for an organization or community. For more information, visit www.empowermentinstitute.net/ctg.

CHAPTER 7
IMPROVING THE PERFORMANCE CAPACITY OF SOCIETY:
DESIGNING AND IMPLEMENTING
A TRANSFORMATIVE SOCIAL INNOVATION

Empowerment Institute Certification Program. See Chapter 5 in this resource section for a description of the Institute. For more information, visit www.empowermentinstitute.net/ei.

CHAPTER 8
SYNERGY AS THE ACCELERATOR OF SOCIAL CHANGE:
THE ART OF BUILDING A UNITIVE FIELD

Empowerment Institute Certification Program. See Chapter 5 in this resource section for a description of the Institute. For more information, visit www.empowermentinstitute.net/ei.

CHAPTER 9
TAKING A SOCIAL INNOVATION TO SCALE:
THE LEVERAGE OF DISPROPORTIONATE INFLUENCE

Empowerment Institute Certification Program. See Chapter 5 in this resource section for a description of the Institute. For more information, visit www.empowermentinstitute.net/ei.

CHAPTER 10
BUILDING LEADERSHIP CAPACITY TO CHANGE THE WORLD:
A SCHOOL FOR TRANSFORMATIVE SOCIAL CHANGE

Empowerment Institute Certification Program. See Chapter 5 in this resource section for a description of the Institute. For more information, visit www.empowermentinstitute.net/ei.

The Empowering Organization, led by David Gershon. This training is designed to help an organization increase its performance capacity through empowering employees to develop their full potential. The training is customized for an organization. For more information, visit www.empowermentinstitute.net/eo.

CHAPTER 11
EMPOWERING A CLIMATE CHANGE MOVEMENT:
LOW CARBON DIET AND THE COOL COMMUNITY

Low Carbon Diet: A 30 Day Program to Lose 5,000 Pounds, by David Gershon, Empowerment Institute. The book shows readers how to reduce their CO_2 footprint and help their workplace and community do the same. To learn more or to purchase the book, visit www.empowermentinstitute.net/lcd.

Cool Community Capacity Building Program. This customized program, including social architecture design consultation, training, coaching, and monthly master classes, builds the capability of local organizers in bringing Low Carbon Diet to scale in their community. It can be designed for single or multiple community participation and initiated by a local government, nonprofit organization or business. For more information, visit www.empowermentinstitute.net/lcd.

Empowerment Institute Certification Program. Offers two global warming certification programs for practitioners: Cool Community Leadership Program—builds transformative leadership capabilities to implement a community campaign; and Low Carbon Diet coaching—a turnkey four-session coaching program to help households reduce their carbon footprint. To learn more, visit www.empowermentinstitute.net/ei.

Cool School Program. This program can be used as part of a Cool Community campaign to empower children ages 8 to 12 to reduce their personal carbon footprint. It uses *Journey for the Planet: A Kid's Five Week Adventure to Create an Earth Friendly Life* and a teacher's curriculum. (See Chapter 2 in this section for a brief description of the books.) To learn more or to purchase the books, visit www.empowermentinstitute.net/journey.

Cool Community Corps. This is implemented by colleges and high schools to support students in participating in a Cool Community campaign. For a description, visit www.empowermentinstitute.net/lcd.

Cool Corporate Citizen. This program, using Low Carbon Diet, helps employees of a company reduce their carbon footprint and then translate this carbon literacy into helping the organization reduce its footprint. Motivated employees, through the organization's volunteer program, are then supported to participate in a Cool Community campaign. For a description, visit www.empowermentinstitute.net/lcd.

Global Warming Café. This workshop engages participants in a conversation about global warming and then invites them to take personal action to reduce their carbon footprint using the Low Carbon Diet. The Global Warming Café Organizers Toolkit is available for free online and provides everything needed to host and promote a café. To view, visit www.empowermentinstitute.net/lcd.

Cool Community Teletraining. led by David Gershon. For those interested in empowering residents in their community to lower their carbon footprint using Low Carbon Diet, this two-hour free training is an opportunity to learn how to mount a Cool Community campaign. To learn more and register, visit www.empowermentinstitute.net/lcd.

Low Carbon Diet CO_2 Calculator. To calculate your CO_2 footprint, visit www.empowermentinstitute.net/lcd

Chapter 12
Transforming the Paradigm of War:
The Emergence of a Unitive Consciousness

A Dream for Our World, by David Gershon, High Point. See Chapter 1 in this resource section for a description. To purchase the book, visit www.empowermentinstitue.net/dream.

A Dream for Our World Web Initiative. The goal of this web-based transformative strategy is to disseminate the First Earth Run story and set of seven practices to accelerate the growth of a unitive consciousness on the planet. To participate, visit www.empowermentinstitue.net/dream.

First Earth Run Video. See Chapter 1 in this resource section for a description. To learn more, visit www.empowermentinstitue.net/dream.

First Earth Run Photo Gallery. See Chapter 1 in this resource section for a description. To learn more, visit www.empowermentinstitue.net/dream.

FURTHER READING

These are some of the books that have sparked my imagination or deepened my knowledge in the creation of Social Change 2.0. I recommend them.

The Age of the Unthinkable: Why the New World Disorder Constantly Surprises Us and What We Can Do About It. Joshua Cooper Ramo. Little, Brown, 2009.

American Sphinx: The Character of Thomas Jefferson. Joseph Ellis. Vantage, 1998.

As a Man Thinketh. James Allen. DeVorss and Company, 1979.

Biomimicry: Innovation Inspired by Nature. Janine Benyus. Harper Perennial, 2002.

Blessed Unrest: How the Largest Movement in the World Came Into Being and Why No One Saw It Coming. Paul Hawken. Viking, 2007.

Blue Ocean Strategy: How to Create Uncontested Market Space and Make the Competition Irrelevant. K. Chan Kim and Renee Mauborgne. Harvard Business Press, 2005.

Collapse: How Societies Choose to Fail or Succeed. Jared Diamond. Viking, 2005.

Creating a Climate for Change: Communicating Climate Change and Facilitating Social Change. Edited by Susanne C. Moser and Lisa Dilling. Cambridge University Press, 2007.

Democracy's Edge: Choosing to Save Our Country by Bringing Democracy to Life. Frances Moore Lappe. Jossey-Bass, 2006.

Diffusion of Innovations. Everett Rogers. Free Press, 1983.

The Experience Economy: Work Is Theatre and Every Business a Stage. Joseph Pine and James Gilmore. Harvard Business Press, 1999.

Group Genius: The Creative Power of Collaboration. Keith Sawyer. Basic Books, 2007.

Hot, Flat, and Crowded: Why We Need a Green Revolution and How It Can Renew America. Thomas Friedman. Farrar, Straus and Giroux, 2008.

How to Change the World: Social Entrepreneurs and the Power of New Ideas. David Bornstein. Oxford, 2004.

Mission Inc: The Practitioner's Guide to Social Enterprise. Kevin Lynch and Julius Walls. Berrett-Koehler, 2009.

The Necessary Revolution: How Individuals and Organizations Are Working Together to Create a Sustainable World. Peter M. Senge, Joe Laur, Sara Schley, and Bryan Smith. Doubleday, 2008.

The Power of Unreasonable People: How Social Entrepreneurs Create Markets That Change the World. John Elkington and Pamela Hartigan. Harvard Business Press, 2008.

The Rhythm of Compassion: Caring for Self, Connecting with Society. Gail Straub, High Point, 2008.

The Search for Social Entrepreneurship. Paul Light. Brookings Institution Press, 2008.

The Starfish and the Spider: The Unstoppable Power of Leaderless Organizations. Ori Brafman and Rod Beckstrom. Portfolio, 2006.

The Tao of Power: Lao Tzu's Classic Guide to Leadership, Influence and Excellence. Translation R.L. Wing. Broadway Books, 1986.

The Timeless Way of Building. Christopher Alexander. Oxford University Press, 1979.

The Tipping Point: How Little Things Make a Difference. Malcolm Gladwell. Little, Brown, 2000.

INDEX

Tables and photos indicated by bold page numbers.

ABOUT THE AUTHOR

David Gershon, founder and president of the Empowerment Institute, is one of the world's foremost authorities on behavior-change and large-system transformation, and applies this expertise to issues requiring community, organizational, and societal change. His clients include cities, government agencies, large organizations, and social entrepreneurs. He has addressed a wide diversity of issues, ranging from environmentally sustainable lifestyles, livable neighborhoods, and disaster-resilient communities to organizational talent development and cultural transformation. Over the past thirty years the empowerment programs he has designed have won many awards, and a major academic research study described them as "unsurpassed in changing behavior."

David used this proficiency to conceive and organize, in partnership with the United Nations Children's Fund and ABC Television, one of the planet's first major global consciousness-raising initiatives, the First Earth Run. At the height of the Cold War, using the mythic power of relaying a torch of peace around the world, this simple and profound act of global unity engaged the participation of twenty-five million people in sixty-two countries, the world's political leadership and, through the media, an estimated 20 percent of the population on the planet. Millions of dollars were raised to enable UNICEF to provide care to the neediest children of the world.

Gershon is the author of ten other books, including *Low Carbon Diet: A 30 Day Program to Lose 5,000 Pounds*, winner of the 2007 "Most Likely to Save the Planet" Independent Publisher Book Award; and, with his wife, Gail Straub, the best-selling *Empowerment: The Art of Creating Your Life As You Want It*. Considered a master social architect and trainer, he co-directs the Empowerment Institute Certification Program—a school for transformative social change. He has lectured at Harvard, MIT, and Duke University, and served as an advisor to the Clinton White House and the United Nations on empowerment and sustainability issues.